Student's Book

Virginia Evans-Jenny Dooley

Express Publishing

Contents

	Topics	Vocabulary	Reading
Module 1			
UNIT 1 My Home is my Castle (pp. 6-19)	dwellings	dwellings & appliances; household chores; colours & rooms; home safety	- In Search of the Perfect Home (multiple choice) - The Charming Past: *Blarney Castle - Dunnottar Castle*
UNIT 2 While there's life, there's hope (pp. 20-33)	life events	facial features; feelings; stages in life; family relationships; work	- A Dream Come True (gapped text) - Extract from *Jack & Jill*
Self-Assessment Module 1 (pp. 34-37)			
Module 2			
UNIT 3 Travel Broadens the Mind (pp. 38-51)	travel; holidays; festivals	weather; types of holidays & holiday equipment; holiday resorts; holiday troubles; traveller's tips; festivals	- Getting away from it all (multiple matching) - Spectacular Nature: *White Cliffs of Dover - The Rockies*
UNIT 4 Earth is Dearer than Gold (pp. 52-65)	environment; energy	planet Earth; environmental problems; conservation; energy crisis; preservation of animals & plants	- The Answer is Blowing in the Wind (gapped text) - *The Little Land* (poem)
Self-Assessment Module 2 (pp. 66-69)			
Module 3			
UNIT 5 Early to Bed … (pp. 70-83)	health; daily routines	health problems; daily routines; stress & relaxation; describing feelings; character adjectives	- Can you feel the rhythm? (multiple choice) - Naturally Hot: *Rotorua - Ainsworth Hot Springs*
UNIT 6 Better Safe than Sorry (pp. 84-97)	technology; crime	technology at home; electrical appliances; types of offence; descriptions of objects	- No More Secrets (matching headings to paragraphs) - Extract from *The Time Machine*
Self-Assessment Module 3 (pp. 98-101)			
Module 4			
UNIT 7 Penny Wise, Pound Foolish (pp. 102-115)	shopping; advertising	shops & department stores; clothes; products; credit cards; shopping complaints; online shopping	- Picking the Perfect Present (multiple matching) - In the Market for a Bargain: *Portobello Road Market - Queen Victoria Market*
UNIT 8 You Are What you Eat (pp. 116-129)	food; healthy eating; eating habits	types of food; recipes; kitchen utensils; ways of cooking; places to eat; diners' complaints	- How to burn fat all day long (gapped text) - Extract from *Oliver Twist*
Self-Assessment Module 4 (pp. 130-133)			
Module 5			
UNIT 9 Every Man to his Taste (pp. 134-147)	sports & entertainment	types of sports; qualities; places & equipment; free-time activities; types of entertainment; the paralympics	- Daredevil Shaun (multiple choice) - Trophy Hunters: *Wimbledon - The Super Bowl*
UNIT 10 Spead the News (pp. 148-161)	the media; disasters	the news; natural/man-made disasters; newspapers; TV Guide; cinema; types of films	- E-books the books of the future? (gapped text) - Extract from *Robinson Crusoe*
Self-Assessment Module 5 (pp. 162-165)			

Grammar Reference Section (pp. 166-180)
Irregular Verbs (p. 181)
Appendices (pp. 182-188)
Tapescripts (pp. 189-215)
Word List (pp. 216-222)

Grammar	Listening	Speaking	Writing
present tenses; adverbs of frequency; state verbs Phrasal verbs: *BREAK, BRING*	note-taking; T/F statements; matching speakers to statements	compare types of houses; suggest ways to make houses safe for children; renting a house; expressing sympathy; requesting services	- an advertisement - an informal letter describing a house for rent
past tenses; used to/would Phrasal verbs: *CARRY, COME*	matching speakers to statements; T/F statements	discuss important things in life; express opinions on family matters; talk about memories of early childhood; breaking the news; describing people; introducing people	- famous people's profiles - a narrative
future tenses; Conditionals Type 0 & 1; the definite article Phrasal verbs: *CUT, DO*	note-taking; T/F/ Doesn't say; multiple choice	discuss weekend activities; speculations; holiday experiences; accepting/refusing invitations; cancelling a hotel reservation; renting a vehicle	- a letter of complaint - a semi-formal transactional letter
comparisons; too/enough; -ing form/ infinitive Phrasal verbs: *FALL, GET*	note-taking; matching speakers to statements	suggest ways to protect animals from extinction; suggest solutions to improve the environment; complaining; offering solutions to problems; expressing hesitation	- a set of rules - an essay providing solutions to problems
-ing/-ed participles; modal verbs; making deductions; question tags Phrasal verbs: *GIVE, GO*	Yes/No statements; multiple choice; matching speakers to statements	discuss ways to relax; speculating; give advice; losing your temper; making an appointment; describing symptoms	- an informal letter describing a personal problem - a for and against essay
order of adjectives; the passive; relatives; relative clauses Phrasal verbs: *HOLD, KEEP*	multiple matching; note-taking; matching speakers to statements	discuss pros & cons of using computers; discuss effects of modern technology on our lives; "filler" phrases; reporting a theft; giving instructions	- a news report - an opinion essay
causative form; reported speech (statements, questions, orders) Phrasal verbs: *LET, LOOK*	note-taking; Yes/No statements; multiple choice	ask for information; discuss pros/cons of advertising; discuss dress code; expressing opinions; making complaints; buying clothes	- describe clothes for a fashion magazine - an article describing a visit to a place
quantifiers (some, any, no, (a) little, (a) few); countable/uncountable nouns; reported speech (special introductory verbs) Phrasal verbs: *MAKE, PUT*	T/F statements; multiple matching; multiple choice	give advice; compare junk food to home cooked food; accepting/refusing invitations; doing your shopping; ordering a meal/fast food	- a recipe - an assessment report
Conditionals Type 2 & 3; wishes; would rather Phrasal verbs: *RUN, SEE, SET*	note-taking; T/F statements; matching speakers to statements	give opinions; guess content; talk about hobbies; asking for permission & polite requests; taking a phone message; inviting a friend to a sporting event	- instructions for a magic trick - a letter to the editor
future perfect; linkers & quantifiers (either/neither, although, both, all, none) Phrasal verbs: *STAND, TAKE, TURN*	multiple matching; note-taking	compare types of films; express preferences; talk about disasters; gossip; making arrangements; making excuses	- a news report - a formal transactional letter

People & Homes

UNIT 1 My Home is my Castle

UNIT 2 While there's life, there's hope

Module 1

Units 1-2

Before you start ...

How long have you been studying English?
Why are you studying?

Listen, read and talk about

- dwellings
- home appliances
- household chores
- rooms
- colours
- home safety
- stages in life
- life events
- types of families
- facial features
- feelings
- working lives

Learn how to ...

- make houses safe for children
- describe a room/a house
- request services
- express sympathy
- decide on a house
- describe people
- express feelings
- express your opinion
- spread the news
- introduce people

Phrasal verbs

- break
- bring
- carry
- come

Write ...

- an advertisement for a house
- an informal letter describing a house for rent
- a description of a person
- a narrative

Practise ...

- present tenses
- adverbs of frequency
- prepositions of place
- linkers
- state verbs
- past tenses
- used to/would

My Home is my Castle

Lead-in

1 The title above is taken from an English proverb. What do you think it means?

A
B
C
D

2 a. Which of the houses in the pictures:

has: five storeys and a house on top; a fibreglass shark; brick walls; a thatched roof; a chimney; a rock on the roof; wooden stairs up to the front door; stone walls; a pitched roof; a tiled roof?

is: built underground; a castle; built on stilts?

b. Use the adjectives to describe each house. Give reasons.

• economical • impractical • cold • spacious • cramped
• airy • comfortable • attractive • eccentric

House A is economical to maintain because it doesn't cost very much to heat and cool.

c. Listen and match the houses to the countries.

five-storey building	Suffolk, England
terraced house	Zimbabwe
hut on stilts	Portugal
rock house	Headington, England

d. Describe the houses A-D. Think about:

• type of house • location • special features
• general description

The house in picture A is a hut on stilts. It is located in Zimbabwe. It has got a thatched roof and wooden stairs up to the front door. It's cramped but it's probably quite airy.

e. Which house would you/wouldn't you like to live in? Give reasons.

I'd like to live in the hut on stilts because it looks very attractive to me. I wouldn't like to live in the rock house because it must get very cold.

How would you like to live in a castle, a tree house or even underground? This might not be as unusual as you think. It seems that these days more and more people want to live somewhere special and **out of the ordinary**, and if they can't buy what they want they are quite prepared to build it **from scratch**.

For John Mew and his wife Josephine their home really is their castle. They have built their own English castle in the Sussex countryside. The building is **brand new** with all the luxuries you would expect from a house that cost more than £350,000 to build. However, when you first see it from the outside it would be easy to think that you are looking at an ancient monument. The building has a lot of the features of a traditional castle, including a **keep**, a **moat** and a **drawbridge**. "My choice of house is somewhat eccentric and building it was very hard work, but we've got the perfect place to live," Mew says. Although some would say that the building is impractical and may be cold in harsh British winters, he certainly has got a unique and spacious home.

If you don't look carefully, you might not even see the home that Jonathan Ridley-Jones and Shanon Ridd built at all! That's because the house is a converted underground water tank. The only thing that can be seen from the surface is a door leading into the hillside. "We've never wanted to live in an ordinary house," Shanon says. "Living below ground means that our home is quiet and very cosy – none of the usual **draughts**. It doesn't damage the local surroundings and has very low **fuel bills**. Some of our friends find it dark and feel shut in when they first visit, but they soon get used to it!"

In Search of the Perfect Home

If an underground home doesn't **appeal to** you, how about living in the tree tops? Dan Garner, a tree surgeon from Gloucestershire, certainly thinks that this is the way to go up in the world.

"When our family **became short of** space at home our solution was to build a luxury tree house in the garden. The tree house is built into a **spruce tree** six metres **above the ground**. It has one main room, a bedroom and a balcony running around two sides." Garner is so happy with this practical **extension** to his home that he thinks he can convince more people of the benefits of living in the trees. He wants to set up his own enterprise making more of the deluxe tree dwellings, saying, "Tree houses are **airy**, secure and comfortable and the only disadvantage is that they might not be **suitable for** people who **suffer from hay fever** or a fear of heights!"

Even people who live in more ordinary **settings** sometimes can't resist doing something to make them **stand out** from the crowd. One extreme example of this is Bill Heines' house in Headington, Oxfordshire. Until one morning in 1986, his house looked much like all the others in his street, when suddenly overnight a 7.5 m long **fibreglass shark** appeared to have crashed through the roof. The shark was a **sculpture** by local artist John Buckley. At first some people complained that it might be dangerous or that it spoilt the look of the neighbourhood, but engineers checked that the sculpture was safe and the 'Headington shark' has become a well-known and popular landmark. It seems that no matter where you live, you can always do something to make sure your house says something about who you are.

Reading

3 a. Look at the title of the article. What do you think it is about? Where might you read it? Say words you expect to find in it.

Tip Read the text quickly to get a general idea of what it is about. Look at the first part of the question, then find the part of the text the question refers to. Go through the choices and choose the answer that best fits. Keep in mind that the information may be rephrased. Even if you think you know the correct answer, always check that the others are not appropriate. Check your answer against the text.

b. Read the article and answer the questions.

c. Explain the words in bold, then suggest synonyms for the highlighted words.

1 More and more people build their own home
   A so that they can live underground.
   B so that they can have exactly the home they want.
   C because it is cheaper than buying a new house.
   D because they want all the modern luxuries you find in a new home.

2 John and Josephine Mew
   A know that their choice of home is unusual.
   B found that creating their dream home was easy.
   C wanted to live like people would have in traditional castles.
   D converted an ancient building into a modern home.

3 What do Jonathan Ridley-Jones and Shanon Ridd say about their home?
   A It's just an ordinary house.
   B They always wanted to live underground.
   C It doesn't harm the environment.
   D They don't pay anything for heating and lighting.

4 Why did Dan build a tree house in his garden?
   A He wants to persuade people to buy one.
   B His family wanted to live in a tree house.
   C He builds them for a living.
   D His family needed more room.

5 The 'Headington shark'
   A was created by Bill Heines.
   B crashed into the roof of Bill Heines' house one night.
   C was immediately popular with everyone in the town.
   D was built without any warning.

Follow-up

4 a. List the advantages and disadvantages of Mew's, Ridd's and Garner's dwellings, then talk about them.

b. What would your ideal house be? Describe it giving reasons.

My ideal house would be a castle. It would be made of ...

Vocabulary Practice

Dwellings and Appliances

5 a. Go through the table and look up the words you don't know in your dictionary.

b. Listen and underline the words that best describe Ann's house. Circle the ones which best describe John's house.

STYLE:	traditional, modern, apartment/flat, (semi) detached, terraced house, cottage, villa, 1/ 2/3 storey building, castle
LOCATION:	village, city, centrally located, residential area, close to the shops, in the suburbs, on the outskirts, isolated, in the country
SIZE:	small, tiny, spacious, large, huge, average, family-sized, 1-/2- bedroomed
COST:	cheap, low-priced, overpriced, expensive, economical
GENERAL DESCRIPTION:	cosy, comfortable, secure, luxurious, well-maintained, fully furnished, airy, noisy, cold

c. Use the words to describe Ann's and John's houses, then describe your house.

Ann lives in a traditional cottage in the country. The cottage is ...

6 a. Read the advertisements, then, in pairs, list the special features of each property under the headings: *Inside - Outside*

A FOR RENT 3-bedroomed semi-detached house, Paddington. Large lounge/dining room with fireplace, entrance hall, modern fitted kitchen, attic, central heating, built-in wardrobes. Garage and driveway. Large front garden with shared fence, rear patio and pool. Close to shops and public transport. Available for long let. £430 per month. Contact Mrs Wilson Tel: 020 8360 7289

A: Inside: large lounge/dining room ...
Outside: garage, driveway ...

B FOR SALE £399,986 Golders Green, London. A superb first-floor 2-bedroomed flat. Fully-furnished with a large balcony, double glazing and air conditioning. Fully-equipped kitchen and modern security system. Minutes from tube station. Full details at Primary Properties: 020 8731 6889

b. What features are there inside/outside your house?

7 a. Which of these items are in your house? In which room?

- refrigerator • vacuum cleaner • electric heater
- washing machine • microwave • humidifier
- air conditioner • hairdryer • dishwasher • cooker

refrigerator – kitchen

b. Match the columns. Which of these have you/haven't you got in your house?

built-in	system
central	hall
fitted	glazing
double	wardrobes
entrance	kitchen
private	parking
security	heating

There are built-in wardrobes in our house. We haven't got ...

8 a. Complete the dialogue, then listen and check.

A: Hello!
B: Good morning. I'm calling about the house advertised for rent in Paddington.
A: Oh yes?
B: I wonder 1) .... give me a bit more information, please.
A: Of course. 2) .... like to know?
B: First of all, 3) .... exactly where the house is situated?
A: Yes, it's on 15, Bayswater Drive.
B: And the lounge and dining room – are they separate?
A: Yes, but they're joined by a sliding glass door.
B: And do all the bedrooms have fitted wardrobes?
A: No, only the two largest bedrooms.
B: One last question. Is the garage large enough for two cars?
A: Oh, definitely.
B: It sounds perfect. 4) .... I could see it?
A: 5) .... 6 o'clock this evening?
B: That's fine — see you then.

b. In pairs, take roles and act out dialogues about each of the advertisements in Ex. 6.

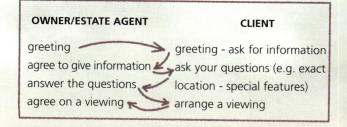

OWNER/ESTATE AGENT	CLIENT
greeting	greeting - ask for information
agree to give information	ask your questions (e.g. exact location - special features)
answer the questions	
agree on a viewing	arrange a viewing

9 a. Use the prompts and the linkers to make up sentences for each house, as in the examples.

- both • as well as
- also • besides
- whereas • but
- although • however

	A	B		A	B
• driveway	✓	✓	• balcony	✓	✗
• chimney	✓	✗	• air conditioning	✓	✓
• garage	✓	✓	• security system	✓	✓
• pool	✓	✗	• cellar	✗	✓
• garden	✓	✓	• fireplace	✓	✗
• attic	✓	✓	• built-in wardrobes	✗	✓
• patio	✓	✗	• central heating	✓	✓
• fence	✗	✗	• fitted kitchen	✓	✗

Both house A and B have got a driveway.
House A has got a chimney, but house B hasn't got one.
House A has got a driveway as well as a garage.
Besides having a garage, house A has got a driveway.

Writing Project

b. Look at the pictures A and B and write an advertisement for each house. Say if it is for rent/sale, what kind of house it is, how much it costs, what special features it has got and give a telephone number for contact. Use the advertisements in Ex. 6a as models to help you.

Household Chores

10 a. Match the verbs to the nouns.

wash	the beds
dust	the carpets
make	the clothes
iron	the dishes
vacuum	the windows
clean	the floors
mop	the lawn
mow	the furniture

Which of these household chores do you do? How often? Which do you like/not mind/hate doing?

I sometimes wash the dishes in the evenings.

b. Which of these verbs can be changed to *do + ing* form of the verb? Make up sentences about your family using these phrases.

*Mum always **does the ironing** on Saturday.*

Colours & Rooms

11 a. Listen and circle the words that are mentioned in connection with each colour.

red — competitive, romantic, active, excited
orange — conservative, talkative, adventurous
yellow — shy, reliable, cheerful, generous, impatient, creative
blue — calm, confident, stressed, relaxed, peaceful
green — relaxed, peaceful, refreshed, depressed
white — cheerful, isolated, withdrawn

b. Listen again. What colour would you paint these rooms? Why?

- a dining room • a child's bedroom
- a play area • a living room • a classroom

I would paint a dining room orange because it stimulates the appetite.

12 Use the prepositions and the words in the list to describe the living room.

- in front of • next to • behind • opposite • on
- between • above • in the middle of

- fireplace • candlesticks • carpet • paintings • sofa
- armchair • cushions • plant • glass coffee table
- window • lamp

There is a glass coffee table in front of the sofa.

Grammar in use

Present tenses
Grammar Reference

13 Identify the tenses in bold, then match them to their use.

1. The Earth **revolves** round the Sun. ....
2. The train **leaves** at 5:30. ....
3. John **is looking for** a new house. ....
4. She can't play. She **has broken** her leg. ....
5. He **is** always **biting** his nails. ....
6. I **have been trying** to call you for an hour. ....
7. He **is flying** to Madrid tomorrow. ....
8. It**'s getting** colder and colder. ....

a action which started in the past and continues up to the present with emphasis on duration
b law of nature
c expressing irritation
d action happening around the time of speaking
e result/consequence of a past activity in the present
f fixed arrangement in the future
g timetable
h gradual development

State verbs
We do not normally use **believe, forget, hate, know, like, love, need, prefer, realise, remember, suppose, understand, want, appear** in continuous tenses.
I believe you. NOT *I'm believing you.*
The verbs **think, taste, see, look, smell, feel** and **have** can have continuous tenses, but there is a difference in meaning.
I think he is desperate. (= I believe) BUT *I'm thinking about moving house.* (= I'm considering)
---

14 Put the verbs in brackets into the correct present tense, then identify their use.

1. She .... (move) house next week.
2. Carl and Mary are looking for a new house. The landlord .... (evict) them from their flat.
3. .... (you/wait) a long time?
4. They .... (convert) the old mill into a beautiful new home at the moment.
5. Water .... (freeze) at 0° C.
6. Her flight .... (arrive) tonight at 7pm.
7. .... (you/sign) the contract for the house next week?
8. The Earth .... (become) warmer and warmer.
9. The bus .... (come) every ten minutes.
10. Jack and Maggie .... (still/search) for the perfect house.
11. Bob can't move house now because he .... (sign) a two-year contract.

15 Fill in the correct tense of the verb in brackets.

1. A: ....
   (Jane/still/think) of renting the house?
   B: Yes, why?
   A: Well, some people .... (think) that it is haunted.
2. A: Mark .... (taste) the curry to see if we need to add any more spices.
   B: I don't think we do. It .... (taste) delicious as it is.
3. A: Why .... (you/smell) the milk? I only bought it this morning!
   B: Well, it .... (smell) off to me!

16 a. Talk about British homes, using adverbs of frequency, as in the example.

British homes always have running water.
There is always running water in British homes.
You can always find running water in British homes.

b. In pairs draw a similar chart about homes in your country, then present it in class.

17 In pairs, talk about:
- what you do/don't do in your free time
- what you are doing this weekend
- what you have done so far today

18 How much have you changed since you were five years old? Make up sentences, as in the example.

I've grown my hair long.

19 In pairs, act out dialogues, as in the example.

- sleep outdoors • visit a castle • be in a tree house
- stay at a campsite • redecorate your own bedroom
- stay in a house with its own swimming pool
- have a power cut at your home • move house

A: Have you ever slept outdoors?
B: No, I haven't. Have you ever visited a castle?
A: Yes, I have.
B: Really? When was that?
A: Two years ago. Have you ever ...? etc

20 Use the prompts to act out dialogues, as in the example.

1. exhausted – work/garden
   - plant/flowers (✓)
   - prune/bushes (✓)
   - water/lawn (✗)

   A: You look exhausted. What have you been doing?
   B: I've been working in the garden.
   A: What have you done?
   B: Well, I've planted some flowers and pruned the bushes but I haven't watered the lawn yet.

2. tired – do/homework
   - finish/Maths (✓)
   - write/composition (✓)
   - study/test (✗)

3. excited – organise party
   - send out/invitations (✓)
   - book/caterers (✓)
   - book/band (✗)

21 Make up sentences about yourself, using present tenses and the time adverbs in the list.

- yet • still • already • for
- since • at the moment
- every day • now
- next Saturday

I haven't done my homework yet.

22 Use the prompts to write sentences, as in the example. Use *present perfect* or *present perfect continuous*.

1. Ann can't get into the house. **(lose/her key)**
   Ann can't get into the house. She has lost her key.
2. Tom's sunburnt. **(sit/in the sun/all morning)**
3. My eyes hurt. **(watch TV/hours)**
4. John passed his Maths exam. **(study/hard)**
5. Nick has lost a lot of weight. **(be on a diet)**
6. Amy looks so happy! **(buy/new house)**

23 Circle the correct tense.

1. I'm afraid I can't make it tonight. I .... the estate agent at 7 o'clock.
   A see B am seeing C have seen D have been seeing
2. The film .... at 7:30.
   A has been starting B has started C is starting D starts
3. He .... to find a cleaning woman for a month now.
   A has been trying B tries C is trying D has tried
4. Look! You .... coffee all over my desk!
   A have been spilling C were spilling
   B have spilt D spill
5. He .... the property section of the newspaper every day, but he still hasn't found anything.
   A has been reading B is reading C have read D read

Prepositions
Appendix 1

24 a. Fill in the correct preposition, then explain the phrases.

1. Ann has been **absent** .... work for two weeks.
2. It has taken Mark a long time to become **accustomed** .... the Australian climate.
3. They **accused** him .... stealing the car.
4. We need to **agree** .... a time to meet.
5. He **apologised** .... Mary .... being late last night.
6. Emma has **applied** .... Leeds University .... a place on the History course.
7. Some people don't **approve** .... the council's plan to build a new shopping centre in town.
8. The old man was **begging** .... food.
9. Do you **believe** .... magic?
10. Rob has been **busy** .... the redecorating all week.

b. Chain Story. Read the beginning of the story, then, one after the other, continue the story using the phrases in bold from Ex. 24a.

*John Smith worked as an office manager. He was very good at his job, but unfortunately he wasn't able to go to work because he was very ill. He was **absent from** work for three weeks.*

Grammar in use

25 Fill in the correct prepositions. Then choose any five phrases and make up sentences using them.

1 .... the ordinary; 2 .... scratch; 3 .... the countryside; 4 to expect sth .... sb; 5 .... the winter; 6 to appeal .... sb; 7 to live .... a tree top; 8 to become short .... space; 9 an extension .... his home; 10 to convince people .... sth; 11 the benefits .... sth; 12 suitable .... sb; 13 to suffer .... hay fever; 14 fear .... heights

Phrasal Verbs
Appendix 2

26 a. Replace the words in bold with the appropriate phrasal verb formed with **break** or **bring**.

1 My computer has **stopped working**. (= *broken down*)
2 My favourite band have just **released** their new album.
3 Schools **finish** for the summer holidays tomorrow.
4 She was **raised** by her grandma.
5 The burglars **entered by force** and stole all our valuables.
6 A fire **began suddenly** on the second floor of the building.
7 Visiting my old neighbourhood always **makes me recall** memories of family holidays.
8 The two countries **ended** diplomatic relations with each other two years ago.

Competition Game

b. Choose one of the phrasal verbs in Ex. 26a and draw a picture about it. In teams, show your picture to the class. The team which guesses the phrasal verb first gets one point. Continue the game until all of you have shown your pictures. The team with the most points is the winner.

Word Formation

27 Fill in the correct word derived from the word in bold.

Tip Read the title of the text to get an idea what the text is about. Read the text once quickly. For each gap decide what the missing word is (e.g. noun, verb, adverb, etc.) You may need to write the word in the plural or with a negative meaning. Think of possible prefixes and suffixes. Fill in the gaps. Check the spelling. Read the completed text to check if it makes sense.

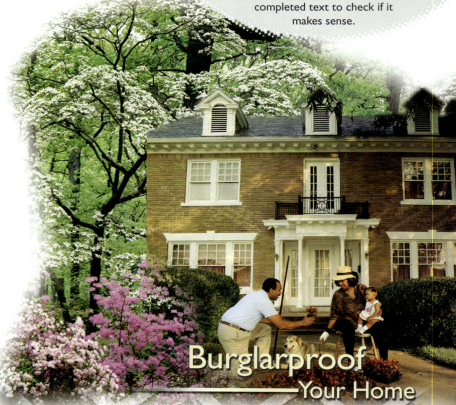

Burglarproof Your Home

Can you imagine anything worse than returning home to find that burglars have broken into your house? 0) *Unfortunately*, this happens to about 1 million people in Britain 1) .... However, if you want better 2) .... against burglars there are several things you can do. To improve 3) ...., check all the locks on your doors and windows. The 4) .... of lighting all around the house will make sure a burglar is 5) .... to hide in the shadows. An alarm system is another good 6) .... measure you can take.

Starting a 7) .... watch group is also a very 8) .... way to prevent crime in your area. Since most 9) .... take place when people are away on holiday, this is when your neighbours' help is most 10) .... Ask them to collect your mail, open and close your curtains every day, switch your lights on and off and even mow your lawn to make your house look occupied.

FORTUNE
ANNUAL
PROTECT

SECURE
INSTALL

ABLE
PREVENT

NEIGHBOUR
EFFECT
BURGLAR

VALUE

Error Correction

28 Read the text below and look carefully at each line. If the line is correct, put a tick (✓).
If it has a word that should not be there, write this word on the lines, as in the examples.

TIP Read the title of the text to see what the text is about. Read the text once quickly, then read it sentence by sentence. Look for mistakes with articles, auxiliary/modal verbs, prepositions, pronouns, comparative forms etc. The extra words are **wrong**, not just unnecessary. Mark your answers. Check the whole text.

An Unusual Home

Why would a basketball player to have an exact copy of a	0	*to*
pirate ship in his backyard? The basketball player is LA	00	✓
Laker's star, Kobe Bryant, who he has created an	1	....
adventure wonderland in his California home. There are	2	....
many of tropical gardens around the house, complete	3	....
with waterfalls, and the pirate ship is in one of these. The	4	....
ship it not only fits in with the garden, but also gives	5	....
to the home a fun-park theme.	6	....
The house is over 16,000 square feet in the size, with ten	7	....
bedrooms and over twelve bathrooms. A huge guest	8	....
house stands next to a theatre and a billiards room. Even if	9	....
the guests need something else to look at, apart from the	10	....
rest of the decor, there are so beautiful ceilings which	11	....
have to been carefully hand-painted. These give Kobe's	12	....
house a casual but elegant look. Kobe didn't want to buy	13	....
a ready-built home, so that he had this one specially built	14	....
for him – at a cost of about $13.5 million!	15	....

Key-word Transformations

29 Complete the second sentence using the word in bold. You can use two to five words including the word given. Don't change the word given.

TIP Read the whole sentence, then look at the key word. Try to work out what the question is testing (passive, indirect speech, part of speech, etc). Complete the sentences without changing the word given. Check that you have written two to five words. Also check for spelling.

1 I've never seen such a tiny house.
ever It's the .... seen.

2 It's a long time since he last visited us.
for He .... a long time.

3 It's a year since he started working here.
been He .... a year now.

4 His new book will be on the market next March.
out His new book .... next March.

5 Two men forced their way into Sally's flat last night.
broke Two men .... last night.

Idioms & Fixed Phrases

30 Fill in the correct colour(s). Then explain the expressions in bold.

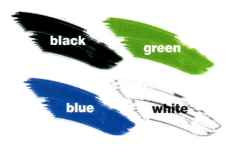

1 Sophie goes to the cinema **once in a** .... **moon**. She doesn't like it much.
2 Jack fell down the stairs and he **is** .... **and** .... **all over**.
3 Angela definitely has .... **fingers** – everything in her garden grows really well.
4 He **is a bit** .... – he hasn't got much experience in this kind of work.
5 They knew that if she found out the truth it would hurt her feelings so they told her a **little** .... **lie**.
6 She doesn't want to say anything until she has seen the facts **in** .... **and** ....

31 Underline the correct word, then explain the phrases.

1 Ian is very active. He is always **out and *about/around***.
2 After the argument they both did their best to **clean/clear the air**.
3 I can't find my keys anywhere – they seem to have **vanished into *thin/delicate* air**.
4 Matt is very determined to buy the cottage. He **won't accept/take no for an answer**.
5 They wanted to build a holiday resort here, but the owners of those beachfront cottages **refused/denied to play ball**.
6 They knew they would have to **drive a *difficult/hard* bargain** if they wanted to buy the house at a price they could afford.

Listening & Speaking skills

32 You will hear five people talking about problems they are having with their houses. Listen and match the problems (A-F) to the speakers (1-5). There is one extra problem which you do not need to use.

Tip: Read the instructions to understand what the speakers have in common. Read the list A-F and underline the words you have to listen for. Listen for clues to match each speaker to the prompts. Remember the extracts may have distracting information so listen to the whole part before you decide. Listen again and check your answers.

A badly fitting window   Speaker 1 ☐
B central heating doesn't work Speaker 2 ☐
C air conditioner doesn't work Speaker 3 ☐
D leaking roof   Speaker 4 ☐
E not enough space   Speaker 5 ☐
F driveway needs repairing

b. Listen again and mark the sentences as true (T) or false (F).

1 Marsha Ward is a writer and a parent. ....
2 1,000 children in Britain have accidents at home each year. ....
3 Young children have more accidents than older children. ....
4 The bathroom is the most dangerous room in the house. ....

33 Look at the pictures. Compare and contrast them. You can use the expressions below to help you.

Both pictures show ...
Picture A ... but picture B ...
Picture A ... . In addition, ...
Picture B, on the other hand, ...
Although/While picture A ..., picture B ...

- Which house would you like to live in? Give reasons.
- How is your house similar to/different from the ones in the pictures?
- What problems might you face in each type of house? Think about: *noise, neighbours, distance from shops/facilities, space, heating* etc.

34 a. You are going to hear a woman talking about home safety. Which of these words do you expect to hear and in what context? Listen and check.

• headache • falling • burning • drowning
• choking • toothache • poisoning • scalding
• cutting • electrocution • indigestion

*I wouldn't expect to hear the word headache.
I would expect to hear the word 'falling'.
"Falling down the stairs is a common household accident."*

35 Look at the pictures and in pairs talk about:
- the dangers children face at home
- how to make our houses safe for children

Use the prompts below to help you.

- electrical sockets/hot stoves – safety covers
- chemicals/cleaning products/medicine – locked cupboards
- cupboards & drawers – safety catches on
- swimming pools – guard rails
- staircases – safety gates
- knives/irons – keep out of reach

Electrical sockets are very dangerous because children can be electrocuted. Safety covers should be put on.

36 Listen to an estate agent talking to a client on the phone and complete the form, then talk about the house.

Main Requirement: big garden
Type of house: 1 ....
Price: 2 ....
When built: 1930s
Parking: large double 3 ....
Number of bedrooms: 4 ....
Number of bathrooms: 5 ....
Extra features: 6 ....

14

37 Your friend, who's got a family of four, has inherited £10,000 and she is thinking of making some improvements to her house. In pairs, decide which would be the best and why.

A: I think she should add a second bathroom.
B: Yes, she's got a big family so another bathroom would be very useful.

Deciding on a house

38 a. Listen to the dialogue. Where does it take place?

b. Complete the dialogue, then use the prompts to act out similar dialogues.

A: How do you **1)** .... it, then?
B: Well, it's nicely decorated and the garden is lovely, but the kitchen is very **2)** ....
A: That's true. But it is **3)** .... equipped.
B: And there are only two bedrooms.
A: Mmm, yes. But we can use the **4)** .... as another bedroom.
B: I think it will suit our needs. And it's not so expensive, either.
A: Okay, then. Let's tell the estate agent that we are definitely **5)** ....

- nice area (+) • four-bedroomed (+) • a long way from the shops (-)
- a bus stop nearby (+) • no central heating (-) • log fire (+)
- well maintained (+) • garden (+) • no garage (-)
- park on the street (+) • no fence (-) • modern security system (+)

Requesting services

39 a. Listen to the dialogue. Who's worried? Now match the exchanges.

1	b	Brown & Sons. How can I help you?
2		Hello, Ms Smith. What can I do for you?
3		What's wrong with it?
4		I'll send someone to look at it right away.
5		What is your address, please?

a Well it doesn't lock properly.
b Hello. My name's Ann Smith.
c 21, Market Street.
d I've got a problem with my front door.
e Thank you, that would be great.

b. Use the prompts to make up similar dialogues.

A	B
name of company	full name
ask for problem	describe the problem
suggest sending sb	thank
ask for address	give address

Expressing sympathy

40 a. Listen and say what each dialogue is about.

b. Read the exchanges and underline the phrases that express sympathy.

1 A: I'm afraid that the plumber won't be able to come today. He's had a car accident.
   B: How awful! Will he be all right?
2 A: Oh, no. I locked myself out!
   B: That's too bad.
3 A: The Smiths are going to be evicted.
   B: I'm sorry to hear that.

c. Use the phrases to make up dialogues expressing sympathy in the following situations.

- How terrible/awful/sad!
- That's terrible/awful/a pity/a shame/too bad!
- You must be very worried/upset.
- I'm (really) sorry about that/ to hear that

1 fire in the basement
2 an aunt fell down the stairs
3 not getting the flat you wanted
4 a friend's daughter burnt her hand on the cooker.

Intonation

41 Listen, then, read out the exchanges in pairs.

- A: I have to move out!
  B: That's a shame.
- A: My flat was broken into last night.
  B: I'm sorry to hear that.
- A: I can't afford the rent.
  B: You must be very worried.
- A: My antique table is ruined.
  B: How sad!

The Charming Past

42
a. How does the title relate to the pictures?

b. In what context do you expect to find the following words in the texts?

Blarney Castle
- tourist attraction • in ruins • battlements
- well-kept grounds • interesting historical site

Dunnotar Castle
- cliffs • exciting past • the Scottish Crown Jewels
- the strongest fortresses • lodgings • stables
- storehouses • popular with birdwatchers

*Blarney Castle is a famous **tourist attraction**.*

43
a. Think of three questions you would like to ask about each castle. Read the texts and see if you can answer them.

b. Read the texts again and answer the questions. Write *A* (for Blarney Castle) or *B* (for Dunnottar Castle).

Which of the castles ...
1. was used to hide sth precious?
2. has a special stone?
3. is associated with a famous film star?
4. has something that nobody really understands?
5. stands on a cliff?

c. Explain the words in bold. Which words are similar to words in your language? Where could you read such pieces of writing?

d. Find the synonyms.

Text A	Text B
• payment (l. 9)	• situated (l. 3)
• endure (l. 13)	• deserted (l. 11)
• merit (l. 24)	• modern (l. 15)

A BLARNEY CASTLE

Eight kilometres north of the city of Cork you will find Blarney Castle, home of the famous Blarney Stone. This stone is traditionally believed to give whoever kisses it the gift of **eloquent** speech. **Built
5 in** 1446 by Dermot McCarthy, King of Munster, Blarney Castle has a **rich history**. It is believed that a past king of Munster sent 4,000 men to help Robert the Bruce win the Battle of Bannockburn in 1314. His reward was said to be half of the Stone of Scone,
10 which was **renamed** the Blarney Stone.

Blarney Castle today is a very popular tourist attraction although most of it is in ruins. Many **features** remain, though, like the tower and the narrow **spiral** staircases. Visitors who wish to kiss
15 the stone must climb up a very narrow **winding** staircase to the top of the battlements, then lie on their back and lean slightly over the edge of the tower to reach the stone. Visitors can also enjoy a walk through the beautiful, **well-kept grounds**,
20 where they will find the Rock Close. This is a mysterious place with ancient stones and trees that were used by the **druids**.

Blarney Castle is a very interesting historical site and definitely well worth a visit. It is one place you
25 must not miss if you get the chance to go to Southern Ireland.

Culture Clip 1

44 a. Which of the two buildings would you most like to visit? Why?

b. Are there any buildings like these in your country? Talk about them. Think about:
- location
- historical details
- exterior/interior

Writing

45 Write a short article for your school magazine about a famous historic building in your country. In the first paragraph, write its *name* and *location*. In the second paragraph, write its *historical details*. In the third paragraph, write a *description of its exterior/interior*. End your article with a *recommendation*.

B DUNNOTTAR CASTLE

Scotland is full of castles, each with its own **myths** and **legends**. One such castle is Dunnottar Castle on Scotland's east coast, 15 miles from the city of Aberdeen. Located on a huge **outcrop** of flat rock with **sheer cliffs** on three sides, it is the perfect place for a **fortress**, and there has been one here since
5 the 13th century.

Dunnottar has a long and **exciting past**. William Wallace, Mary Queen of Scots, King Charles II and the Marquis of Montrose have all played a part in its rich history. The Scottish Crown Jewels, the "Honours of Scotland", were hidden here in the 17th century so that Oliver Cromwell couldn't destroy them.

10 Dunnottar used to be one of the strongest fortresses in Scotland. However, the castle was abandoned in the 18th century and it fell into **decay** until 1925, when Viscountess Cowdray began repairs. Visitors can see the 14th century keep, which was built by Sir William Keith in 1392 and is still **intact**. There are also **barracks**, **lodgings**, stables and storehouses.

15 The castle has become a lot more popular in recent years since the site was used as one of the locations for the film "Hamlet" starring Mel Gibson. It is also popular with **birdwatchers** because of its location. Whatever the reason for your visit, it will certainly be memorable.

Writing an informal letter describing a house for rent

Tip

When we write an informal letter to a friend describing a house for rent, we can divide it into five paragraphs. We start our letter with *Dear + our friend's first name*.

Introduction
In the **first paragraph** we write our **opening remarks** and the **reason** for writing our letter.

Main Body
In the **second paragraph** we describe **the location** of the house and give details of the **rent**.
In the **third paragraph** we describe **the exterior** of the house (what it is made of, garden, etc).
In the **fourth paragraph** we describe **the interior** of the house (e.g. floors, rooms, furniture, special features, etc). We start each main-body paragraph with a topic sentence i.e. a sentence which introduces or summarises the paragraph.

Conclusion
In the **last paragraph** we write our **closing remarks** and sign off using *Yours, Best wishes, etc + our first name*.

We can use a variety of adjectives to make our descriptions more interesting to the reader.

Analysing the Rubric

46 Read the rubric, look at the underlined phrases and answer the questions.

> Peter has been looking for a <u>summer house</u> to <u>rent</u> on the coast for August. He has asked <u>his friend</u>, Laura, to find a house for him. Laura has found a suitable house and is going to write Peter a <u>letter</u> <u>describing the house</u> and <u>giving rental details</u>.

1. Who is going to write a letter? To whom? What is their relationship?
2. What style is appropriate?
   formal – to someone in authority
   semi-formal – to someone you do not know very well
   informal – to someone you know very well
3. Which of the following would you expect to find in Laura's letter? Tick (✓) accordingly.
   - description of the outside ☐
   - description of the inside ☐
   - location of the house ☐
   - historical details ☐
   - weather conditions ☐
   - rent ☐

Analysing a Model Text

47 a. Read the letter and underline the topic sentences, then replace them with your own topic sentences.

> Dear Peter,
> ① How are you? Hope everything's OK. I'm writing to let you know that I think I've found the perfect summer cottage for you.
> ② It's in a really nice location. It's a quiet area, but the best thing about it is that it is less than a kilometre from the sea. Also, the rent for the cottage is only £150 a week.
> ③ The house is really charming outside. It's an old brick farm building which has been converted into a holiday cottage. It's got a patio and is surrounded by a beautiful garden.
> ④ Inside, the house is nice and comfortable. It has two floors. On the ground floor there is a cosy living room and a kitchen with all the modern equipment you would expect, as well as a dining room and a WC. Upstairs there are two small bedrooms and a bathroom. The house is fully furnished so you don't need to worry about that.
> ⑤ Let me know if you like the sound of it. I can easily talk to the owner, Mr Smith, for you. I hope I'll see you here soon. I'll tell you all of my news then.
> Yours,
> Laura

b. Which words/phrases does Laura use to describe the interior/exterior of the house? In which paragraphs does she mention these?

Style

c. Study the table, then find examples of informal style in Laura's letter.

Informal style
• abbreviations *e.g. I've got*
• simple linking words *e.g. but, so, and*, etc.
• shorter sentences *e.g. I'd like to see you*
• personal tone *e.g. I've got some great news*
• everyday expressions *e.g. Thanks a lot.*
Formal style
• no abbreviations *e.g. I have got*
• formal linking words *e.g. despite*
• longer sentences
• impersonal tone *e.g. passive*
• formal expressions *e.g. I look forward to hearing*

Opening/Closing Remarks

d. What are Laura's opening and closing remarks? Which of the following can you use instead? Why can't you use the others?

a Thanks for your letter.
b I feel obliged to write to inform you ...
c Sorry I haven't written for so long.
d Get in touch with me soon.
e Looking forward to hearing from you.
f I look forward to receiving a prompt reply.

Descriptive Writing

48 Use the phrases to describe the building where you live.

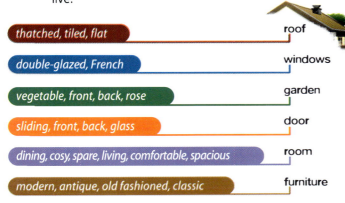

- thatched, tiled, flat — roof
- double-glazed, French — windows
- vegetable, front, back, rose — garden
- sliding, front, back, glass — door
- dining, cosy, spare, living, comfortable, spacious — room
- modern, antique, old fashioned, classic — furniture

I live in a detached house. It's got ...

Discuss & Write

49 a. Read the rubric and underline the key words. Then, answer the questions.

> Your friend wants to move to your area and is looking for a house to rent. He/She has asked you to help. Write a letter to your friend describing a house you have seen and giving further details.

1 What type of writing is it?
2 Who is sending the letter? What is the relationship between you and the recipient of the letter?
3 What style is appropriate? Justify.
4 What information do you need to include?
5 What opening and closing remarks can you use?

b. Listen to the conversation you had with an estate agent and complete the table.

Location	1) .... Beech Lane, Deighton
Exterior	large 2) .... at the front; garage
Interior	fully-furnished; upstairs: two bedrooms; a 3) .... downstairs: bathroom; living room; old 4) ....; dining room; large kitchen
Rent	5) £ .... a month

c. Use your notes to ask and answer questions, as in the example, then talk about the house.

A: Where is the house located?
B: It is located ...

50 Use the information in Ex. 49b to answer the questions in the plan. Then write your letter. You can use the letter in Ex. 47a as a model.

Dear (your friend's first name)

Introduction
(Para 1) opening remarks

Main Body   *(Suggest topic sentences)*
(Para 2) Where exactly is the house? How much is the rent?
(Para 3) What is the exterior like? (material, garden, etc)
(Para 4) What is the interior like? How many floors/rooms/furniture?

Conclusion
(Para 5) What should you do next: give phone number/book it?
          closing remarks

Yours,
your first name

51 Explain the sentences below in your own words.

- A man travels the world over in search of what he needs, and returns home to find it.
  George Moore (Irish author/poet)
- Strength of character may be learned at work, but beauty of character is learned at home.
  Henry Drummond (1851-1897) (Scottish naturalist)

While there's life, there's hope

Lead-in

1 **a.** Which of the following life events match the pictures (1-4)? What other life events can you think of?

- engagement • moving house • having a baby
- retirement • graduation • wedding

b. In pairs, think of words related to each life event in the pictures. Use the words to describe the pictures.

The man in picture 1 is moving house. He is carrying a large box. He looks happy.

2 **a.** Listen and match the people to the events. How does each person feel?

Marta	losing your job
Steve	moving house
Laura	having a baby
Tony	leaving school
Bill & Terry	retirement

b. In pairs, use the adjectives below to talk about some important events in your life.

- sad • happy • scared • thrilled • excited
- worried • disappointed • pleased • irritated

*I'll never forget my first day at school. I felt very scared.
I was so happy at my sister's wedding. She looked gorgeous in her white dress. It was unforgettable!*

3 **a.** Look at the chart and see what American adults consider to be the top ten stressful life events. Then make up sentences, as in the examples.

73%	Divorce
63%	Death in the family
53%	Personal injury or illness
50%	Marriage
45%	Retirement
39%	Bringing up children
36%	Changing jobs
26%	Starting/leaving school
23%	Trouble at work
20%	Moving house

Seventy-three percent of Americans consider divorce to be the most stressful event in life. Sixty-three percent of Americans consider a death in the family to be the second most stressful event in life.

b. Which are the three most stressful life events for you? Give reasons.

A Dream Come True

The young professor was working in his workshop in a narrow street in Boston, not far from Scollay Square. It was a very hot afternoon in June, but the man did not notice. **0)** [F] Suddenly he heard an almost inaudible sound, the first sound ever **transmitted** through a wire. The machine was the very first telephone and the young man was Alexander Graham Bell.

Although he was only 28 years old at the time, Alexander had been working in the fields of speech, **anatomy**, electricity and **telegraphy** for over 11 years. **1)** [ ] In fact, his whole family had been involved in the study of speech and sounds. Alexander's father had also written several books on how to speak correctly as well as creating a form of sign language called '**visible speech**'.

At the age of 16 Alexander started to help teach young deaf mutes; children who could not hear or speak. He used his father's system of 'visible speech' and achieved amazing results. A few years later, while working in London, Alexander met two men who would play an important role in his life. **2)** [ ] Unfortunately, it was around this time that the **fatal** disease called the **white plague**, spread through Britain and both Alexander's brothers died. **3)** [ ] Alexander was teaching to a tribe of Mohawk Indians in a small Canadian town called Brantford, when the Boston Board of Education asked him to come and work in the USA at a new school for deaf mutes. Alexander was very happy to move to Boston and continue the work he had started in Britain. **4)** [ ] However, he was so busy there that he did not have the time to work on his inventions.

Then, two years later, he agreed to give private lessons to a young boy whose family allowed him to use their **basement** as a workshop. This gave Alexander the opportunity to **resume** his experiments with sound transmitters. He used to spend all his free time, and most of his money, on his inventions. **5)** [ ] She was a young girl who had lost her **hearing** and the ability to speak because of a childhood illness. Her name was Mabel Hubbard, and four years later they got married. Although many people thought that the plan to invent a human voice transmitter was a **waste** of time, Alexander refused to give up his dream. He continued his experiments with sound **vibrations**. He even copied the design of the human ear using **iron rods** and **electrical wires** to produce the same effect.

Alexander was spending so much time and energy on his inventions he did less and less work with his students and soon **ran out of** money. He was about to give up when he met Professor John Henry, an expert on the **telegraph** and electricity. **6)** [ ] In order to **survive financially** Bell had to work on the musical telegraph, but he also continued working on his **mechanical voice transmitter**. **7)** [ ] Almost a year later, in March 1876, the first words were heard coming through the phone.

On his 29th birthday Alexander Graham Bell **registered** his invention with the **patent office** and, because they had never seen anything like it before, they registered his invention as 'an improvement in telegraphy'. The name 'telephone' came later.

Tip: Read the text through. Think of what information might be missing. Read the list of missing sentences. Cross out the one used in the example. Remember there is one extra sentence. Start fitting the sentences into the gaps. Match the topic of the missing sentence with the topic of the sentence before and after each gap. Look for clues such as reference words (he, there, it etc) or linking words before or after each gap. Check that the sentence you choose fits grammatically and makes sense. Read the completed text to see if it makes sense.

Reading

4
a. What do you know about Alexander Graham Bell? What did he invent? When? Did he come from a big family? Read the article and find out.

b. Choose from sentences, (A-I), the one that best fits each gap (1-7) to complete the text. There is one extra sentence you do not need to use.

A Professor Henry realised immediately that Alexander had made an amazing discovery and encouraged him to continue with his experiments.

B At that time he had another student who greatly influenced his life.

C His grandfather had invented a system to help people with speech problems.

D He was inspired by the Baron's work and refused to give up his dream.

E Mr Alexander Ellis, a professor of philology, and Sir Charles Wheatstone, an expert in telegraphy, started him thinking about sending sounds through a machine.

F He was totally absorbed in his strange machine which he had been working on for about three years.

G As a result Alexander and his parents left the country and moved to Canada.

H On that summer afternoon in 1875, when Alexander heard the first sound transmitted over his machine, he realised that he had finally achieved his goal.

I He became so successful that he soon opened his own school called "The School of Vocal Physiology".

c. Read the article again and explain the words in bold. Give synonyms for the highlighted words.

d. Which of the following words best describe Alexander Graham Bell? Give reasons.

• persistent • sensitive • daydreamer • stubborn
• hardworking • patient • indifferent

Follow-up

5 Read the article again and make notes about Alexander Graham Bell's life. Then, talk about his life. How has his invention changed our lives?

Vocabulary Practice

Describing People

6 a. Look at the pictures. Who's got: *wrinkles, freckles, spiky hair, dimples, a centre parting, crooked teeth, a beard, bushy eyebrows, glasses, straight hair, a wide forehead, frizzy hair, sideburns, a moustache, a pointed chin*?

Tony, Jean, Bill, Mr Harris, Peter

b. In pairs, complete the table with as many adjectives or phrases as possible. Then, use the words to describe yourself.

Age:	in his teens,
Height/Build:	broad-shouldered,
Hair:	wavy,
Face:	oval,
Cheeks:	rosy,
Eyebrows:	arched,
Eyes:	green,
Eyelashes:	thick,
Nose:	snub,
Mouth:	wide,
Chin:	pointed,

I am in my early teens. I am tall and slim and …

7 a. Look at the pictures, then use the words from Ex. 6 to describe each one.

A – Michelle Pfeiffer (1958)
B – Rod Stewart (1945)
C – Harrison Ford (1942)
D – John Malkovich (1953)
E – Sting (1953)

b. Listen and match the jobs to the famous people above.

English teacher ………. checkout clerk ……….
forest fire fighter ………. footballer ……….
carpenter ……….

c. Talk about each person, as in the example.

A: When was Michelle Pfeiffer born?
B: She was born in 1958?
A: What does she look like?
B: She has got long blonde hair and blue eyes.
A: What did she do before she became an actress?
B: She was a checkout clerk.

Project

Prepare a poster of famous people. Write their job, age and a short description of each. Decorate your project with pictures.

Stages in Life

8 a. Listen and fill in the average ages for people in the USA, then make up sentences, as in the example.

EVENT	AGE
start elementary school	
go to college/university	
leave home	
get married	
have first child	
buy a house	
retire	

Americans usually start elementary school at the age of five.

b. Make a similar table for your country. How does your country differ from the USA?

c. Study the diagram and in pairs, think of two events typical of each stage.

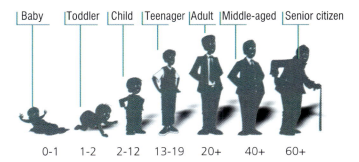

A baby learns to crawl.
A toddler learns to walk.

Feelings

9 a. Write the adjectives on the correct line.

- terrified • bored • delighted • worried
- impatient • calm • annoyed • cheerful • sad
- depressed • ecstatic • furious • miserable
- pleased • nervous • relaxed • frustrated

b. Choose one adjective from each column. When was the last time you felt like this? What had happened to cause this feeling?

The last time I felt annoyed was when the train was late.

Listening

10 Listen and write how each speaker felt. Why did each speaker feel that way?

Speaker 1: ....
Speaker 2: ....
Speaker 3: ....
Speaker 4: ....
Speaker 5: ....

11 Listen to these sounds and match them to how you would feel. Then, make up sentences, as in the example.

siren wailing	irritated
dogs barking	nervous
waves splashing	scared
message notification	eager
thunder crashing	relaxed

Whenever I hear a siren wailing, I feel nervous.
A siren wailing makes me feel nervous.

12 These symbols, or *emoticons*, are used in e-mails and chat rooms to suggest feelings. Study them and then use the symbols to respond to the comments.

1 Can you believe it? He gets paid $ 1 million a film! :-/
2 Guess what? I got engaged!
3 He's in hospital. He's very ill.
4 They won 3-0!
5 I've applied to London University.
6 I DIDN'T GET THE JOB.

13 Fill in *be* and/or *feel*. Then use the collocations to make up sentences about yourself.

1 .... convinced	6 .... expressive
2 .... exhausted	7 .... easy-going
3 .... kind	8 .... forgiven
4 .... pathetic	9 .... interested
5 .... worried	10 .... responsible

He felt/was convinced that she didn't like him.

Grammar in use

Past tenses

Grammar Reference

14 a. Identify the tenses in bold, then match them to their use.

1. She **left** university six years ago.
2. He **was waiting** for the bus when the accident happened.
3. He **had just finished** his report when his boss asked to see him.
4. She **had been working** as a clerk for two years before she got promoted.

a happened before another past action with emphasis on continuation
b happened at a specific time in the past
c happened before another past action
d was in progress at a certain time in the past

b. Underline the time adverbs used with each tense. What other adverbs can you think of which can be used with these tenses? Make up three sentences using them.

15 Match the prompts from each column to make sentences.

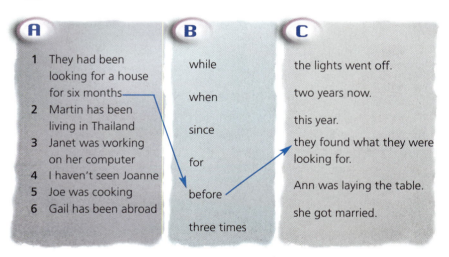

16 Put the verbs in brackets into the correct past tense. Justify your answers.

1. Paul .... (break) his arm while he .... (paint) the wall.
2. Sandra finally .... (pass) the exam. She .... (study) really hard for months.
3. A: How long .... (Mary/work) here before she .... (retire)?
   B: More than twenty years.
4. While I .... (walk) home last night, I .... (bump) into Sally.
5. The sun .... (shine) and the birds .... (sing) as we .... (drive) towards the village.
6. We .... (finish) the main course and .... (wait) for dessert when the fire alarm .... (ring).

7. "...................... (you/work) late last night?"
   "Yes, actually I .... (not/leave) until 11 pm."
8. She .... (visit) France before but she only .... (go) to Paris last month.
9. A: .... (you/see) Jamie at the party last night?
   B: No, by the time I .... (get) there, he .... (already/leave).
10. Amy .... (walk) home when she .... (hear) her mobile phone ring.

17 Underline the correct words.

1. When she entered her flat she **had found/found** that someone **had broken/broke** in.
2. He **had been driving/was driving** home **when/after** he crashed into a tree.
3. When Laura **arrived/had arrived** at the restaurant, Tony **had gone/had been gone** home.
4. **When/While** I walked into the room, they had **just/yet** finished their dinner.
5. After they **had been living/lived** there **since/for** two years they decided to build an extension to their house.
6. He **didn't shave/hadn't been shaving** this morning because he **hadn't had/didn't have** time.
7. **While/After** he graduated from university, he **joined/was joining** the army.
8. She **had been watching/watched** TV **when/since** Tom came home.
9. He **was having/had** a bath when the lights **had gone/went** out.
10. She had **never/ever** been to South America **before/after**.

Game

Look at the cartoons, then in teams try to explain what happened to each of the people using past tenses. Each correct sentence gets 1 point. The team with the most points is the winner.

He fell off the ladder while he was painting the wall and broke his arm. He had been playing football for an hour when ...

Used to / Would

Grammar Reference

18 a. Study the examples. In which of the sentences (1-6) can you use *would* instead of *used to*? Tick (✓) accordingly.

> He **used to/would** go jogging before breakfast. (past routine)
> He **used to** live in York as a student. (past state)
> NOT: He ~~would~~ live in York as a student.

1 I used to come here when I was young.
2 Jack's parents used to live in Canada.
3 Louise used to have a motorbike but I think she has a car now.
4 Caroline used to play tennis every week when she was a child.
5 When they were younger, they used to go for long walks in the countryside.
6 Grandma used to make porridge for breakfast.

b. Listen to Sam and Sarah and tick (✓) the things that they used to do when they were children and cross (✗) the things that they didn't use to do. Then make up sentences, as in the example.

✗ play with computers	☐ lock their doors
☐ have their own private telephone lines	☐ do lots of chores
☐ play outdoors	☐ have early nights
☐ play with their friends in the street	☐ wear a uniform to school
☐ go fishing	☐ go to school six days a week
☐ go swimming in the river	☐ visit their grandparents in the school holidays

Sam and Sarah didn't use to play with computers.

c. Talk about what you used to do during your childhood.

19 a. Study the two examples. Which sentence refers to the past?

a. They met ten years ago.   b. They have been together since then.

b. Put the verbs in brackets into the *past simple* or the *present perfect*.

Alex Morton is a talented writer who 1) .... (lead) a very interesting life. He was born in 1945 in Manchester, and he was the youngest of six children. From the moment he could read, he was never without a book in his hands. He was an avid reader throughout his schooldays, and he soon 2) .... (show) his talent for writing, too. In fact, his teachers 3) .... (give) him extra assignments just to be able to read more of his work.
After he 4) .... (leave) school he went to Manchester University. By the time he got his BA, he had already published a number of short stories, and his first novel was almost finished. Over the next few years he 5) .... (write) non-stop and each of his books was more successful than the last. Despite being so busy with his work, Alex still 6) .... (find) time for romance. He met Fiona Jones while he was at university and they were married in 1971. They have two children. He 7) .... (always/be) a devoted husband and father.
Alex Morton 8) .... (write) over twenty books so far and his name 9) .... (be) on the best seller list more times than he can remember. However, the pinnacle of his career was when he 10) .... (win) the Booker Prize for Fiction in 1995. Since then, Alex 11) .... (continue) to write and many of his books 12) .... (be/made) into films.

c. Talk about one of your older relatives. You can talk about his/her:

• childhood • education • work • family (e.g. marriage/children)
• achievements • later years

My grandfather is called Harry. He was born in Brighton in 1920. When he left school he joined the local fire brigade. He got married when he was twenty-six. He and his wife Ada had seven children. He says that his family was his most important achievement in life. My grandfather retired three years ago. Since then, he and my grandmother have spent their time travelling and gardening.

Grammar in use

Prepositions
Appendix 1

20 a. Underline the correct preposition, then explain the phrases in bold.

1. Julie is **capable** *of/for* doing it on her own.
2. You can **depend** *to/on* Simon. He's very reliable.
3. He shouldn't **comment** *on/to* that when he doesn't know all of the facts.
4. It was very unfair that Paul was **dismissed** *from/of* his job.
5. The criminal has been **charged** *for/with* burglary.
6. They're always **complaining** *of/about* something.
7. Children are very **curious** *for/about* the world they live in.
8. Julian is very serious and **dedicated** *to/at* his work.
9. She is finding it difficult to **concentrate** *on/to* her studies.
10. Sally is amazing. I don't know how she **copes** *with/at* her job, and her kids at the same time.

b. Fill in the correct preposition. Then choose any three phrases and make up sentences using them.

1 .... fact; 2 to be involved .... sth; 3 to move .... Boston; 4 to spend time and money .... sth; 5 a waste .... time; 6 an expert .... sth

Phrasal Verbs
Appendix 2

21 a. Fill in the correct particle and explain the phrasal verbs.

• out (x2) • up with • into
• across • round • away • on
• off • down with

1. The fans got completely **carried** .... when their team scored in the last minute.
2. Neil was reading the newspaper when he **came** .... an article about an old friend of his.
3. When Lucy's uncle died she **came** .... a lot of money.
4. Sue asked Rick and Claire to **come** .... for dinner tonight.
5. Danny **carried** his speech .... perfectly.
6. Jason is going to **carry** .... the business after his father retires.
7. The author has a new novel **coming** .... next week.
8. Liz has **come** .... an excellent solution to our problem.
9. Doctors will **carry** .... more tests to find out what the problem is.
10. John is ill; he has **come** .... chickenpox.

b. Look up other meanings of *come out* and *come (a)round* in your dictionary. Then make up sentences using these meanings.

Word Formation

22 Fill in the correct word derived from the word in bold.

Although the 0) *majority* of people say that they work, 'for the money', the 1) .... reward isn't actually the only thing that they think about. 2) ...., research has shown that people consider many different factors to be of 3) .... when they make their 4) .... A worldwide survey of students showed that after 5) .... they would be looking for jobs that allowed them to balance their 6) .... lives with their work lives.

It's not just the younger generation who think like this either. There has even been an increase in the number of middle-aged 7) .... who are moving away from highly-paid executive positions into less 8) .... jobs. They are looking for something which is more 9) .... and gives them more leisure time. All this has meant that 10) .... are realising that they need to do more than just offer good wages if they are going to keep their workers happy and motivated!

MAJOR
FINANCE
RECENT
IMPORT
CHOOSE
GRADUATE
PERSON

WORK

STRESS
ENJOY
EMPLOY

Working Lives

Open Cloze

23 Read the text and think of the word which best fits each gap. Use only ONE WORD in each gap.

Tip: Read the title of the text. It is a summary of what you are going to read. Read the text once quickly to get the general meaning. Read the text again. Pay attention to the words before/after each gap. These will help you decide what word is missing. Missing words can be adverbs, articles, modal/auxiliary verbs, conjunctions, prepositions, pronouns, phrasal verbs etc. The word that you choose must be grammatically correct and make sense in context. When you have filled in the gaps read the text again to see if it makes sense.

The Importance of Family

In Western Europe and the USA, family life **0) has** changed dramatically over the last forty years. The number of families that depend **1)** .... both parents going out to work, or where **2)** .... is one parent raising the children alone, is much greater than it **3)** .... to be. Also, many more people move away from their families **4)** .... ever before. **5)** .... these changes, most people still think **6)** .... their family as one of the most significant parts of **7)** .... lives.

A recent American survey showed that **8)** .... people think that spending time **9)** .... home is more important **10)** .... earning a high salary or having a challenging job. The majority of young people surveyed said that they **11)** .... be happy to earn less money if they had more time to **12)** .... with their loved ones. Older people also commented that they had worked **13)** .... hard in the past when they should have **14)** .... with their families. **15)** .... if the typical family doesn't follow the traditional model today, it is still a vital part of our lives.

Key-word Transformations

24 Complete the sentences using the words in bold. You must use between two and five words, including the word given.

1. He started to play golf five years ago.
   for   He .... five years now.

2. How long is it since you moved here?
   ago   How .... here?

3. We haven't had a holiday for years.
   ages   It's .... a holiday.

4. We haven't been out since last summer.
   time   The .... was last summer.

5. After hours of discussion, they finally succeeded in reaching an agreement.
   managed   They .... after hours of discussion.

6. She wasn't involved in the argument at all.
   nothing   She had .... the argument at all.

Idioms & Fixed Phrases

25 Underline the correct word, then try to explain the idioms.

1. Let's put on some music. It's **as *silent/quiet* as the grave** in here.
2. He's got food poisoning and he's been **as sick as a *dog/cat*** all week.
3. Don't worry about Maggie; she's **as tough as old *shoes/boots***.
4. The Martin children are not at all alike. They're **as different as chalk and *cheese/milk***.
5. I'll look after Jo anytime. Really, she's **as good as *silver/gold***.
6. Ben can't wait to get started on the project. He's **as keen as *ketchup/mustard***.

26 Circle the correct word, then explain the expressions in bold.

1. Things are going very well at work at the moment, I think a promotion might even be **on the** ....
   A books   B cards   C letters   D papers

2. Chris does lots of work for charity. He's always doing something for **a good** ....
   A aim   B example   C cause   D reason

3. You have to **make it** .... to her exactly how you feel.
   A easy   B straight   C clean   D clear

4. Helen is a lovely girl, but she always **has her head in the** .... She never notices what's going on around her.
   A sky   B stars   C clouds   D air

5. It was only a silly argument, but they were both getting very .... **under the collar**.
   A hot   B red   C heated   D warm

Listening & Speaking

27 a. You will hear five people talking about the most important thing in their lives. Listen and match the speakers to the statements. There is one statement which does not match any of the speakers.

A We have a great relationship.
B Financial security is very important to me.
C Nothing is as important as your health.
D They're like my family.
E My family is everything to me.
F My career is my life.

Speaker 1 ☐
Speaker 2 ☐
Speaker 3 ☐
Speaker 4 ☐
Speaker 5 ☐

b. Listen again and write one reason why each person feels this way.

28 Look at the survey results and the visual prompts. Then, in pairs, discuss the following:

- Which of these things do you consider to be important in your life? Why/why not?
- Are some things just as important as other things? Which ones? Give reasons.

A: I think family life is the most important thing in my life because my family help and support me.
B: Really, I think friendships are the most important thing because I share everything with my friends. etc

29 a. Listen and mark the sentences *T* (true) or *F* (false).

1 Rachel gets plenty of attention from her parents. ....
2 Her parents spoil her. ....
3 She never feels lonely. ....
4 She sometimes wishes she had a brother. ....
5 She doesn't want to share things with anyone. ....
6 She likes having her own room. ....
7 She thinks that friends can be as good as sisters. ....

Tip Read the statements before you listen and underline the key words. Try to match the key words with similar words in the script.

b. In pairs talk about your family. How big is your family? What does each member of your family look like? Which family member do you admire most? Who is your favourite relative? Why? How often do you see your relatives?

30 Describe the pictures. Then, in pairs, express your opinions about:

- the advantages and disadvantages of each type of family
- the problems the children in each type of family might have
- how each family compares to your own

EXPRESSING OPINIONS

Picture A shows ..., whereas ..., I think ..., I believe ..., In my opinion ..., It seems to me ...

AGREEING	DISAGREEING
You´re right/That's true/ I quite agree with you.	Do you (really) think so? No, I'm afraid I can't agree with you.

A: Picture A shows a large family. There are the parents and three children; two girls and a boy. They look European or American. What do you think?
B: I think you're right. They look very happy. etc

31 You'll hear five people talking about a past experience. Decide which of the statements (A-F) matches what the speaker says. There is one extra statement which you do not need to use.

A I simply didn't want to do it.
B It was an unforgettable experience.
C I've never been so afraid.
D It was the best day of my life.
E I was really excited.
F I didn't know what was going on.

Speaker 1 ☐
Speaker 2 ☐
Speaker 3 ☐
Speaker 4 ☐
Speaker 5 ☐

Moments in Life

100 people were questioned about what they thought was the most important thing in their lives. This is what they said.

- family life 28%
- career 24%
- relationship 20%
- friendships 18%
- good health 10%

32 Look at the pictures and identify what they show. Which of these bring back memories of your early childhood? Talk about your memories.

I'll never forget my first fancy dress party. I was dressed as a cowboy. It was ...

Spreading the news

33 a. Listen and identify which extracts give good/bad news.

b. Read the exchanges and practise the intonation. Then, use the prompts to act out similar dialogues.

- Your sister has got engaged.
- Your brother has been promoted.
- Your friend was in a car accident.
- You passed your exams.
- You got your driving licence.
- Your friend lost his job.

1 A: **I've got something to tell you.** I'm afraid I failed my driving test.
   B: **That's a pity.** You must be really disappointed.
2 A: **Have you heard?** I won a trip to Florida.
   B: **Wow! Congratulations!** You must be thrilled!
3 A: **Guess what!** I've got a new job!
   B: **That's brilliant!** You must be very happy.
4 A: **I'm afraid I've just heard something terrible.** Simon crashed his motorbike
   B: Oh no! **How awful!**

Intonation (contrastive stress)

34 Listen, mark the stressed words, then repeat.

- A: Did you make a chocolate cake?
  B: No, I made a fruit cake.
- A: Do you want three boxes of chocolates?
  B: No, I want two boxes.
- A: Did you ask Mr Johnson?
  B: No, I asked Miss Johnson.

Describing people

35 a. Listen to the dialogue. Who does Simon want to meet?

b. Match the columns to form a dialogue. Then, in pairs, act out similar dialogues for the people in the pictures.

A	This is a great party, Fred.	1	No problem. Let's go over and I'll introduce you.
B	Yes, I am, but who's that over there?	2	Oh, that's Diana. She's just started working in my office. Do you want to meet her?
C	The girl with the long blonde hair.	3	Thanks. Are you having a good time?
D	Yes, please. That would be great.	4	Who?

Introducing people

36 a. Listen to the dialogue. Where does it take place?

b. Read the dialogue. Then use the expressions in the box to introduce:

- your new friend to your parents
- your husband/wife to your employer
- two business associates to each other

A: Miss Lane, I'd like to introduce you to a colleague of mine.
B: Certainly.
A: Miss Lane, this is my colleague, Mr Kent. Mr Kent this is Miss Lane.
B: How do you do? It is a pleasure to meet you Mr Kent.
C: It is a pleasure to meet you too, Miss Lane.

INTRODUCTIONS	
Formal	Informal
May I introduce ...	This is ...
I would like you to meet ...	Come and meet ...
I would like to introduce you to ...	Hi, how are you?
How do you do?	Hi there!
It is a pleasure to meet you.	Pleased to meet you.

Jack & Jill

Louisa May Alcott (1832-1888) was born in Germantown, Pennsylvania, the second of four sisters. At an early age, Louisa and her family moved to Massachusetts, where she lived for most of her life. Her father was a teacher, and he encouraged Louisa to keep a diary. She started to write at the age of 16. Alcott used her diary to help her write about her own life and experiences. One of her most famous books is *Little Women*, which is based on the life of her family. She wrote *Jack and Jill: A Village Story* in 1880. Alcott has been called the 'novelist of children' for her ability to reflect the teenage point of view. *Jack and Jill* tells the story of life in rural New England at the turn of the century. It tells of how the friendship between the two main characters is tested by a terrible accident. With the help of their friends and family, they put their bad luck behind them and get on with their lives.

37 Read the title and the author's biography. What do you think the novel is about? How could Alcott's own experiences have helped her write the novel? Look at the picture. What time of year is it? What are the children doing?

38 a. Read the extract and match the characters with their descriptions, then make up sentences about them. Finally explain the words in bold.

1	Frank Minot	a	white teeth, golden hair
2	Little Boo	b	short legs, round face
3	Ed Devlin	c	tall, keen sparkle in his eye
4	Jack	d	black eyes, red cheeks
5	Jill	e	sweet-faced, rosy cheeks

b. Which of the characters is: **serious; clever; good-natured; popular; protective; patient**? Underline the words/phrases/sentences which imply the character.

c. Which of the characters can you see in the pictures? Describe them.

d. Match the highlighted words to their synonyms in the list.

• boy • serious • smarter • guy • gathered • playful • generously
• first-rate • protected • shy

39 a. This chapter is called **The Catastrophe**. What catastrophe do you think might happen? In pairs, predict what you think is going to happen next.

I think there is going to be a fight between Joe and Jack.

b. Listen and check if your guesses were correct.

Project

You have decided to enter the Louisa May Alcott drawing competition. Read the extract again, then choose a scene to draw for the competition.

Literature Corner

Chapter 1
The Catastrophe

"Clear the lulla!" was the general cry on a bright December afternoon, when all the boys and girls of Harmony Village were out enjoying the first good snow of the season. Up and down three long coasts they went as fast as legs and sleds could carry them. One smooth path led into the meadow, and here the little folk **congregated**; there was a group of lads and lasses sitting or leaning on a fence to rest after an exciting race, and, as they **reposed**, they amused themselves with **criticising** their mates.

"Here comes Frank Minot, looking as **solemn** as a judge," cried one, as a tall fellow of sixteen spun by, with a set look about the mouth and a keen sparkle of the eyes, fixed on the distant goal with a **do-or-die expression**.

"Here's Molly Loo and Little Boo," sang out another; and down came a girl with flying hair, carrying a small boy behind her, so that his short legs **stuck out** from the sides, and his round face looked over her shoulder like a full moon.

"There's Gus Burton; doesn't he go it?" and such a very long boy **whizzed** by, that it looked almost as if his heels were at the top of the hill when his head was at the bottom!

"Hurrah for Ed Devlin!" and a general shout greeted a sweet-faced **lad** with a laugh on his lips, a fine colour on his brown cheek, and a gay word for every girl he passed.

"Laura and Lotty keep to the safe coast into the meadow, and Molly Loo is the only girl that dares to try this long one to the pond. I wouldn't for the world; the ice can't be strong yet, though it is cold enough to freeze one's nose off," said a **timid** damsel, who sat **hugging** a post and screaming whenever a **mischievous** lad shook the fence.

"No, she isn't. Here's Jack and Jill going like fury."

"Clear the track for jolly Jack!" sang the boys, who had rhymes and **nicknames** for nearly everyone.

Down came a gay red sled, bearing a boy who seemed all smile and sunshine, so white were his teeth, so golden was his hair, so bright and happy his whole air. Behind him **clung** a girl, with black eyes and hair, cheeks as red as her hood, and a face full of fun and sparkle, as she waved Jack's blue **tippet** like a **banner** with one hand, and held on with the other.

"Jill goes wherever Jack does, and he lets her. He's such a **good-natured** **chap**, he can't say *No*."

"To a girl," **slyly** added one of the boys, who had wished to borrow the red sled, and had been politely refused because Jill wanted it.

"He's the nicest boy in the world, for he never gets mad," said the timid young lady, recalling the many times Jack had **shielded** her from the terrors which beset her path to school, in the shape of cows, dogs, and boys who made faces and called her 'Fraidcat'.

"He doesn't dare to get mad with Jill, for she'd take his head off in two minutes if he did," growled Joe Flint.

"She wouldn't! She's a dear! You needn't sniff at her because she is poor. She's ever so much **brighter** than you are, or she wouldn't always be at the head of your class, old Joe," cried the girls, standing by their friend with a **unanimity** which proved what a favourite she was.

Joe subsided with as scornful a curl to his nose as its chilly state permitted, and Merry Grant introduced a subject of general interest by asking abruptly, "Who is going to the candy-scrape tonight?"

"All of us, Frank invited the whole set, and we shall have a **tiptop** time. We always do at the Minots'," cried Sue, the **timid** trembler.

"Jack said there was a **barrel** of **molasses** in the house, so there would be enough for all to eat and some to carry away. They know how to do things **handsomely**", and the speaker licked his lips, as if already tasting the feast in store for him.

"Mrs Minot is a mother worth having," said Molly Loo, coming up with Boo on the sled; and she knew what it was to need a mother, for she had none, and tried to care for the little brother with maternal love and **patience**.

"She is just as sweet as she can be!" declared Merry, enthusiastically.

Writing a story

Tip

To write a story we first decide on the type of story, the plot and the main characters. Our story can be a comedy, a spy story, a thriller, an adventure story, a detective story, a fairy tale etc.

Introduction
In the **first paragraph**, we write when and where the event happened, who the people in the story were and what happened first.

Main Body
In the **main body paragraphs**, we describe the events in the order they happened. One of the events should be the climax event. We can use *so, because, and, also* etc to join our sentences or ideas.

Conclusion
In the **last paragraph**, we write what happened in the end and how the people in the story felt. We can use a variety of adjectives or adverbs to make our story more interesting. We normally use past tenses in stories.

Analysing a Rubric

40 Read the rubric and answer the questions.

> **ENTER NOW AND HAVE YOUR STORY PRINTED IN TEENS!**
>
> What is your most unforgettable childhood experience?
> Send in your story (120-180 words) for your chance to win a two-week all-expenses paid trip to **Disneyland, Paris**. Runners-up will receive a one-year subscription to **TEENS**!
> Closing date: 10th December.
> Results announced: 17th February.

1. Where would you see this announcement published?
2. What is the announcement about?
3. Who are you going to write about?
4. What could your story be about?

Analysing a Model Text

41 a. Read the story and fill in the linkers. What tenses has the writer used?

• by the time • while • then • but • as soon as • as

b. Which scene does the picture show? What happened before/after it? Who do you think the writer is?

The best day of my life

Whenever I look at that photograph, it takes me back to those early years when every new experience was so important that it was almost unbearable. It was towards the end of the school year – my first year at primary school – that it happened. I had been looking forward to that day with such eagerness.

I can still remember the shouts of the spectators as I went out onto the sports field with my classmates. Earlier that week I had qualified for the finals of the 100 metres. Now, looking around, I was determined to win.

1) .... I was walking across to the start, I began to feel more and more nervous. I looked at the bustling crowd of spectators, and I saw my proud parents waving enthusiastically. My heart was pounding fast **2)** .... I lined up with the other eager competitors. I felt so excited that my whole body was shaking. I braced myself, took some deep breaths and waited for the signal. **3)** .... the starting pistol sounded and I set off down the track.

I could hear the crowd shouting excitedly, **4)** .... the noise seemed very far away. I sprinted as fast as I could, not looking at anything except the finishing line. **5)** .... I crossed the line I was so exhausted I could hardly breathe. **6)** .... I heard the result announced, I realized I had won! Overjoyed, I collapsed on the soft grass with a broad grin on my face.

"Well done!" said the Headmaster later, as he presented me with the winner's certificate. I had never felt so happy and proud in my life.

Sequence of events

c. Read the story again and put the events in the correct order.

a He set off. .....
b The runners lined up for the race. .....
c He finished the race. .....
d He was presented with a certificate. .....
e He walked to the start. .....
f The result was announced. .....
g He went very fast. .....
h The starting pistol sounded. .....
i He collapsed on the grass. .....
j He entered the sports field. .....

Descriptive Techniques

42 a. Fill in the adjectives from the story. In pairs, think of synonyms for each adjective.

1 .... competitors
2 .... parents
3 .... grin
4 .... crowd
5 .... grass
6 .... breaths
7 .... pistol
8 .... line

b. Underline the verb/adverb collocations the writer used. Can you think of other adverbs used with these verbs? Write them down, then make up sentences using them.

c. The writer used his senses to describe the event. Read the story and find examples.

the shouts of the spectators

43 a. Use the adjectives and adverbs in the list to make the paragraph more interesting.

- deafening • heavy • winding • brilliant • gloomy • huge

- suddenly • luckily • nervously • loudly • slowly

We were driving along the road through the forest, on the way to my grandmother's house. The rain made it difficult to see where we were going. There was a flash of lightning followed by a crash of thunder. A tree crashed into the road in front of us. My father stopped the car in time. We all looked at each other. What were we going to do now?

b. Underline the words and phrases that use the senses to make the story interesting.

Beginnings/Endings

44 Read the beginning of the story in Ex. 41 again. What does the writer say about the place/time his story took place? people involved? event?

To start/end a story you can:
- Use direct speech. (e.g. *"Hurry up!" Jim shouted, as he ran down the stairs. "We are going to be late!"*)
- Ask a rhetorical question. (e.g. *Have you ever wondered what it would be like to escape for a day?*)
- Refer to feelings/moods. (e.g. *It was a bright, clear Sunday afternoon, and I was excited by the thought of the adventure ahead.*)
- Use our senses to begin a story. (e.g. *The sun was shining brightly, and the birds were singing as Jim pulled on a light jacket and ran out of the house.*)

45 What techniques has the writer used to start/end his story? In pairs, rewrite the first and last paragraph using different techniques.

Discuss & Write

46 a. You have read the rubric in Ex. 40 and you have decided to enter the competition. Plan your own story by answering the questions below.

Introduction
(Para 1) Where were you? When did it happen? What happened?

Main Body
(Paras 2-4) What exactly happened? (List the events in chronological order.)
What was the climax event?

Conclusion
(Para 5) What was the outcome? How did you feel?

b. Write your story. Check you have:
- made your beginning interesting by applying one of the techniques mentioned
- used a variety of adjectives and adverbs
- put the events in the correct chronological order
- ended your story by using one of the techniques mentioned
- given it a suitable title

47 Explain the sentences below in your own words.

- It takes courage to grow up and become who you really are.
 e e cummings (US poet)
- Live your beliefs and you can turn the world around.
 H D Thoreau (US poet)

Self-Assessment Module 1

Vocabulary & Grammar

1 Fill in the missing word.

1 A fire broke .... in the school cafeteria last night.
2 They're tired. They .... been painting all morning.
3 Are you .... a good time, Jim?
4 Bill is nineteen, so he's still in his ....
5 When he reached 65 he .... from work.
6 Oh no! I haven't finished my homework ....!
7 He usually .... the lawn on Sundays.
8 Peter was washing the dishes .... the phone rang.
9 .... Janet thinking of moving to Italy?
10 We .... to play football every day when I was a teenager.
11 Jason was accused .... cheating on the test.
12 Did you know that John was dismissed .... his job?
13 I don't know how she copes .... a full-time job and a family.
14 I go to the theatre once in a .... moon.
15 Sarah was cleaning the attic when she came .... her grandmother's silver necklace.
16 Because of a childhood illness she .... her hearing. Now she can't hear at all.
17 My wallet has disappeared into .... air!
18 Reading my old diaries always .... back memories of my childhood.
19 I'm afraid I just don't approve .... this kind of behaviour!
20 The fans got really carried .... when Beckham scored a goal.

(10 marks)

2 Circle the correct item.

1 They couldn't find what they wanted, so they had to build it from ....
   A begin   B scrape   C scratch   D first
2 Her .... leaped when she heard the news.
   A head   B heart   C mind   D stomach
3 She is very pretty, with rosy .... and big eyes.
   A nose   B mouth   C face   D cheeks
4 My new flat has central ...., so it's really warm.
   A heating   B system   C wardrobe   D parking
5 Jane became .... as she was waiting for Tom to turn up.
   A easy-going   C impatient
   B exhausted   D depressed
6 Listen! A siren is ....
   A barking   B wailing   C crashing   D splashing
7 Ann has got frizzy hair and a .... chin.
   A wide   B pointed   C crooked   D spiky
8 Bill has got a wide .... and wrinkles.
   A forehead   B build   C chin   D face
9 Jim has come .... the flu, so he won't be able to come.
   A down with   B up with   C on with   D in with
10 He gives private lessons for a small ....
    A fee   B money   C payment   D receipt

(10 marks)

Use of English

3 Complete the second sentence using the word in bold. You can use two to five words including the word given. Don't change the word given.

1 It's a month since he started working here.
   been   He .... a month.
2 How long is it since you went to Russia?
   ago   How .... to Russia?
3 Their new album will be on the market next month.
   out   Their new album .... next month.
4 She succeeded in passing her exams.
   managed   She .... her exams.
5 They haven't been out for months.
   ages   It's .... out.

(5 marks)

4 Fill in the correct word derived from the word in bold.

1 Jim seems to have .... problems.   **FINANCE**
2 Jenny is an .... woman in her early thirties.   **ATTRACT**
3 They decided to have a .... system installed.   **SECURE**
4 He was .... to find a solution so he asked for help.   **ABLE**
5 After .... he started looking for a job.   **GRADUATE**

(5 marks)

34

Self-Assessment Module 1

5 Read the sentences. If a sentence is correct put a tick (✓). If it has a word which should not be there, write this word on the line.

1. The Smiths' house, which it is in the suburbs, ...
2. was broken into the last night. The owners ....
3. were at the theatre at the time to celebrating ....
4. their tenth wedding anniversary. Surprisingly ....
5. the alarm didn't go off although it was on. ....

(5 marks)

Communication

6 Complete the dialogue.

A: Hi Ben, it's Janet. **1)** ....?
B: Oh hi, Janet. I'm fine. How **2)** ....?
A: I'm okay. Look, are you busy on Saturday night?
B: No, as a matter of fact, I'm not.
A: I'm having a party at my house. Would **3)** ....
   ....?
B: I'd love to. **4)** ....?
A: Anytime after 8.
B: Sounds great. **5)** ....
   on Saturday, then.
A: I'll be there.

(5 marks)

7 Complete the exchanges.

1. A: ....?
   B: She's got short fair hair and green eyes.
2. A: Mr Smith, this is Mrs James.
   B: ....? It is a pleasure to meet you.
3. A: ....the post office?
   B: It's on Apple Street, five minutes from the tube station.
4. A: Hello, Mr Smith. .... you?
   B: Yes. I've got a problem with the roof.
5. A: ...., please?
   B: 21 Blueberry Street.

(5 marks)

Listening

8 a. You will hear five people talking about their childhood homes. What do you think they will talk about?

b. Listen and match the speakers (1-5) to the statements (A-F). Use the letters only once. There is one extra letter which you do not need to use.

A Memories of unusual houses   Speaker ☐ 1
B Hand-made furnishings   Speaker ☐ 2
C Large but almost empty   Speaker ☐ 3
D Built for another purpose   Speaker ☐ 4
E Expensive fittings everywhere Speaker ☐ 5
F An escape from city life

(10 marks)

Speaking (prioritising)

9 Leo has decided to go on a ten-day tour of Portugal. Look at the visual prompts, then, in pairs, decide what he needs to take with him and what he doesn't, giving reasons. You can also suggest other things he can take with him.

Useful phrases	
Inviting speaker:	**Agreeing/Disagreeing:**
• What do you think?	• I couldn't agree more.
• Isn't that right?	• I think you're wrong.
• Don't you agree?	• Yes, you're right.
	• I don't agree.

(10 marks)

35

Self-Assessment Module 1

Reading

10 You are going to read a brief summary of the book "Black Beauty". Choose the most suitable heading from the list (**A-H**) for each part (**1-6**) of the article. There is one extra heading which you do not need to use. There is an example at the beginning (0).

BLACK BEAUTY
THE LIFE OF A HORSE IN NINETEENTH CENTURY ENGLAND

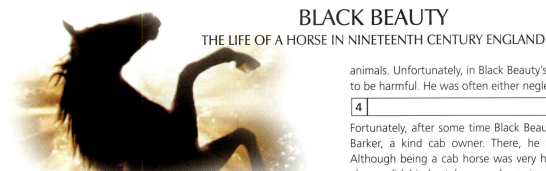

Anna Sewell (1820-1878) wrote only one novel during her lifetime, a book describing the life of a beautiful, black horse, Black Beauty. Sewell was very concerned about animals and used the book to write about the terrible treatment of horses in England at the time. The book is written from the point of view of the horse, which helps us to understand the influence that good and bad treatment had on the horses in the story. Black Beauty had a great effect on the treatment of animals and changed the way that people thought about horses.

| 0 | D |

Black Beauty spent his early years in a picturesque, green field with his mother and some other young colts. When it was time for him to be trained to serve men, he was gently and patiently broken in by his master. He learned to wear a saddle and bridle, and carry a human quietly on his back.

| 1 | |

Black Beauty learnt about the way horses can suffer because of men very early in life. He witnessed a hunting expedition in which a horse was pushed too hard and fast by an inexperienced and overconfident rider. The consequences were tragic. The rider took a fall that killed him and the fine horse broke his leg and was then shot.

| 2 | |

At his next home, one of the horses with whom he shared a stable, had the reputation of being wild and aggressive. This horse, Ginger, said this was because she had been treated very badly at a young age. Ginger was taken away from her mother, not long after birth, and was trained to work, in a very rough manner, by men who did not care for horses. Although her new master and his employees were very kind, she could not help being suspicious of men.

| 3 | |

Black Beauty's kind owner was forced to move abroad for the sake of his wife's health. This marked the beginning of a string of owners with different personalities. Some were well-intentioned but allowed their grooms full control of their animals. Unfortunately, in Black Beauty's case, this often proved to be harmful. He was often either neglected or misused.

| 4 | |

Fortunately, after some time Black Beauty was bought by Jerry Barker, a kind cab owner. There, he was treated very well. Although being a cab horse was very hard work, Black Beauty always did his best because he enjoyed pleasing his master. Black Beauty was very well cared for. He was given good food to eat, a warm stable to sleep in and lots of kind words. Black Beauty learned many things from his new owner, such as the advantages of not being greedy and of being fair and kind to all creatures. Black Beauty spent a couple of very happy years there.

| 5 | |

This pleasant life came to a sudden end when Jerry was forced to sell his horses. After several other owners, Black Beauty was sold to Nicholas Skinner. He had to work every day with no rest, insufficient food and poor accommodation. Although he was still a cab horse, it was a different world. Black Beauty's various drivers would swear at him and whip him. Eventually, Black Beauty became very ill from all this hard work and bad treatment. His owner wanted to have him killed when he could no longer do the job. Luckily, a vet convinced Skinner to allow Black Beauty to rest and recover, and then sell him, so that he would make a bigger profit. The owner agreed to have the horse's life spared, but only for the sake of money.

| 6 | |

After spending years on London's streets, Black Beauty's next home was a pleasant farm, with a caring master. After nursing him back to good health, the farmer decided that Black Beauty needed to be in a place more appropriate than a farm. He sold Black Beauty to two kind young sisters, who lived on a pleasant country estate with a large, green meadow. Here the weary but content horse finally found the rest and peace of mind that he so desired and deserved.

- A A cruel and greedy owner
- B Unable to trust
- C Time to take it easy
- D A gentle teacher
- E In the wrong hands
- F Hard but satisfying work
- G Life as a cart horse
- H A fatal accident

(15 marks)

Self-Assessment Module 1

Writing a first-person narrative

11 Use the notes to write a short story entitled *"A Day Out to Remember"* (120-180 words). Use the notes as well as your own ideas.

Introduction
(Para 1) one afternoon last summer – friend came to your home – invitation – a bike ride

Main Body
(Para 2) made sandwiches – set off – early morning – country lanes – open fields – nice weather
(Para 3) field – stop for lunch – picnic – bull ran at us – left picnic – ran away – bull ate sandwiches – we watched from a distance

Conclusion
(Para 4) hours later – back home – felt happy – tired – very hungry

(20 marks)

(Total = 100 marks)

12 a. Look at the picture. What could Jimmy be dreaming about?

b. What are your dreams? What do you think you should do to make them come true?

Sing Along!

c. Listen and fill in. Then, listen again and sing.

Jimmy worked in an office
From eight o'clock **1)** .... four
His job was satisfying
But he **2)** .... for something more

He was waiting for a sign
And he knew there'd come a time
When a turning point would change his life
And bring a chance for him to shine

Jimmy had an old guitar
People
3) .... to hear him play
And he knew he could be
4) ....
If he could only find a **5)** ....

He was waiting for a sign ...

When Jimmy played at a party
His dream **6)** .... became real
A **7)** .... producer heard him
And offered him a **8)** ....

He was waiting for a sign ...

Jimmy made a record
It went straight to **9)** .... one
He'd found the life he wanted
He'd found his **10)** .... in the sun

He'd been waiting for a sign ...

A TURNING POINT

Progress Update

How do you rate your progress? Tick (✓) the box that applies to you.

	Excellent ****	Good ***	OK **	Could do better *
Vocabulary & Grammar				
Listening				
Speaking				
Reading				
Writing				
Communication				

Planet Earth

UNIT 3 Travel Broadens the Mind

UNIT 4 Earth is Dearer than Gold

Module 2

Units 3-4

Before you start ...

What would your ideal house be? Describe it. Which has the most important event in your life been? Talk about it

Listen, read and talk about ...

- weather
- holidays/holiday destinations
- holiday troubles
- traveller's tips
- festivals
- weekend activities
- planet Earth
- environmental problems
- conservation
- endangered species
- the Tundra

Learn how to ...

- make invitations/ accepting - refusing
- cancel a hotel reservation
- rent a vehicle
- offer solutions to problems
- make suggestions
- complain
- show hesitation

Practise ...

- future tenses
- conditionals Types 0 & 1
- the definite article
- comparisons
- too - enough
- -ing form/infinitive

Phrasal verbs

- cut
- do
- fall
- get

Write ...

- a letter of complaint
- a short article about a natural area in your country
- a semi-formal transactional letter
- a short article about global warming
- a short poem
- an essay providing solutions to problems

Travel Broadens the Mind

Lead-in

1 a. How is the title related to the pictures? In which continent is each place in the pictures? What do you know about these places? Have you ever visited them? Which would you like to visit? Why?

b. Which of the following do you think you can do in each place? You can add your own ideas.

- visit galleries/museums/ancient castles/historical sites
- see animals in their natural environment
- go scuba diving/snorkelling/hiking/kayaking/white-water rafting
- walk along white sandy beaches
- try delicious local cuisine
- see spectacular falls
- take leisurely strolls
- buy handmade souvenirs
- see people in traditional dress
- admire interesting architecture

In Russia you can visit galleries, museums, ancient castles and historical sites. You can also ...

2 a. Listen and match the people to the type of holiday. Which of the places in the pictures is each person going to?

Carl	adventure holiday
Sonya	cultural holiday
Rick	package holiday
Moira	island holiday

b. Listen again and write down what each person is going to do, then make up sentences, as in the example.

Carl is going on a cultural tour of Russia. He is going to visit the Hermitage Museum.

c. Where do you like spending your holidays: by the sea? on an island? Why? Which country would you most like to visit? Why?

Getting away from it all

Tip: Read the questions carefully and underline the key words. Scan the texts for the information you need. As you are reading, underline parts of the texts which are related to the questions. When you finish reading, go back to the questions and try to answer them one by one referring to the texts. Keep in mind that some information may be rephrased.

Reading

3 a. Look at the subheadings of the article. In which country are these places situated? What information do you expect to read?

b. Ask questions about the hotels, using the key words: situated? shops? countryside? sea? modern? room service? activities? facilities?

c. Read the article and answer the questions 1-13. Write **A, B, C** or **D**.

Which place(s):

- is not a hotel?
  0 | D |
- are perfect for a luxury break?
  1 [ ] **2** [ ]
- offers the chance to visit a famous person's home?
  3 [ ]
- is situated on a hill?
  4 [ ]
- are not far from shops?
  5 [ ] **6** [ ]
- offers the chance to eat outdoors?
  7 [ ]
- is suitable for fitness fanatics?
  8 [ ]
- is near the sea?
  9 [ ]
- is not in the countryside?
  10 [ ]
- was built more than 100 years ago?
  11 [ ] **12** [ ] **13** [ ]

d. Read the article again and explain the words in bold. Then, give a synonym for the highlighted words. Can you find any words in the text similar to your language?

e. Which place would you like to stay at? Why?

A Radisson SAS Portman Hotel, London

For those who enjoy **the finer things in life**, a break at the Radisson SAS Portman Hotel will be right up your street. This deluxe four-star hotel is just a minute's walk away from Marble Arch and **a stone's throw** from the stylish boutiques of Oxford Street. After spending a day shopping and sightseeing in London's trendiest area, you can relax in your room, watch cable TV and enjoy something from the **extensive** room service menu. At this hotel, you will also be in the ideal place to visit the many sights of London such as Buckingham Palace and the Houses of Parliament. You must also be sure to allow yourself the time to enjoy the leisure facilities of the hotel itself. The hotel has a **fully equipped** gym and two fantastic restaurants where you can sample gourmet cuisine.

B Langley Castle Hotel, Northumberland

For a touch of medieval magic why not take the time to visit Langley Castle Hotel. Set in its own ten-acre **woodland** this fabulous castle hotel **dates back to** 1350. All guest rooms have got private facilities and are luxurious. Some have special features such as four-poster beds, **stained glass** windows and window seats. The hotel is the perfect base from which to explore Hadrian's Wall and the Northumberland countryside, as well as the Scottish Borders and the Lake District. At night, relax in the hotel lounge in front of the **roaring** log fire or dine in style in the **award-winning** restaurant. During your stay, you can go hot-air ballooning or try your hand at **archery**. You can even have a picnic especially prepared for you by the hotel's chefs. However you choose to spend your time, you will never forget your stay.

C The Metropole Hotel, Cornwall

This Victorian Hotel, situated in one of the most **scenic** areas of the British Isles, stands on a hilltop with an amazing view out over Padstow Harbour. Walk along the **waterfront** or one of the area's many **unspoiled** beaches. Try some fabulous seafood – the local speciality. Wander through Padstow's narrow streets and buy some **handmade** souvenirs from one of the many colourful shops. This is an area with a fascinating history. Take a short trip to Tintagel where you can visit the ruins, claimed to be those of the legendary King Arthur's castle. You can end the day with a swim in the hotel's heated outdoor pool. The Metropole Hotel is ideal for those who want to experience the mystery of Cornwall.

D Old Oxenhope Hall Cottage, West Yorkshire

Fans of English Literature should not miss the opportunity to spend a few days at Old Oxenhope Hall Cottage. This attractive 17th century building is just five minutes from the village of Haworth, where the famous Brontë sisters lived. Their house, *Haworth Parsonage*, is **open to the public** and is well worth a visit. The **moors**, where they would wander for hours, are perfect for those who enjoy walking. The cottage itself is fully **self-contained** and has been **restored** to a high standard of comfort. It is furnished with all the **modern conveniences**, and will certainly appeal to history lovers and **aspiring** writers alike.

Follow-up

4 a. Read the article again, choose one hotel and make notes under the headings below. Then, use your notes to talk about it.

• name • location • description • facilities • things to see/do

b. Make notes under the same headings for a place you have stayed on holiday. Then use your notes to write a short article about it. You can use the article in Ex. 3 as a model.

Vocabulary Practice

Weather

5 a. Listen to the weather forecast and fill in the gaps, then talk about the weather in these places.

A

B

Havana: hot, dry, ..., temperature high thirties

Hong Kong: rainy season, hot, ..., temperature 35°C

C

D

Cape Town: wet, ..., temperature below freezing

Geneva: warm, dry, ..., temperature 18°C

In Havana it's hot, dry and sunny. The temperature is in the high thirties.

b. Imagine you are a weather reporter. Report tomorrow's weather.

❄ *snowy* ☀ *sunny* 🌧 *rainy* ☁ *cloudy* 🌫 *foggy*

35°C *boiling hot*; 30°C *hot*; 25°C *warm*; 15°C *cool*; 10°C *chilly*; 5°C *cold*; -5°C *freezing cold*

Athens 🌧 15°C	Istanbul 🌧 10°C	Moscow ❄ 4°C
Barcelona ☀ 17°C	Kiev ☀ 8°C	Prague ☀ 5°C
Budapest ☀ 10°C	Madrid ☀ 20°C	Singapore ☀ 33°C
Chicago ❄ 2°C	Milan ☀ 17°C	Warsaw 🌧 12°C

It will be cool and rainy in Athens with a temperature of 15°C.

Holidays

6 In pairs discuss which of the items below you would pack if you were going to each of the places in Ex. 5a.

sunglasses umbrella boots gloves
rucksack goggles insect repellent
T-shirt money belt umbrella
sandals shorts first aid kit credit card
guidebook swimsuit binoculars
sunscreen laptop computer mobile phone
camera hairdryer raincoat

A: If I visited Cape Town, I would definitely take my boots because it is cold and wet there.
B: I couldn't agree more. A raincoat is absolutely ...

7 What type of holiday suits you best? Do the quiz to find out.

HOLIDAY QUIZ

1 How do you feel when you go shopping or sightseeing during your holiday?
A trapped
B hot and bothered
C excited
D bored

2 You're trying to enjoy your holiday but the weather is terrible. What do you do?
A Get out into the countryside.
B Stay in and get warm with a cup of tea.
C Take your umbrella and do some window shopping.
D Pack up and go home.

3 You're staying in an old family friend's house for your summer holiday. How do you thank them?
A Invite them on an adventure weekend.
B Invite them to your house for a long weekend.
C Invite them for a weekend out on the town.
D Invite them to a health spa.

4 A friend suggests a trip to a country you've never visited before. What do you ask him about first?
A the national parks
B the beaches
C the nightlife
D the best restaurants

5 What's your ideal spring break?
A Walking over the rugged Yorkshire moors.
B Wandering along the beach in Tahiti.
C A stopover in New York city.
D A luxurious Mediterranean cruise.

Now check your answers

Mostly A)'s, you enjoy adventure and wide open spaces. You would be happiest out hiking in rocky mountains, canoeing across deep blue lakes or camping under the stars in the middle of a green forest.

Mostly B)'s, you enjoy gentler pastimes. You would be happiest somewhere where you can relax. A secluded mountain resort or a sandy, palm-fringed beach where you need do nothing but lie back and relax is the perfect spot for you.

Mostly C)'s, you want to be with people. You would be happiest in a bustling city centre where you can fill your days shopping in elegant boutiques and your evenings sampling the non-stop nightlife of the area's trendiest hot spots.

Mostly D)'s, you appreciate comfort and luxury. Glamorous resorts, upscale hotels and first-class cruises were created with you in mind. Your holidays are the time when you want to experience all the finer things in life.

8 Guess the noun which goes with the adjectives, then use them to describe the place you spent your holidays last year.

1. clean, sandy, dirty, secluded b <u>e a c h</u>
2. trendy, expensive, second-hand, souvenir s __ __ __
3. narrow, busy, winding, cobbled s __ __ __ __ __
4. luxury, family, five-star, Victorian h __ __ __ __
5. delicious, local, gourmet c __ __ __ __ __ __
6. rocky, snow-capped m __ __ __ __ __ __
7. exotic, tropical, desert i __ __ __ __ __

1 *Last year I went to a tropical island in the Caribbean. It was great. I spent most of my days on the sandy beaches.*

9 a. Listen and match the speakers to the places.

hotel	Speaker 1
hostel	Speaker 2
caravan	Speaker 3
cruise liner	Speaker 4

b. Listen again and complete the spidergrams with words which match each place. Use any four words to make up sentences.

HOTEL
- lounge
- suite
- ....

CRUISE LINER
- cabin
- ....
- captain's table
- ....

CARAVAN
- mobile
- ....
- pack
- ....

HOSTEL
- cheap
- ....
- basic accommodation
- ....

Some hotels have got a swimming pool and a gym.

Holiday Troubles

10 a. Listen to the speakers and underline the problems they had while on holiday. What other unpleasant holiday experiences can you think of?

Claire	travel sickness, flight delay, lost luggage, engine trouble
Tim	small room, noisy guests, terrible food, overcharged
Pam	flat tyre, ran out of gas, power cut, flat battery

b. Talk about one of your bad holiday experiences. Say *where you were, when it happened*, then *describe what happened to you in detail*.

Writing

Imagine that you are Tim. Write a letter of complaint to the Manager of The Milton Hotel. Include these points: • **exact dates of stay** • **complaints** • **action expected to be taken**

Traveller's Tips

11 a. Join the items from the two columns with **in case** or **so that** to form sentences, as in the examples.

1	Be careful in crowded areas or at night	a	they/get in touch with you/emergency
2	Let your family know your travel plans	b	they/be replaced/more easily if lost
3	Take out travel insurance	c	something serious/go wrong at/destination
4	Find out the local address of your country's embassy or consulate	d	any of your belongings/be lost or stolen
5	Make photocopies of your tickets and passport	e	there/be pickpockets or muggers about

1 e – Be careful in crowded areas or at night in case there are pickpockets or muggers about.

2 a – Let your family know your travel plans so that they can get in touch with you in an emergency.

b. In pairs, think of other traveller's tips and write them down giving a reason.

Festivals

12 a. Match the festivals with the events. Then make up sentences, as in the example.

Festival	Events
• Holi (India)	• decorate towns with paper lanterns
• Rocket Festival (Thailand)	• throw dye-filled water bombs
• Moomba (Australia)	• make rockets/set off fireworks
• Star Festival (Japan)	• decorate trams/parade through streets

The Holi Festival takes place in India. The Indian people celebrate it by throwing dye-filled water bombs.

b. In pairs, talk about a festival in your country. Say when it takes place and how you celebrate it.

41

Grammar in use

Future tenses

13 Look at the question, then read sentences 1 to 4. Which suggests: a future action already arranged? an intention/plan? an uncertainty/possibility? a prediction based on evidence?

1 The weather is getting hotter and hotter. **I'm going to** spend the summer on my yacht.
2 **I'm touring** Malta.
3 I don't know yet. I think **I'll go** to Rio.
4 I'm working all summer but **I'm going to** spend a few days in Majorca in September.

14 In pairs discuss your plans for your next holiday. Talk about:

- destination
- means of transport
- people to go with
- length of stay
- place to stay
- things to do

A: Are you doing anything on your next holiday?
B: Yes, I'm visiting a friend in Edinburgh.
A: That will be nice. Is anybody going with you?
B: I think my brother will come but he's not sure yet. etc

15 a. Read the sentences below. Which expresses: a request, a promise, a hope, a fear, an offer? Which tense is used in all of these sentences?

1 I'm afraid he will be fired if he keeps coming late to work.
2 I'll definitely call you tomorrow.
3 Will you help me with the suitcases?
4 I'll translate it if you like; I speak a little Italian.
5 I hope she won't be late. We haven't got much time today.

b. Think of another sentence for each use.

> The present simple tense can also be used to talk about future events with time words, such as **after, while, before, as soon as, until, unless, when** etc.
> e.g. *I'm going to meet some friends after I finish work.*
> *Call me as soon as you know what you are going to do.*
> Compare:
> *I'll phone you when I am ready.* (time word)
> *Do you know when he'll be back?* (question word)

16 Put the verbs in brackets into the correct tense.

1 Jenny is going to finish her essay before she .... (meet) her friends.
2 When .... (Sam/finish) work tonight?
3 He'll pay us back when he .... (get) a job.
4 We're not going out now. We're going to wait until Sandra .... (arrive).
5 As soon as he .... (come) back, I'll tell him to call you.

17 Fill in the correct future form of the verbs in brackets.

1 A: Are you doing anything this afternoon? I .... (go) to Marco's for lunch if you're interested.
   B: Oh that sounds good. I .... (be) in town this morning. I .... (meet) you after I .... (finish) my shopping.
2 A: I .... (go) to the baker's. Do you need anything?
   B: Yes, please, a loaf of bread.
   A: OK, I .... (get) you one.
3 A: We .... (go) to the park later.
   B: Are you crazy? Look at the clouds. It .... (rain). You .... (get) soaked.
4 A: .... (you/help) me clean the house today?
   B: Yes of course. I .... (pick) Jane up from the station at three o'clock, but I .... (help) you as soon as I .... (get) back.

18 Put the verbs in brackets into the correct tense. How do you feel about holidays in space?

FAR FROM EARTH

Do you want a holiday that is really out of this world? Well how about booking tickets for two weeks in outer space. This 1) .... (be) a dream of science-fiction writers for decades but some scientists are predicting that soon this dream 2) .... (become) a real possibility. It seems that big business 3) .... (also/realise) that there is plenty of money to be made from taking tourists into orbit. The race is on to build a cheap and reusable spacecraft to carry passengers and freight. Once they 4) .... (be) in space, these tourists 5) .... (need) somewhere to stay. A Japanese company 6) .... (already/make) plans to build the first space hotel. They say that they 7) .... (be) ready to accept the first guests in as little as five years. The guests 8) .... (pay) more than £40,000 and many 9) .... (suffer) from space sickness, but this isn't expected to put off people who 10) .... (look for) the ultimate adventure holiday.

19 Write two sentences about your:
1. plans for next year
   Next year I am going to Portugal for my holidays.
2. ambitions
3. predictions about the future of the world
4. hopes/fears for the future

Conditionals Types 0 and 1
Grammar Reference

20 Fill in the correct tense, then say what type of conditional each sentence is.

1. She will miss the train unless she .... **(come)** now.
2. If you mix red and blue paint, you .... **(get)** purple.
3. I .... **(come)** to the concert if there are any tickets left.
4. If you wear that coat, you .... **(be)** too hot.
5. He'll go to university unless he .... **(fail)** his exams.
6. If you .... **(pour)** oil on water, it floats.

21 a. Use *if/when* to make up sentences, as in the example.

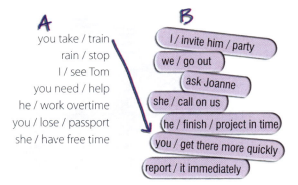

A
you take / train
rain / stop
I / see Tom
you need / help
he / work overtime
you / lose / passport
she / have free time

B
I / invite him / party
we / go out
ask Joanne
she / call on us
he / finish / project in time
you / get there more quickly
report / it immediately

If you take the train, you will get there more quickly.

Competition Game

b. **Chain story:** In teams continue the story using type 1 conditionals. Each correct sentence wins a point. The team with the most points is the winner.

If Tom wins the competition ...
Team A S1: If Tom wins the competition, he'll win lots of money.
Team B S1: If Tom wins lots of money, he'll buy a sports car. etc

22 a. Use the diagram to make up sentences about yourself.

more possible
less possible

will definitely
will probably
could
may
might

I'll definitely go to Paris this spring. – I'll probably visit the Eiffel Tower. – I could stay in a 5-star hotel. – I may visit the Louvre. – I might hire a car.

b. Use the prompts to make sentences about yourself.

If I find a well paid job, I — may — get good job
If I get my university degree, I — might — buy a house
If I become famous, I — could — have children
If I get some time off work, I — will probably — be on TV
If I get married, I — will definitely — go to New York

If I find a well paid job, I will probably buy a house.

The Definite Article
Grammar Reference

23 Fill in *the* where necessary, justifying your answers. Where might you find a text like this?

Holiday Destinations

1) .... Venezuela is a beautiful country in 2) .... South America which has something to offer to every visitor. There are tropical beaches where 3) .... land meets 4) .... Caribbean Sea and 5) .... Atlantic Ocean. To 6) .... east there are 7) .... snow-capped peaks of 8) .... Andes Mountains and in 9) .... south there is 10) .... Amazonian rainforest.

Most tourists come into 11) .... country by 12) .... air, landing in 13) .... capital city, 14) .... Caracas. While you are there, 15) .... Plaza Bolívar with its architecture from 16) .... 17th century is well worth a visit as is 17) .... busy 18) .... Parque Central.

Most people, however, come to see 19) .... natural wonders on offer. Two of 20) .... favourite destinations are 21) .... Angel Falls, 22) .... highest waterfall in 23) .... world, and 24) .... Lake Maracaibo. More adventurous travellers can take a canoe trip up 25) .... Orinoco River, climb 26) .... Pico Bolívar, 27) .... country's highest mountain or take a boat trip along 28) .... Carrao River to 29) .... Hacha Falls. It will be 30) .... experience of a lifetime.

Grammar in use

Prepositions

Appendix 1

24 a. Fill in the correct prepositions, then explain the phrases in bold.

1 On the day of the sale, crowds of people gathered before the shop opened, all **eager** .... a bargain.
2 Anne has really **put a lot of effort** .... planning this holiday, so she hopes she will have a really good time.
3 The management always **puts** special **emphasis** .... the comfort of its guests.
4 The whole class was really **enthusiastic** .... the trip to Disneyland Paris.
5 Are you **familiar** .... this part of town?
6 San Francisco is **famous** .... its magnificent Golden Gate Bridge.
7 All of our agents are **experienced** .... all aspects of the business.
8 Let's speak to Jeff. He's an **expert** .... travel in Asia.

b. Fill in the correct preposition, then choose any five of the phrases and make up sentences using them.

1 to date back 1350;
2 to dine .... style;
3 situated .... an area;
4 to stand .... a hilltop;
5 trip .... a place; 6 ideal .... sb; 7 open .... the public; 8 to be furnished ....; 9 to appeal .... sb

Phrasal Verbs

Appendix 2

25 Fill in the correct particle, and explain the phrasal verbs.

1 Tom always **cuts** .... the park on his way home.
2 John is trying to **cut** .... the amount of sweet food he eats every day.
3 She forgot to pay the bill, and now her phone's been **cut** .... !
4 When he read the article, he found that the most exciting part had been **cut** .... !
5 It's cold today, so make sure you **do** .... your coat.
6 I could really **do** .... a cup of coffee right now.
7 Sooner or later we will have to **do** .... room keys and have only card keys.

Multiple Choice Cloze

26 Read the text and circle the answer A, B, C or D, which best fits each gap (1-15). There is an example at the beginning (0).

Tip: Look at the title of the text to get an idea of what the text is about. Read the text once to get the general idea. Read the text again, looking at the words before and after each gap. Then, look at the choices and decide which word fits best. Do not leave any blanks. Finally, read the completed text to see if it makes sense.

The four-hour rail journey to Machu Picchu is nothing 0) *short* of spectacular. On either 1) .... of the tracks you will see steep mountains towering above. As the outlines of the 2) .... site loom out of the mist, you will 3) .... your first glimpse of the silent ruins of the 'lost city', which stand on a high ridge with a great 4) .... of the Andes Mountains. 5) .... opposite sides of the ruins, you will be able to 6) .... straight down at different river valleys. You can follow an ancient stone road, 7) .... leaves the site to climb to a gap 8) .... as the 'Gate of the Sun'. 9) .... the climb is exhausting, the astonishing scenery 10) .... an unforgettable experience. Even though the Incas left 11) .... clues behind when they abandoned Machu Picchu some 500 years 12) ...., it's believed to have been one of the homes of the royal 13) .... A walking 14) .... of the site will take you about four and a half hours, but the experience will be 15) .... worth the effort.

0	A	except	B	short	C	less	D	other
1	A	side	B	bank	C	edge	D	part
2	A	previous	B	past	C	ancient	D	old
3	A	grasp	B	take	C	catch	D	hold
4	A	picture	B	sight	C	scene	D	view
5	A	On	B	From	C	Over	D	For
6	A	watch	B	view	C	look	D	see
7	A	which	B	whose	C	where	D	who
8	A	called	B	understood	C	thought	D	known
9	A	When	B	Although	C	Even	D	Despite
10	A	makes up	B	makes for	C	makes off	D	makes of
11	A	little	B	few	C	many	D	much
12	A	ago	B	before	C	later	D	after
13	A	team	B	group	C	people	D	family
14	A	tour	B	trip	C	journey	D	travel
15	A	fairly	B	rather	C	well	D	quite

Error Correction

27 Read the text below and look carefully at each line. If the line is correct, put a tick (✓). If it has a word that should not be there, write this word on the line, as in the examples.

Up Up and Away!

On October 6th, I am going to the International 0 ✓
Balloon Fiesta which will get on underway 00 on
in Albuquerque, New Mexico. It is a colourful festival 1 ....
which it started in 1972 with just 15 balloons. Now, 2 ....
it has been grown into one which attracts more 3 ....
than 1,000 balloons from countries as far away from 4 ....
as Brazil, South Africa, Turkey and more. More 5 ....
than 800,000 people they come to this spectacular 6 ....
event in every year. I am going to volunteer as a 7 ....
member of for one of the ground crews. We will 8 ....
meet before dawn in the morning and inflate the 9 ....
hot air balloons. When the sun has rises, the 10 ....
balloons will be released so to float into the crystal 11 ....
clear morning sky. The fiesta also includes in the 12 ....
International Gas Balloon Race, several night 13 ....
ballooning events and other activities such as 14 ....
an arts and crafts fair, the fireworks, parties and 15 ....
much more. I know I will have a great time. 16 ....

Key-Word Transformations

28 Complete the second sentence using the word in bold. You must use between two and five words, including the word given.

1. We are grateful for all your help in the matter.
   appreciate   We really .... the matter.

2. He will never use that travel agent again.
   last   It's the .... that travel agent.

3. I'll leave my mobile phone on so that you can call me.
   case   I'll leave my mobile phone on .... to call me.

4. If you don't leave immediately, you'll miss your flight.
   unless   You'll miss your flight .... right away.

5. The first thing I'll do when I get to the hotel is to have a hot shower.
   soon   I'll have a hot shower .... to the hotel.

6. You needn't wait for me. I'll be a long time.
   point   There's .... for me. I'll be a long time.

Idioms & Fixed Phrases

29 a. Fill in the words from the list. Then try to explain the phrases in bold.

- feet • time • suitcase
- move • line • weather

1. This new job in sales means that I'll have to **live out of a** .... for months.

2. I'll **drop you a** .... as soon as I get there and let you know what's going on.

3. I can't wait to **put my** .... **up** and forget about work.

4. Come on! If you don't **get a** .... **on**, we'll miss the train.

5. I've been **feeling a bit under the** .... all week.

6. We arrived **in the nick of** .... The show was about to start as we sat down.

b. Are there similar idioms in your language? What are they?

30 Underline the correct word and then explain the phrases.

1. That's what we like about Phoebe. She's willing to **lend an** *ear/eye* and give her advice.

2. It's **early** *days/times* yet. Pete has not yet made his decision.

3. I can't believe you're going on a cruise this summer; it must be **costing the** *fortune/earth*!

4. You have to see that new film at the Rialto; I was **on the** *corner/edge* **of my seat** until the very end.

5. We're finding it really difficult to **make ends** *meet/together* since Jason lost his job at the factory.

45

Listening & Speaking skills

31 Listen to the advertisement for a holiday in Wales and fill in the missing information. Do not use more than three words in each gap.

Tip Read each sentence carefully. Try to think of what information is missing e.g. a name, a number etc. Listen and start filling in. Remember you can write up to three words. What you write must fit grammatically in the sentence and make sense. Listen again and fill in the other answers. Check what you have written.

Breakaway is offering family **1** _____ at a hotel.
The weekend costs **2** _____
The hotel was built in the **3** _____
Don't miss a visit to Snowdonia's many **4** _____
Snowdonia is a good place to go **5** _____ and rock climbing.
Exercise in the hotel's **6** _____ or the **7** _____ in the restaurant.
Try traditional **8** _____
Book before **9** _____ 4th. SPECIAL OFFER
Call now on 0180 2278954.

32 a. Look at the pictures and, in pairs, discuss the points listed.

WEEKEND ACTIVITIES
- ways of spending your free time
- how young people relax
- sports for pleasure
- alone or with friends

b. Talk about your most exciting weekend. Who were you with? What did you do? What made it exciting?

33 You will hear a conversation between two friends talking about a recent trip to Brazil. For questions 1-6, decide which of the following choices A, B or C is the best answer.

1 Why did Dave go to Rio?
  A On a business trip.
  B To go to the beach.
  C To experience Carnival.

2 What was the first place he went?
  A To the beach.
  B To the hotel.
  C To the Carnival.

3 What does Dave say about the dancers?
  A They were tireless.
  B They were tiring.
  C They were tired.

4 How long does Carnival last?
  A 10 hours.
  B 10 days.
  C 5 days.

5 What does Dave say about the nightlife?
  A It's an interesting mix.
  B He didn't go out much.
  C The nightclubs were great.

6 What is Janet going to do?
  A Take some photos.
  B Look at some photos.
  C Get some photos developed.

34 You have just come back from a trip. Tell a friend of yours:
- why you went there
- how you got there
- how long you stayed and where
- what you did during your stay

A: *So why did you decide to go there?*
B: *Well, I had been dreaming of ... etc*

35 You are going to listen to two news items. For questions 1-6, decide which of the sentences are true, which are false and which are not mentioned. Mark each statement as *True/False/Doesn't say* by ticking the appropriate box.

		True	False	Doesn't say
1	The Williams' luggage never reached Mexico.			
2	The suitcase was mislabelled in LA.			
3	Mr Williams is having problems with his insurance company.			
4	Mr Sor will go to court.			
5	Mr Sor claims he had no choice other than to leave the boys.			
6	The boys missed the boat by accident.			

36 You had a bad experience while you were on holiday. Now you are back, relate:
- what the problem was
- where you were and what you were doing
- who helped you and how the problem was solved

One of the worst experiences I had was .... . I was ...

Invitations - Accepting and Refusing

37 a. Listen to the dialogues and write **A** (accepted), **R** (refused) or **NS** (not sure) for each one.

1 .... 2 .... 3 .... 4 ....

1   A: Oh hi Steve. How are you?
    B: Fine. Listen, I'm meeting George and Mary for lunch in an hour. **Would you like to** join us?
    A: **Thanks, I'd love to but** I'm working this afternoon.

2   A: Hi Matt!
    B: Oh, hi Ann. I haven't seen you for ages.
    A: I know, **have you got time for** a coffee?
    B: **That's a great idea**.

3   A: **Shall we** go to that new restaurant for dinner tonight?
    B: No, **I'd rather not. I'm not keen on** Chinese food.

4   A: I heard that there's a really good film on at the Odeon. **Why don't we go**?
    B: **I don't know**. I've got to finish this report. I'll let you know how I'm getting on later.

b. In pairs act out similar dialogues using the prompts and the phrases in the box.

- go to the theatre
- have dinner at an expensive restaurant
- spend the weekend in Cornwall

Inviting	Accepting/Refusing
Let's/Shall we ...	I'd love to ... but ...
Why don't we/you ...	I'm afraid I can't.
How/What about ...	I suppose so.
I think we should ...	(not) fancy, (not) keen on, (not) like
We could ...	I don't really feel up to it.
Would you like to ...	I'd love to.
I was wondering if ...	That would be great.
	Another time perhaps.
	I'm not sure I can.

Intonation (short answers)

38 a. Listen and repeat.

A: The plane will be on time.
B: I hope so.
A: Josh is coming with us, isn't he?
B: I think so.
A: Is Vicky coming too?

B: I hope not.
A: Has Beth cancelled the milk?
B: I don't think so.
A: Has Tim been there before?
B: I suppose so.

b. In pairs act out similar dialogues. Mind the intonation.

Cancelling a hotel reservation

39 a. Listen to the dialogue. Who are the speakers?

b. Read and match the exchanges.

A	B
[1] Good afternoon. The Palace Hotel, how can I help you?	a I thought so. That's not a problem.
[2] Just a minute, please. Ah, yes. You reserved a double room for two nights.	b Yes, that's right. I'm very sorry but can you cancel it, please?
[3] Certainly, although you do realise the deposit you paid is non-refundable?	c Hello. I made a reservation with you about two weeks ago. My name's Vanessa Bryce.

c. Use the prompts to act out similar dialogues.

- Azar Airlines/2 months ago/Tina Charles/ 2 seats/10 am flight to Madrid/22nd August
- Monsieur's Bistro/6 weeks ago/table/Barry White/ table for 6/New Year's Eve

Renting a vehicle

40 a. Listen to the dialogue. Where does this conversation take place?

b. Read the dialogue and change the questions in bold into indirect questions as appropriate.

A: Good morning. **How can I help you?**
B: Hello. I'd like to hire a car for the weekend, please.
A: Certainly. **What type of car would you like?**
B: A small hatchback, please. **How much is it going to cost?**
A: Well, including the insurance, it will cost £100.
B: That's fine.
A: **May I see your driving licence, please?**
B: Of course. Here you are.
A: Now, if you will sign the contract here, I'll get the keys.

c. Use the prompts to act out similar dialogues.

motorcycle 125cc/£50

speed boat £175

47

Spectacular Nature

41 a. Look at the pictures. What do these places have in common? Where do you think they are?

b. In what context might you find these words in the texts?

Text A: • stunning views • chalk • coastline
• shipwrecks • strategic location
• shipping lanes

Text B: • slopes • spectacular scenery
• wild game • Indian tribes
• railroad route • snow-capped peaks

*The White Cliffs of Dover offer **stunning views** of the English Channel.*

42 a. Read the texts and write **A** or **B** for each question.

Which natural feature(s) ...

1. contains the remains of ancient animals? ....
2. has been used to guard the country? ....
3. allows you to see another country? ....
4. is made up of several different ranges? ....
5. allows you to see local wildlife? ....
6. contains tunnels? ....
7. made it difficult for travellers to move west? ....

b. Which text may be from an encyclopaedia? a tourist brochure?

43 Explain the words in bold. Then, match the synonyms below to the highlighted words.

• visit • pioneers • because of • sight
• passes • section • obstructed

44 Read the texts again and in pairs, talk about the similarities and differences of these places. Then say which place you would like to visit and why.

Writing Project

Write a short article about one of the most interesting natural areas in your country for your school magazine. Write about:

- its location
- size
- historical details
- what you can do/see there
- recommendation

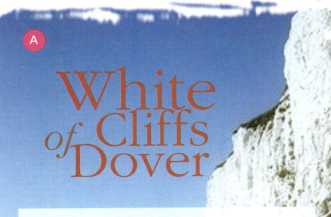

A

White Cliffs of Dover

When crossing the English Channel from **continental** Europe to Dover, England, the first sight you see is the famous White Cliffs of Dover. They are almost 70 million years old and have been in existence since dinosaurs were **roaming** the earth. Their characteristic white colour is **due to** the fact that they are made of **chalk**. They are believed to grow 15 metres every million years and are now around 250 metres high.

Due to their strategic location they have been used to help **defend** the coast from **invasion** throughout England's history. During the time of Napoleon, tunnels were dug into the cliffs so that soldiers could attack the invading French armies. These tunnels were used as recently as World War II. There are many **shipwrecks** to be found in the bays and along the beaches below the cliffs because the sea is exceptionally rough along this stretch of the coast.

What's more, there is plenty to see and do in the surrounding area. You can visit one of Dover's many spectacular heritage castles or even the Roman fort at nearby Richborough. The White Cliffs themselves are an excellent place for hiking, and offer stunning views of one of the world's busiest **shipping lanes**. On a clear day, you can even see the French coastline. A visit to England would not be complete without a stopover at this magnificent natural feature.

Culture Clip 3

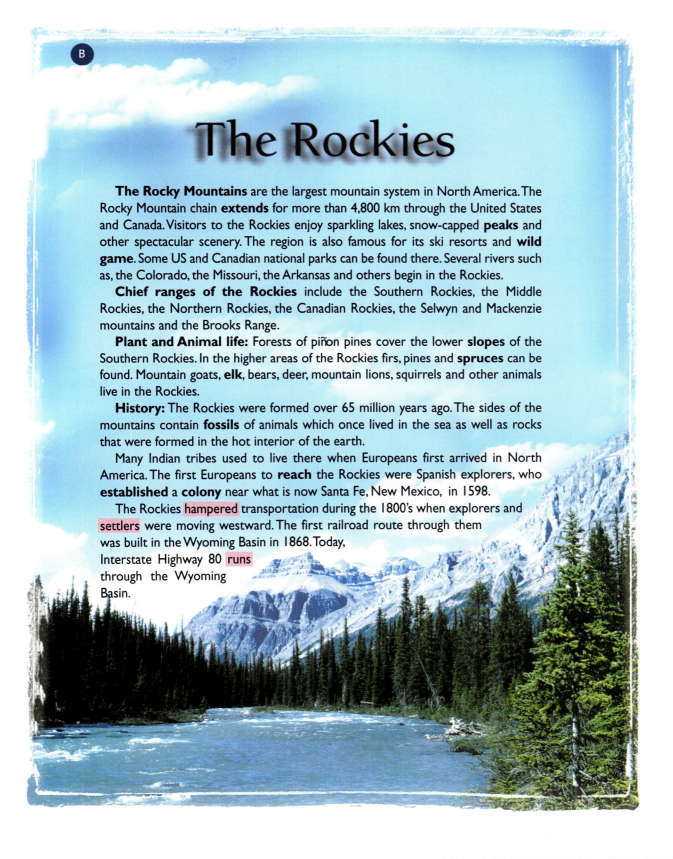

The Rockies

The Rocky Mountains are the largest mountain system in North America. The Rocky Mountain chain **extends** for more than 4,800 km through the United States and Canada. Visitors to the Rockies enjoy sparkling lakes, snow-capped **peaks** and other spectacular scenery. The region is also famous for its ski resorts and **wild game**. Some US and Canadian national parks can be found there. Several rivers such as, the Colorado, the Missouri, the Arkansas and others begin in the Rockies.

Chief ranges of the Rockies include the Southern Rockies, the Middle Rockies, the Northern Rockies, the Canadian Rockies, the Selwyn and Mackenzie mountains and the Brooks Range.

Plant and Animal life: Forests of piñon pines cover the lower **slopes** of the Southern Rockies. In the higher areas of the Rockies firs, pines and **spruces** can be found. Mountain goats, **elk**, bears, deer, mountain lions, squirrels and other animals live in the Rockies.

History: The Rockies were formed over 65 million years ago. The sides of the mountains contain **fossils** of animals which once lived in the sea as well as rocks that were formed in the hot interior of the earth.

Many Indian tribes used to live there when Europeans first arrived in North America. The first Europeans to **reach** the Rockies were Spanish explorers, who **established** a **colony** near what is now Santa Fe, New Mexico, in 1598.

The Rockies hampered transportation during the 1800's when explorers and settlers were moving westward. The first railroad route through them was built in the Wyoming Basin in 1868. Today, Interstate Highway 80 runs through the Wyoming Basin.

Writing a semi-formal transactional letter

> **Tip**
> We write a transactional letter to respond to some kind of written input. This input may be a letter, an advertisement, an invitation, notes, etc, or a combination of these.
> When we write a transactional letter, we have to:
> - Read the rubric carefully, underlining the key words/phrases
> - Choose a writing style depending on who we are writing to (informal, semi-formal or formal)
> - Cover all the points in the rubric in full sentences.
> We should use our own words.

Analysing the Rubric

45 Read the rubric, underline the key words and answer the questions.

> You are a teacher and you are taking a group of students on a skiing trip to France. You have made a preliminary booking at the hotel and now the assistant manager has contacted you for more details. Read part of the letter and the notes you have made, then write a letter answering his questions.

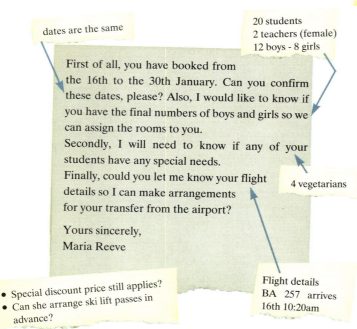

1. Who are you writing to?
2. What style will you use to write this letter? Why?
3. Which of the following pieces of information should you include in your letter?
   - date of arrival • time of arrival • duration of stay
   - flight number • number of students
   - number of boys/girls • students' special needs
4. What questions would you ask?

Analysing a Model Text

46 a. Read the letter and cross out the inappropriate phrases in bold. Justify your choices.

> Dear Maria,
> **1** Thank you for your letter. 1) **Here's what you need to know/I have the information you requested** and I also have a few questions of my own.
> **2** Firstly, 2) **the dates stay as they are/we haven't changed the dates**. We shall be coming from the 16th January to the 30th. Also, 3) **here are our flight details/our flight details are as follows**, we will arrive on flight BA 257 at 10.20am. 4) **Our party will consist of/There will be twenty students in total**, twelve boys and eight girls. There will also be two adults, myself and another female teacher. 5) **With regard to/And the** special requirements, there will be four vegetarians in our party.
> **3** Also, 6) **can you tell me/could you kindly inform me** if the special discount price is still available? Finally, 7) **would it be possible for you to/ can you** organise our ski lift passes in advance.
> **4** I hope this covers everything. 8) **I am looking forward to seeing you soon/I can't wait to see you**.
>
> 9) **Yours truly/Love from**,
> Jennifer Taylor

b. Look at the notes. Have the exact words been used in the letter? Have all the points been included? What is the topic of each paragraph?

Style

47 Match the informal sentences to the semi-formal ones of the same meaning. Then, identify the type of letter each pair came from – *accepting / refusing an invitation, thank-you letter, asking for / giving information, apologising, giving advice*.

INFORMAL STYLE

1. Thanks a lot for lending me your motorbike.
2. Do you have a free room in the beginning of May?
3. I'd love to come to your school play.
4. Sorry for not being able to make it last Saturday.
5. I think you should book soon.
6. I'm 20 years old. I'm at university this year.

SEMI-FORMAL STYLE

a. I would be happy to attend the school play.
b. If I were you, I would make the bookings as soon as possible.
c. Thank you very much for the use of your vehicle.
d. I'm a twenty-year-old university student.
e. I'd like to apologise for not managing to meet you at last Saturday's conference.
f. I would like to know if you have any vacancies in early May.

48 Rewrite the following sentences in semi-formal style.

1. Are there any flights to Portugal on 2nd April?
2. We weren't very pleased with our cabin.
3. I'm sorry the children were so noisy during their visit to the museum.
4. Can you tell me what time I should get to the station?
5. Let me know what time the people will get here.

Indirect Questions

49 Rewrite these direct questions as indirect questions, as in the example. Use the phrases below to help you.

- Could you (tell me/let me know) ...
- I would like to know if/whether ...
- I would be grateful if ...
- I would appreciate it if ...

1. Can we hire a car at the hotel?
   Could you tell me if we can hire a car at the hotel?
2. How much will it cost altogether?
3. Are there any school discounts available?
4. Does the hotel have facilities for young children?
5. What time will the plane arrive?
6. Will somebody meet us at the airport?

Discuss & Write

50 a. Read the rubric and underline the key words/phrases. How well does the person who is going to write the letter know the recipient? What would you expect to read in the letter?

> You are a teacher taking a group of students on a school trip. You have had a telephone conversation with the centre where you plan to stay. Now the Activity Leader has sent you a fax asking you to confirm the details you discussed on the phone. Read the fax and the notes you made carefully. Then write a letter in response.

b. Read the fax carefully. Then, listen to the conversation about the school trip and complete the notes.

From: ....
To: ....

From: Joe Benson, (Activity Leader)
To: Kate Peterson
Re: Trip Details

Dear Kate,
Regarding our recent telephone conversation, I'd like you to confirm a few details in writing so that we can move ahead with the arrangements for your school trip.

- The dates of your stay.
- The proposed time of arrival / means of travel.
- Size of party / number of rooms required.
- Any questions?

I look forward to hearing from you in the near future.
Yours truly,
Joe Benson

At: ....
By: ....

.... teachers
.... students
.... rooms

c. Look at your notes. Then, in pairs, ask and answer questions, as in the example.

A: When will they arrive at Hawthorn Park?
B: On 6th September.
A: When will they leave? etc

d. Rewrite the questions the teacher is going to ask in a semi-formal style.

51 Which of the following are *opening* and which are *closing remarks*? Which are appropriate for this letter?

1. I am writing to confirm the arrangements for our school visit to Hawthorn Park.
2. Call me if you want to know anything else.
3. Please do not hesitate to contact me should you require any further information.
4. You asked me to give you some details in writing.

52 Answer the questions in the plan, then write your letter (120-180 words). You do not need to include any addresses. Use the letter in Ex. 46 as a model.

Introduction

Dear (+ recipient's full name,)

(Para 1)   Why are you writing the letter?
           How can you start the letter?

Main Body

(Para 2)   What information are you giving?
(Para 3)   What questions do you want to ask?

Conclusion

(Para 4)   How can you end the letter?

Yours sincerely / Yours truly,
(Your full name)

53 Explain the sentences below in your own words.

- He who travels west, travels not only with the sun but with history.   *Hal Borland (US journalist)*
- The world is a book, and those who do not travel, read only a page.   *Saint Augustine (Roman philosopher)*
- A rolling stone gathers no moss.   *(traditional)*

1 What ....
  do they have?
2 Can he arrange a visit
  from ....?

Earth is Dearer than Gold

Lead-in

1
a. Look at the pictures (1-5) and say as many words as you can related to each one. How is the title related to the pictures?

b. Which of the problems in the pictures exist in your country? Use the prompts to make up sentences as in the example. You can use your own ideas.

- cars • factories • greenhouse gases • smog
- trees • water • people

There are more and more cars on the roads.
There are more and more people living in the cities.

2
a. Look at the list of where we get our energy from today. Which of these are mostly used in your country? Which of these are renewable and which are non-renewable?

- wood • coal • water • gas • oil
- wind • sun

b. Listen and write **S** (for solar energy), **W** (for wind power) and **H** (for hydropower) next to each use. Then, make up sentences as in the example.

• run small gadgets	S
• create electricity for whole cities	…………
• power grain mills and sawmills	…………
• heat water	…………
• run homes and communities	…………
• heat and cool factories	…………
• power batteries	…………
• pump water	…………

We can use solar energy to run small gadgets.

52

Reading

3 a. Which of the words below can you see in the picture on p. 53?

- fossil fuels • generate power
- wind power • wind farm
- nuclear power stations
- alternative form of energy
- wind turbines • slim towers
- rotor blades • unoccupied sites
- monitor wind direction

b. Read the article and fill in the sentences (A-H) which best fit each paragraph (1-6). There is one extra sentence which you do not need to use.

A At the moment there are only around sixty wind farms in Britain both on land and offshore.

B More importantly, though, these methods of electricity generation are harmful to the environment.

C In fact, the stronger winds generated at sea make offshore wind farms a practical alternative.

D In fact, today it is the world's fastest-growing source of energy.

E This new alternative source of energy must also be practical, cheap to set up and maintain, highly productive and above all kind to our planet.

F Well, as people are increasingly coming to realise, the answer is all around us.

G Wind power has been used for many years to pump water.

H This pole is connected to a generator, where the electricity is made.

c. Explain the words in bold, then give synonyms for the highlighted words. Where could you read such an article?

d. Find words similar in your language.

Follow-up

4 Read the article again and underline the advantages of wind power. Can you think of any others? Is wind power used in your country?

The Answer is Blowing in the Wind

Britain is in the middle of a serious energy crisis! We are desperately in need of a new form of energy which will be capable of **generating** enough power to see the country's homes, businesses and industries into the twenty-first century. But, that's not all! **0** **E** This is certainly a tall order!

At the moment, more than 90% of Britain's energy needs are met by burning **fossil fuels** or generated in nuclear power stations. Unfortunately, these are not **renewable** sources of energy, and once they have run out, that's it. **1** They emit harmful **greenhouse gases**, which contribute to **global warming** and **climate change**.

How then can we produce enough energy to power an entire country without damaging the environment? What can we use as an alternative, reliable form of energy, which will generate as much power as fossil fuels and nuclear energy, but have none of the **drawbacks**? **2** Wind power!

Wind power is an alternative energy source which has been used for many years in countries like Holland and Denmark. **3** Strangely enough, even though it is one of the windiest countries in Europe, Britain has been slow to **take advantage of** wind power. The strong winds which blow around Britain's coastline could easily be used to provide us with all our energy needs. All we need to do now is set up some wind farms.

Wind farms are actually **arrays** of electricity-generating **wind turbines**, which are tall, slim towers with two or three **rotor blades** at the top. The wind turns the blades, which spin a pole. **4** There can be as few as one and as many as thousands of wind turbines in a single array. Computers monitor the wind direction and speed, and can shut down the turbines if the wind becomes too strong.

What is more, wind turbines make hardly any noise and they are not unpleasant to look at, certainly not as ugly as nuclear power stations! Although wind farms do take up a lot of space, they are often located on **unoccupied sites** or in areas that can also be used for farming. Building wind farms at sea is also possible. **5** Offshore wind farms also mean that much larger turbines can be built, without **objections** from the public.

A single wind turbine can produce enough electricity to power 375 homes and these wind farms are already making a small but significant difference. **6** As this number increases, we may well see wind power supplying as much as 10% of world's electricity **demands** and up to 20% of Britain's total.

So, why delay? Wind power offers a solution to all our energy problems by being a renewable, clean and safe source of energy which is easy to live and work with. Isn't it about time we started building more wind farms in Britain and protecting our environment for future generations?

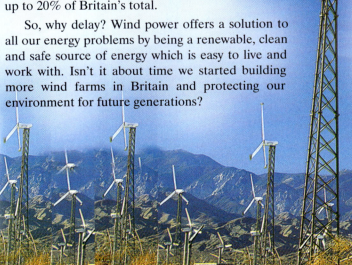

Vocabulary Practice

Planet Earth

5 🎧 Listen and underline the correct piece of information about the Earth, then talk about it.

Circumference: 40,000/14,000 km
Diameter: 17,260/12,760 km
Percentage of surface area covered by oceans: 40% / 70%
Highest point: Mt Everest 8,848/4,888 m
Lowest point: Dead Sea – 800/400 m below sea level

The Earth's circumference is ...

Environmental Problems

6 a. Match the headlines to the environmental problems.

A **Push for whale sanctuary in South Pacific**
B **Greenhouse gases blamed for sudden storms**
C **World to face water shortages by 2025**
D **More land off limits for loggers**
E **Population will rise to 10 billion people in next 50 years**

Problems
Overpopulation .... Deforestation ....
Lack of resources .... Endangered species ....
Global warming ....

b. Which of these problems do you think is the most worrying? Who do you think is responsible for solving these problems?

c. Find headlines from newspapers related to environmental problems and present them to the class.

7 a. Match the problems to their effects and their solutions. Then in pairs discuss, as in the example.

Problems	Effects	Solutions
A Global warming	3	d
B Pollution	....	....
C Hunting/Overfishing	....	....
D Deforestation	....	....

Effects
1 destruction of the rainforest
2 many animals and fish wiped out
3 change in world's climate – ocean levels rising – extreme weather conditions
4 very poor air quality in cities – rivers and lakes full of industrial waste

Solutions
a Have stricter laws and harsher punishments for illegal hunting and fishing.
b Encourage countries to control the number of trees that are cut down.
c Reduce gases emitted from factories. Use public transport instead of cars.
d Reduce use of aerosols. Use alternative sources of energy.

A: What is the effect of global warming?
B: Global warming is causing a change in the world's climate. Ocean levels are rising and we are seeing more extreme weather conditions. We need to do something before it's too late.
A: What can we do?
B: We could reduce the use of aerosols. We could also use alternative sources of energy. etc

Writing

b. Use ideas from Ex. 7a as well as information from other sources to write a short article about global warming. State the problem, then write what has caused it. Finally, write what we can do about it.

8 Match the columns to form compound nouns and explain them. Finally make up sentences using them.

rubbish — effect
gas — rain
acid — dump
greenhouse — layer
ozone — path
urban — mask
cycle — sprawl

rubbish dump: *a place where rubbish is left. The rubbish dump on the outskirts of town is an eyesore.*

9 Answer the questionnaire to see if you are environmentally aware.

Are you part of the problem?

1 When you leave a room, do you
 a turn off all the lights?
 b leave one light on?
 c never bother to turn off the lights?

2 Do you
 a take short showers (less than 10 minutes)?
 b have baths?
 c take long showers (more than 10 minutes)?

3 Do you
 a walk or ride a bike for short journeys?
 b take public transport when you can?
 c travel everywhere by car?

4 Do you
 a separate all your rubbish and recycle what you can?
 b recycle some of your rubbish?
 c never recycle anything?

5 Do you
 a only use heating and air conditioning when you really need them?
 b use heating and air conditioning now and again?
 c have the heating on all winter and the air conditioning on all summer?

6 When you are outside, do you
 a always put your litter in a rubbish bin?
 b usually try and find a bin for your litter?
 c throw your litter away on the ground wherever you are?

What your answers mean:

Mostly a's — Well done! It sounds like you are doing all you can to help our planet. Keep up the good work.

Mostly b's — It seems like you know about the problems that are facing our environment and try to do what you can. There are still some more things that you could do though.

Mostly c's — There is a lot more you could do to help the environment. Why don't you read through the a and b answers and see if you could do any of the things mentioned here? Every little bit can help make our world a better place for everyone.

Conservation

10 a. There are many things we can do to conserve our non-renewable resources. Match the following suggestions (1-6) to the correct headings below. Then make up sentences, as in the example.

1 switch off the lights when we leave a room
2 wear warmer clothes in the winter
3 ride a bicycle
4 insulate our houses
5 use fluorescent light bulbs
6 use public transport

a To use less petrol for transportation we can: 3
b To use less electricity inside our houses we can: ....
c To use less coal, gas, petrol and electricity to heat our homes we can: ....

To use less petrol for transportation we can ride a bicycle.

b. Can you think of any other ways to reduce consumption of our non-renewable resources?

11 In pairs think of two ways that we can: **save on water**; **create less litter**; **reduce air pollution**. Then, ask and answer, as in the example.

Making Suggestions
Why don't we ...
We can ... / could also ...
It would be a good idea to ...
If ..., then ...

A: What can we do to save on water?
B: A good idea would be to take shorter showers.
A: That's true, we could also ...   etc

Writing

12 Use ideas from Ex. 10 as well as information from other sources to write your own set of rules on how to save on water. Write at least five rules and pin them up on your class noticeboard.

Grammar in use

Comparisons
Grammar Reference

13 Underline the comparative and superlative forms in the sentences. How are *more* and *most* used?

1. Jenny is taller than Kate.
2. The exam was easier than we expected.
3. This restaurant is more expensive than the one we went to last night.
4. The train was going faster and faster.
5. The roads in the city are becoming more and more crowded.
6. He thinks that the richer he becomes, the happier he will be.
7. The African elephant is the biggest land mammal.
8. London is the busiest city in the UK.
9. She is the most beautiful woman I know.
10. Tony is more capable than Billy.

14 Make up as many sentences as possible, as in the example.

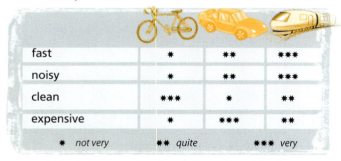

	🚲	🚗	🚄
fast	*	**	***
noisy	*	**	***
clean	***	*	**
expensive	*	***	**

* not very   ** quite   *** very

A bicycle is not very fast. A car is faster than a bicycle. A train is the fastest of all. A car is quite fast. A train is very fast.

15 Complete the sentences using the correct forms of the comparative or superlative.

1. Ruth seems much ....(happy) today than yesterday, doesn't she?
2. Some scientists think that global warming is .... (big) problem facing the world today.
3. It's becoming .... (hard) and .... (hard) to find a job nowadays.
4. Steve is definitely .... (good) player in the team.
5. Venice is .... (beautiful) city I have ever visited.
6. He feels much ....(healthy) since he started that diet.
7. Tim finds history .... (interesting) than maths.
8. It was one of .... (difficult) things he has ever had to do.
9. The .... (early) we leave, the .... (soon) we'll arrive.
10. I'm sure you can do .... (good) than that. Try harder.

16 In pairs, use the pictures and the prompts to compare life now and in the past. Think about: *life*; *people*; *dwelling*; *transportation*; *work*; *cities*; *streets*.

- hard/easy • work short/long hours • noisy/quiet
- healthy/unhealthy • slow/fast • exciting/boring
- inconvenient/convenient • safe/dangerous

People used to ... ;
These days ...
Most people in the past/nowadays ... ;
(The) ... used to be ... but now ...

A: Life used to be harder in the past than it is now.
B: I agree. These days life seems to be quite easy.

17 In pairs use the prompts to ask and answer questions about the animals listed, as in the example.

• elephant • lizard • mouse • cobra • centipede • tiger

• many legs • large • tall • small • fast • slow
• loud • poisonous

A: Which animal has got the most legs?
B: I think it's the centipede. Which animal ...

Too / Enough
Grammar Reference

18 Complete the sentences using either *too* or *enough*.

1. Tom hasn't got .... money to move to a bigger flat.
2. The river is .... polluted to swim in.
3. Erica's old .... to make her own decisions.
4. Do you think that it's .... heavy to carry?
5. It might be .... late to save some endangered species.
6. Is it warm .... for you in here?
7. The exam was .... difficult for me.
8. The hole in the ozone layer means that parts of the earth do not get .... protection from ultraviolet radiation.

-ing form / Infinitive

19 Match the items in the two columns to make complete sentences. Underline and label the *-ing form;* the *to-infinitive form;* the *infinitive without to form*.

• I can't stand people	to join an environmental group.
• We can all	throwing rubbish in the streets.
• I'd like	help save endangered species.

20 What does each group of words take: *to-inf*, *inf without to* or *-ing form*? Give an example for each.

1. go (+ activity) + *-ing form*
2. verb + preposition + ...
3. would love/like/hate + ...
4. like/love/hate + ...
5. modal verbs + ...
6. can't stand/help, look forward to + ...

I often go swimming at weekends.

21 Put the verbs in brackets into the correct form.

1. He goes .... (swim) every morning before work.
2. George isn't here; he must .... (be) on his way to work.
3. We're still waiting for him .... (arrive).
4. I would love .... (visit) India one day.
5. Lisa is looking forward to .... (meet) you.
6. He only finished the essay on time by .... (work) all night.
7. Come here. I would like .... (tell) you something.
8. Laura didn't want to leave without .... (speak) to Dan.
9. We should .... (do) more to help endangered species.
10. He is thinking about .... (change) jobs.

22 Fill in the *-ing form* or *to-inf*. Then explain the words in bold.

1. He **forgot** *to put* (put) out the fire. *(forget = not remember to do sth)*
2. I'll never **forget** .... (visit) Italy for the first time.
3. Jamie couldn't **stop** .... (think) about what had happened the night before.
4. Sorry I'm a bit late. I had to **stop** .... (buy) petrol on the way over here.
5. Did you **remember** .... (get) some milk when you were out?
6. I **remember** .... (talk) to your friend Debbie at the party.
7. He **wanted** .... (catch) the 8 o'clock train but he was too late.
8. Sandra **tried** .... (write) him a letter but he didn't answer.

23 Complete the sentences using *to-inf*, *inf without to* or *-ing form*.

1. Josh isn't interested in ....
2. He refused ....
3. Paula's keen on ....
4. If they've got enough time, they'll ....
5. These days we can ....
6. She really hates ....
7. Jason can't help ....
8. Do you like .... ?
9. You should ....
10. We're looking forward to ....

Game

Chain Story. In turns use the words in the list to make up a story using *-ing form* or *infinitive forms*. Cross out the words used each time so that you won't use them again.

- like • love
- manage • mind
- write • threaten
- hope • must
- start • finish
- hate • regret
- avoid • arrange
- afford • look forward to
- want • can't stand • decide

John likes travelling abroad. One day ...

57

Grammar in use

Prepositions
Appendix 1

24 a. Fill in the correct preposition, then explain the phrases in bold.

1. She was **grateful** .... all the volunteers .... their help.
2. The chemical factory's owner was found **guilty** .... dumping barrels of chemicals into the river.
3. Did you **hear** .... the Environmental Weekend at Woodford in June?
4. Local authorities are anxious to **hear** .... anyone who may have seen the waste being dumped in the park.
5. Have you ever **heard** .... the greenhouse effect?
6. He has always been **hopeless** .... speaking in public.

b. Fill in the correct prepositions, then choose any five phrases and make up sentences using them.

1 in need ....; 2 capable ....; 3 to be generated ....; 4 to contribute ....; 5 to protect sth .... sb; 6 to take advantage .... sth; 7 to provide sb ....; 8 to be used .... sth

Phrasal Verbs
Appendix 2

25 Replace the words in bold with the correct phrasal verb formed with *fall* or *get*.

1. You can always **rely on** me for help.
2. Do you think that they are going to **escape without punishment for** their crime?
3. I really **like** Alice, she's such a friendly person.
4. It took Tony a long time to **recover from** his illness.
5. I can't believe they **were deceived by** that old trick.
6. The plans for the new sports centre **failed to be completed**.
7. He's going to try to **finish** the first half of that report tonight.

Word Formation

26 Fill in the correct word derived from the word in bold.

Treasuring the Tundra

The tundra is a cold, dry, 0) *treeless* region with very cold temperature and little rain. One of its most 1) .... characteristics is the 2) .... frozen layer of ground called permafrost. 3) ...., these extreme conditions can support a wide 4) .... of wildlife. In fact, several groups of Inuit people live there, relying on hunting and fishing for their 5) .... The animal life includes such species as arctic foxes, reindeer, wolves and seals. In spring, 6) .... flowers cover the ground. The snow offers 7) .... to such plants, allowing them to resist the cold temperatures. However, it is 8) .... for trees and larger plants to live in this environment.

The tundra is extremely fragile, so any changes caused by increasing temperatures and high 9) .... levels will have a 10) .... effect on the environment. We need to safeguard this delicate environment for the future.

TREE
DISTINCT
PERMANENT
SURPRISE
VARY

SURVIVE

COLOUR
PROTECT

POSSIBLE

POLLUTE
CONSIDER

Key-word Transformations

27 Complete the second sentence using the word in bold. You must use between two and five words including the word given.

1. Emma is finding it difficult to manage on the money she earns now.
   difficulty Emma ....
   .... on the money she earns now.
2. No one seemed to want to join the theatre group this year.
   interest There seemed to ....
   .... the theatre group this year.
3. She didn't say goodbye last night.
   without She left ....
   .... last night.
4. Ian has managed to give up smoking.
   succeeded Ian ....
   smoking.
5. Richard is 18, so he can vote.
   old Richard ....
   .... vote.

6 It's too cold for us to go to the park today.
   not   It's ....
   .... to go to the park today.

7 The tickets for the concert were more expensive than I had expected.
   as   The tickets for the concert were ....
   .... I had expected.

Open Cloze

28 Read the text and think of the word which best fits each gap. Use only ONE WORD in each gap.

SOWING THE SEEDS FOR SURVIVAL

When people mention endangered species the **0) first** things that come **1)** .... mind are probably whales, pandas or tigers. Not **2)** .... people would think of plants, but, in **3)** ...., there are far more threatened species of plants **4)** .... of the threatened mammals, fish, birds and insects combined.

One of the **5)** .... threats to the survival of many plants is industrialisation. This causes pollution and acid rain, **6)** .... destroy forests and harm many species of plant. Another threat is man! Many products that man uses **7)** .... from plants. For instance, many plants **8)** .... collected from the Amazon and are used to make medicines. Other plants, **9)** .... as mahogany trees, are valued **10)** .... their timber and are very popular building materials. There are even plants that **11)** .... become desirable collectors' items.

Luckily, **12)** .... and more people are becoming aware **13)** .... the problem and change is on the way. **14)** .... are now a number of organisations that are working to protect endangered plants as **15)** .... as animal species and preserve all living things for the future.

Idioms & Fixed Phrases

29 Match the phrases in bold to the definitions. Have you got any similar idioms/ phrases in your language? How do they compare with those in the exercise below?

- criticise • busy and active • be kind
- not show gratitude for • admire • remain calm
- become disappointed • not move

1 I really **take my hat off to** those eco-warriors. At least they are standing up for what they believe in.
2 He's exhausted, he's been **on the go** all day.
3 If you just **hold still** for a minute, I can explain everything to you.
4 She may seem strict but underneath she **has a heart of gold**.
5 I don't know why she **was having a go at** Steve. It wasn't his fault.
6 Environmentalists mustn't **lose heart** even when it seems like some people are ignoring them.
7 I'm happy to help her out but I don't want to **be taken for granted**.
8 Martin **kept his head** and didn't panic despite the chaos around him.

30 Fill in the correct animal from the list, then explain the phrases in bold. In pairs, think of other idioms with animals.

1 Ben was so nervous he **had .... in his stomach** before he gave his speech.
2 If I go into town to visit Mark, I might as well **kill two .... with one stone** and do some shopping on the way home.
3 I don't want to tell Liz the truth but I suppose it's time to **take the .... by the horns** and get it over with.
4 I'm sure Jean wasn't really upset; those were just .... **tears**.
5 Peter has done most of the work, so he should get **the ....'s share** of the money.

Listening & Speaking Skills

31 🎧 Listen to the people talking about problems on their island and write **S** (for Sandra), **B** (for Bill) or **J** (for Janet).

Which speaker:
- didn't hear a warning ....
- thinks the factory causes air pollution ....
- expected a warning ....
- believes that everyone is responsible ....
- saw somebody littering ....
- mentions a new building project ....
- is worried about wildlife ....
- suggests doing something ....

32 a. Look at the pictures and describe them. Then, in pairs, discuss the problems faced by Sandra's island.

b. Use the prompts below, as well as any ideas of your own, to suggest possible solutions, as in the example.

- fit filters to factory chimneys
- plant more trees
- write to the government
- fine people who drop litter
- improve public transport

Useful language for making suggestions
A good idea would be ...; Why don't we ...; We should/ could ...; If we ..., then ...; Perhaps we should ...; I think ...

A: One of the problems which the island faces is air pollution.
B: I couldn't agree more. You know, if factory owners fitted filters to the factory chimneys, then there wouldn't be so much air pollution.

33 🎧 You will hear part of a radio talk about endangered species. For questions (1-6), complete the notes which summarise what the speaker says.

1. John McKenzie is an ☐ activist.
2. John is working to raise ☐ about the problem of our endangered species.
3. We are wiping out the ☐ of many animals.
4. We need to be more careful about the ☐ we buy.
5. If we look after the ☐, more animals will survive.
6. We should report people who ☐ and ☐ animals to the police.

34 a. Look at the pictures and answer the questions.

1. What dangers do these animals face?
2. How is the title related to the pictures?
3. What can we do to protect animals?
4. What do you think this quotation implies: "The more I know people, the more I like animals"?

b. Give a one-minute monologue suggesting ways to protect animals.

35 🎧 You will hear five people talking about recycling ideas. Match the speakers to the sentences. There is one sentence which does not match any of the speakers.

A This will save lives. Speaker 1 ☐
B Teaching the public about recycling. Speaker 2 ☐
  Speaker 3 ☐
C Providing work and helping the environment. Speaker 4 ☐
  Speaker 5 ☐
D Things can be used more than once.
E Reasons why we should all recycle.
F This helps cut down energy use.

36 Look at the poster. In pairs, talk about what we can recycle and how. Then, explain why it is important for everyone to recycle.

A: First of all, we can recycle newspapers and magazines.
B: Yes, we can put them into the recycling bins in our neighbourhood. Then, they can be used to make recycled paper.

Offering solutions to problems

37 a. Listen to the dialogue. What is the problem?

b. Read the dialogue and fill in the missing phrases.

- Let's • Have you thought about
- I can't believe • I know • That's a great idea

A: 1) .... how much traffic there is on the roads these days.
B: 2) .... It took me two hours to drive into the city centre today.
A: You know, I've just had a brilliant idea. 3) .... starting a car pool?
B: 4) ....! We would save money and help reduce the amount of traffic at the same time!
A: 5) .... start right away. Who is going to drive tomorrow?

c. Use the prompts to act out similar dialogues.

- litter everywhere/start a clean-up campaign/pick up litter/clean up neighbourhood
- concrete everywhere/start a tree-planting campaign/make our town a more pleasant place to live

Complaining

38 a. Listen to the dialogue. How are the speakers related?

b. Match the sentences to form a dialogue.

A	B
1 ☐ John, could I have a word with you, please?	a Yes, you're right. I'll get right on it.
2 ☐ Well, I was wondering if you could do something about all that rubbish in front of your house.	b Sure, Linda. What's up?
3 ☐ I would appreciate it if you could sort it out as soon as possible, please.	c Oh right, yes. I've been meaning to do something about it, but I keep forgetting.

c. Follow the pattern and use the prompts to act out similar dialogues.

- greet/ask for a discussion → • return greeting/ask what
- state problem ←   the problem is
- ask politely for solution ← • make an excuse
                              → • agree politely

- dirty garden pond
- piles of bottles at the back of the house

Showing hesitation

39 a. Listen to the dialogues. Which of the sentences show hesitation?

b. Read the dialogue and underline the words which suggest hesitation.

1 A: Are you busy tonight, Bob?
   B: Let me see ... erm ... I don't think so. Why?
2 A: Shall we go out next Saturday?
   B: Oh ... Well ... I don't know.
3 A: Have you made up your mind yet?
   B: Mmm ... but I'm not sure about it.

c. In pairs, act out similar dialogues using the prompts.

- going to the beach
- planting some trees
- cleaning up the back garden

Intonation (key word stress)

40 Listen and underline the words that are stressed.

1 The thing that worries me most is global warming.
2 The main problem in this city is air pollution.
3 The cleanest form of energy is wind power.
4 A bicycle is something everyone should use.
5 Many rare species are in danger of extinction.

Robert Louis Stevenson (1850-1894) was a Scottish novelist, essayist and poet. Stevenson began to write at an early age and published his first essays while he was still at university. He is best known for his novels such as *Treasure Island*, *Kidnapped* and *The Strange Case of Dr Jekyll and Mr Hyde*. His childhood, near the Royal Botanic Garden, inspired many of his charming poems, published in *A Child's Garden of Verses* (1885). He is admired for his style and imagination.

Reading

41 a. Look at the title of the poem and the picture. What could the poem be about?

b. Read the first verse of the poem, then read the author's biography. What kind of experiences do you think might have inspired Robert Louis Stevenson to write this poem?

42 a. Listen to the poem and follow the lines. Read the poem verse by verse and answer the questions.

verse 1
1. Who is "I"? How old do you think he is?
2. Where does he dream of going?
3. Who lives there?

verse 2
1. Which animals/insects does the poet mention? Which of these can you see in the picture?
2. Which of these are busy? What are they doing?

verse 3
1. Where does the poet see a reflection of himself?
2. What is "his boat"?

verse 4
1. Where is the poet?
2. What can he see?

verse 5
1. Where is the poet now?
2. How does he feel? What makes him feel this way?

b. How does this poem make you feel? Why?

43 Study the theory boxes to answer the questions a - d.

> There are three main kinds of poetry: **lyric** (any short poem); **narrative** (poems which tell a story, either epic or ballad); and **dramatic** (poems which tell a story and in which the poem's characters act out the story).

a. What kind of poem is *The Little Land*?

> The rhythm and rhyme scheme of poetry is very important. Without these we could not read the poems with the same enjoyment and understanding.

b. Look at the first verse. It consists of sixteen lines. The first two lines rhyme with each other.

"When at home alone I **sit**
And am very tired of **it**"

Is this consistent throughout the first verse? Where does it change?

> Rhythm is created with stressed and unstressed syllables.

c. Listen to the first two lines of the poem and underline the stressed syllables. Listen again and repeat to feel the rhythm.

> Stevenson uses detailed descriptions, so that we can imagine what "The Little Land" looks like. This is called imagery.

d. Read the first verse and find an example of imagery. Look at the picture and underline the lines in the poem which create these images.

Project

Draw a scene from *The Little Land* for your class drawing competition.

Writing

44 Use the following words to write your own poem for your school's poetry competition.

- bed – red – head – said – fed
- see – bee – free – tea – agree
- ship – lip – slip – equip – skip
- eyes – skies – wise – tries – rise

Literature Corner

The Little Land

When at home alone I sit
And am very tired of it,
I have just to shut my eyes
To go sailing through the skies –
To go sailing far away
To the pleasant Land of Play;
To the fairy land afar
Where the Little People are;
Where the clover-tops are trees,
And the rain-pools are the seas,
And the leaves, like little ships,
Sail about on tiny trips;
And above the Daisy tree
Through the grasses,
High o'erhead the Bumble Bee
Hums and passes.

In that forest to and fro
I can wander, I can go;
See the spider and the fly,
And the ants go marching by,
Carrying parcels with their feet
Down the green and grassy street.
I can in the sorrel sit
Where the ladybird alit.
I can climb the jointed grass
And on high
See the greater swallows pass
In the sky,
And the round sun rolling by
Heeding no such things as I.

Through that forest I can pass
Till, as in a looking-glass,
Humming fly and daisy tree
And my tiny self I see,
Painted very clear and neat
On the rain-pool at my feet
Should a leaflet come to land
Drifting near to where I stand,
Straight I'll board that tiny boat
Round the rain-pool sea to float.

Little thoughtful creatures sit
On the grassy coasts of it;
Little things with lovely eyes
See me sailing with surprise.
Some are clad in armour green –
(These had sure to battle been!) –
Some are pied with ev'ry hue,
Black and crimson, gold and blue;
Some have wings and swift are gone; –
But they all look kindly on.

When my eyes I once again
Open, and see all things plain:
High bare walls, great bare floor;
Great big knobs on drawer and door;
Great big people perched on chairs,
Stitching tucks and mending tears,
Each a hill that I could climb,
And talking nonsense all the time –
O dear me,
That I could be
A sailor on the rain-pool sea,
A climber in the clover tree,
And just come back a sleepy-head,
Late at night to go to bed.

Writing an essay providing solutions to problems

Tip

Essays providing solutions to problems are pieces of writing in which we present a problem and its causes, then discuss our suggestions as well as their expected results.

Introduction
In the **first paragraph**, we present the problem and its causes.

Main Body
In the **second, third** and **fourth paragraphs**, we write our suggestions and their expected results. We write each suggestion and its results in separate paragraphs. We should link our ideas using appropriate linking words.

Conclusion
In the **last paragraph** we summarise our opinion.

Such essays are normally written in semi-formal or formal style, depending on who is going to read them and where it is going to be published. They are usually found as articles in magazines, newspapers, etc.

To make our piece of writing more interesting to the reader, we can use certain techniques to start or end it such as:

- **addressing the reader directly.** *If **you** want to help the environment, there are lots of things that **you** can do.*
- using a **quotation** (a sentence/phrase from a book, a play, etc). Don't forget to mention the name of the person who said / wrote it.
  ... as American anthropologist Margaret Mead said "We have nowhere else to go ... this is all we have."
- using a **rhetorical question** (a question that makes a statement rather than expecting an answer).
  Is it important to protect endangered species?

USEFUL VOCABULARY

To make suggestions:
It would help if / be a good idea if ...;
A / Another useful suggestion would be to ...;
The situation could be improved if / by ...;
Steps / Measures should be taken in order to solve / deal with ...

To present results and consequences:
In this way ...; This would ...; Then ...; If ... , the result would be ...; The effect / consequence / result of ... would be ...

Analysing the Rubric

45 Read the rubric and underline the key words. Then answer the questions.

> A local newspaper has asked its readers to write articles entitled "How can we make our planet a safer place for animals?" to be published in the newspaper.

1. Who is going to read your piece of writing?
2. What problems do animals face nowadays? Think about their *habitats*, *who hunts them* and *why*, the *effects of environmental problems* such as various forms of pollution etc.
3. Can you think of any ways to help animals?

Analysing a Model Text

46 a. What words can you think of related to the title of the article?

b. Read the article and put the paragraphs in the correct order, then answer the questions.

How can we make our planet a safer place for animals?

A ☐ Another solution is to promote education about endangered species. If people are aware of the problem, then they will buy fewer products made of materials such as ivory or fur.

B ☐ In conclusion, there are many ways to make our world a better place for animals. We all need to do whatever we can. As Malcolm Bradbury said "If you're not part of the solution, you're part of the problem."

C ☐ Is our planet a safe place for animals? Unfortunately, it doesn't seem like it. Thousands of species have become extinct and many more are now endangered. We need to do something fast before it is too late for them.

D ☐ Firstly, measures need to be taken to protect our wildlife. The destruction of threatened animals' habitats should be illegal, with long prison sentences for people who break these laws. This would protect animals and the environments they live in.

E ☐ Finally, we should create more national parks and conservation areas. This would allow animals to live and breed safely in their natural habitats. As a result, their numbers would increase and species would not die out.

1. Underline the topic sentences in each of the paragraphs in the main body. What supporting sentences does the writer give?
2. What are the writer's suggestions? Which linking words has he used to introduce each one? What results does he expect?
3. How does the writer start and end the article: with a rhetorical question? a quotation? addressing the reader directly? Suggest another beginning or ending to the article.

Beginnings – Endings

47 Read the extracts below. Which are beginnings? Which are endings? Which writing technique has been used in each?

A What would you like to learn about in school? In my opinion schools should focus on practical skills as well as on academic subjects.

B All in all, I think that banning cars from the city centre is an excellent idea. It will make shopping safer and healthier for pedestrians as well as reducing traffic jams. What more could the people of this city want?

C As Thomas Jefferson said, "Our liberty depends on the freedom of the press." However, nowadays with celebrities claiming that their private lives should remain private the issue is no longer so straightforward.

Suggestions & Results

48 Match the suggestions to the results, then make sentences, as in the example.

Suggestion
1. [d] Use renewable energy sources.
2. [ ] Insulate your house and use energy efficient products.
3. [ ] Create more nature reserves and wilderness areas.
4. [ ] Don't use aerosol sprays.

Result
a Use less fuel to heat and cool our houses.
b Protect endangered species' habitats.
c Prevent damage to the ozone layer.
d Use fewer fossil fuels, which would reduce air pollution and acid rain.

1 d – It would help if we used renewable energy sources. This way, we would use fewer fossil fuels, which would reduce air pollution and acid rain.

Topic & Supporting Sentences

49 Read the topic sentences; then use the prompts to write appropriate supporting sentences.

1 Using fossil fuels to generate power has several major disadvantages.
   non-renewable / burn fossil fuels / cause environmental problems / acid rain / global warming
   Firstly, fossil fuels are non-renewable resources. Also, ...

2 Hunting, pollution and the destruction of food sources mean that many species of whales are now endangered.
   said to be / less than 5,000 blue whales / 9,000 bowhead whales / worldwide / soon none left

Discuss & Write

50 Read the rubric and underline the key words. In pairs think of the causes of air pollution and make a list, then discuss the suggestions you would make.

> Your teacher has asked you to write an article for the school magazine entitled: "How can we reduce air pollution levels in our cities?" (120-180 words)

51 a. Match the causes to the suggested solutions and results.

Cause	Suggested Solution	Result
too much traffic in the city centre	create industrial park	less rubbish being burned
factories polluting the air	introduce a recycling scheme	less smoke over the city
too much rubbish being burned	introduce park and ride scheme	fewer cars in the city centre

b. Use your answers to Ex. 51a to answer the questions in the plan. Then write your article for the school magazine. You can use the article in Ex. 46b as a model.

Introduction
(Para 1) What is the problem?
          What has caused it?

Main Body
(Para 2) What is your first suggestion?
          What would its results be?
(Para 3) What is your second suggestion?
          What do you expect to happen?
(Para 4) What is your third suggestion?
          What results would it have?

Conclusion
(Para 5) How can you summarise your opinion?

52 Explain the quotations, then choose one to start/end your article in Ex. 51b.

- The only thing we have to fear on this planet is man.
  Carl Jung (Swiss psychologist)
- Treat the Earth well, it was not given to you by your parents, it was loaned to you by your children.
  Kenyan proverb

Self-Assessment Module 2

Vocabulary & Grammar

1 Fill in the missing word.

1 Many countries use fossil ...., such as coal, to generate electricity.
2 Global .... is caused by high levels of dangerous gases in the atmosphere.
3 It's freezing .... Do up your coat.
4 Wind is a renewable .... of energy.
5 Many species of fish have been wiped .... by overfishing.
6 Many forests in Europe have been damaged by .... rain.
7 Tony is .... reliable than Billy.
8 She will be late for class .... she doesn't leave now.
9 He is .... young to drive.
10 He doesn't have .... money to buy a new car.
11 Wind power .... a solution to energy problems.
12 Pandas are considered a(n) .... species.
13 Jeff didn't pay his bill, so now his electricity has been .... off.
14 Big Ben dates .... to the mid-1800s.
15 That was the .... interesting film I have ever seen.
16 I can't .... people who tell lies.
17 We should protect animals' .... habitat.
18 .... you drive more carefully, you'll have an accident.
19 The museum is .... to the public daily from 9:00am to 6:00pm.
20 The ozone .... protects the earth from the sun's harmful rays.

(10 marks)

2 Circle the correct item.

1 The old Victorian building has been .... to its original condition.
   A redecorated   C refurbished
   B restored   D renovated
2 Anita is always willing to .... an ear when I've got a problem.
   A give   B provide   C offer   D lend
3 Pete had .... in his stomach the whole time he was on stage.
   A birds   C flies
   B butterflies   D insects
4 He can't help .... slowly.
   A speaking   C speak
   B to speak   D to be speaking
5 He .... to Malta next month.
   A will have gone   C be going
   B goes   D is going
6 We're looking forward .... Mr Brown.
   A meeting   C to meeting
   B meet   D be meeting
7 He put a lot of .... into the project.
   A exertion   B sweat   C effort   D struggle
8 I'll drop you a .... when I arrive.
   A letter   B line   C note   D memo
9 The rainforest is .... to many species of birds and animals.
   A place   B house   C home   D hotel
10 There are lots of .... shops to look in.
   A popular   B style   C fashion   D trendy

(10 marks)

Use of English

3 Complete the second sentence using the word in bold. You can use two to five words including the word given. Don't change the word given.

1 It's not worth trying to grow oranges in England.
   point There is .... to grow oranges in England.
2 Julia couldn't drink the tea as it was very hot.
   too   The tea .... Julia to drink.
3 We have never travelled by bus.
   first It's .... travelled by bus.
4 Jenny is as old as Alain.
   same   Jenny .... Alain.
5 If you don't leave now, you'll be late for work.
   unless You'll be late for work .... now.

(5 marks)

4 Fill in the correct word derived from the word in bold.

1 .... travellers can go on a trip down the river.   **ADVENTURE**
2 There is a great .... of plants you can choose from.   **VARY**
3 It's .... for me to do it as it is very difficult.   **POSSIBLE**
4 We should use .... sources of energy.   **ALTERNATE**
5 Visiting Malta will be an .... experience.   **FORGET**

(5 marks)

Self-Assessment Module 2

5 Read the sentences. If a sentence is correct put a tick (✓). If it has a word which should not be there, write this word on the line.

1. A visit to the Rio will never be complete ....
2. if you don't take part in the carnival ....
3. celebrations. It is the world's most biggest ....
4. street party in where you can enjoy fantastic ....
5. costumes, bright decorations and a lots of ....
   dancing.

(5 marks)

Communication

6 Find the question which matches the answers.

1. (hotel)? — Not really. / I do, actually.
2. (beach)? — Why not? / It depends.
3. (bike ride)? — Yes, sure. / I can't.
4. (rubbish)? — Oh right, yes. / No problem.
5. (weekend)? — I don't think so. / No, I'm not.

(5 marks)

7 Complete the exchanges.

1. A: ....
   for a game of tennis after work?
   B: No, I'm afraid not. I have to finish this report.
2. A: ....?
   B: Well, it costs £50 per day or £200 for a week.
3. A: ....?
   B: Yes, sir, we accept Visa, Mastercard and American Express.
4. A: ....?
   B: You can come and pick it up tomorrow morning.
5. A: There are too many cars on the roads these days.
   B: It .... for more people to take the bus.

(5 marks)

Listening

8 🎧 You will hear an interview with a member of an environmental protection group. Listen and mark the sentences *T* (for true) or *F* (for false).

1. Dan is an aggressive person. ....
2. The 'Act Now' group planted flowers to show people how they feel. ....
3. 'Act Now' is for children. ....
4. Dan wants to teach people how to use fertilizers and pesticides. ....
5. 'Act Now' arranges public protests and demonstrations. ....
6. Dan knows lots of famous people. ....
7. Dan and his group spend a lot of time on the computer. ....

(10 marks)

Speaking (making decisions)

9 Your school has decided to join in a project to help the environment. Look at the pictures and, in pairs, decide which activities you could participate in, giving reasons.

Let's all help!!!!

plant flowers — collect rubbish — stray dogs — recycling

Useful phrases		
• I think ...	• It would be a good idea to ...	• So that ...
• We should ...		• Then ...
• Why don't we ...?	• That way ...	

(10 marks)

67

Self-Assessment Module 2

Reading

10 You are going to read some geographical information about different English-speaking countries. For questions (1-12), choose the country (A-C). There is an example at the beginning.

A JOURNEY
THROUGH THE ENGLISH-SPEAKING WORLD

A Ireland

LAND: The Republic of Ireland takes up about 83% of the island of Ireland, which is located in north-western Europe. Ireland is a small country with an area of just 70,285 km². Although there are high mountains near the coasts, the central part of Ireland is flatter and used for farmland.

CLIMATE: Most of Ireland is mild and wet throughout the year, giving Ireland its green countryside and earning it the name *The Emerald Isle*.

PEOPLE: Dublin is both the capital and the largest city. However, only about 57% of the Irish people today live in urban areas. The first Irish people probably came from Scandinavia to Scotland and then to Ireland about 8,000 years ago. Since then, Ireland has been invaded and colonised by Celts, Vikings, English and Scots. Today, most of Ireland's 3,590,000 population are of Celtic origin. It was the Celts who first introduced the language we know today as Irish, which is one of the country's official languages. English is the other official language.

B New Zealand

LAND: Located in the southwest Pacific Ocean, New Zealand is a small country of about 270,543 km². It is made up of two main islands, the North Island and the South Island, as well as a number of smaller islands. The North Island is famous for its volcanoes and many hot springs as well as its many forests, hills and mountains. The South Island has many high, snow-capped mountains.

CLIMATE: Most of the country is mild and rainy throughout the year, with the South Island much cooler than the North.

PEOPLE: Although Wellington is the capital city, it is not the largest. About one third of New Zealand's population lives in Auckland, the largest city in New Zealand. Today, only about 15% of all New Zealanders live in rural areas.
Most of New Zealand's 3,683,000 population are descendants of British settlers. There are also increasing numbers of people of Asian and Pacific island descent living in New Zealand. About 526,000 Maoris also live in New Zealand. Their ancestors came from the Polynesian Islands about 1,000 years ago. Today, the official language of New Zealand is English, although many Maoris speak their own language, Maori, as well.

C Canada

LAND: Canada, with an area of 9,970,610 km², is the second largest country in the world, spread across the top of North America. Canada is perhaps best known for its vast size, and variety of natural wilderness areas. The high mountains in the west of Canada are covered with green forests and crystal clear lakes, while in the centre are flat lands known as prairies. Further south, there are rolling hills.

CLIMATE: The climate ranges from temperate in the south to arctic in the north. In fact, the far north arctic landscape is so cold that trees cannot grow there. In the north the winters are cold and summers are short and quite cool, whereas in the south the winters are cold, and the summers are warm. It is wet on the coasts and dry in the centre.

PEOPLE: Ottawa is the capital of Canada, but Toronto is the largest city, with a population of over 4 million. More than one third of Canada's population of 29,450,000 are the descendants of British immigrants and there are almost as many descendants of French immigrants. This is why both English and French are the official languages of Canada. Other large immigrant groups include German, Italian and Asian people. Native American Indians and Inuit make up only a small part of Canada's population.

Which country(ies)

- is smaller than only one other country? **0** *C*
- are islands? **1** .... **2** ....
- has one official language? **3** ....
- have a constant climate throughout the year? **4** .... **5** ....
- has an area where there are no trees? **6** ....
- are made up of many different cultural groups? **7** .... **8** ....
- have a population of about three million? **9** .... **10** ....
- have minority racial groups? **11** .... **12** ....

(15 marks)

Self-Assessment Module 2

Writing

11 Your local council is going to publish a brochure called *Cleaning Up Our Town*. The brochure will include short articles on how to improve the environment in your town. You have been asked to write a short article for this brochure on improving the quality of the water in the local rivers and lakes. Use the plan below to write your article. (120-180 words)

Introduction
(Para 1) state problem: rivers and lakes polluted – people throw litter – factories dump industrial waste – can't swim – can't drink the water – must do something

Main Body
(Para 2) organise a clean up campaign – volunteers clean up rivers and lakes – put out more rubbish bins – less litter in water

(Para 3) fine factories that dump industrial waste into lakes and rivers – water pollution will decrease – cleaner water

Conclusion
(Para 4) restate opinion: local people and industry work together – clean up our lakes and rivers – can swim and use the water again

(20 marks)

(Total = 100 marks)

Sing Along!

12 a. Look at the pictures and the title of the song. Which of these problems do you expect to hear about? Listen and check.

b. Listen again and fill in, then sing.

There's so much pollution
Poisoning the 1) ....
There is so much 2) ....
We can see it everywhere
3) .... is disappearing
While everyone stands by
The world we love is dying
And we're the
4) .... why

Why are we killing our world
Why aren't we doing our share
We can save our planet
We can help it survive
All it needs is a little care

If we all work together
Something can be done
We need a 5) .... campaign
Which involves everyone
We can slow down global 6) ....
We can stop the acid rain
We can heal our 7) ....
We can help it live again

Why are we killing our world ...

If we don't act quickly
Our world will soon be dead
We must leave our 8) .... at home
And use bicycles instead
We must stop using chemicals
And 9) .... fossil fuels
We must recycle all our 10) ....
It's so easy to do

We must stop killing our world ...
We must start doing our share ...

Progress Update

How do you rate your progress? Tick (✓) the box that applies to you.

	Excellent ****	Good ***	OK **	Could do better *
Vocabulary & Grammar				
Listening				
Speaking				
Reading				
Writing				
Communication				

Module 3

Units 5-6

Before you start ...

When was the last time you went on holiday? Talk about it.
What can you do to protect the environment?

Listen, read and talk about ...

- daily routines
- health problems & symptoms
- stress & relaxation
- feelings
- character adjectives
- ways to relax
- technology & leisure time
- technology at home
- crime
- computers

Learn how to ...

- express preferences
- describe your feelings
- describe a person's character
- make deductions
- speculating
- give advice
- make an appointment
- express your loss of temper
- describe symptoms

Practise ...

- modal verbs (must, ought to, need, mustn't, have to, should, could, would, may, might)
- past & perfect modals
- clauses of reason
- question tags
- the passive
- relatives
- relative defining – non-defining clauses

Phrasal verbs

- give
- go
- hold
- keep

Write ...

- a letter to a friend about a health problem you had
- a set of school rules
- a short article about a famous health spot
- a for and against essay
- an inventor's short biography
- a newspaper article
- a diary entry
- an opinion essay

Early to Bed...

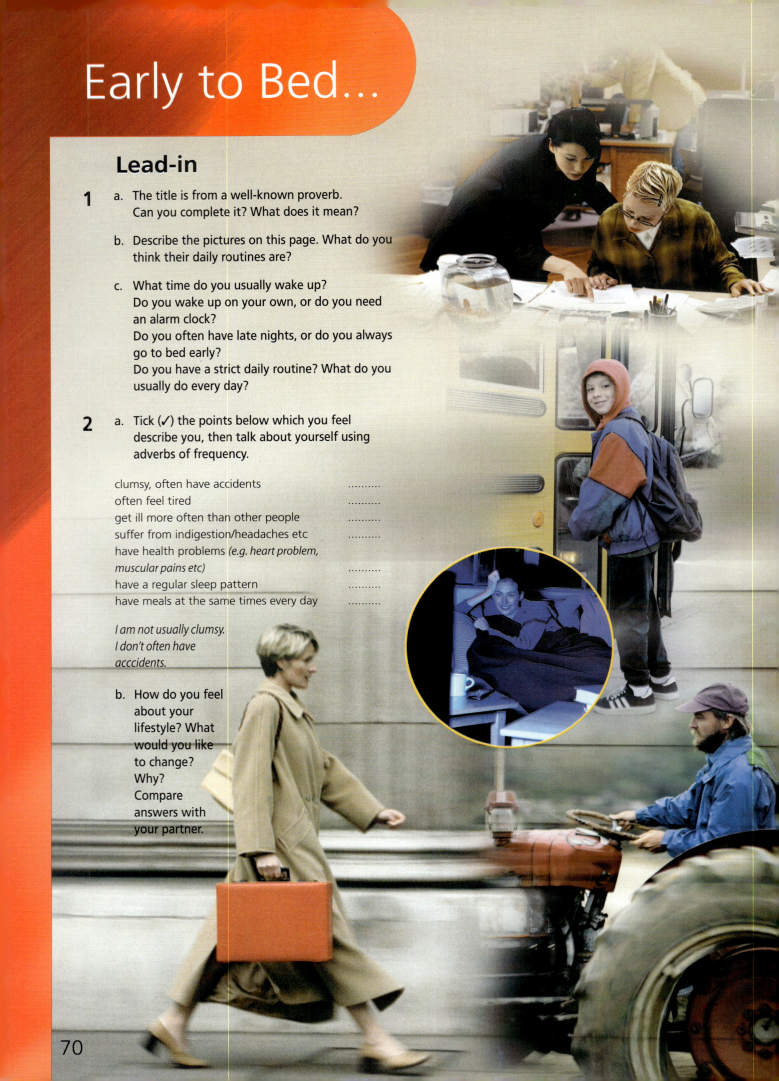

Lead-in

1. a. The title is from a well-known proverb. Can you complete it? What does it mean?

   b. Describe the pictures on this page. What do you think their daily routines are?

   c. What time do you usually wake up?
   Do you wake up on your own, or do you need an alarm clock?
   Do you often have late nights, or do you always go to bed early?
   Do you have a strict daily routine? What do you usually do every day?

2. a. Tick (✓) the points below which you feel describe you, then talk about yourself using adverbs of frequency.

   clumsy, often have accidents ....
   often feel tired ....
   get ill more often than other people ....
   suffer from indigestion/headaches etc ....
   have health problems *(e.g. heart problem, muscular pains etc)* ....
   have a regular sleep pattern ....
   have meals at the same times every day ....

   I am not usually clumsy. I don't often have acccidents.

   b. How do you feel about your lifestyle? What would you like to change? Why? Compare answers with your partner.

Can you feel the rhythm?

'Routine' is usually seen as a negative term nowadays, largely because we no longer belong to a society of nine-to-fivers. We live in what is fast becoming a 24-hour society, where everything is open all hours. You can buy your groceries at midnight, book your holiday on the Internet at 3 am, and do business online at the crack of dawn. Before you join the 24-hour **revolution**, however, take a minute to listen to what your body is trying to tell you – that a round-the-clock lifestyle is not what nature intended.

In an area of our brains called the hypothalamus, we have a 'body clock' that controls our body's natural rhythms. It tells us when it's the right time to eat, sleep, work and play. It plays an important part in our **physical** and **psychological** well-being. It is, in fact, what makes us tick and it controls many things including our **hormones**, temperature, immune functions and **alertness**. It **synchronises** all these like a conductor with an orchestra; it regulates tempo and brings in all the different instruments on time to make music rather than **random** noise. If we try to ignore our body clocks, or even to switch them off for a while, we not only **deprive** ourselves of much needed rest but we also run the risk of seriously damaging our health.

Ignoring your body clock and changing your body's natural rhythms can not only make you **depressed**, **anxious** and **accident prone**, it can lead to much more serious health problems. For example, **heart disease**, fatigue, **ulcers**, **muscular pain**, and **frequent viral infections** can all result from trying to **outsmart** our body clocks. Altering our patterns of sleeping and waking dramatically affects our **immune system**. While we sleep the body's **repair mechanisms** are at work; when we are awake natural killer cells **circulate** around our bodies and cause more damage. Our **digestive system** is affected, too – high levels of **glucose** and fat remain in our **bloodstream** for longer periods of time and this can lead to heart disease.

Unfortunately, we were not designed to be members of a 24-hour society. We can't ignore millions of years of **evolution** and stay up all night and sleep all day. We function best with a regular pattern of sleep and wakefulness that is **in tune with** our natural environment. Nature's cues are what keep our body clocks ticking rhythmically and everything working in **harmony**. So, next time you think a daily routine is boring and **predictable**, remember that routine may well save your life in the long run.

line 12 *line 14*

Reading

3
a. What is the man below looking at? How do you think he feels? Why?

b. Is it important to have a standard daily routine? Why/Why not? Read the text to find out.

c. Read the text again and choose the correct answer, A, B, C or D, for questions 1-6.

1 What does *it* in line 12 refer to?
 A our body's natural rhythms
 B the hypothalamus
 C our body's biological clock
 D our brain

2 What does the word *tick* in line 14 mean?
 A check
 B motivate
 C select
 D function

3 In what way is our body clock like the conductor of an orchestra?
 A The hypothalamus controls our actions.
 B It makes all the body's functions work together at the right time.
 C The body clock is very precise.
 D We have a special programme.

4 If we change our sleep patterns, we
 A will get an infection.
 B will disturb our immune system.
 C will get heart disease.
 D get high levels of dangerous cells.

5 According to the text, we should
 A do things when our body tells us to.
 B organise our body clock according to a strict schedule.
 C use the natural environment to work out a regular routine.
 D have a boring, slow-paced lifestyle.

6 According to the text, our body clock
 A can be changed without harm.
 B determines when we should do things.
 C helps us to fight sleep.
 D is a boring routine.

d. Explain the words/phrases in bold. Which words in the text do you think come from another language? Are there any words in the text that are the same in your language?

Follow-up

Why has the writer written this article? Are there any points in the article you disagree with? Is there any information you did not know before reading the article? Compare answers with your partner.

Vocabulary Practice

Health Problems

5 a. Look at the table and match the problems to their symptoms and causes.

Symptoms	Problem	Common Cause
can't sleep	indigestion	not getting enough sleep
a bloated, painful stomach	asthma	a virus
headache, fever, aching muscles	insomnia	spending too much time in the sun
high temperature, nausea, dizziness	overtired	bacteria under the skin
a painful muscle contraction	flu	eating too much or too quickly
difficulty breathing, wheezing	cramp	doing too much exercise
can't stop yawning	acne	stress, anxiety
runny nose, sore eyes, sneezing	heat stroke	an allergy to pollen
spots and red lumps on the face and neck	hay fever	an allergy to dust or animals

b. In pairs, use the table to talk about health problems, as in the example. Which of these problems have you experienced?

If you have a bloated, painful stomach, then you've probably got indigestion. This is usually caused by eating too much, too quickly.

c. What medical problems could you suffer ...
- on a very hot day?
- if you get wet on a cold day?

6 a. Match the words in column A to those in column B to make collocations, then say what might give you each problem.

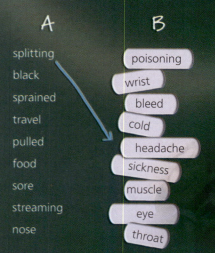

You may get a splitting headache if you work on a computer for too long.

b. Match the collocations to the advice.

- take an aspirin
- put it in a sling
- pinch your nose
- put some ice on it
- get some fresh air
- drink plenty of fluids
- ask the doctor to prescribe some medicine
- rest the injured part
- suck on a throat lozenge

If you have a splitting headache, you should take an aspirin.

c. In pairs, act out dialogues, as in the example.

A: I've got a splitting headache.
B: Really? Why?
A: I've been working on the computer all day.
B: You should take an aspirin.

Writing

7 Write a letter to a friend about a health problem that you have had recently. Write what caused it, when/where it happened and what you did about it.

Stress and Relaxation

8 Look at the list below and rank the stressful situations from 1 to 9, where 1 is the least stressful and 9 the most stressful. Compare your list to your partner's and talk about the situations.

- a ☐ being stuck in a traffic jam
- b ☐ doing the housework
- c ☐ waiting in a queue for a long time
- d ☐ being late for school/work
- e ☐ missing the bus/train to school/work
- f ☐ walking home alone at night
- g ☐ going to the dentist
- h ☐ taking an exam
- i ☐ not being able to sleep at night

A: To me, going to the dentist is the most stressful situation. I can't stand drills! What about you?
B: Well, I just hate being stuck in traffic jams. I really get stressed when I have to sit and wait for ages.

9 a. Look at the pictures. Which would you do to help you relax when you are stressed? You can add your own ideas.

go shopping · play music · get together with friends · go cycling · paint · go to the gym

I **prefer** playing tennis **to** going to the gym.
I**'d rather** watch TV **than** play computer games.

b. In pairs, discuss what you prefer doing to relax. Use the table below.

POSITIVE	NEGATIVE
I (really) enjoy/like/love/prefer	I don't like ...
I'm fond of/interested in/keen on	I hate/detest/can't stand ...
I find ... quite exciting/relaxing/fascinating etc	I'm not very fond of/interested in/keen on ...
	I find ... a bit/rather boring/tiring etc

A: I find painting quite relaxing.
B: Really? I'm not very fond of drawing, but I enjoy playing squash.

Describing Feelings

10 a. Study the table, then choose words from the list and make up pairs of sentences, as in the examples in the table.

> **Present/Past Participles**
> We use **-ed** participles to describe how we feel/felt:
> I **felt satisfied** when I passed the test.
> We use **-ing** participles to say what an experience is/was like: Passing the test **was satisfying**.

- satisfied · disappointed · thrilled · tired
- embarrassed · frightened · excited
- annoyed · fascinated · confused · worried
- relaxed · bored · pleased · relieved

b. Listen and say how each speaker sounds, using words from the list above.

A .... B .... C ....

11 Talk about two things – one pleasant and one unpleasant – that happened to you. Say what happened and how you felt about it, as in the examples.

When my dog went missing I felt very **worried**.
When my dog came home again I felt **relieved**.

Character Adjectives

12 a. Match the character adjectives to the definitions.

1 ☐ sociable	a want things to be perfect
2 ☐ sentimental	b like going to parties
3 ☐ conservative	c show pity/love
4 ☐ perfectionist	d can be trusted
5 ☐ arrogant	e hate change/new ideas
6 ☐ confident	f can't wait for long
7 ☐ moody	g make sensible decisions
8 ☐ reliable	h be sure of your abilities
9 ☐ practical	i change feelings frequently
10 ☐ impatient	j think you're better than others

b. Which of the adjectives above best describe you/your friends? Give reasons. Use adjectives of your own as well.

I think I'm quite sociable, because I like going to parties and being with friends.
I wouldn't say I'm shy, because I don't feel uncomfortable with people I've just met.

Grammar in use

Obligation, Prohibition, Suggestion, Necessity

Grammar Reference

13 Read the sentences and match the verbs/modals in bold to their meanings. Which express: *obligation*? *prohibition*? *suggestion*? *necessity*? *lack of necessity*?

1. ☐ Surgeons **must** wear masks during an operation.
2. ☐ You **ought to** have an annual check-up.
3. ☐ You **must** clean your teeth every day.
4. ☐ You **need to** sleep for at least 7 hours a night.
5. ☐ You **mustn't** smoke in here.
6. ☐ You **don't have to** drive me to the station.
7. ☐ You **shouldn't** be rude to your mother.
8. ☐ In the UK you **have to** be 17 to get a driving licence.

a It would be a good idea to do this.
b This is a rule.
c You are not allowed to do this; it is forbidden.
d It is important that you do this.
e It's not necessary, but you can if you want to.
f This is necessary.
g It would be a good idea not to do this.
h This is very important; it is essential.

14 a. Use the prompts and make up three sentences each about doctors and nurses.

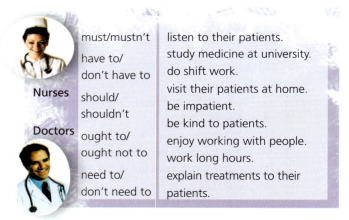

Doctors should listen to their patients.

b. Write three sentences about patients, using the verbs **listen**, **tell** and **visit**.

15 Expand these signs into full sentences in as many ways as possible. Where might you see each sign?

You must not smoke.
Smoking is forbidden.
You are not allowed to smoke.
We might find this sign in a public place.

16 Join the sentences. Can you suggest another ending to each sentence?

Students have to study hard	in case	of an emergency.
Athletes have to exercise regularly	otherwise	they will have a heart attack.
Everyone should have a first-aid kit at home	because	they must keep fit.
Patients with a heart condition must avoid stress	or else	they won't pass their exams.

Writing Project

Write a set of five rules about what students need to do while at school.

Permission, Request, Ability, Possibility

Grammar Reference

17 Match the modals in bold to the functions below.

• possibility • lack of ability • permission
• request • ability • lack of permission

1 **Could/Would** you help me with my homework?
2 You **can't/mustn't/may not** smoke in here.
3 You **can/may** borrow my dictionary.
4 He **can** play the piano really well.
5 He **could/may/might** have the flu.
6 I **can't** speak French.

18 Underline the correct modal, then explain its use.

1 **Could/Would** it be OK if I left early today?
2 He **won't/can't** see without his glasses.
3 No, you **would not/may not** borrow my car.
4 She isn't inside; she **might/can** be in the garden.
5 You **will/may** go home if you aren't feeling well.

Past & Perfect Modals
Grammar Reference

19 Match the modals in bold to their meaning.

1. ☐ I **should have** phoned my mum on her birthday.
2. ☐ You **needn't have** bought a ticket, because we had an extra one.
3. ☐ He **ought not to have** shouted at his neighbour.
4. ☐ Jim drove me to work, so I **didn't have to** walk.
5. ☐ He **couldn't/wasn't able to** play football until his leg healed.
6. ☐ He **didn't need to** go to the supermarket, because his wife had already done the shopping.

a He didn't do it, because it became unnecessary.
b He did it but it was the wrong thing to do.
c He didn't have the ability to do it.
d He didn't do it, although it was necessary.
e He didn't do it, because it wasn't necessary.
f He did it, although it wasn't necessary.

20 Fill in *could(n't) have*, *ought (not) to have*, *needn't have*, *should(n't) have* or *didn't need to*.

1 We took our time because we .... be there until 11 o'clock.
2 You .... gone to see a doctor if you were feeling so ill.
3 Andy .... said that to Julie. He really upset her, didn't he?
4 I was busy last Saturday, so I .... gone to his party even if I'd wanted to.
5 You .... come to pick me up – there are plenty of taxis.
6 He .... arrived by now, because he left at least an hour ago.
7 We .... rushed, because we got there with plenty of time to spare.
8 If you had sprained your ankle, you .... walked here.
9 You .... let Paul know what we were doing – he was waiting for us.
10 We .... take an exam at the end of the course.

Making Deductions
Grammar Reference

21 Which of the sentences express certainty/uncertainty?

Present	Past
He must be tired.	He must have been at work.
He might be tired.	He might have been at work.
He can't be tired.	He can't have been at work.

22 Look at the pictures. Write sentences using *must*, *could*, *shouldn't*, *ought*, *can't*, etc, as in the examples.

*He must be stressed.
He shouldn't work so hard.
He may have got a parking ticket.
He ought to relax.
His work can't be going very well. etc*

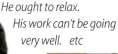

Game

In teams, think of three sentences about the following situations, using appropriate modals. Each correct set of sentences gets a point. The team with the most points is the winner.

Suggested situations

A your friend is in bed with a bad cold
B your friend is upset because she has put on weight
C your brother has failed his exam
D your uncle has been fired from his job

Team A S1: You shouldn't go to school.
       S2: You ought to see a doctor.   etc

Question Tags
Grammar Reference

23 a. Look at the examples and underline the question tags. Which asks for confirmation? Which asks for information? How are they formed?

FALLING/RISING INTONATION
He isn't in today, is he? (sure of the answer)
She left yesterday, didn't she? (not sure of the answer)

b. Fill in the correct question tags.

1 They bought some flowers, ...?
2 He hasn't called yet, ...?
3 Ann looks tired, ...?
4 Stop talking, ...?
5 Let's have dinner together, ...?
6 He will keep our secret, ...?
7 You booked the tickets, ...?
8 We are going out tonight, ...?
9 Dad will be on time, ...?
10 She won't forget, ...?

Prepositions
Appendix 1

24 a. Underline the correct preposition, then explain the phrases.

1 Look! That dress is **identical *to/with*** the one Jane was wearing last night.
2 I think he is **jealous *for/of*** Sally because of all the money she's making these days.
3 We offered to help her but she **insisted *for/on*** doing the whole thing herself.
4 James thinks it's an excellent plan but I'm not so **keen *on/to*** the idea.
5 Everyone has been very **kind *to/of*** me since the accident.

75

Grammar in use

6 That book made a really strong **impression** *with/on* Emma. She can't stop talking about it.

7 Come to the fair – everyone is welcome to **join** *in/to* the fun.

8 In recent years there has been a large **increase** *of/in* the number of people who take no regular exercise.

b. Fill in the correct preposition, then choose five phrases and make sentences using them.

1 .... the crack of dawn; **2** to play a part .... sth; **3** .... fact; **4** to deprive sb .... sth; **5** to run the risk .... sth; **6** to lead .... sth; **7** .... example; **8** to be .... tune .... sth; **9** .... harmony; **10** .... the long run

Phrasal Verbs
Appendix 2

25 Fill in the correct particles, then explain the phrasal verbs.

1 I've seen this film before. Don't worry, though – I won't **give** .... the ending.

2 The fire was **giving** .... a lot of heat.

3 The car was running fine this morning but on the way home the engine suddenly **gave** ....

4 It was obvious that they would lose, but they still wouldn't **give** ....

5 He said he would do it – I can't believe he **went** .... his word.

6 I feel really ill today; I hope I'm not **going** .... flu.

7 Erica left a bit suddenly, maybe you should **go** .... her and check she's OK.

8 The dog **went** .... him when he tried to open the gate.

9 I'm afraid there won't be enough food to **go** ....

Multiple Choice Cloze

26 Read the text and decide which answer – A, B, C or D – best fits each space (1-15). There is an example at the beginning (0).

An Early Bird or a Night Owl?

Owls are nocturnal creatures. They're wide **0)** *awake* at night and they sleep during the day. If this **1)** .... like bliss to you, then, like about 20 percent of the population **2)** .... find themselves most active at around 9 pm, you may fall into the same category **3)** .... our feathered friend. Night owls often have difficulty waking up in the morning, and like to be up late at night. **4)** .... of animal behaviour indicate that being a night owl may actually be **5)** .... into some people's genes. This would explain **6)** .... those late-to-bed, late-to-rise people find it so difficult to change their behaviour.

The trouble for night owls is that they just **7)** .... to be at places such as work and school far **8)** .... early. This is when the alarm clock becomes the night owl's most important survival tool. Experts **9)** .... that one way for a night owl to beat their dependence **10)** .... their alarm clocks is to sleep with the curtains open. The theory is that if they do so, the morning sunlight will awaken them gently and naturally.

The **11)** .... is that, unlike the feathered owl, human owls can't claim that a nocturnal existence is their **12)** .... lifestyle. They are programmed to be at their best **13)** .... the day. **14)** .... if we try to change our schedules and work at night, Mother Nature isn't fooled. Night is still the time when our body **15)** .... down. Night owls simply start and finish a little later than average.

0	A	aware	B	wakeful	C	awake	D	alert
1	A	sounds	B	hears	C	listens	D	looks
2	A	when	B	whose	C	which	D	who
3	A	like	B	as	C	with	D	for
4	A	Research	B	Examinations	C	Enquiries	D	Studies
5	A	constructed	B	built	C	erected	D	made
6	A	why	B	when	C	how	D	where
7	A	ought	B	have	C	must	D	should
8	A	too	B	enough	C	from	D	away
9	A	tell	B	speak	C	inform	D	say
10	A	in	B	on	C	to	D	for
11	A	truth	B	honesty	C	real	D	reason
12	A	usual	B	expected	C	ordinary	D	natural
13	A	while	B	throughout	C	through	D	during
14	A	Also	B	Even	C	Yet	D	As
15	A	slows	B	moves	C	goes	D	falls

Error Correction

27 Read the text below and look carefully at each line. If the line is correct, put a tick (✓). If it has a word that should not be there, write this word on the line, as in the examples.

Eat to Relax

We all know that eating of healthy foods helps us to	0	*of*
live longer and to ward off the danger of strokes or	00	✓
heart disease. A healthy lifestyle, which includes and	1	....
regular exercise and a diet with lots of fruit and	2	....
vegetables, not only keeps the doctor away but also	3	....
makes us to feel good. Being in good health is an	4	....
important way for to reduce stress, but this is not the	5	....
only benefit of eating properly. In particular, the types	6	....
of food that we eat influence on our moods. Eating	7	....
carbohydrate-rich foods like breads, cereals, rice and	8	....
pasta it causes the production of seratonin, which	9	....
makes us feel calm. Fruit and vegetables also set off	10	....
the production of this chemical, but in too smaller	11	....
doses. Milk, cheese and the yoghurt can also help,	12	....
especially when they eaten together with	13	....
carbohydrates. The next time you feel stressed, try a little	14	....
piece bread and a glass of milk and you'll feel relaxed in	15	....
no time.		

Key-word Transformations

28 Complete the second sentence using the word in bold. You can use two to five words, including the word given.

1. It was wrong of him not to tell us as soon as he found out.
   should   He .... as soon as he found out.

2. Anna didn't go to hospital; it was only a minor injury.
   have   Anna .... to hospital; it was only a minor injury.

3. It isn't necessary to make an appointment – come in any time tomorrow morning.
   need   You .... an appointment – come in any time tomorrow morning.

4. His speech had an effect on everyone who was there.
   impression   His speech .... everyone who was there.

5. Patients must be accompanied by a nurse when they leave the ward.
   allowed   Patients .... the ward unless accompanied by a nurse.

6. You mustn't reveal the secret to anybody.
   away   You aren't allowed to .... to anybody.

Idioms & Fixed Phrases

29 Fill in the words from the list then explain the phrases in bold.

- mouth • finger • stomach
- tooth • chest • bones

1. Martin loves chocolate and biscuits – he's really got **a sweet** ....

2. Thanks for listening. I needed to **get that off my** ....

3. There's something wrong with the car, but I just can't **put my** .... **on** what it is.

4. Surgeons need to have **a strong** .... , because they can't let the sight of blood and injuries upset them.

5. I'm sure something is going to go wrong today. I can **feel it in my** ....

6. I didn't say that. Please don't **put words into my** ....

30 Underline the correct word then explain the phrases.

1. At the start of the meeting the boss told a few jokes **to break the** *ice/pace*.

2. She's really funny, she can *do/make* **impressions** of all sorts of famous people.

3. He said that he would think about it, but in fact he **had no** *plan/intention* **of** going.

4. Debbie **has itchy** *feet/boots* – she never stays in one place for more than a year or two before she goes travelling again.

5. I think the professor has really *knocked/hit* **the jackpot** with his latest invention.

Listening & Speaking skills

31 You are going to listen to four people talking about how they have improved their quality of life. Match the statements which best summarise their ideas (A-E) to the speakers (1-4). There is one statement which you do not need to use.

A Be with friends.   Speaker 1 ☐
B Get back to nature.   Speaker 2 ☐
C Be satisfied with less. Speaker 3 ☐
D Focus on the family   Speaker 4 ☐
E Help those in need.

32 Look at the table and the pictures, then, in pairs, talk about:

- different ways to relax;
- pros & cons of active and passive relaxation

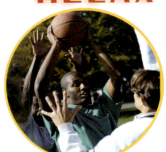

Survey results for 500 teenagers

- 27% watch TV
- 24% spend time with friends
- 12% read a book
- 10% listen to music
- 8% play sports
- 6% play a musical instrument
- 5% go shopping
- 3% go to cinema
- 3% go out for a meal
- 2% play computer games

A: Watching TV is a form of passive relaxation.
B: Yes, you can sit quietly ...

Tip Read the instructions to find out what the listening text is about. Read the question stems and underline any key words. Read the options (A, B, C) for each question. Do not predict the answers. Listen and mark your answers. Listen again and check. Do not leave any questions unanswered.

33 You will hear five short dialogues about people's health. Listen and circle the correct item: A, B or C.

1 What happened to the girl?
  A She crashed her bicycle.
  B She crashed her car.
  C She crashed her mother's car.

2 What is wrong with the man?
  A He has got food poisoning.
  B He is allergic to seafood.
  C He ate too much.

3 What has the man been doing?
  A fighting
  B dressing his children
  C jogging

4 What is the doctor's advice?
  A To exercise more.
  B To exercise less.
  C To do some weightlifting.

5 How did the woman hurt her hand?
  A She burnt it.
  B She trapped it in the kitchen door.
  C The man hurt it.

Speculating

34 a. Look at the pictures. Who: is in a hurry? has a splitting headache? has had an accident?

Jack   Jean   Bill

b. What do you think caused each problem?

Jack might have been playing football. He could have tripped and fallen down. He must be in pain.   etc

Giving Advice

c. What advice would you give each person? Use the phrases below, as well as your own ideas.

If I were you, I ... / You should(n't) ... / Why don't you ...

Jack – You should be more careful.

35 a. You are going to hear someone giving advice on how to reduce stress. Listen and say where you might hear this dialogue. How do the speakers sound? Why?

b. Listen again and write *Yes* or *No* for each statement (1-7).

1 The woman is suffering from stress.   .....
2 She often goes out with her friends.   .....
3 She thinks her work is causing her stress. .....
4 The man suggests that she find another job. .....
5 The woman can work fewer hours.   .....
6 The man suggests she take some medicine. .....

36 Your friend is feeling stressed out and wants to make some changes to his/her lifestyle.

- suggest ways to change his/her lifestyle in order to help reduce stress
- reject his/her reasons for not being able to follow your advice, and suggest alternatives
- express your hope that everything will work out well

Writing

Use your ideas from Ex. 36 to write a letter of advice to your friend on how to reduce stress. Start with your opening remarks. In the main body write your advice. End your letter with closing remarks.

Losing your temper

37 a. You will hear four short exchanges about various problems. Listen and match the exchanges (1-4) to the problems listed.

untidiness ....   noise ....
overwork ....   faulty appliance ....

b. Read the exchanges and replace the expressions in bold, which show the speaker has lost their temper, with appropriate ones from the list.

- For crying out loud! • I'm fed up with this!
- I don't believe it! • I don't know what to do!
- Good grief! • I can't put up with this!
- I'm sick of this! • I've had all I can take!

1 A: **I've had enough!** Go on – *you* fix this machine. I give up!
  B: OK, I'll do it. Just calm down.

2 A: **I can't stand it any more!** Don't you know it's late and I'm trying to sleep? Turn down the music or I'll call the police.
  B: Alright, alright. Don't go on about it. I'll turn it down.

3 A: Haven't you finished that report yet?
  B: **You must be joking!** The phone hasn't stopped ringing all day and I've been running around after you. When do you expect me to do it?

4 A: **For goodness' sake!** I won't tell you again – clean up this mess *immediately*, please.
  B: Oh come on, Mum. It's my room after all. You never stop nagging me.

Pronunciation

38 a. Read the words and say which language each comes from. Write **G** (for Greek), **L** (for Latin) or **B** (for Both). Do you use any words in your language which are similar to these?

stethoscope	....	physical	....
pneumonia	....	temperature	....
thermometer	....	patient	....
asthma	....	medicine	....
diarrhoea	....	muscle	....

b. Listen and repeat, then make up sentences using the words. Be careful how you pronounce them.

Making an appointment

39 a. Listen to the dialogue and fill in the questions. Who is Tina speaking to?

A: Good afternoon. Meadows Surgery. 1) ....?
B: Oh yes, I'd like to make an appointment with Doctor Michaels, please.
A: I'm afraid Dr Michaels is on holiday at the moment. 2) ....?
B: Erm ... yes, alright. That would be fine.
A: Right. The first available appointment is on Thursday at 10 o'clock. 3) ....?
B: Yes, that should be okay.
A: Good. 4) ....?
B: Tina, Tina Wilcox.
A: 5) ....?
B: I've been having trouble sleeping lately.
A: Right then, we'll see you on Thursday at 10 o'clock.
B: Thank you. Goodbye.

b. Use the prompts below to act out similar dialogues.

Friday	Monday
2:30pm	9 o'clock
Carol Ormerod	Brian Powell
(bad cough)	(earache)

Describing symptoms

40 a. Listen to the dialogue and fill in the missing words. What's wrong with Betty?

• aches • the flu • pale

A: Are you okay, Betty? You look a bit 1) ....
B: Actually, I feel terrible.
A: Oh! What's wrong?
B: I'm burning up and my whole body 2) ...., too.
A: Sounds to me like 3) .... If I were you, I would go to bed.

b. Use the prompts to act out similar dialogues.

- burning feeling in my chest
  heartburn – take an antacid tablet
- can't stop yawning
  you're overtired – get an early night

Naturally Hot

41 a. Look at the pictures. What do these places have in common?

b. The words/phrases below are used in the texts. In what context do you expect each to be used? Make up sentences, as in the examples.

Text A: ancient limestone - high mineral content - relaxation and therapeutic purposes - dark and humid - caves - natural steam bath

Text B: bubbling geysers - active volcano areas - mud pools - hot springs - pain-relieving qualities - arthritis, rheumatism and neuralgia - spas

Text A: The caves contain ancient limestone.
Text B: There are lots of bubbling geysers in New Zealand.

c. How do you think the title above is related to the pictures?

42 Which of the following can you find in your country: *mud pools? hot spring? active volcanic areas? caves in mountains? natural steam baths? health spas?* Why might a person visit such places?

43 a. Read the articles and decide which health spot each statement refers to. Write *R* (for Rotorua) or *A* (for Ainsworth Hot Springs). Then, explain the words in bold.

Which place:
1 was once used by miners? ....
2 has water that comes from deep below the ground? ....
3 has got caves? ....
4 is famous for its volcanoes? ....
5 can be found in an area of natural beauty? ....

b. Read the articles again and find one similarity and one difference between each of the resorts.

c. Find synonyms for the highlighted words. Then, find words in the articles which are similar in your language.

d. In pairs, think of alternative titles for the articles.

44 What similar resorts are there in your country? What can you do there? Imagine you are a tourist guide, and give a talk to the class about one such resort.

Writing

45 Write a short article about a famous health spot in your country. Write about:
- brief description of location / what it is famous for
- historical details (if any)
- special features
- what to do there / recommendation

A
Ainsworth Hot Springs

The Selkirk Mountains in British Columbia, Canada, are famous for the Cody Caves System with its ancient **limestone** and natural hot springs. The springs have a naturally high mineral content and have long been used for relaxation and therapeutic purposes.

The native Indians originally discovered the springs, but now they form part of one of the country's favourite **holiday resorts**. The springs got their name from George Ainsworth from Oregon, who founded Hot Springs Camp in 1882. At that time the only visitors were local **miners** and **prospectors**, but in the 1920s the springs were developed and **caves** and a pool were constructed. Meanwhile the mining industry declined, and all the mines were closed by the 1960s.

From its source in the Cody Caves, the water works its way down through the rock, and the deeper it goes, the hotter it gets. It finally **surfaces** at Ainsworth Hot Springs, where the water temperature varies from 35°C to 42°C. The caves are dark and humid and with the hot spring water at waist height they act as a natural **steam bath**.

The surrounding area is of great natural beauty. There are fantastic views of Kootenay Lake and the Purcell Mountains, and visitors can go hiking in Kokanee Provincial Park.

Culture Clip 5

B Rotorua

Rotorua in New Zealand is famous as one of the world's most active volcanic areas. It is filled with bubbling **geysers**, mud pools and natural **hot springs**. The springs are famous for their relaxing and **pain-relieving** qualities. The waters can help people with arthritis, rheumatism and neuralgia, as well as improve their general health.

Throughout history, people have visited the area and bathed in the mineral rich hot springs to relieve their aches and pains. The **healing properties** of the hot springs were discovered by the native Maori people a long time ago but were only made known to the rest of the world in 1878 when they were discovered by a travelling priest. He found that his arthritis was cured after bathing in the waters, and the spring became known as the Priest Spring.

The water from the Priest Spring is **acidic**. It flows from the volcanic rock deep below the surface of the earth, and its temperature varies from 33°C to 43°C. This is totally different from the other springs in the area where the water is **alkaline** and comes from nearer the surface.

There are many spas to visit in the region that have a number of pools with different temperatures. Other attractions include visiting a volcanic crater, hiking in a national park or visiting a **wildlife** reserve.

Writing a for and against essay

Tip

We usually write a for and against essay in a formal style. When we write the essay, we need to discuss both sides of the argument to give a balanced view.

Introduction
In the **introduction** we present the topic, but do not give our opinion.

Main Body
In the **second paragraph** we give the arguments for the topic together with justifications and examples.
In the **third paragraph** we give the arguments against the topic. We start each paragraph with appropriate topic sentences.

Conclusion
In the **last paragraph** we write a balanced personal opinion, or summarise the main arguments for and against.

We also need to use appropriate linkers to connect similar ideas and introduce opposing ideas.

Analysing the Rubric

46 Read the rubric, underline the key words and answer the questions.

- Your school newspaper has asked you to write an article discussing the pros and cons of exercising to reduce stress.
- Write your article in about 120-180 words.

1. What are you going to write?
2. Who is going to read your piece of writing?
3. Should you use informal language? Why (not)?
4. In pairs, think of two positive and two negative aspects of exercising to reduce stress. Compare your answers with the rest of the class.

Analysing a Model Text

47 a. Read the article and underline the correct linkers. Which:
- list/add points
- introduce reasons/examples
- show contrast
- introduce a conclusion

b. What is each paragraph about?

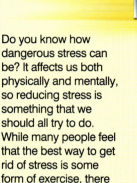

More exercise, less stress?

Do you know how dangerous stress can be? It affects us both physically and mentally, so reducing stress is something that we should all try to do. While many people feel that the best way to get rid of stress is some form of exercise, there are other ways which are just as effective.

The benefits of physical exercise are obvious. **1) Moreover/First of all**, keeping fit helps your body stay strong and healthy. **2) Therefore/Because** you are less likely to get sick or suffer from stress-related health problems **3) such as/in addition to** heart attacks and cancer. **4) Furthermore/However**, exercise is a good way to get rid of frustration and anger, because after exercise the brain produces hormones called endorphins which make us feel good.

5) On the other hand/Moreover, if you are out of shape, exercise can be quite painful. You may pull a muscle or injure yourself. **6) Due to the fact that/Furthermore**, exercising may even cause more stress **7) what is more/since** it will add to your already hectic schedule.

8) Last but not least/In conclusion, the best way to combat stress in our lives is to live a healthy life. As James Freeman Clark says, "Never hurry. Take plenty of exercise. Always be cheerful. Take all the sleep you need. You may expect to be well."

48 a. Read the article again and list the points *for* and *against* the topic. Are they similar to yours? What justifications/examples does the writer give to support each point?

b. What topic sentences has the writer used in the main body? Suggest other appropriate ones.

c. What techniques has the writer used to start/end his article: *a quotation? addressing the reader directly? a rhetorical question?* Can you suggest another beginning/ending?

Topic Sentences

49 a. Choose the appropriate topic sentence 1-4 for the paragraph.

1. Society teaches women that good health matters more than body shape.
2. Women are getting the message that they are judged by their weight.
3. A woman's physical appearance is less important than it used to be.
4. Nowadays, a woman's intelligence and her personality are considered more important than her looks.

.... On TV, in films and magazines, only thin women are considered beautiful, popular and successful. As a result, many women feel that their lives will improve only if they lose weight. Our society not only encourages women to become thin but almost insists on it.

b. Suggest a topic sentence for the paragraph.

> .... For instance, obesity can put a strain on the heart which can lead to heart disease. The extra weight also puts extra pressure on joints and bones, which makes it painful as well as difficult to move

Supporting Sentences & Linkers

50 Expand the prompts into full supporting sentences using appropriate linkers.

1. There are many arguments against taking diet pills.
   - put on weight when you stop taking them
   - not enough vitamins and minerals
   - might have side effects/endanger health

2. Cosmetic surgery has certainly got its advantages.
   - surgeons can repair people's faces if they are injured in an accident
   - people can have scars or blemishes removed
   - people can change parts of their bodies which make them unhappy/depressed

Discuss & Write

51 Read the rubric and underline the key words, then answer the questions.

> Your school magazine has asked its readers to write an article discussing the advantages and disadvantages of fast food. Write your article for the magazine in about 120-180 words.

1. What type of composition are you going to write?
2. What will the topic of each paragraph be?
3. Think of two pros/cons which you can include.
4. In which paragraph can you write your opinion?
5. Which techniques can you use to start/end your essay? Suggest a full beginning/ending.

52 a. Match the points to their justifications. Which are positive, and which are negative?

1		our bodies need a balanced diet
2		not healthy
3		convenient
4		large amounts of additives

a. full of saturated fats and other chemicals
b. we need some fats, sugars and salt in our diet
c. it's available whenever you want it
d. doesn't provide you with enough vitamins/minerals

b. Join the ideas into full sentences.

53 a. Look at the plan below, and use your answers to Exs 51 and 52a to answer the questions.

Introduction
(Para 1) How can you present the topic?
What general remarks can you make?

Main Body
(Para 2) Which are the pros?
What examples can you think of?
(Para 3) Which are the cons?
What examples can you think of?

Conclusion
(Para 4) What is your opinion?

b. What linking words can you use to list/add points; introduce pros/cons; introduce examples; show contrast; introduce a conclusion?

c. Will you write your personal opinion?
d. What style will you use? Why?
e. What topic sentences will you use?

54 Use your answers to Ex. 53 to write your article for the magazine. You can use the article in Ex. 47 as a model.

55 Try to explain these quotations in your own words. How do they relate to the theme of the unit?

- To get rich, never risk your health. For it is the truth that health is the wealth of wealth.
  Richard Baker
- Health is the first muse, and sleep is the condition to produce it. *Ralph Waldo Emerson*
  (US philosopher)
- The first wealth is health. *Ralph Waldo Emerson*

83

Better Safe than Sorry

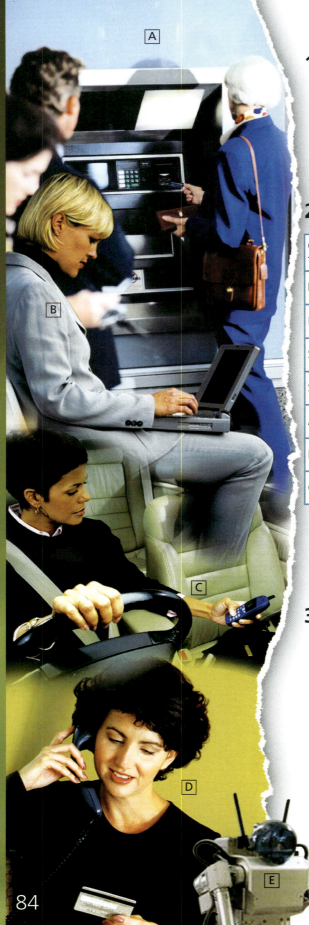

Lead-in

1 Which of the following can you see in the pictures?

- mobile phone • credit card • ID card • ATM • CCTV
- laptop computer • satellite dish • robot • radar screen

Which item do you think is the most/least useful?
How often do you/your parents use these items?
What other pieces of equipment do you use daily?

2 Match the columns to make sentences.

CCTV (closed circuit TV) cameras		to store and organise information.
ID cards		to store large amounts of information on circuits.
Radars		to monitor roads and public areas.
Security systems	are used	to identify you.
Satellites		to locate ships and planes when we can't see them.
ATMs		to collect and send information to and from space.
Microchips		to protect a building from burglars.
Computers		to allow you to take money out of the bank.

CCTV cameras are used to monitor roads and public areas.

Reading

3 a. Read the headings A-H and the title of the article. What do you expect to read in the text? Read the article and check your guesses.

b. Read the text again and match the headings A-H to each part 1-6 of the article. There is one heading which you do not need to use. There is an example at the beginning.

- A A single card
- B A difficult decision
- C The positive side
- D Nothing is hidden any more
- E Keeping watch is expensive
- F Captured on film
- G New forms of identification
- H Nowhere to hide

No More Secrets

c. In pairs, think of other appropriate headings.

d. Explain the words in bold, then answer these questions, according to what the text says.
   1. How can surveillance increase public safety?
   2. In what ways can ID technologies offer greater convenience?
   3. What is the disadvantage of increased surveillance?

Follow-up

4. Read the article again and list all the surveillance technologies mentioned, making notes on what each does. Then talk about the two technologies that you think are the most useful in your society. Justify your answers.

Tip: Read the list of headings quickly. Read the text once and try to understand the main point of each paragraph. Look at the headings again and underline the key words. Read the text again, paragraph by paragraph, and try to find words/phrases that match the headings. The information might be phrased in different words. Each time you choose a heading, cross it out.

---

0 — **D**

Did you know that somebody somewhere knows everything about you – what you buy at the supermarket, who you call on the phone, which videos you rent and even what you like on your pizza? Most of us are **aware of** the fact that every time we use a credit card, phone card, cash card or supermarket card, our personal information is being recorded somewhere. This is the **price we pay** for the **convenience** of using cards instead of cash. We have even accepted the fact that nothing we do on our computer is ever completely private.

1

You might think that you have never been on TV, but you are wrong. CCTV (closed circuit TV) cameras are everywhere! They are in shopping centres, at ATMs, outside buildings and even on our roads and motorways. They are **operated** by the police and private **security** companies, and they are there to discourage crimes such as **muggings**, shoplifting, and carjackings. They also watch the roads for people speeding, and more. In some buildings there are even cameras in smoke detectors, clocks and exit signs. They **keep track of** where you are and what you are doing all day, every day.

2

In the very near future you will no longer have to worry about forgetting your computer password, your cash card number or even your keys, because your body will be your ID. **Finger scanning**, which is similar to **fingerprinting**, is already being used by large companies to **identify** employees. **Face recognition** is another growing area of ID technology, as are voice and eye recognition. Something quite new on the market is **footstep identification**. Using special floor tiles, computers are able to identify people from the way they walk. This technology will let your employer or your teacher know exactly where you are and what you are doing while you are at work or at school.

3

Locating you when you are not at work or at school is also becoming easier. GPS (Global Positioning Systems) technology already exists, and in less than a minute it can find out, **via satellite**, exactly where you are. Some car rental companies are already using this technology to keep track of their vehicles. Mobile phone companies are even planning to use this technology in all their phones. This means that when someone makes a call on their mobile phone, or even if they simply have their phone turned on, they can easily be **located**.

4

Identity cards are also getting 'smarter'. Many countries already have a system which requires their citizens to carry **identification cards**. These cards usually include personal information such as name, address and birth date as well as a personal identification number. However, in the near future, these cards will also contain a microchip, which will be able to store a lot more information. Using this technology, one card will be able to replace your driving licence, student card, medical card, library card, credit card, **birth certificate** and most of the other pieces of ID that we have to carry around with us.

5

The benefits of all these new ID systems are obvious. Imagine walking into your office at work. The floor will know you have arrived and your computer will recognise your voice and **automatically** log you on. You will be able to walk up to your ATM, smile sweetly and say hello, and it will give you your money. Your family will know exactly where you are, and you will always know where your car is. Criminals are going to find it a lot more difficult to commit crimes, and the police will find it a lot easier to catch them.

6

The question that we have to ask ourselves now is how the rights of the individual will be **preserved**. We must ask ourselves whether increased public safety and convenience will come at the cost of our **privacy**, and whether or not this is a price we are **willing** to pay. Is convenience worth the loss of privacy as all our personal data from bank records to health information and employment history is on file and more readily available every day? Are we really ready to live in a world where our every move is being watched?

Vocabulary Practice

Technology at Home

5 a. Are you a technophile or a technophobe? Choose A, B or C to complete each sentence in the way that best describes you.

A	B		C	
I never	always	use a mobile phone	only in an emergency	C
I seldom	often	use an answering machine	only if I have no choice	
I don't	love to	play computer games	when I'm in the mood	
I can't	usually	send e-mails	whenever I need to	
I won't	frequently	use the Internet	now and again	

I use a mobile phone only in an emergency.

Mostly A's: You are definitely technophobic. There is nothing to be scared of. Try it – you might like it!

Mostly B's: You are without doubt a technophile. Be careful you don't forget how to use pen and paper!

Mostly C's: You seem to have the technical world under control. Well done! It's important to be able to use technology to help you, but not let it run your life.

b. Now, use the words and phrases to talk about how often you:

- watch DVDs • listen to MP3s • buy something online
- watch satellite TV • cook with a microwave oven
- withdraw money from an ATM

I never watch DVDs, because we haven't got a DVD player.

6 a. Which of these have you got at home?

1 fax machine 2 iron 3 camcorder 4 kettle 5 microwave oven 6 blender

b. Match the appliances above to their uses listed below, then make up sentences, as in the example.

- video events • cook food • liquidise food
- boil water • iron clothes • send faxes

A fax machine is used for sending faxes.

7 a. Fill in: **turn on, plug in, log off, create, send, install.**

1 The battery in my laptop is running out. I need to .... it .... and recharge it.
2 I'm going to .... an e-mail to my mother, because it's cheaper than calling her on the phone.
3 Can you help me .... this new computer game on my PC?
4 I'm going to .... a "birthday" file to store my friends' birthdays.
5 Your printer isn't broken – you just forgot to .... it ....
6 Don't forget to .... when you have finished using the Internet, or your phone bill will be huge.

b. Find the opposites of the verbs above.

8 Add words to each of the spidergrams, then make up sentences using the words.

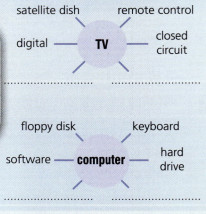

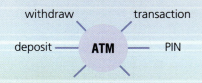

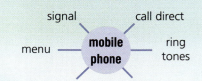

signal — call direct
menu — **mobile phone** — ring tones

Writing Project

Collect information about various inventors (e.g. date of birth/death, nationality, etc) and their inventions (e.g. year, reason/use, etc). Find or draw pictures and prepare a poster of famous inventors and their inventions.

Game

Divide into two teams. One team says a word related to technology. The other team makes up a sentence using the word. Each correct sentence gets a point. The team with the most points is the winner.

Team A S1: ATM
Team B S1: An ATM is used to allow us to get money out of the bank.

Crime

9 a. Match the criminals 1-8 to the definitions a-h, then make sentences, as in the example.

1	c	burglar	5		kidnapper
2		smuggler	6		hijacker
3		shoplifter	7		thief
4		arsonist	8		forger

a sets fire to buildings/forests/etc on purpose
b takes someone by force and doesn't release them until a ransom is paid
c breaks into a building in order to steal things
d copies works of art/documents/signatures/etc to deceive people
e takes things into or out of a country illegally
f steals things from a shop while pretending to be a customer
g illegally takes control of a plane or other vehicle using force
h steals another person's property

A burglar breaks into a building in order to steal things.

b. Give the name of the crime and the verb related to each of the criminals above.

burglar – burglary – to burgle

10 a. Underline the correct word or phrase, then use your dictionary to help you explain the meaning.

Car thief claims innocence

24-year-old Sam Thorn of Leeds was **1) charged with/sentenced to** 5 years in prison yesterday for car theft.
After Thorn was stopped for **2) speeding/skidding** last July, the police discovered that the car which he was driving was stolen.
Although Thorn pleaded not guilty at his **3) court/trial**, there were three **4) statements/witnesses** who saw him smash the window of the car and drive it away.
Thorn told the **5) judge/trial** that it was his car but he had lost his keys. Unfortunately, he could not produce **6) defence/proof** that the car was his and it was discovered that the real owner had reported it **7) stolen/robbed** the same day.
"I'm innocent" is all Thorn would say to the reporters outside the **8) courtroom/courtyard**.

b. Match the columns to make correct sentences.

He was charged — for murder.
He was robbed — out of his money.
He was accused — of assault.
He was sentenced — with burglary.
He was cheated — to two years' imprisonment.
He was tried — of a family heirloom.

Writing

Read the headline below, then write a news report.

75-year-old caught shoplifting in supermarket

Write:
• where/when it happened
• what happened in detail
• what the criminal said

You can use words from Ex. 10.

11 Study the table, then rewrite the descriptions below, putting the adjectives in the correct order.

When two or more adjectives are used together to describe the same noun, they usually follow this order:

Opinion	expensive	elegant	pretty
Size	miniature	large	small
Age	brand-new	antique	old
Shape	rectangular	round	square
Colour	silver	brown	grey
Origin	Japanese	American	Irish
Material	plastic	wooden	stone
Use	mobile	dining	holiday
NOUN	phone	table	cottage

a a(n) **oval/jewellery/blue/enamel** box
b a **prehistoric/clay/cooking/brown** pot
c a **striped/new/small/canvas** bag
d a pair of **triangular/ugly/plastic/orange** earrings
e a(n) **antique/enormous/Chinese/beautiful** vase

12 a. You will hear someone describing his stolen bag and what it contained. Listen and tick (✓) which of the objects below he describes.

b. Describe each of the objects shown above.

c. Take roles and act out a dialogue between a police officer (A) and a person (B) who is reporting the theft of their travel bag.

A	B
ask B's name/address	give name/address
ask when/where/how the theft occurred	say when/where/how the theft occurred
ask B for description of bag and contents	describe stolen bag and contents in detail

Grammar in use

The Passive
Grammar Reference

13 Read the sentences a-h and underline the passive forms, then answer questions 1-6.

a   Customers are requested to refrain from smoking inside the store.
b   The motorist was fined £80 for illegal parking.
c   Breakfast is now being served in the Garden Room.
d   "Guernica" was painted by Picasso.
e   The theft was committed with high-tech equipment.
f   Rentals should be returned to the main garage.
g   The telephone was invented by Alexander Graham Bell.
h   This is clearly a case of arson, because the fire was started with rags soaked in petrol.

1   Where might you see/read the sentences above? Are they formal or informal in style?
2   How do we form the passive?
3   Which sentence(s) contain(s) the agent? Why? How is the agent introduced?
4   Why is there no agent in the other sentences?
5   How do we form the passive of modal verbs?
6   When do we use *with* to introduce the agent?

14 Use the prompts to make complete passive sentences, as in the example.

1   A: my office / break into / last night
    My office was broken into last night.
    B: Oh no! Did they take anything?
2   A: you / invite / to Bill's birthday party?
    B: No, I wasn't.
3   A: Can I have my bill, please?
    B: Of course, sir. Your bill / prepare / now.
4   A: the new CCTV camera / install / yet?
    B: No, not yet.
5   A: Is their website information up to date?
    B: Maybe ... but I visited the website last week, and / it / not / update / for months.
6   A: Why is everyone lined up?
    B: Our ID cards / check / the security guards.

15 Study the examples. How do the two passive sentences differ?

> Active • *People say that he escaped to Brazil.*
> Passive • *He is said to have escaped to Brazil.*
> • *It is said that he escaped to Brazil.*

16 Use the patterns in Ex. 15 to make sentences, as in the example.

1   People believe he has stolen £1m.
    It is believed that he has stolen £1m.
    He is believed to have stolen £1m.
2   They say he is working on a new software package.
3   We expect the company will set up a computer network this year.
4   The police think he was involved in the theft.
5   Everyone thinks she is the creator of the robot-pet.

17 Expand the newspaper headlines into full sentences using the passive, as in the example.

Laptops are being tried out in the classroom by schools.

18 Complete the text by putting the verbs into the correct tense/form of the active or passive voice.

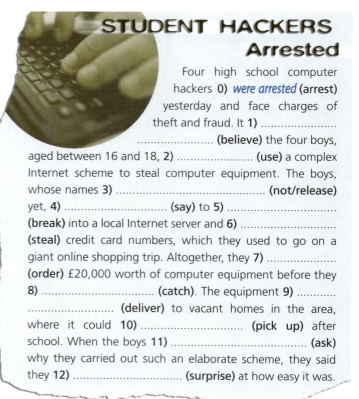

STUDENT HACKERS Arrested

Four high school computer hackers **0)** *were arrested* (arrest) yesterday and face charges of theft and fraud. It **1)** .... (believe) the four boys, aged between 16 and 18, **2)** .... (use) a complex Internet scheme to steal computer equipment. The boys, whose names **3)** .... (not/release) yet, **4)** .... (say) to **5)** .... (break) into a local Internet server and **6)** .... (steal) credit card numbers, which they used to go on a giant online shopping trip. Altogether, they **7)** .... (order) £20,000 worth of computer equipment before they **8)** .... (catch). The equipment **9)** .... (deliver) to vacant homes in the area, where it could **10)** .... (pick up) after school. When the boys **11)** .... (ask) why they carried out such an elaborate scheme, they said they **12)** .... (surprise) at how easy it was.

Relative Pronouns in Defining/Non-Defining Relative Clauses

Grammar Reference

19 a. Use appropriate relative pronouns to match the main clauses to the relative clauses. When do we use *who*, *which/that* or *whose*?

Main clause	Relative pronoun	Relative clause
Lucy likes people Lucy likes things That's Lucy,	who which / that whose	are useful. aren't arrogant. she can talk to. family you have met. she can make something with. bicycle was stolen yesterday.

b. Study the rule below. Can we leave out the relative pronoun in any of the sentences above? Which sentences, and why?

> 'We can leave out the relative pronouns **who**, **which** and **that** if they are used as the **object** of a **defining** relative clause.

20 Make sentences with *who/which* about the people/things in the pictures, as in the example.

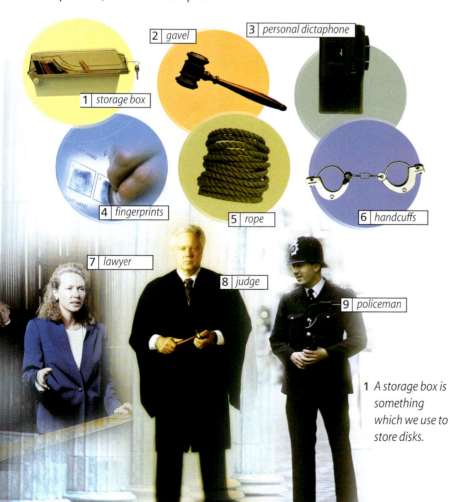

1 storage box
2 gavel
3 personal dictaphone
4 fingerprints
5 rope
6 handcuffs
7 lawyer
8 judge
9 policeman

1 *A storage box is something which we use to store disks.*

21 Fill in *who*, *whose* or *which*. In which sentences could you leave out the relative pronoun? Why?

1 The man .... she was talking to used to live here.
2 He's got a new job, ... is much better than his last one.
3 That's the man .... wife works with Steve.
4 The police arrested the burglar .... broke into their house.
5 Sarah, ... dog I'm looking after, is on holiday in Spain.
6 We're looking for a restaurant .... serves Italian food.
7 Is that the girl .... bought your car?
8 The train .... we were going to take has just left.
9 My video recorder, ... I bought last week, cost £200.
10 I gave Joan, ... car had broken down, a lift to the office.

> **... of whom / ... of which**
>
> **Whom** (for people) and **which** (for things) can be used with *none of ...*, *all of ...*, *most of ...*, *any of ...*, *many of ...*, *some of ...*, *both of ...*, *each of ...*, *neither of ...*, *either of ...*, *one of ...* etc.
>
> He bought three **jackets**, all of **which** were exactly the same colour.
> He's got two **brothers**, both of **whom** live in England.

22 Join the sentences using *which* or *whom*, as in the example.

1 Mary has three sisters. One of them is married.
   Mary has three sisters, one of whom is married.
2 He has three cars. One of them is a Jaguar.
3 Louise invited fifty people to the party. Most of them said that they would come.
4 The police arrested six men. Two of them are suspected of organising the crime.
5 Two prisoners escaped. They were both later recaptured by the police.

Grammar in use

23 Fill in *where*, *when* or *why*.

1. Do you remember the day .... we first met?
2. His office is in the street .... Mary lives.
3. Do you know the reason .... she didn't come?
4. The house .... he was born has been broken into.
5. 1914 was the year .... World War I broke out.

Competition Game

In teams, think of definitions for the nouns below using relative pronouns. Each correct sentence gets a point. The team with the most points is the winner.

- CCTV • judge • court • arsonist
- microchip • satellite • burglar
- prison • ID card • shoplifter
- hijacker • courtroom • gavel

Team A S1: *CCTV is a system which is used to monitor roads and public areas.*
Team B S1: *A judge is a person who ... etc*

Prepositions
Appendix 1

24 a. Underline the correct preposition, then explain the phrases in bold.

1. He was given the job, despite his **lack** *in/of* experience.
2. Stop **laughing** *at/to* him.
3. Be careful. This area is **notorious** *for/of* street crime.
4. Please don't **lean** *at/on* the table – it isn't very strong.
5. Jo is **married** *to/with* Jack.
6. She's really **nervous** *about/for* the exam, because she hasn't studied for it.
7. I often **mistake** Lyn *from/for* Anna – they look so alike!
8. The new product was **named** *for/after* its inventor.

b. Fill in the correct preposition, then choose five of the completed phrases and make up sentences using them.

1. be aware .... sth
2. to pay .... sth
3. to do sth .... your computer
4. to be .... TV
5. to have a problem .... sth
6. to worry .... sth
7. to keep track .... sth
8. to make a call .... your mobile phone
9. .... the near future
10. to be .... file

Phrasal Verbs
Appendix 2

25 Replace the words or phrases in bold with the correct form of a phrasal verb using *hold* or *keep*.

1. Can you **wait** for a minute? I'll see if Mr Walker is available.
2. I haven't fixed the problem, but I'll **continue** trying to find a solution.
3. The children were **made to stay behind** by the teacher after school.
4. They built a fence so that people would **not intrude on** their land.
5. The bad weather **delayed** departure of the flight for a couple of hours.

Word Formation

26 Fill in the correct word derived from the word in bold.

It's All on Film!

The 0) *frequency* with which surveillance cameras are used is increasing 1) .... all the time, and due to the 2) .... of improved technology they are being used in a 3) .... of new and unusual ways.

CCTV cameras improve public 4) .... , it is said, because they help the police to identify 5) .... , which makes the 6) .... of crime much easier. Traffic cameras film those 7) .... of speeding or 8) .... driving, so reducing the risk of accidents.

Despite the general 9) .... of CCTV cameras, some people 10) .... of their use, because they feel that any surveillance is an invasion of privacy.

FREQUENT
STEADY
INTRODUCE
VARY

SAFE
CRIME
PREVENT
GUILT
DANGER

POPULAR
APPROVE

Open Cloze

27 Read the text and think of the word which best fits each gap. Use only ONE WORD in each gap.

THE MICROWAVE MISHAP

Did you know that microwaves were first used **0)** *by* the British Army in World War II **1)** .... identify enemy warplanes? In fact, it was **2)** .... accident that made people aware that microwaves could also cook food.

In 1945, Percy LeBaron Spencer, **3)** .... work involved the testing of radar waves, became the first person to **4)** .... this connection. **5)** .... day at work, Spencer was standing near a machine which was emitting radar waves. Later **6)** .... , when he felt like a snack, he reached **7)** .... the chocolate bar he had in his pocket – **8)** .... to find that it had melted! When he thought about it, he realised **9)** .... had happened. The radar waves coming from the machine **10)** .... he had been standing next to had melted his chocolate. Later, experiments showed that radar waves contain microwaves that could heat food **11)** .... faster than traditional ovens.

His company went **12)** .... to develop and market the first microwave ovens in 1954. They **13)** .... huge, bulky and expensive, but since **14)** .... , microwave ovens have become smaller, giving **15)** .... the compact models we see in our kitchens today.

Key-word Transformations

28 Complete the second sentence using the word in bold. You can use two to five words, including the word given.

1 They don't expect you to finish all that work today.
   expected   You ....
   .... all that work today.

2 They are building a new cinema in Cannon Street.
   built   A new cinema ....
   .... Cannon Street.

3 That's the school which we attended when we were young.
   go   That's the school we ....
   .... when we were young.

4 The weather was so hot that they went to the seaside.
   such   It was ....
   .... they went to the seaside.

5 Nobody apart from Bill thought that it would work.
   only   Bill ....
   .... thought that it would work.

6 Experts have estimated that more than half the population of the UK now own a mobile phone.
   been   It ....
   .... more than half the population of the UK now own a mobile phone.

7 Two men wearing ski masks carried out the robbery, which was the third such crime in less than a month.
   was   The robbery, ...
   .... two men wearing ski masks, was the third such crime in less than a month.

8 People say that the ancient Babylonians knew a lot about astronomy.
   said   The ancient Babylonians are ....
   .... a lot about astronomy.

Idioms & Fixed Phrases

29 Match the pairs of words joined with *and*, then use the phrases to complete the sentences.

• safe • alive • clean • hit • law • right
... and ...
• run • order • tidy • wrong • sound • well

1 The missing climber was found two days later, *safe and sound*.
2 Children have to be taught the difference between .... at a young age.
3 She was knocked over in a(n) .... accident.
4 A policeman's job is to maintain ....
5 I haven't seen him since he went to America twenty years ago, but I know he's ....
6 She spends a lot of time doing housework. Her flat is always ....

30 Underline the correct word, then explain the fixed phrases.

1 I think if you interfere you will only *make/do* matters worse.
2 I only see my grandparents once in a blue *sky/moon*.
3 Sales staff use mobile phones to call the office when they are **on** the *round/road*.
4 Keep in *mind/head* that most software soon goes out of date.

Listening & Speaking skills

31 🎧 Listen to the people talking about computers and mark the sentences as *M* (for Martha), *B* (for Bob) or *S* (for Sally).

Who:
1. has been working longer hours to store information? ....
2. says that computers save on office space? ....
3. thinks computers save time? ....
4. says people can keep up to date while on the road? ....
5. wishes their children would spend less time using computers? ....
6. thinks that some children don't get much chance to practise their computer skills? ....
7. mentions that computers damage people's eyes? ....

32 a. Look at the pictures and describe them.

Picture A shows a young woman in an Internet café. etc

b. Answer the questions.

- When do you use a computer?
- What are the advantages and disadvantages of using computers?
- How have computers affected various areas of your life (e.g. work, home, health, etc)?

33 🎧 Listen to a police officer giving advice on how to protect our houses while we are away, and complete the form.

Always lock your **1** _____ and _____.
Put all your **2** _____ in a safe.
Leave a **3** _____ on in the living room or bedroom while you are away.
The best thing is to get a **4** _____ installed professionally.
Ask your **5** _____ to check your house for you when you go on holiday.
Neighbourhood **6** _____ schemes can help to prevent burglaries.
Get a **7** _____ to protect your home from fire.

34 You are going away for a two-week holiday and you are worried about your house being burgled while you are away. Visit your neighbour and

- explain your problem.
- ask your neighbour to check on your house while you're away.
- thank your neighbour and offer to return the favour.

35 🎧 Listen and match the speakers to the ways in which they relax. There is one way of relaxing which you do not need to use.

A Internet   Speaker 1 ☐
B Gameboy   Speaker 2 ☐
C TV   Speaker 3 ☐
D Board games   Speaker 4 ☐
E Exercising   Speaker 5 ☐
F DVD

36 Look at the survey report below. Then, in pairs, discuss the following:

- How has technology influenced our leisure time?
- Have we become "couch potatoes"?
- Has technology brought people closer?

SURVEY RESULTS

We asked members of the public for their opinions on how modern technology affects our lives. This is what they said:

	Yes	No
Is modern technology turning us into "couch potatoes"?	45%	55%
Will books be replaced by the net?	32%	68%
Do you use the Internet every day?	56%	44%
Do you watch more than one hour of TV every day?	67%	33%
Do you spend less than an hour a day with your family?	71%	29%
Do you use the Internet to keep in touch with friends and relatives?	53%	47%

Reporting a theft

37 a. Listen to the dialogue. Where does it take place?

b. Match the columns to form the dialogue.

	A		B
1	b	Good afternoon, sir. What can I do for you?	a	Michael Crawford.
2		Right. I'll just take some details. What is your name?	b	I want to report a theft. My briefcase was stolen.
3		When and where did the theft take place?	c	I don't think so.
4		Now, can you tell me exactly what happened?	d	Well ... I was drinking a cup of coffee. My briefcase was under the table. I left the table for a moment and when I returned my briefcase was gone.
5		Did anyone witness the theft, sir?		
6		Please fill in this form with your details, a description of the briefcase and a full list of the contents.	e	About 15 minutes ago, at the Cornmill Café on Chapel Street.

c. Take roles and make up similar dialogues about the objects in the pictures. Think about:
- what was taken
- when/where it happened
- the event in detail

Intonation (stress in lists of adjectives)

38 Listen and repeat.
- dress – party dress – red party dress – long red party dress
- car – sports car – blue sports car – new blue sports car
- bag – leather bag – black leather bag – big black leather bag
- vase – china vase – white china vase – beautiful white china vase

"Filler" Phrases in Conversation

39 a. Listen to two interviews with students of English. Who uses "filler" expressions? Who leaves long pauses in the conversation?

b. Listen again and label the following items as *A* or *B*, according to which speaker says each one.

1 I'm sorry – I didn't catch what you said. ....
2 I really haven't got a clue, I'm afraid. ....
3 What? ....
4 It's – oh, what's the word? – it's ... .
5 I don't know. ....
6 In other words, ...
7 Er ... er ... .
8 I'm afraid I'm not sure what you mean. ....

c. What phrases/expressions could you use in the following situations in a conversation? You can use your own ideas.

- you didn't hear/understand what was said
- you can't remember a word/name/etc
- you want to give an example/explanation
- you don't know the answer to a question

Giving instructions

40 a. Listen to the dialogue. What is Judy's problem?

b. Complete the dialogue with *finally*, *first*, *now*, *then*.

A: What's the problem, Judy?
B: I'm trying to send an e-mail, but I can't do it.
A: Here, let me see. Well, 1) .... you have to click on "Create mail".
B: Okay. I've done that.
A: 2) .... you have to type your friend's e-mail address in the box marked "To".
B: All right. I've got her address here. Now what?
A: 3) .... just start typing in the box below. 4) ...., when you've finished, just click on the "Send" button at the top.
B: Is that all? I thought it'd be more difficult than that.

c. Use the instructions to act out a similar dialogue.

SAVING YOUR VOICE MAILBOX NUMBER

1 Press **Menu** 122 (Messages - Voice messages - Voice mailbox number).
2 Enter your voice mailbox phone number.
3 Press **OK**.
4 Press **Yes** if you want to save your voice mailbox password in your phone. Press **No** if you don't.
5 If you selected **Yes**, enter your security code.
6 Press **OK**.
7 Enter your voice mailbox password.
8 Press **OK**.

The Time Machine

Herbert George Wells (1866-1946) was a British novelist, journalist, sociologist and historian, who is best known for his science-fiction novels. His rather romantic interest in science came from his years studying at the Normal School of Science in London. **The Time Machine** was his first novel and was very successful at the time. The novel is about a man who invents a time machine and devotes his life to travelling through time. His attention to detail makes his work realistic even today.

41 Read the title and the short biography. What do you expect to read in this extract? What do you think made Wells write about this topic? Read and check your answers.

42 Read the extract and match the characters 1-6 to their positions a-f.

1	The Time Traveller	a	next to the Provincial Mayor
2	Filby	b	on the left of the Time Traveller
3	The Medical Man	c	behind the Time Traveller
4	The Provincial Mayor	d	behind the Psychologist
5	The Very Young Man	e	in front of the model time machine
6	The Psychologist	f	on the right of the Time Traveller

43 Explain the words in bold in the text, then match the highlighted words to the synonyms below.

a unusual, strange
b amazing, unbelievable
c lit
d completely
e shining, sparkling
f copied

44 Read the extract again and put the sentences in the correct order.

- [ ] The Time Traveller said that the model had taken two years to make.
- [ ] The Time Traveller put the object on a small table.
- [ ] The Psychologist pressed the lever on the object.
- [ ] The Time Traveller held a small metal object in his hand.
- [ ] The others gathered around the table and watched.
- [ ] The object disappeared!
- [ ] The Time Traveller explained how the machine worked.
- [ ] The Time Traveller said that the object was the model for a time machine.

45 Which paragraph contains a description of the inside of a room? Use the information to draw a picture, then use words from the text to talk about your picture.

46 How do you think everyone felt when the model vanished? How would you feel? Do you think time travel is really possible? Why/Why not?

Writing Project

Imagine that you have just returned from a visit to another time. Write a diary entry describing what time period you visited, what you saw there, who you met and how you felt about it.

94

Literature Corner

The thing the Time Traveller held in his hand was a **glittering** metallic **framework**, no larger than a small clock, and very delicately made. He took one of the small octagonal tables that were **scattered** about the room, and set it in front of the fire. On this table he placed the mechanism. Then he drew up a chair and sat down. The only other object on the table was a small lamp. There were also perhaps **a dozen** candles about, so that the room was brilliantly **illuminated**. I sat in a low armchair nearest the fire, and I drew this forward so as to be almost between the Time Traveller and the fireplace. Filby sat behind him, looking over his shoulder. The Medical Man and the Provincial Mayor watched him **in profile** from the right, the Psychologist from the left. The Very Young Man stood behind the Psychologist. We were all **on the alert**. It appears **incredible** to me that any kind of trick could have been played upon us under these conditions.

The Time Traveller looked at us, and then at the mechanism. "Well?" said the Psychologist.

"This little affair," said the Time Traveller, resting his **elbows** upon the table and pressing his hands together above the **apparatus**, "is only a model. It is my plan for a machine to travel through time. You will notice that it looks quite uneven, and that there is an **odd twinkling** appearance about this bar, as though it was in some way unreal." He pointed to the part with his finger. "Also, here is one little white **lever**, and here is another."

The Medical Man got up out of his chair and looked into the thing. "It's beautifully made," he said.

"It took two years to make," said the Time Traveller. Then, when we had all **imitated** the action of the Medical Man, he said: "Now, I want you clearly to understand that this lever, being pressed over, sends the machine into the future, and this other **reverses** the motion. This saddle represents the seat of a time traveller. Presently I am going to press the lever, and off the machine will go. It will vanish, pass into future Time, and disappear. Have a good look at the thing. Look at the table too, and satisfy yourselves there is no **trickery**. I don't want to waste this model, and then be told I'm a **quack**."

There was a minute's pause, perhaps. The Psychologist seemed about to speak to me, but changed his mind. Then the Time Traveller put forth his finger towards the lever. "No," he said suddenly. "Lend me your hand." And turning to the Psychologist, he took that individual's hand in his own and told him to put out his **forefinger**, so that it was the Psychologist himself who sent forth the model Time Machine on its voyage. We all saw the lever turn. I am **absolutely** certain there was no trickery. There was a breath of wind, and the lamp flame jumped. One of the candles on the **mantel** was blown out, and the little machine suddenly swung round, became **indistinct**, was seen as a ghost for a second perhaps; and it was gone – **vanished**! Save for the lamp, the table was **bare**.

Writing an opinion essay

Tip

An opinion essay presents our personal opinion on a particular topic. We need to state our opinion clearly and support it with examples or reasons.

INTRODUCTION
- In the **first paragraph** we present the topic and state our opinion clearly.

MAIN BODY
- In the **second** and **third paragraphs** we present our viewpoints and give reasons/examples. We present each viewpoint, with reasons/examples, in a separate paragraph.
  In the **fourth paragraph** we present the opposing viewpoint and give examples/reasons.

CONCLUSION
- In the **last paragraph** we restate our opinion using different words.

We usually use present tenses in this kind of writing and avoid using informal language such as contractions (*I've, she's*) and colloquialisms (*What's up?*) etc. We can use phrases like *In my opinion; I (strongly) believe that; It seems to me that* to introduce our opinion. We can find opinion essays in newspapers and magazines as articles or letters to the editor, etc.

Analysing the Rubric

47 Read the rubric, underline the key words and answer the questions.

> Your local newspaper is asking readers to write an article giving their opinion on the following statement: *Students should not be allowed to have mobile phones at school.*

1. What type of writing is it?
2. Who is going to read it?
3. What style should you use?

Analysing a Model Text

48 a. Read the article and put the paragraphs into the correct order. What is each paragraph about?

NO MOBILE PHONES AT SCHOOL

☐ **Furthermore,** parents who work may need to contact their children. **For example**, if a parent has to work late, the student has to be told if arrangements have been made for a relative or neighbour to look after them.

☐ **In conclusion,** I feel that students should be allowed to take mobile phones to school for use in an emergency. **However,** all phones should certainly be turned off during lessons.

☐ Nowadays more and more students bring their mobile phones to school. **While** I believe that students should carry mobile phones in case of an emergency, I am strongly opposed to these phones being used at school, particularly in the classroom.

☐ **On the other hand,** nothing is more disruptive during a lesson than the sound of a mobile phone ringing or playing an annoying tune. **Moreover,** students who send and receive text messages in class are not paying attention to the lesson.

☐ **Firstly,** many students travel to and from school without their parents. **Therefore,** it is important for them to have a mobile phone in case they need help or have an accident on the way to school or home.

Linkers

b. Identify the function of the linking words in bold, then replace them with synonyms from the list below.

- in addition • also • to sum up • although • as a result
- to begin with • nonetheless • in contrast • for instance

49 Underline the correct linking words.

1. There are several reasons why we should all install burglar alarms in our cars. **To begin with/ Furthermore**, car theft is a big problem in the city.
2. Mobile phones are becoming smaller and more efficient. **Although/In addition**, many models allow you to access the Internet.
3. It is up to parents to teach a child right from wrong. **In conclusion/For example**, they must learn not to take things that don't belong to them.
4. To sum up, while I agree that shoplifting is a crime, it is not nearly as serious as other crimes **such as/apart from** murder or kidnapping.

Register

50 a. Which register is each paragraph written in (formal, semi-formal, informal etc)? Give reasons for your answer. Which paragraph is suitable for an opinion essay? Why?

> A I strongly believe that we rely too much on technology today. This means that we are losing important skills such as personal communication. For instance, people who spend long hours in front of a computer no longer know how to talk to other people, and may even feel uncomfortable in the company of others.
>
> B I think computer games are good stuff. They help us learn all about technology. This is important 'cause it'll help us to get ready for our future jobs. You know, all jobs in the future will need computer skills.

b. Rewrite the incorrect paragraph in the correct register.

Paragraph Structure

51 a. Match the newspaper headlines 1-3 to the topic sentences a-f. There are two sentences for each headline. Say which topic sentence agrees with the headline, and which does not.

a Many people think that using a computer is an enjoyable pastime.
b Soon all art will be created on computers.
c If we replace human teachers with computers, we will develop the skills we will need to live and work in the office of the future.
d Computers cannot teach creative subjects, such as art, music and poetry, as well as a human teacher can.
e Computers and computer labs are very expensive to set up and maintain.
f Sitting in front of a computer screen all day can make students feel lonely and bored.

b. In pairs, think of supporting sentences for each of the topic sentences above.

52  Listen to the dialogue and fill in the gaps. Then, match each reason/example to one of the topic sentences above.

A Schools should use 1) .... in the classroom as students will need computer 2) .... when they are looking for 3) ....

B Computers use 4) .... , cartoons and 5) .... to help students understand the material. Students will think classes are more like a 6) .... rather than a lesson.

C Techniques for the 7) .... of the future can be taught in the computer lab. Students can learn to create 8) .... effects and how to use computer graphics.

Discuss and Write

53 Read the rubric and underline the key words, then answer the questions.

> You have been asked to write an article for a monthly news magazine giving your opinion on the topic "Schools should provide computers for students to use for all their school subjects".

1 What type of writing is it?
2 Who is going to read it?
3 Should you use formal or informal language? Why?
4 Can you think of an appropriate title?
5 Do you agree or disagree with the statement?
6 What arguments can you use to support your opinion?

54 Look at the plan below, then use your answers to Exercises 51, 52 and 53 to answer the questions.

Introduction
(Para 1)   *What is the topic? What is your opinion?*

Main Body
(Para 2)   *What is your first viewpoint? What are your reasons and examples?*

(Para 3)   *What is your second viewpoint? What are your reasons and examples?*

(Para 4)   *What is the opposing viewpoint? What are the reasons and examples?*

Conclusion
(Final Para) *What is your opinion again?*

55 Write your article for the magazine. You can use the article in Ex. 48a as a model.

56 Explain the sentences below in your own words.

Famous words

- Modern science and techniques have taught mankind at least one lesson: Nothing is impossible.   *Lewis Mumford (US philosopher)*
- It is only when they go wrong that machines remind you how powerful they are.
  Clive James (Australian critic)
- As machines get to be more and more like men, men will come to be more like machines.
  Joseph Wood Krutch (US naturalist)

Self-Assessment Module 3

Vocabulary & Grammar

1 Fill in the missing word.

1 I've got a splitting .... I think I'll take an aspirin.
2 Could I pay by .... card?
3 She was named .... her great-aunt.
4 A shoplifter .... things from shops.
5 You should carry a pump with you in .... you have a puncture.
6 The TV isn't broken, you just forgot to .... it in.
7 Try not to make matters .... by failing.
8 People must carry .... cards with them in some countries.
9 John prefers tennis .... squash.
10 That's the man .... sister was on TV.
11 Mr Jones insisted .... cooking the meal himself.
12 Recently, there has been an increase .... the number of people using a credit card.
13 Thanks to ATMs we can .... money from a bank whenever we want to.
14 That gas heater doesn't give .... enough heat.
15 Twenty people came to the party, three of .... I've known since childhood.
16 You must have been aware .... the dangers.
17 That style of jacket has gone out of ....
18 He was .... to two months imprisonment.
19 My flat was .... into last night, and my stereo was stolen.
20 I'd rather watch TV .... read a comic.

(10 marks)

2 Circle the correct item.

1 It is believed that the forest fires were lit by ....
   A smugglers   C arsonists
   B shoplifters   D kidnappers
2 He got a £50 .... for speeding in the centre of town yesterday.
   A sentence B charge C arrest D fine
3 He .... be in Paris, I saw him in the library this morning.
   A might B can't C shouldn't D ought to
4 The battery is flat. We need to .... it.
   A install B operate C recharge D liquidise
5 If you have a .... muscle, you should rest it.
   A pulled B strained C broken D sore
6 That essay is .... to the one that Peter wrote.
   A identical B matching C alike D the same
7 If you have ...., you have a painful muscle contraction.
   A cramp   C insomnia
   B indigestion D sunburn
8 He suffers from heart ....
   A infection B attack C disease D pain
9 He was released due to .... of evidence.
   A need B lack C point D necessity
10 She has been married .... James for almost twenty years.
   A with B for C to D by

(10 marks)

Use of English

3 Complete the second sentence using the word in bold. You must use two to five words including the word given. Don't change the word given.

1 This puzzle will need a lot of patience.
   have This puzzle .... done very patiently.
2 A fishmonger's is a shop that sells fish.
   where A fismonger's is a shop .... fish.
3 It is thought that the company is expanding rapidly.
   be The company .... rapidly.
4 Turn off the electricity in case of fire.
   turned The electricity .... in case of fire.
5 It was wrong of them to give false information.
   given They ....false information.

(5 marks)

4 Fill in the correct word derived from the word in bold.

1 The .... of new technology has helped us a lot. **INTRODUCE**
2 The springs have been used for .... for years. **RELAX**
3 He was found .... of theft. **GUILT**
4 This place is one of the country's .... holiday resorts. **FAVOUR**
5 Measures should be taken to help the .... of crime. **PREVENT**

(5 marks)

98

Self-Assessment Module 3

5 Read the sentences. If a sentence is correct put a tick (✓). If it has a word which should not be there, write this word on the line.

1 Computers they play an important role   ....
2 in our lives today. Children are been taught   ....
3 how to use them at school, as they have   ....
4 become part of the school curriculum. In the   ....
5 years to come everybody will be able to   ....
   use one.

(5 marks)

Listening

6 🎧 You will hear people talking in six different situations. For questions (1-6), choose the best answer A, B or C.

1 You hear a conversation between two people in a waiting room. How does the woman feel?
   A suspicious   B angry   C nervous
2 A man is talking on the phone. What does he want to do?
   A to buy some oil
   B to make an appointment
   C to complain about migraines
3 A man is taking part in a radio chat show. Why has he phoned in?
   A to discuss a health problem
   B to complain about vitamins that he bought
   C to talk about health food shops
4 A girl approaches you at a shopping centre. What does she want you to do?
   A to enrol in a course
   B to talk about painting
   C to participate in something
5 While visiting an exhibition, you hear a man talking. How can yoga help you?
   A It will help you to relax.
   B It will help you to lose weight.
   C It will help you breathe.
6 A man is talking on the phone. Where has he called?
   A a florist   B a college   C a clinic

(10 marks)

Communication

7 Complete the questions.

A: DMI Technology, Shirley speaking. 1) ....?
B: I'd like to speak to Charles Lawton.
A: 2) ....?
B: Yes. My name is Martin Banks.
A: Hold the line please, Mr Banks. I'll see if he's available.
B: Thank you.
A: I'm afraid he's not available at the moment.
   3) ....?
B: Yes. Could you tell him to call me at ICP, please.
A: Of course, Mr Banks. 4) ....?
B: It's 823 764.

(5 marks)

8 Think of a question which matches the answers.

1 (restaurant)?   Not really. / Why not?
2 (crime)?   I don't think so. / Actually yes.
3 (junk food)?   Always. / Never.
4 (bill)?   Of course. / In a minute.
5 (machine)?   No, I can't. / OK, I'll do it.

(5 marks)

Speaking

9 Describe the photographs, then, in pairs, compare and contrast them. Which type of job would you prefer? Why?

- work alone/meet lots of people/monthly salary/ weekly wage
- 9-5/flexible hours/uniforms/smart clothes
- part time/full time/work long hours/have a standard daily routine

(10 marks)

Self-Assessment Module 3

Reading

10 You are going to read an article about rockets. For questions (1-5) choose the correct answer A, B, C or D.

THE HISTORY OF ROCKETRY:
FROM FIREWORKS TO THE MOON

At first glance you might think that there couldn't possibly be anything in common between a 13th century festival in China and the Apollo 11 moon landing in 1969. However there is a **link** and that is that they both relied on the use of rockets.

The Chinese first developed **rockets** by filling bamboo tubes with an explosive made from **saltpetre**, charcoal, and sulphur. The sealed tubes would be thrown onto fires during celebrations because it was thought that the loud explosions would protect them. When these tubes were not perfectly **sealed** though they would fly out of the fire and could explode some distance away. It wasn't long before the ancient Chinese realised the military potential of these **devices** and **primitive** rockets were used to repel a Mongol invasion in 1232 AD. Word of these amazing new weapons quickly spread around the world and soon rockets were being used in military operations in North Africa and Europe. During the 15th and 16th centuries they were widely used in naval battles to set fire to enemy ships. Around this time they also started being used for more peaceful purposes again. In 16th and 17th century Europe firework displays using rockets became a very popular form of public entertainment.

In the late 18th century the British army suffered two serious defeats at battles in Seringapatam, in India. The main reason for these defeats was that the Indian prince, Haidar Ali's army included a **corps** of rocket throwers. They used very large bamboo rockets which had a range of hundreds of metres. The British were determined to learn from their mistakes and a British officer, William Congrieve, began work on developing even bigger and better rockets. Within a few years Congrieve had developed 14 kg iron rockets that could be fired over 3200m. These rockets were successfully used against Napoleon at the battle of Waterloo and during the US War of Independence.

By the 1880s other applications for rockets were being developed. They were used for signalling, for whaling, and even for rescuing people from **sinking** ships. If a boat got into trouble near to the shore, a rocket with a thin rope tied to it would be fired out over the boat, survivors in lifeboats could use the ropes to pull themselves **ashore**. These traditional rockets are still used as **distress signals** on boats and planes.

However in the 1920s and 30s a great leap forward in the use of rockets took place with the introduction of **liquid fuel**. This made rockets much more powerful. The new rockets were so impressive that for the first time people began to seriously think about using rockets to take people into space.

It didn't take long for these dreams to become a reality. In the 1950s the Soviet Union and the USA invested large amounts of money in their new space programmes. This lead to the launch of Sputnik 1, the first artificial satellite, by the USSR in 1957. Less than a month later they followed this with Sputnik 2 which carried a dog, Laika, into orbit. The USA sent its first satellite, Explorer 1, into space early the next year. The next step, putting a man in space followed in 1961 when Yuri Gagarin orbited the Earth in Vostok 1. Eight years later Neil Armstrong took those famous first steps on the **lunar** surface. This was possibly mankind's greatest scientific achievement and it was all due to rockets whose basic design had been thought up hundreds of years before.

---

1 Why did the Chinese first use rockets?
 A They wanted to fire one to the moon.
 B They wanted to frighten their enemies.
 C They wanted to protect themselves.
 D They wanted to make explosives.

2 The ancient Chinese military used rockets
 A to defeat an invading army.
 B in order to invade Mongolia.
 C against the North Africans and Europeans.
 D to burn enemy boats.

3 William Congrieve designed a new type of rocket
 A so that the British could capture Seringapatam.
 B which was made of bamboo and could travel for hundreds of metres.
 C with the help of an Indian prince, Haidar Ali.
 D which was used in later military campaigns.

4 What does 'it' refer to in line 28?
 A a boat
 B a rocket
 C the shore
 D a survivor

5 Early in the 20th century rockets improved greatly because
 A scientists started experimenting with new types of fuel.
 B people stopped using petrol as a fuel.
 C a number of different countries wanted to send rockets into space.
 D people began thinking of different uses for rockets.

(15 marks)

Self-Assessment Module 3

Writing an opinion essay

11 Your class has had a discussion about modern technology. Your teacher has asked you to write an essay, giving your opinions on the following statement.
Computers are an essential part of our daily lives.
Use the plan below to write your essay (120-180 words).

Introduction
(Para 1)   state topic & your opinion: *computers are used in all parts of our lives – work, school, leisure – make our lives easier – better organised – can't live without them*

Main Body
(Para 2)   *computers make our working lives easier – accurate – save time – keep a lot of information in one place – everything we need is right there in front of us*
(Para 3)   *use the Internet for research, for work and school and pleasure – helps us keep in contact with people around the world – have fun as well as work or study*
(Para 4)   *not healthy to spend too much time sitting at a computer – can damage our eyes – we don't exercise as much – don't talk to other people*

Conclusion
(Para 5)   *restate your opinion: computers are an important part of our lives today – help us to work and study more effectively – we shouldn't spend all of our time in front of a computer screen*

(20 marks)

(Total = 100 marks)

Sing Along!

12 a. Look at the picture. What are they doing? Why? How is the picture related to the title of the song?

b. Listen and fill in. Then, listen again and sing.

You know someone is watching
Although they are discreet
You can feel the 1) .... upon you
As you're walking down the street
You don't know where they're 2) ....
Or just how much they know
But you know that they can see you
No 3) .... where you go

Wherever you go
Whatever you say or do
Always remember
Big Brother is watching you

There are cameras in the 4) ....
There are cameras in the shops
Big Brother has eyes everywhere
The watching never 5) ....
They know about your every move
And what you do each day
They're recording every 6) .... you take
And every 7) .... you say

Wherever you go ...

They know how you spend your money
They know what you like to 8) ....
They know exactly where you are
They know exactly who you meet
There's no use trying to 9) ....
They will find you anyway
You are under observation
Every 10) .... , every day

Wherever you go ...

c. Have you ever been photographed by a surveillance camera? Where? How did you feel?

Progress Update

How do you rate your progress? Tick (✓) the box that applies to you.

	Excellent ****	Good ***	OK **	Could do better *
Vocabulary & Grammar				
Listening				
Speaking				
Reading				
Writing				
Communication				

Shopping and Eating around the

UNIT 7 Penny Wise, Pound Foolish

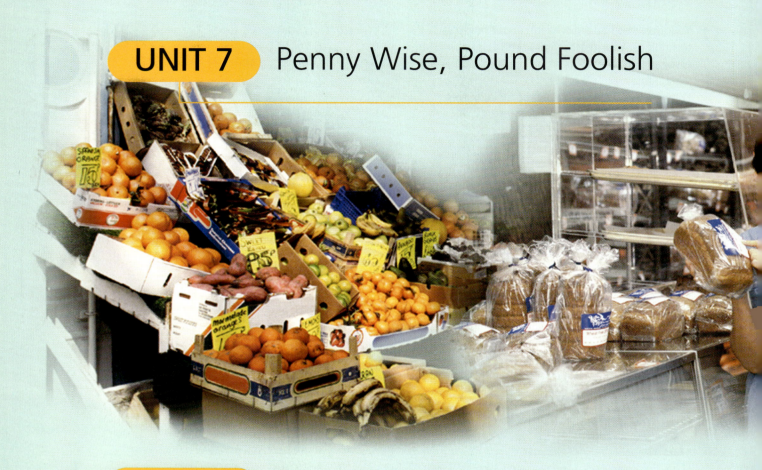

UNIT 8 You Are What you Eat

World

Module 4
Units 7-8

Before you start ...

Are you a techno maniac or a techno phobic? Justify your answer.
Describe your most favourite possession.
Have you got a standard daily routine? Talk about it.

Listen, read and talk about ...

- shops & departments
- products
- shopping centres
- clothes
- shopping complaints
- advertising
- credit cards
- healthy eating
- food/drinks
- kitchen utensils
- recipes
- places to eat
- ways of cooking
- diners' complaints

Learn how to ...

- ask for/give directions
- express preference
- describe people's clothes
- express your opinion
- make complaints
- buy clothes
- accept/refuse invitations
- do your shopping
- order fast food

Practise ...

- the causative form
- reported speech (statements – questions – orders – special introductory verbs)
- quantifiers (some, any, no, (a) little, (a) few, a lot of, much, many, plenty of)
- countable/uncountable nouns
- containers & contents
- clauses of concession

Phrasal verbs

- look
- let
- make
- put

Write ...

- a fashion section for a women's magazine
- a short article about a market
- an article describing a visit to a place
- a recipe
- an assessment report

Penny Wise, Pound Foolish

Lead-in

1.
   - How often do you/your parents/your friends go shopping?
   - Where do you/your parents/your friends do your shopping: *at supermarkets; department stores; shopping centres; online?*
   - How do you/your parents/your friends pay: *in cash; by cheque; by credit card*?

2. Do you enjoy buying presents? What would you buy for your: *six-year-old brother/ best friend/grandparents/boss on their birthday?* Choose from the list, giving reasons.

   • jewellery • an antique ornament/clock • clothes • a CD
   • a piece of art (e.g. a painting) • an expensive pen • a diary
   • a leather wallet • a bunch of flowers • bath oils • a book
   • tickets to the theatre • perfume

3. a. Listen to the people. What was the best present ever given to them? Who gave it to them?

   Tony ....; Linda ....; Helen ....;

   b. What was the best present ever given to you? Who gave it to you? On what occasion?

Reading

4. a. When were you born? What is your star sign? Describe your personality.

   b. What do you take into consideration when you choose a present for someone: *their position; their star sign; their preferences; their hobbies?* Do you believe that knowing someone's star sign can help you decide on an appropriate present? Read the article and find out.

   c. Read the article again and for questions 1-14, choose from the star signs A-F. Some of the star signs may be used more than once.

   Who ...
   - is too well-mannered to complain?   0 *B*
   - would appreciate something old?   1 ......   2 ......
   - is job-oriented?   3 ......
   - dreams of receiving some property?   4 ......   5 ......
   - likes to have their days planned?   6 ......
   - loves gifts with a personal touch?   7 ......
   - appreciates practical gifts?   8 ......
   - likes items from abroad?   9 ......
   - appreciates the best that money can buy?   10 ......
   - is likely to remember a gift?   11 ......
   - would welcome a trip or an outing?   12 ......   13 ......
   - likes exercising?   14 ......

   d. Read the article again and explain the words in bold. Then find the opposites of the highlighted adjectives.

Follow-up

5. List the characteristics of each star sign as well as the most appropriate presents for them. Then, in pairs, talk about each sign.

PICKING THE PERFECT PRESENT

If you spend hours wondering what to buy your friends and loved ones, why not look to the stars. Knowing someone's star sign can give you a clue about what they would most like to unwrap on their birthdays!

A Cancer (22 June - 22 July)
Cancer's ideal gift would be a house or a boat, but don't worry if you don't have that kind of money to spend! All people **ruled by** Cancer love anything to do with the "good old days", so an antique ornament or piece of jewellery is certain to make them smile. Almost every Cancerian collects something, and if you find out what the **Crab** in your life collects, you will never run out of gift ideas. Another of their passions is cooking for their friends and family, and they will definitely appreciate anything which will help them in the kitchen, such as cooking utensils or tableware. If you are on a **tight budget**, remember that Cancer people are sensitive and love to receive presents which have **sentimental** value. A favourite family photograph in a simple frame will make them just as happy as that expensive yacht!

B Libra (23 September - 23 October)
Librans are diplomatic and will tell you that they love whatever you buy them, because they are just too polite to hurt your feelings! However, if you want to make them **genuinely** happy, **bear in mind** that anyone born under the sign of Libra loves beauty. A piece of art, an ornate mirror, or a marble statue will guarantee a warm response. A gift which allows them to **enhance** their personal beauty will also be well-received, such as a trip to a beauty salon, or a **shopping spree** for a new outfit. Make sure you go along with them to offer a second opinion – Librans are hopeless at making decisions!

C Capricorn (22 December - 19 January)
Capricorns are not usually very sentimental, but they all like to feel materially and financially secure. They enjoy being given gifts with designer labels, as they appreciate high quality goods. All Capricorns are ambitious, hardworking and **dedicated** to their careers, so a business-related present is always a good idea. They are also **obsessed** with time and will be delighted with a watch or an antique clock. If you are thinking of buying clothes for the Capricorn in your life, make sure they are stylish classics, and not **wacky** fashion statements, as Capricorn people are somewhat traditional!

D Taurus (20 April - 20 May)
Taureans have **conservative** tastes, but they do enjoy a **touch of luxury** now and then. They will always be grateful for fine leather goods or fresh flowers. What they really hope to receive is a **piece of land** or even cash, but they will be equally pleased with a wallet, a mirror, or a family memento. Give the Taurean in your life a chance to pamper themselves with gifts of lotions, bath oils or perfumes, or treat them to a night at the opera or a performance of classical music. That will appeal to their romantic side and definitely bring a smile to their face. And remember a quality gift is never wasted on a Taurean – they make warm and faithful friends who will never forget what you have given them.

E Virgo (23 August - 22 September)
It is true that Virgos always appreciate a bargain, so if you can find a great gift at a low price, they will be thrilled. Nevertheless, don't forget that all Virgos are perfectionists, and will not be impressed by imperfect products. The practical Virgo loves to receive useful presents, such as socks, shirts and other items of clothing which they may need. Virgos are also **creatures of habit** and like to follow routines, so a gift which will help them to organise their lives (a diary or a bookcase, for example) will be a huge success. Anything connected to health and cleanliness will also appeal to your Virgo friends. Bath products and diet books are always on their list of wanted items.

F Sagittarius (22 November - 21 December)
Sagittarians love to play games and take risks. Sport is an obsession with them, so a new pair of rollerblades or skis will always be appreciated. A typical Sagittarian is open-minded and optimistic. They love travelling so foreign gifts are ideal, particularly if you have had them **imported**. For the truly perfect present, though, you should send the Sagittarian in your life on an adventure holiday. They will love every minute of it!

Cancer   Leo   Gemini   Taurus

Vocabulary Practice

A chemist's
B shoe shop 
C bakery 
D butcher's 
E florist's 
F boutique 
G department store 
H supermarket 
I greengrocer's 

Shops and Departments

6   a. Match the items to the shop(s) where you can buy them. Then, make up sentences, as in the example.

1 packet of aspirin   A
2 bunch of flowers ....
3 sugar ....
4 black shoe polish ....
5 mangoes ....
6 lamb chops ....
7 pair of black gloves ....
8 pair of black leggings ....
9 bar of soap ....
10 bread ....
11 fish ....
12 packet of biscuits ....
13 washing-up liquid ....
14 carrots ....
15 pair of tights ....
16 toothpaste ....
17 chocolate cake ....
18 beef steaks ....
19 tinned soup ....
20 thermometer ....

You can buy a packet of aspirin at a chemist's.

b. In pairs, ask and answer, as in the example.

A: I'm going to the butcher's. Do you need anything?
B: Yes, please. Could you pick up six lamb chops?
A: Sure! Anything else?
B: No, thanks.

7   In pairs, complete the table. You can add your own ideas. Then make up sentences as in the example.

• cooker • hammer • envelopes • carpet • toothpaste • fruit • jacket
• washing powder • bracelet • ketchup • vacuum cleaner • deodorant • pen
• lamp • furniture polish • washing machine • shirt • ring • rice • birthday card • mirror
• shampoo • dress • bleach • necklace • screwdriver • cornflakes • nails • tie

Electrical Appliances	*cooker* ....
Furnishings	....
Stationery	....
Cleaning Products	....
Toiletries	....
Groceries	....
Clothing	....
Jewellery	....
Hardware	....

Cookers, ... are electrical appliances.

8 a. Here is a floor plan of the Lewston Shopping Centre. Listen and fill in the spaces.

Lewston Shopping Centre

Ground Floor
- W H Smith – newsagent's
- Boots – 1) ....
- Tesco – 2) ....
- Starbucks – coffee shop
- McDonald's – fast food restaurant
- Next – clothing

First Floor
- Debenhams – 3) ....
- Habitat – 4) ....
- Dixons – electrical goods
- Homebase – DIY
- HMV – CDs
- Payne and Son – jeweller's

b. In pairs, use words from Exs 7 & 8 to act out dialogues, as in the example.

A: I've got to buy **a birthday card for my aunt**. Any ideas where to go?
B: Try the stationery department at **W H Smith**. It has a great selection of **cards**.
A: Where's that?
B: On the **ground floor**.

Clothes

9 a. Look at the pictures. Say who is wearing something:
- striped ....
- polka-dot ....
- denim ....
- loose/baggy ....
- plaid ....
- flowery ....
- tight ....

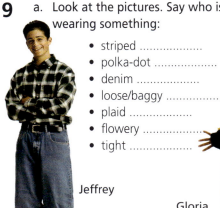

Jeffrey

Mark
Suzy
Gloria
Nancy

b. Using the prompts, describe the clothes in the pictures.

STYLE/PATTERN
- straight • flared • baggy/loose
- tight • long sleeved • plaid
- short sleeved • plain • pinstriped
- flowery • checked • polka-dot

MATERIAL
- leather • cotton
- suede • wool
- nylon • denim

FOOTWEAR
- boots • sandals
- trainers
- flat shoes
- high-heeled shoes

TYPE OF CLOTHING
- jacket • sweater • blouse • anorak
- evening dress • tuxedo • waistcoat
- T-shirt • skirt • jeans • shirt • suit
- dress • jumper • socks • leggings
- shorts • tights • trousers

Gloria is wearing a black and yellow nylon anorak, a white T-shirt, tight black trousers and black leather boots.

c. Write down five items of clothing that only women wear, then compare your list with your partner's.

d. Which clothes would you wear to:
- go skiing • a wedding
- the beach
- a friend's birthday party

I'd wear a sweater, jeans, a jacket and boots to go skiing.

Writing Project

Design your own fashion section for a women's magazine. Cut out pictures from fashion magazines and write a description of the clothes. Write about: *the material; if it is formal/casual; occasion suitable for; price; where you can buy it.*

Shopping Complaints

10 a. Listen to the dialogue and tick (✓) the problems that the man has with his new jacket. How does he sound?

1 broken zip ....
2 missing buttons ....
3 torn lining ....
4 loose stitching ....
5 loose buttons ....
6 stained sleeve ....
7 uneven sleeves ....
8 uneven pockets ....

b. Listen and match the objects to the problems. How does the woman sound? In pairs, act out dialogues, as in the example.

1	table	A	cracked
2	mirror	B	stained
3	carpet	C	scratched
4	cushions	D	broken
5	TV	E	torn

1 A: Good afternoon, Madam. How can I help you?
B: I want to return this table. When it was delivered this morning, I found that it was scratched.
A: Oh I'm terribly sorry, Madam. Would you like us to repair it for you?
B: No. I would prefer to have a refund.

105

Grammar in use

Causative Form
Grammar Reference

11 a. Study the examples. Who did the action himself/herself?

> Jane **cleaned** her coat.
> Sue **had** her coat **cleaned**.
> Mike **had** his car **repaired**.
> Steve **repaired** his car.

b. Complete the rule.

> To say that we arrange for someone else to do something for us we use
> .... + object + ...

12 In pairs, ask and answer questions, as in the examples.

1. cut/hair (✗)
   A: Did you cut your hair?
   B: No, I had it cut.
2. tidy/bedroom (✓)
   A: Did you tidy your bedroom?
   B: Yes, I tidied it myself.
3. wash/dishes (✓)
4. decorate/living room (✗)
5. iron/skirt (✓)
6. change/tyre (✗)
7. install/air conditioning (✗)
8. fix/bike (✗)

13 In pairs use the prompts to ask and answer questions, as in the example.

- barber's • laundrette
- jeweller's • garage • optician's

1. watch/fix
   A: Where can I have my watch fixed?
   B: At the jeweller's.
2. eyes/test
3. car/repair
4. clothes/wash
5. moustache/trim

14 Complete the sentences using the causative.

1. Andy's suit was dirty so he took it to the cleaner's.
   Andy *had his suit cleaned*.
2. Jane is in the hairdresser's at the moment. She is changing her hair colour.
   She is ....
3. Claire's TV isn't working so she is taking it back to the shop to be repaired.
   Claire is going ....
4. This is the third time Steve's flat has been decorated since he moved in.
   Steve ....
5. Chris is being measured for a new suit at the tailor's today.
   Chris ....

Reported Speech
Grammar Reference

15 Fill in the correct verb *said*, *told*, *asked*, to change the sentences from direct speech into reported speech. How do we use these verbs in reported speech?

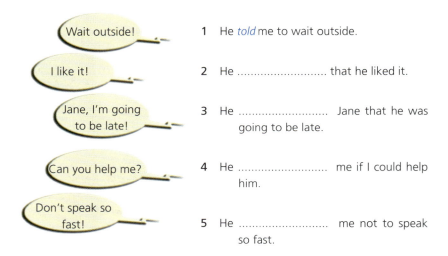

- Wait outside!
- I like it!
- Jane, I'm going to be late!
- Can you help me?
- Don't speak so fast!

1. He *told* me to wait outside.
2. He .... that he liked it.
3. He .... Jane that he was going to be late.
4. He .... me if I could help him.
5. He .... me not to speak so fast.

16 Underline the correct tense. What were the speakers' exact words?

1. A: Where's Ann?
   B: She's gone home. She said she **wasn't feeling/isn't feeling** well.
2. A: Is Mike coming to the party tomorrow?
   B: He told me that he **will come/would come** straight after work.
3. A: Are you going to the supermarket tonight?
   B: No, John said that he **would do/have done** the shopping this week.
4. A: Sarah asked me to help her with her essay.
   B: Yes, she told me that she **was having/has** problems with it.
5. A: When I saw Julie this morning she said that she **was going/went** into town.
   B: Yes, I bumped into her at the bus stop. She said that she **was doing/is doing** her Christmas shopping.

17 Rewrite the shop assistant's comments as reported speech.

1 Jane asked if she would like anything else.

18 Read the dialogue, then report the conversation that Mark had with James.

> Mark: Oh, hi James. How are you?
> James: I'm fine.
> Mark: Why aren't you at work?
> James: I've taken a day's holiday because I have so much to do.
> Mark: Are you still looking for a new flat?
> James: Actually, I found a place on Porter Street yesterday. That's why I'm so busy, I'm moving in this afternoon. I've just come into town to collect the van I've hired to move all my things ...

Mark asked James how he was.

19 Rewrite the direct questions as reported speech.

1 "Do you know what time the bank closes on Saturdays?" Lucy asked Jenny.
2 "Has anyone seen Jill this morning?" Jack asked.
3 "Where are you going tomorrow night?" Pete asked Joan.
4 "Who is coming to lunch today?" Laura asked Tony.
5 "Have you ever been here before?" Richard asked Ann.

Prepositions

Appendix 1

20 a. Fill in the correct preposition. Then in your own words explain the prepositional phrases.

1 He is very **proud** .... his daughter, especially now she is at university.
2 Many people **object** .... the council's plan to build a new road through the town centre.
3 She was wearing a long thick coat and a scarf to **protect** herself .... the cold.
4 Mark **takes great pleasure** .... doing the Christmas shopping.
5 Jane can't **part** .... this ring. Her mother gave it to her when she graduated from university.
6 He's a good teacher and very **popular** .... his students.
7 Heather **prides** herself .... her honesty.
8 Graham **takes pride** .... his job.
9 The thought had never **occurred** .... Malcolm before.
10 She has very sensitive skin and is **prone** .... getting all sorts of rashes.
11 The doctors need to **operate** .... him.
12 The government is introducing new laws to **prevent** people .... getting away with online crime.

b. Fill in the correct preposition. Then, choose any five phrases and make sentences using them.

1 to be .... a tight budget; 2 to bear sth .... mind; 3 to be hopeless .... sth; 4 to be dedicated .... sth; 5 to be delighted .... sth; 6 to be grateful .... sth; 7 to be pleased .... sth; 8 to appeal .... sb; 9 to be .... a list

Phrasal Verbs

Appendix 2

21 Fill in the correct particles. Then explain the phrasal verbs.

1 I'm **looking** .... my niece at the weekend. Her parents are going away.
2 Since it was his first offence, they **let** him .... a caution.
3 The police are **looking** .... the theft at the school.
4 You have to come tonight. Dawn will be really upset if you **let** her ....
5 Charlie spoke to the estate agent and we're going to **look** .... the flat this afternoon.
6 I must have put on weight. I'll have to **let** these trousers ....
7 She's so arrogant. She always seems to be **looking** .... the rest of us.
8 James **looked** .... his essay again before he handed it in.

107

Grammar in use

Error Correction

22 Read the text below and look carefully at each line. Put a tick (✓) next to the lines which are correct. If it has a word which should not be there, write this word on the line. There are two examples at the beginning.

Shopping Online

I really love to shopping online. I buy everything on	00	*to*
the Internet: books, CDs, even my groceries. It wasn't	0	✓
always about like this, though. I have had my computer	1	....
for years and I always enjoyed surfing the Net but I	2	....
had never used it to buy anything. Even as though I	3	....
knew most sites were more safe and trustworthy, I was	4	....
worried about who might get hold out of my credit	5	....
card number and whether anything I paid for would	6	....
actually arrive. Finally, one of my friends convinced me to	7	....
give it up a try and so I decided to do my Christmas	8	....
shopping online. It was so many easy; everything I	9	....
wanted was there at the touch of a button. I didn't have	10	....
to fight my way through the crowds in the bad weather	11	....
or struggle to carry through my shopping home at the	12	....
end of the day. Everything arrived in plenty time and in	13	....
perfect condition and since to then, I've been hooked. It	14	....
saves me time and makes shopping a real pleasure.	15	....

Open Cloze

23 Read the text and think of the word which best fits each gap. Use only ONE WORD in each gap.

Ads Everywhere!

Advertising has become a part **1)** *of* everyday culture. People are exposed **2)** .... hundreds of adverts every day whenever they switch **3)** .... the TV or radio or open a newspaper or magazine. This means that we know all **4)** .... the tricks that advertisers use to sell us their products and so they need to work harder **5)** .... ever to keep us interested. The latest trend designed to do this is known **6)** .... ambient advertising. This is the practice of putting ads in unusual places to make the product stick **7)** .... people's minds. It also allows the advertisers to **8)** .... flexible and to try all sorts of new approaches to advertising. Ambient ads started out on the sides of taxis and the backs of bus tickets but even these **9)** .... now become commonplace. One recent award-winning campaign advertised a modern art agency **10)** .... putting stickers on everyday objects **11)** .... as lamp-posts and paving stones, describing them as **12)** .... they were works of art. Another involved projecting images of an English football team onto the White Cliffs of Dover **13)** .... promote a brand of trainers. It seems that wherever you go **14)** .... days some advertising agency will have got **15)** .... first and will be desperately trying to grab your attention.

Idioms & Fixed Phrases

24 Complete each sentence with the correct word from the list. Then explain each of the phrases. Are there any similar idioms in your language? What are they?

hat, glove, shirt, trousers, shoes

1. I love your new dress, it's such a beautiful colour and it **fits you like a** ....

2. Elaine doesn't want anybody to know about her new job yet, so **keep it under your** ....

3. She's so bossy. I think it's obvious who **wears the** .... in her family.

4. I wouldn't want **to be in Mike's** .... when his boss finds out he wasn't really sick last week.

5. If the deal goes wrong, he's going to **lose his** ....

Competition Game

In teams, say the name of a product (e.g. a piece of clothing, an electrical appliance, etc) and its definition/use. Start with the letter A and continue to W in order. Each correct answer gets 1 point. The team with the most points is the winner.

Team A S1: **a**norak:
It's a piece of clothing we wear when it's rainy.

Team B S1: **b**oots:
They are footwear which we wear when it's cold and rainy.

25 a. Fill in the correct word from the list. Then explain each of the fixed phrases in bold.

- night • name • trouble • nerve
- here • tail • dearest

1 I better go and talk to her now before I **lose my** ....

2 Technology is the .... **of the game** these days, isn't it?

3 What I think is **neither** .... **nor there**, it's what Jack says that is important.

4 At a difficult time like this it makes sense to spend time with your **nearest and** ....

5 Those kids seem to have a **nose for** .... They're always getting into mischief.

6 She went to complain to the neighbours because recently they have been playing really loud music **day and** ....

7 It took us hours to get home, the traffic was **nose to** ....

b. Can you guess where the phrase in number 7 came from?

Word Formation

26 Fill in the correct word derived from the word in bold.

Buying on CREDIT!

It can be a huge 0) *temptation* to apply for a credit card, 1) .... if you are having problems managing your money. They can 2) .... be very 3) .... if you are travelling, if you need to 4) .... make a big purchase, or if you shop online. However, before you fill in your 5) .... form remember that there are 6) .... too. It can be very easy to get into 7) .... buying things that you don't 8) .... need or can't really afford on credit. It's also 9) .... not to pay off the whole balance every month as the interest 10) .... can soon get the better of you.

TEMPT
PARTICULAR
CERTAIN
USE
EXPECTED

APPLY
ADVANTAGE
DIFFICULT
ACTUAL
DANGER

PAY

Key-word Transformations

27 Complete the second sentence using the word in bold. You must use two to five words, including the word given. Don't change the word given.

1 That's the garage where they repaired Andy's motorbike.
   had   Andy ....
   .... at that garage.

2 "I'll call you later, Pete," he said.
   told   He ....
   .... call him later.

3 "Did you buy a new coat in the sales?" she asked.
   asked   She ....
   .... bought a new coat in the sales.

4 The birthday present made Pam happy.
   pleased   Pam ....
   .... the birthday present.

5 "Are you a university student, Ben?" she asked.
   whether   She asked ....
   .... a university student.

6 When was the last time you went to the hairdresser's?
   have   When ....
   .... your hair cut?

7 Sally has got the same name as her aunt.
   named   Sally ....
   .... her aunt.

8 "Do you want a lift?" asked John.
   if   John ....
   .... a lift.

Listening & Speaking skills

28 🎧 Listen and complete the advertisement for Gibson's Mall.

Gibson's Mall
Facilities: • over 100 free **1)** .... spaces, • a roof-garden **2)** .... shop, • a gas station • an indoor **3)** .... area for children
Stores: Kay's **4)** ...., Baxter's Hardware Store, Carter's **5)** ...., dress stores, **6)** .... stores, shoe stores, boutiques, bookstores, a deli, a photoshop, a **7)** .... salon and much more
Opening hours: Monday to Saturday **8)** ...... am - **9)** ...... pm Sunday 10 am - **10)** ...... pm

29 a. You are new to the area and you want your neighbour to tell you where to do your shopping. In pairs discuss:

- where you should do your daily grocery shopping and why;
- where it is and how to get there;
- where the best places to buy specific items e.g. newspapers, milk, medicine, etc. are.

b. Draw a neighbourhood map and mark the shops on it.

30 🎧 Listen to a radio interview about advertising and mark the sentences **YES** or **NO**.

		YES	NO
1	Donna believes advertising is not good.	☐	☐
2	Ads make us feel good about how we look.	☐	☐
3	Ads try to mislead us.	☐	☐
4	Buying certain products will change your life.	☐	☐
5	Ads have little effect on us.	☐	☐
6	Not all adverts are bad.	☐	☐

31 Look at the advertisements and in pairs discuss the following:

- Which of the ads do you like most and why? What does it promote?

> • On the whole, I like/dislike ...; • I prefer ... • Generally speaking, I'd say ... • If I had to choose, I'd say ...

A: Hmm, if I had to choose, I'd say the one with the skateboarder is the best.
B: Oh, really? Why?

- How do you think advertising can benefit/harm the consumer? Think about: *positive/negative images, how ads influence us*

32 🎧 Listen to the people talking and choose the best answer A, B or C.

1. You are in a shop and you hear a conversation between a customer and a sales assistant. How does the customer pay for the jumper?
   A by cheque
   B by credit card
   C in cash

2. You hear someone talking about his shopping habits. Why does he shop in his own neighbourhood rather than in a superstore?
   A Because neighbourhood shopkeepers are friendlier.
   B Because superstores are more expensive.
   C Because neighbourhood shops are cheaper.

3. You hear a conversation between two girls in a clothing shop. One of them is trying on a pair of jeans. Why does she decide to buy them?
   A Because they are a good price.
   B Because they suit her well.
   C Because they are tight.

4. You hear an advertisement on the radio for a new mobile phone. What features does it have?
   A It comes in six colours.
   B It has five computer games and six different ring tones.
   C It has caller ID and a voice dialling feature.

33 Describe the people in the pictures. Then, answer the questions.

1. Do you feel more comfortable in smart or casual clothes? Why?
2. How often do you go clothes shopping? Where?
3. Do you agree that you can tell a person's character by the way they dress?

Expressing Opinions

34 a. Listen and tick (✓) the phrases the speakers use to express their opinion.

1. You should ....
2. How about ....
3. Trouble is ....
4. Anyway ....

b. Read the dialogues, then in pairs act out similar dialogues using the prompts.

1. A: Where do you think we should go to eat tonight?
   B: How about Marco's? We haven't been there for ages.
2. A: When I got home I noticed that the CD was scratched.
   B: You should take it back and exchange it.
3. A: I think I'll wear my new T-shirt to the party tonight.
   B: Trouble is, I think it's going to be quite formal. Maybe you should wear a shirt and tie instead.

- go to new Italian restaurant for dinner? / Chinese / instead?
- go to Italy on holiday this year? / expensive / stay home

Making Complaints

35 a. Listen to the dialogues. Which is a mild complaint? Which is a strong complaint?

b. Read the dialogues. Then, use the prompts to make either a mild or a strong complaint.

1. A: Excuse me.
   B: Yes.
   A: I'm afraid this T-shirt is the wrong size.
   B: Oh I'm sorry. I'll get you another one right away.
2. A: I would like to return this radio.
   B: I'm sorry, but we don't give refunds.
   A: Well, then I want to speak to the manager. It doesn't work and I want my money back.

- given wrong change
- food/cold

Useful language for Complaints	
Mild	**Strong**
I may be mistaken but ...	This just won't do ...
I think there may be a problem with ...	I demand a refund ...
There seems to be something wrong with ...	This is just unacceptable.

Buying Clothes

36 a. Listen to the dialogue. What did the woman buy?

b. Complete the dialogue.

A: Hello. 1) ....?
B: Yes, can I try these on, please?
A: Of course. The fitting rooms are over there.
B: Thank you.
A: What do you think?
B: Actually, they're a bit short. 2) .... the next size up, please?
A: Certainly. Here you are. ... Are they any better?
B: Yes, they fit nicely. 3) ....?
A: They're £35.
B: Okay. I'll take them.
A: Thank you. 4) ....?
B: In cash. Here you are.
A: Thank you very much. Your receipt is in the bag.

c. Use the pictures to make up similar dialogues.

£150/cheque £40/cheque £50/cash £80/credit card

Question Intonation

37 a. Listen and say which sentences have got falling intonation and which have rising intonation. How does this intonation pattern match question intonation in your language?

- What time does the bank open?
- Can you tell me what time the bank opens?
- Do you know where the butcher's is?
- Where is the butcher's?

b. Practise the intonation asking about:

- post office
- supermarket

In the Market for a Bargain

38 a. Listen to the sentences. Where do you think you might hear them?

b. Match the speakers to what they are selling.

A	seafood/fish	Speaker 1 ☐
B	flowers	Speaker 2 ☐
C	glassware/ornaments	Speaker 3 ☐
D	baked goods	Speaker 4 ☐

c. Look at the pictures on p. 113. In pairs, decide what you might find in each place. Choose from the list. Skim the texts to see if you have guessed correctly.

- antiques • coffee • pasta • seafood
- jewellery • bedding • clothes
- household items • cakes • flowers
- souvenirs • rare records • furniture • bread
- specialities • leather goods • handicrafts

I think we can buy antiques in Portobello Road Market.

39 Read the texts again. Fill the gaps with one of the missing sentences below. Then, explain the words in bold.

a Here you can also find many different types of cheese and a variety of game meats, including crocodile and kangaroo.
b It is known as the world's largest antique market and has been around since the 1870s.
c There is so much competition that you are guaranteed the widest range, the highest quality and the most competitive prices that you will find anywhere.
d Saturday is, of course, the busiest day of the week.
e Dating from 1878, it is spread out over two main sites; the lower market and the upper market.

40 To make the texts more interesting to the reader, the writers have used their senses while describing the markets.
Read text A again and find two phrases related to what we can hear.
Read text B again and find two phrases related to what we can smell and taste.

41 a. Read the list of phrases and match them to the senses.

• hearing • smell • sight • taste • touch

1 The air is filled with the voices of traders ...
2 The hustle and bustle of shoppers, traders and tourists ...
3 Many talented street performers to keep an eye out for, too ...
4 The aromatic smells that come from the food court ...
5 So delicious your mouth will water ...
6 Come away empty-handed ...

b. Use the phrases to talk about a street market in your country.

42 a. Make notes about the *age, location, size and specialities* of each market. Then, in pairs, compare and contrast them. Which of these places would you like to visit and why?

A: Both markets are very old, aren't they?
B: That's true. Portobello Road Market and Queen Victoria Market both date from the 1870s.

b. Imagine you are a trader in one of these markets. Talk about a typical day at work.

I've been selling clothes in the market for over thirty years. As you can imagine, I've seen styles come and go. A typical day for me starts bright and early at five in the morning when I ...

Writing

43 Write a short article about a similar market in your own country. Think about:

- opening days and times
- items sold
- specialities
- recommendations

Find pictures to decorate your article.

Culture Clip 7

Portobello Road Market

London has some of the biggest and oldest street markets in the world and Portobello Road in Notting Hill is no exception. **1** **B** It has over 1500 **stalls** which sell all kinds of antiques and **collectibles** ranging in price from one or two pounds to several thousand pounds. People come from all over the world to visit Portobello Road because they know there is no other place like it.

Portobello Market is several markets **rolled** into one. From Monday to Friday the market sells fruit and vegetables. The air is filled with the voices of **traders** shouting and **hawking** their goods. The antique stall holders open on Saturdays. There are many antique and specialist shops along Portobello Road as well as a large number of cafés and restaurants. **2** The market opens at 5.30 am and the **hustle and bustle** of shoppers, traders and tourists continues all day. As well as antiques, you can find clothes, household items, rare records and furniture. There are many talented street performers to **keep an eye out for**, too.

So, next time you are in London, make sure you visit Portobello Market. It's an experience not to be missed.

Queen Victoria Market

The biggest and most culturally **diverse** market in all of Australia is the Queen Victoria Market in Melbourne. **3**

In the lower market you will find the Meat Hall that **houses** 23 butchers and 11 fishmongers. There is also the Food Court that seats over 400 people and **caters** for every taste with dishes from all around the world. The aromatic smells that **come** from the Food Court are so delicious your mouth will water. Then, there is the Deli Hall that contains 17 delicatessens offering cuisine from many countries including France, Italy, Greece, Japan and Poland as well as a range of other shops selling cakes, bread, coffee and pasta. **4**

The upper market sells a great variety of fresh fruit and vegetables. There you can also find clothes, leather goods, flowers, fabric, jewellery, bedding, **handicrafts** and souvenirs.

Queen Victoria Market is the perfect place to shop, and there are many **bargains** to be found. **5** It is impossible to visit Queen Victoria Market and come away **empty-handed**. With over 600 traders in the market itself as well as the speciality shops and boutiques **lining** the surrounding streets, there is something for everyone.

Writing an article describing a visit to a place

Tip

When we write an article describing a visit to a place we usually write four paragraphs.

Introduction
- In the **first paragraph** we write the name and location of the place as well as our reason(s) for choosing it.

Main Body
- In the **second paragraph** we usually write about what the place looks like. In the **third paragraph** we describe the place in detail. We can include the things we can see, feel, hear, smell and taste.

Conclusion
- In the **last paragraph**, we write about our feelings and personal comments and/or our recommendation.

Narrative descriptions of places can be found in tourist magazines, letters, stories etc. We normally use past tenses to describe our visit. However, we use present tenses to talk about the location. We can use a variety of adjectives and adverbs as well as our senses to make our description more appealing to the reader.

Analysing the Rubric

44 Read the rubric, underline the key words and answer the questions.

> A consumer magazine has asked its readers to send in articles about a shopping place they have visited. Write your article including a detailed description of the place and why you recommend it.

1 Who is going to read your article?
2 Tick (✓) the subjects you should include.
...... location; ...... type of shops; ...... prices; ...... public transport; ...... opening hours; ...... emergency services

Analysing a Model Text

45 a. Read the article. Find and correct the eight mistakes. Then, complete the paragraph plan.

A Unique Shopping Experience

I have shopped in some very strange and interesting places. The best place I have ever been to is the Damnoen Saduak Floating Market. It is located about 80 km from Bangkok, in Thailand. The market is over 100 years old and has hardly changed for all that time.

What maked my visit to this market so special is that the whole market is on a canal and the brightly-dressed merchants sell their goods from their colourful boats. The day that I was there, there were hundred of boats crowded together, where you could buy everything from fruit and vegetables to clothes, toys and even cooking meals. If you wanted to buy something, you could either wait on the banks of the canal and the boats to pass by or you could hire your own boat and join in the fun!

It wasn't just the sights, though, that made this visit such an unforgettable experience. This market offers a feast for the senses! All around me were the sounds of wooden boats bumping together and the noisy chatter of the crowd. I had never been to a place with so many different smells: the aroma for freshly ground spices, exotic fruit and vegetables, seafood and meats, all mixed with the mouth-watering fragrance of fresh cooked Thai delicacies.

When I finished my shopping for the day, I felt tired but excited and happy. It was certainly an experience I would never forget. If you are ever in Thailand, you should definitely visit the floating market. It's an unique experience.

| Paragraph 1 name, location | Paragraph 2 | Paragraph 3 | Paragraph 4 recommendations |

b. Underline the topic sentences. Then suggest appropriate alternatives.

c. What senses does the writer discuss in the text? Give examples.

46 a. The following are sections found in a supermarket. Which of these are found in your local supermarket?

1	frozen food	......	8	toiletries	......
2	international foods	......	9	paper goods	......
3	deli	......	10	flowers	......
4	tinned food	......	11	fruit	......
5	bakery	......	12	cafeteria	......
6	fish	......	13	toy department	......
7	tea and coffee	......			

b. Listen to the dialogue and tick the sections of the supermarket mentioned in the conversation.

Using the Senses

47 Match the phrases to the pictures. Then, use them to make sentences.

A   B   C

- wonderful scent of freshly cut flowers   ....
- mouth-watering aroma of freshly baked bread   ....
- colourful displays of fresh fruit and vegetables   ....

Joining Sentences

48 Join the sentences using the words in brackets, as in the example.

1 The cafeteria is a great place for a snack or a hot meal. It has fresh, tasty and inexpensive food. **(with)**
With its fresh, tasty and inexpensive food, the cafeteria is a great place for a snack or a hot meal.
2 You won't be able to resist the wonderful smell coming from the bakery section. They bake all their own bread, cakes and biscuits. **(where)**
3 Don't miss the deli counter. It has an amazing variety of cheeses. **(which)**
4 I didn't need to buy any. I couldn't resist the smell of the freshly-ground coffee. **(although)**
5 I didn't know which brand to buy. The friendly staff helped me. **(when)**

Prepositions

49 Read the text and fill in the correct prepositions.

Paris is home **1)** .... more than seventy street markets and the majority of Parisians shop **2)** .... one every week. The Rue Mouffetard Market is a perfect example, with its lively atmosphere and the wide variety **3)** .... produce available. The market can be found **4)** .... the heart of the Latin Quarter **5)** .... the city, south **6)** .... the River Seine. It runs **7)** .... an old, narrow street **8)** .... the Jardin des Plantes and the Jardin du Luxembourg. A stroll **9)** .... the market is the perfect way to do your weekly shopping. You will find stalls selling everything **10)** .... French cheese to seafood or fresh bread. Then, further **11)** ...., you will find the freshest fruit and vegetables **12)** .... the city. The market is open all day **13)** .... Tuesday to Saturday and **14)** .... Sunday mornings **15)** .... the summer.

Making Recommendations

50 Read the following recommendations. Which are positive and which are negative? Justify your answers.

1 No trip to the city centre is complete without going there.
2 Its out-of-the-way location and poor selection of goods mean that I would think twice before shopping there again.
3 On the whole it has everything you could want and is well worth a visit.
4 Despite all the positive hype, I'm afraid my overall impression was that it was a little disappointing.

Discuss & Write

51 a. Read the rubric and underline the key words. Then, answer the questions in the plan.

- Your local newspaper is running a consumer writing competition. The prize is £200 worth of groceries. Write an article describing a visit to your local supermarket and explain why you would/wouldn't recommend it to others.

Introduction
(Para 1)   Where is it? What is it called?

Main Body
(Para 2)   What is the overall impression?
(Para 3)   What does it have? What features does it have? What can you see, hear, smell?

Conclusion
(Para 4)   Would you recommend it to the readers? Why/why not? Will you shop there again? Why/why not?

b. Use your answers from Ex. 51a to write your article. (120-180 words)

52 Explain the sentences below in your own words.

- Credit cards have three dimensions: height, width and debt.
  Shelby Friedman (US journalist)
- Creditors have better memories than debtors.
  Benjamin Franklin (US statesman)
- Clothes make the man.
  Mark Twain (US novelist)

115

You Are What you Eat

Lead-in

1 Describe the pictures and answer the questions. How is the title related to them?

Melissa

Helen

a Who seems to be a sensible eater? Give reasons.
b Who is more likely to skip breakfast? Why?
c Who prefers home cooked meals to junk food or snacks?
d Which of the following foods/drinks is each person more likely to include in their diet? Which are high in carbohydrates, protein, fat, vitamins?

1 raw vegetables		10 chicken ......
2 kiwi fruit		11 tuna ......
3 banana		12 yogurt ......
4 dried fruit		13 chillies ......
5 rye bread		14 ginger ......
6 white bread		15 coffee ......
7 burger		16 green tea ......
8 chocolate		17 water ......
9 ice cream		18 salt ......

2 Answer the questions about yourself.

a What is a typical breakfast for you? What time do you usually have breakfast?
b Which is the main meal of the day? When do you have it?
c How often do you have snacks during the day? What do you usually have?
d How often do you eat out? What kind of places do you usually go to?

Reading

3 a. Read the title of the article. Which of the following do you expect to read in it? Read and check.

- how to lose weight   • exercise   • spices
- have a healthy diet   • faster reflexes
- have a standard daily routine   • skip breakfast
- have regular checkups   • plan what you eat

b. Read the article and choose the most suitable paragraph from the list A-H that best completes the article. There is one extra paragraph which you do not need to use.

You eat all the right foods and do plenty of exercise, so why aren't you losing any of that extra weight? Perhaps you need to think about a daily diet and exercise plan which tells you when you should be eating, drinking and exercising in order to burn fat more quickly.

| 0 | C |

After your hot drink, think about an early morning workout. This will help to **elevate** your energy levels and keep you **alert** all day long. But wait until your body temperature has risen and give yourself time to wake up. The best time to start exercising is half an hour after you open your eyes.

| 1 | |

As you make your way through the first part of your busy schedule, don't forget that mid-morning **energy boost**. Eating just three meals a day makes the body store more food as fat. The secret of burning fat is to eat little amounts at regular intervals throughout the day. Keep away from unhealthy food like ice cream and chocolate, though! A banana or a kiwi fruit at around eleven will give you all the energy you need.

| 2 | |

It is always important to eat lunch earlier rather than later. The later you leave it, the easier it will be to fill up on fast food to satisfy your hunger. Try to plan your lunch menu and choose light carbohydrates and proteins such as tuna or chicken sandwiches **accompanied by** raw vegetables or fruit.

116

How to burn fat all day long

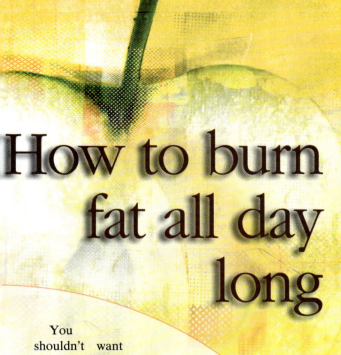

You shouldn't want to eat very much as you have already filled up with water.

| 3 |

Later in the day when you finish work and your body temperature is at its **peak** is the best time to do some fast, powerful exercise. At this time, your muscles are more **flexible** and your **reflexes** are faster than usual, so make the most of it. Go for a run or even a fast walk. Do whatever you enjoy, as long as it gets you moving and burning fat.

| 4 |

If you plan well, this meal can be an important part of your fat-burning day. There are certain foods and spices that will actually help your body to burn up any unwanted calories, such as red peppers, chillies and ginger. These will make your **nervous system** work faster and raise your body temperature, which in turn will burn more calories. Don't leave your evening meal too late, though, as you need to give your body time to **absorb** the food before you sleep.

| 5 |

If you have trouble getting off to sleep, though, don't panic. There are plenty of healthy, low fat alternatives to help you **nod off**. Why not try a glass of warm **skimmed** milk, or even a cup of camomile tea? These natural and low-fat drinks will help you to get to sleep.

| 6 |

A   The next step is to **stock up** on **carbohydrates** and liquids. This will help to give you the energy you need to get moving. Try to eat breakfast an hour after exercising so the carbohydrates will be turned into energy and not be stored as body fat. It's also a good idea to eat plenty of **unprocessed carbohydrates** such as fruit, yogurt and rye bread.

B   Now, by mid afternoon, you will find that your **stress levels** are on the rise again. That means that you are in need of fuel to keep you going through the rest of the afternoon. A small sweet snack would be the perfect choice. Try dried fruit, a banana or some fruit yogurt.

C   Try to start the day with a cup of green tea. Green tea wakes you up and gets you ready for your hectic day ahead. You will feel **upbeat** and active and at the same time your **metabolism** will be off to a good start, burning up those extra calories.

D   It makes sense if you become a calorie counter. Always read the back of packets and cans so that you know exactly what you are eating and what you are likely to gain from it.

E   So, eat regularly, drink lots of water, keep active, relax and sleep well. You too will be well on the way to a fat-burning routine that will keep you healthy and slim.

F   Then, instead of sitting down in front of the TV for those last few hours of your busy day, why not try a few deep breathing relaxation techniques. This will **guarantee** that your body is calm and ready for that deep sleep that you need to get ready for the next day.

G   The next step is the evening meal. It is important to eat an hour or so after your evening workout. This will replace some of the energy you have lost so that you will be able to get up and get going again the next day.

H   At around noon it's vital to drink lots of water. Water will help to **take the edge off** your appetite as it will fill you up. Experts recommend drinking cold water, as your body will have to use up calories just to warm it up!

c.   Read the article again and explain the words in bold. Suggest synonyms for the highlighted words. Then, list all the names of foods/drinks mentioned. Which are the same in your language? How similar are your daily eating habits to what the article says?

Follow-up

   Read the article again and make a timetable for the perfect fat-burning day. List the foods mentioned and the approximate times for eating, exercising etc.

Vocabulary Practice

Food

5 a. Read the lists. Can you add to them? Which of these do you eat every day? Which is your favourite/least favourite?

Meat/Poultry	Vegetables
beef	cauliflower
veal	aubergine
lamb	cabbage
chicken	beans
	peas
Fish	mushroom
tuna	leek
salmon	onion
cod	tomato
trout	carrot
	lentils
Seafood	
oysters	**Dairy**
mussels	milk
shrimps	cheese
squid	yogurt
octopus	eggs
	butter
Fruit	
olives	**Other**
pear	bread
melon	pasta
grapes	rice
pineapple	salt
lemon	pepper
avocado	ketchup
kiwi fruit	mayonnaise
peach	snails

b. What do you need to make
- a chicken salad sandwich?
- an omelette?
- a fruit salad?

c. Which of the fruits and vegetables in Ex. 5a grow in your country? Are they the same in your language? Use the words in the list to say how you usually eat them.

- raw • boiled • steamed
- fried • grilled • baked
- roasted • pickled

Olives grow in my country. I usually eat them pickled.

Kitchen Utensils & Recipes

6 a. Match the verbs to the nouns. Can you think of any more foods to match each verb?

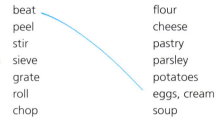

beat	flour
peel	cheese
stir	pastry
sieve	parsley
grate	potatoes
roll	eggs, cream
chop	soup

- Which kitchen utensils do we use to do each of the above? Choose from the pictures, then make up sentences, as in the example.

peeler   sieve   knife   whisk   wooden spoon   grater   rolling pin

We can beat eggs using a whisk.

b. Read the list of ingredients. What do **ml**, **kg** and **g** stand for? Which do we use to measure weight? volume?

SEAFOOD PIE WITH LEEKS

Ingredients
1 kg potatoes
650 g cod
500 ml milk
500 g leeks
35 g butter
325 g large prawns
salt and pepper

for the cheese sauce:
200 g cheddar cheese
75 g butter
80 ml single cream
75 g plain white flour

c. Read the recipe and fill in the appropriate verbs from part a. Then, talk about it using *first*, *next*, *then*, *after that*.

First, you peel the potatoes.

METHOD

- 1) **Peel** the potatoes and cut into slices. Cook for 5 minutes in salted boiling water. Drain thoroughly.
- Poach the fish in 75 ml of milk and then separate into flakes.
- Wash and 2) .... the leeks into small pieces and then fry in the butter.
- To make the cheese sauce: Melt the butter in a pan then 3) .... the flour before adding it to the pan to make a smooth paste. Gradually pour in the rest of the milk, while constantly 4) .... the mixture.
- 5) .... the cheese and slowly add it to the pan and 6) .... well. Add the cream and salt and pepper.
- Mix the fish, prawns, and leeks in a pie dish and cover with half the sauce.
- Layer the potatoes on top and then pour on the remaining sauce.
- Bake at 190° C for about 45 minutes, until it is bubbling and golden.

Serves 4

Writing Project

Write the recipe of a famous dish from your country for an international students' magazine. First write the **list of ingredients**, next write the **steps** that need to be followed. End your recipe saying how many people the dish serves.

7 Match the pairs, then make up sentences.

milk		cream
salt		butter
strawberries	and	sugar
bread		biscuits
cheese		pepper

Do you take milk and sugar in your coffee?

8 Match the opposites, then name foods or drinks which can go with each.

sweet	tough
tender	mild
fatty	bitter/sour
spicy	still
sparkling	lean

sweet chocolate – bitter coffee – sour lemon

9 a. Can you guess what each sentence is about?

1. Oh, well done, please. I can't eat it if it's rare.
2. Would you like still or sparkling, sir?
3. There's no white left I'm afraid, you'll have to have brown.
4. Yes, they do either a continental or a full English.
5. Yes, there's still some in the pot. Would you like milk and sugar?

b. Listen and check if you were correct.

Ways of cooking

10 Look at the pictures. How can each of these foods be prepared? In pairs, act out dialogues.

- boiled • roasted • fried • stuffed • grilled
- baked • poached • steamed

A: How can tomatoes be cooked?
B: They can be fried, stuffed or grilled.

Places to eat

11 Match the words to the pictures. Write **R** (for restaurant), **F** (for fast food) or **B** (for both). Then make up sentences using these words.

1 tablecloth ....; 2 bill ....; 3 tip ....; 4 crystal glasses ....; 5 menu ....; 6 paper napkin ....; 7 counter ....; 8 plastic cup ....; 9 waiter ....; 10 till ....; 11 cutlery ....; 12 plastic chairs ....; 13 three-course meal ....; 14 tray ....; 15 self-service salad bar ....

The tables were laid with expensive, white linen tablecloths.

12 a. Listen and match the speakers to the places. What is each person complaining about?

Speaker 1	fast food
Speaker 2	supermarket
Speaker 3	takeaway
Speaker 4	restaurant

b. Where could you see these signs? In pairs, think of two dishes you can have at each place.

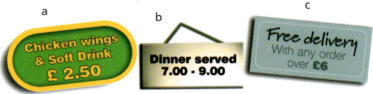

Diner's Complaints

13 Match the adjectives to the nouns, then, in pairs, act out dialogues, as in the example.

dirty	order
chipped	soup
cold	steak
overcooked	knife
wrong	glass

A: Excuse me.
B: Yes, sir?
A: This knife is dirty.
B: I'm sorry, sir, I'll replace it immediately.

Grammar in use

Quantifiers
Grammar Reference

14 Fill in *some, any, no, little* or *few*. How do we use each?

1. Could I have some more coffee please?
2. Have we got .... biscuits? I'm starving.
3. There is very .... milk left; could you get a pint when you are out?
4. Maggie is so fussy, there are very .... things that she will eat.
5. I'm sorry, sir, there is .... lobster left; would you like to try something else?
6. There are .... sandwiches in the fridge if you are hungry.
7. I'm going to the market; would you like .... fruit or vegetables?
8. There are a .... olives left in the bottom of the jar.
9. I think you should add a .... more pepper to the sauce.
10. .... more potatoes for me, thanks, I'm full.

15 Complete the dialogue, then act out similar dialogues using the prompts.

A: Would you like **1)** .... more bread?
B: Yes, please. Is there **2)** .... pasta left?
A: Sorry, there's **3)** .... pasta left but there is a **4)** .... salad if you would like that.
B: No, that's OK. Thanks.

- potatoes/beef/gravy
- water/curry/rice
- cake/tea/orange juice
- chips/fish/sauce

16 a. Read the dialogue and underline the correct item.

A: It shouldn't take too long to do the shopping this week. I don't think we need **1) many/much**.
B: Well, there's **2) no/any** cheese left and only a **3) little/few** bit of butter.
A: Yes, don't worry. They're both on the list. Can you think of **4) something/anything** else?
B: How **5) many/much** eggs have we got left?
A: Oh, there should be plenty. I don't think we need **6) no/any** more.
B: Why don't you get **7) some/any** spaghetti and a **8) little/few** mince and I'll make bolognaise for dinner tonight.
A: Oh, that would be nice. I'll get a **9) few/little** more tomatoes and **10) some/any** mushrooms as well.

b. In pairs, look at the ingredients in Ex. 6b and act out a similar dialogue.

17 Fill in *a lot of, much, many, (a) few, (a) little, plenty of*.

- A: How **1)** .... orange juice have we got left?
  B: There's **2)** .... bit, would you like to finish it?

- A: How **3)** .... more potatoes would you like?
  B: Just one, thanks. I'll have **4)** .... more carrots as well.

- A: You should eat **5)** .... vegetables, they're really good for you.
  B: I know. I try to eat at least **6)** .... portions each week.

- A: There isn't **7)** .... bread left, so I can't make you a sandwich, I'm afraid.
  B: That's OK. There's **8)** .... fruit. I'll eat some of that.

- A: Would you like **9)** .... more lemonade?
  B: No thanks, I'm trying not to drink so **10)** .... sugary drinks these days.

- A: There's **11)** .... cream in this sauce, isn't there?
  B: Yes, maybe I shouldn't have used so **12)** ....

18 Look at the pictures and ask and answer, as in the example.

1 A: *Are there enough biscuits to go round?*
   B: *No, there are only a few left.*

Containers & Contents

19 What can you see in the pictures? Make up sentences using the words *bag*, *box*, *carton*, *tin*, *bar*, *packet*, *bottle*, *jar*. What other foods/drinks can go with each container?

Can I have a bottle of ketchup, please?

Countable/Uncountable Nouns

20 Write **C** (for countable) or **U** (for uncountable) next to each of the nouns, then make up sentences.

Food: roast lamb ......; grape ......; olive ......; olive oil ......; ketchup ....; rice ....; spaghetti ....; bread ....; egg ....; oyster ....; mussel ....; beef ....; biscuit ....; aubergine ......

Drink: milk ....; orange juice ....; lemonade ....; tea ....; Coke ....; coffee ....

Other: accommodation ......; news ....; police ....; traffic ....; advice ....; warning ....; job ....; work ....; Physics ....; furniture ....; coin ....; travel ....; money ....; view ....; scenery ....; journey ......; rubbish ....; bag ......; luggage ....; information ....; weather .... Maths ....; bottle ....;

I'd like some roast lamb, please.

Competition Game

In pairs, think of a recipe and list the ingredients you need. Stand in front of the class and use your list to act out a dialogue as if you are making a shopping list for this dish. Students, in teams, try to guess what you are planning to cook. The first team to guess correctly is the winner.

S1: *Have we got any eggs?*
S2: *No, we need to buy some.*
S1: *All right. What about butter? etc*

Reported Speech: special introductory verbs

21 Match the verbs 1-12 to the direct sentences a-l and then rewrite them as reported speech using the appropriate introductory verb, as in the example.

1	warn	5	offer	9	complain
2	invite	6	order	10	apologise
3	remind	7	boast	11	threaten
4	advise	8	suggest	12 *a*	forbid

a Susan's mum told her, "You are not allowed to go to the party."
Susan's mum forbade her to go to the party.
b "Would you like to come over to dinner tonight?" Ian asked her.
c His secretary said, "Don't forget that the time of the meeting has changed to 11 o' clock."
d "I'm so sorry I was late. My car broke down," Chris said to Angela.
e "The service is very slow in this café, isn't it?" Dave said.
f Mary told Jim, "If you do that again, I'll have to tell your mother."
g "Don't touch the oven or you'll get burned," she said to the children.
h "If I were you, I'd go to Tony's," Andy said to Mark.
i Ben told Helen, "I can help you with the shopping if you like."
j "Let's have fish for dinner," said Tom.
k "I'm definitely the best chef in town," Bob said.
l The policeman said to the criminal, "Stand still."

Prepositions

Appendix 1

22 a. Fill in the correct preposition, then explain the phrases.

1 You can **rely** .... her. She won't let you down.
2 Remember to **reply** .... Mr Jones' letter.
3 Researchers have shown that there is a **relationship** .... a high-fat diet and heart disease.
4 She took a long time to **recover** .... the shock.
5 Citrus fruits are **rich** .... vitamin C.
6 Sarah is **responsible** .... the catering.
7 Using peppers instead of chillies **results** .... a milder, sweeter dish.
8 His doctor told him to **refrain** .... eating fatty foods.

b. Fill in the correct prepositions, then make up sentences using the phrases.

1 to think .... sth (= consider); 2 .... the rise; 3 .... its peak; 4 ready .... sth; 5 .... need of sth

121

Grammar in use

Phrasal Verbs
Appendix 2

23 Replace the verb in bold with the correct phrasal verb formed with *make* or *put*.

1. Let's **postpone** our trip to the countryside until the weather improves.
2. He **invented** an excuse but I'm sure nobody believed him.
3. Tina's dad was away on business on her birthday but he **compensated** for it by bringing her back some beautiful presents.
4. It took the firefighters about two hours to **extinguish** the fire.
5. John **proposed** some really good ideas at the last meeting.
6. I don't think he is going to **tolerate** her complaining for much longer.
7. I could see the sign, but I couldn't **distinguish** exactly what it said.
8. Vicky is **saving** her money at the moment to buy a new car.
9. He **stored** the potatoes in the cupboard.
10. The thieves **stole** about £2000.

Open Cloze

24 Read the text and think of the word which best fits each gap. Use only ONE WORD in each gap.

The Low-Down on Low-Fat Labelling

When you walk around a supermarket **0)** *these* days you can easily be dazzled **1)** .... all the food labels claiming to be 'fat-free' or 'light', but are these foods as healthy **2)** .... they claim to be? Unfortunately, when you look more closely, **3)** .... becomes clear that they are not. For example, a product that claims to **4)** .... 80% fat free is simply a product that contains 20% fat, actually quite a high fat content. The **5)** .... goes for so-called light foods. Products **6)** .... as sausages and mayonnaise that are naturally high **7)** .... fat can be labelled 'light' even if **8)** .... fat content is only slightly reduced. Another problem is that 'low in fat' **9)** .... sometimes also mean low in taste. So, to make **10)** .... for this, some manufacturers add a lot **11)** .... salt and sugar to their low-fat products than is needed. This makes them **12)** .... bad as, if not worse than, the full fat equivalent. In the UK, the government is preparing guidelines that would strictly control **13)** .... use of phrases like 'low fat' and 'light' on food packaging, but until these come **14)** .... effect don't believe everything you read on the label. If something looks **15)** .... good to be true, it probably is.

Idioms & Fixed phrases

25 a. Fill in the gaps with the correct word from the list and then explain the meaning of each expression.

beans
cake
soup
potato
nutshell
tea

1. I thought it would be really difficult to cook that Thai recipe, but in the end it was **a piece of** ....
2. The children had a nap this afternoon so now they are **full of** ....
3. I didn't go to see the film with Alex because it didn't sound like **my cup of** ....
4. It's very simple. **In a** ...., all you have to do is call them and see what they want.
5. Labour relations is a bit of **a hot** .... in our office at the moment.
6. Whenever she opens her mouth, she seems to land right **in the** ....

b. Find other English **food idioms** and present them in class.

26 Underline the correct word and then explain each of the phrases in bold.

1 Publishing his new cookery book has brought him **into the public** *eye/tongue*.
2 His grandparents would tell him all sorts of stories about **the** *good/past* **old days**.
3 Jane is very happy with her new job as a chef. She seems to have found her **place in the** *sky/sun*.
4 The company donated £5000 to Feed the Children, which was very generous but unfortunately **just a drop in the** *sea/ocean* compared to what they actually need.

27 a. Match the American words to their corresponding British ones. Which of these are the same in your language?

American	British
meat grinder	biscuit
candy	sweets
jelly	tin
chips	mincer
can	crisps
cookie/cracker	mincemeat
eggplant	chips
french fries	courgette
zucchini	aubergine
ground meat	jam

b. In a minute make a list of foods which you use in your language but come from another language.

28 Fill in the correct word then make up sentences.

- loaf • bunch • piece • grain
- clove • pinch

1 a *piece* of cake
2 a .... of rice
3 a .... of bread
4 a .... of grapes
5 a .... of salt
6 a .... of garlic

Would you like another piece of cake?

Key-word Transformations

29 Complete the second sentence using the word in bold. You must use between two and five words, including the word given. Do not change the word in bold.

1 There is only a little milk left in the bottle.
 much There .... in the bottle.
2 He said to us, "I can give you a lift to the station if you like."
 offered He .... a lift to the station.
3 "Don't forget to take an umbrella with you," she said to him.
 reminded She ....
 .... an umbrella with him.
4 I'm sorry, there's no coffee left.
 run I'm sorry, we .... coffee.
5 The fridge is almost empty.
 hardly There .... in the fridge.
6 "I'd cut down on salt if I were you, Tim," said Jo.
 advised Jo .... on salt.
7 What is the price of that saucepan?
 much How ...., please?
8 "Why don't we invite Lisa to the party?" Rob asked.
 suggested Rob .... to the party.

Error Correction

30 Read the text below and look carefully at each line. If the line is correct, put a tick (✓). If it has a word which should not be there, write this word on the line, as in the example.

Mood Food

Did you know that what you eat can have been a	0	*been*
drastic effect on how you feel? We all know	00	✓
that what we eat it affects us physically but did	1	....
you know some foods affect us mentally, too? Studies	2	....
have been shown that chocolate can lift your spirits	3	....
and make you feel happier. However, the effect	4	....
lasts only for a short time. The high fibre foods	5	....
on the other hand can be make people feel positive,	6	....
energetic and think quicker. Research shows that	7	....
people who they eat a high fibre diet tend to be less	8	....
stressed, less tired and less depressed than people are	9	....
who don't. Also, they are able to think lots more	10	....
quickly. Nevertheless, other foods can that have a	11	....
negative effect on us such as coffee, eggs, sugar	12	....
and foods that they contain a lot of artificial	13	....
flavourings and preservatives. These all foods can	14	....
make us feel sad, anxious and prone to panic	15	....
attacks. Foods that have been proven to lift up your	16	....
spirits are oily fish, salads, fruit, cereals and nuts.	17	....

Listening & Speaking skills

31 🎧 You will hear a conversation between three friends talking about eating out versus cooking at home. Listen and decide who said what. Write **G** for Gary, **S** for Sarah or **F** for Frank.

1. This speaker wants to go out for dinner. ....
2. This speaker says that eating out is unhealthy. ....
3. This speaker thinks that restaurant food tastes good. ....
4. This speaker says eating out is expensive. ....
5. This speaker thinks someone is making excuses. ....
6. This speaker thinks someone is lazy. ....
7. This speaker can't cook well. ....

32 Describe the pictures. Compare and contrast them, then answer the questions.

Picture A shows a person at a takeaway restaurant whereas Picture B shows a man preparing a salad at home.

a. Why do some people prefer eating out to eating at home?
b. Why is junk food so popular?

33 🎧 You will hear a radio interview with a famous cardiologist. For questions 1-6 decide whether the statements are true (**T**) or false (**F**).

1. Heart attacks are more common now than they were in the past. ....
2. Dr Shaw says most people would eat a healthier diet if they had more time. ....
3. If you have a healthy diet, with lots of fruit and vegetables, you don't have to exercise. ....
4. Dr Shaw recommends joining a gym. ....
5. Dr Shaw says men in their 50s tend to smoke and drink too much coffee. ....
6. Dr Shaw implies men are more at risk of heart attacks than women. ....

34 Your friend has put on a lot of weight recently and wants to do something about it. Talk to your friend and

- advise him/her on what to do in order to lose weight in a healthy way;
- tell him/her about a diet/exercise programme that has worked for you;
- encourage him/her to try it.

35 🎧 You are going to hear a news report on young people's eating habits. Listen and choose the best answer to the questions below.

1. The speaker says young people
   a. had a healthier diet in the past.
   b. think fast food is nutritious.
   c. would be healthy if they didn't eat fast food.

2. Modern day families
   a. prefer to eat out.
   b. don't have time to prepare healthy food.
   c. eat more than they should.

3. The speaker says
   a. people should skip breakfast instead of eating doughnuts or croissants.
   b. home cooked meals are very nutritious.
   c. no fixed meal times lead to bad eating habits.

4. Young people eat junk food at lunchtime
   a. because it is convenient.
   b. because it is filling.
   c. because they can't afford anything else.

5. The speaker says teenagers
   a. eat unhealthy snacks all day long.
   b. sometimes eat nothing healthy all day.
   c. need to learn to cook healthy food.

6. Young people today
   a. don't eat fresh food.
   b. usually have a healthy evening meal.
   c. only drink sugary soft drinks.

36 Lucy's son has invited his friends from the football team over for dinner. In pairs, decide which would be appropriate for Lucy to cook for her guests.

A: I think she shouldn't cook burgers because they're too oily.
B: I couldn't agree more. A good idea would be ...

Accepting/Refusing Invitations

37 a. Listen to the dialogues. In which one is the invitation accepted more enthusiastically?

b. Complete the dialogues 1-4 using one of the expressions from the boxes below.

Accept

Enthusiastically: Thanks, I'd love to ...; Thanks, that sounds great/like fun ...; I'd love to, thank you very much for asking/ inviting me.
Unenthusiastically: I guess so; I suppose so; I might as well; Why not?

Refuse

Politely: Thanks for asking/thinking of me but ...; It sounds lovely/great/wonderful but I'm afraid I ...; Sorry, I can't ...; I would love to, but I'm afraid I can't because ...; Thanks, but I'd rather not/I'm not very keen on ...
Firmly: No thanks, I don't enjoy/fancy/ feel like ...
Impolitely: No, I don't want to/I hate ...

1 A: We are all going out to that new Chinese restaurant tonight. Would you like to join us?
  B: ....
     (accept enthusiastically)

2 A: I'm having a party on Saturday night. I hope you can make it.
  B: ....
     (accept unenthusiastically)

3 A: I'm having a dinner party on Tuesday. Would you like to come?
  B: ....
     (refuse politely)

4 A: It's my daughter's birthday party on Sunday and all the children from her class will be there. You are coming, aren't you?
  B: ....
     (refuse firmly)

c. In pairs, use the phrases from the table and the prompts below to act out similar dialogues.

Invite somebody to:
• a wedding reception • a fancy dress party
• a barbecue • an Italian restaurant

Doing your Shopping

38 a. Listen to the dialogue. Where does it take place?

b. Read the dialogue and fill in the questions, then use the prompts to act out similar dialogues.

• Will that be all? • Who's next, please?
• Would you like anything else?
• What would you like?

A: Number 54, please.
B: Yes, that's me.
A: 1) ....
B: Can I have 250 grams of Camembert cheese, please?
A: Here you are. 2) ....
B: Yes, I'd like half a kilo of smoked salmon and 300 grams of coleslaw, please.
A: Right. 3) ....
B: Yes, that's it. Thank you.
A: Here you are. Thank you very much. 4) ....

• half a kilo of Lancashire cheese/150 grams of potato salad/3 Scotch eggs
• 100 grams of cheese dip/250 grams of sliced roast beef/2 slices of cheese and tomato quiche

Ordering Fast Food

39 a. Listen to the dialogue. How many people is the food for? Listen again and check.

b. Read the dialogue and fill in the missing parts.

A: 1) ....
B: No, I haven't.
A: 2) ....
B: Erm, 2 cheeseburgers and 2 large Cokes, please.
A: 3) ....
B: Yes, 2 medium fries and a child's portion of chicken nuggets.
A: 4) ....
B: No, that's it, thanks.
A: 5) ....
B: Here you are.
A: Thank you. It'll just be a couple of minutes.

c. Use the prompts to act out similar dialogues.

• Margarita pizza with extra cheese/any garlic bread?/yes, 1 and 2 tins of lemonade/£8.20
• 6 pieces of chicken and 2 tubs of coleslaw/any chips/yes, 3 large portions/£10.50

Intonation

40 Listen and repeat, then say how we form exclamations.

• That's expensive!
• How tasty!
• What nice sauce!
• What excellent roast beef!
• What impolite waiters!
• What a delicious dish!

Charles Dickens** (1812-1870) is generally considered to be the greatest English novelist, enjoying immense popularity throughout his career. Dickens wrote novels that exposed the terrible lives of the poor during the nineteenth century in England. Novels such as **David Copperfield, Great Expectations, Bleak House, A Christmas Carol** and **A Tale of Two Cities draw attention to the dreadful conditions in which so many of London's poor lived at that time. These novels reflect Dickens' own childhood, when his father was unable to pay his debts and Dickens himself was sent out to work in a factory when he was just twelve years old. **Oliver Twist** (1838) is set in the underworld of poverty and crime which existed in early Victorian London. It tells the story of an orphan, Oliver, who, after spending his early life in a workhouse is sent to work for a hard taskmaster. Oliver runs away to London, where he joins a gang and becomes a pickpocket. By chance, a wealthy gentleman takes pity on Oliver and takes him into his house. Although Oliver is forced to return for a time to the gang, he eventually is reunited with his family and lives happily ever after.

Reading

41 Read the biography and the title. Who do you think Dickens describes in *Oliver Twist*? Why?

42 a. Look at the pictures and describe them. How do you think people lived in early Victorian London? Was life easy for children then? How do you know?

  b. Look at the pictures again. Who do you think Oliver Twist is? What kind of life did he have? Was it happy? Read the extract and find out.

43 Read the extract again. Which picture is described?

44 Match the opposites in the list to the highlighted words and then explain the words in bold.

• hot • loud • unafraid • indifferent • light • calmly • rosy-cheeked

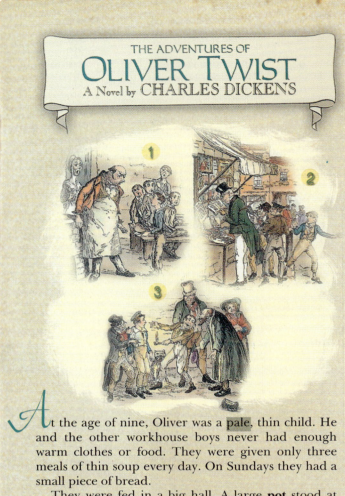

THE ADVENTURES OF
OLIVER TWIST
A Novel by CHARLES DICKENS

At the age of nine, Oliver was a pale, thin child. He and the other workhouse boys never had enough warm clothes or food. They were given only three meals of thin soup every day. On Sundays they had a small piece of bread.

They were fed in a big hall. A large **pot** stood at one end of the room, and the soup was served by the **master**. Each boy had one small bowl of soup and no more. The bowls never needed washing, because the boys cleaned them with their spoons until they shone. But there was not enough food. Oliver and the other boys were always hungry, so one day they decided that one boy would walk up to the master after supper and ask for more soup. Oliver was chosen.

In the evening, the boys sat down at the tables.

45 a. Read the extract again and put the sentences in the correct order.

☐ Mr Bumble put Oliver in a dark room.
☐ The master served the soup.
☐ The boys whispered to each other.
☐ Oliver asked for some more soup.
☐ The boys made signs to Oliver.
☐ Oliver asked for some more soup a second time.
☐ Oliver stood up.
☐ The soup disappeared quickly.
☐ The master was surprised.

Literature Corner 8

The master stood by the pot, and the soup was served. It disappeared quickly. The boys whispered and made signs to Oliver. He stood up from the table and went to the master, with his bowl and spoon in his hands.

"Please, sir," he said, "I want some more."

The master was a fat, healthy man, but he went very pale. He looked with surprise at the small boy.

"What?" said the master at last in a **quiet** voice.

"Please, sir," repeated Oliver, "I want some more."

The master hit Oliver with his spoon, then **seized** him and cried for help. Mr Bumble rushed into the room, and the master told him what Oliver had said.

"He asked for more?" Mr Bumble cried. "I cannot believe it. One day they will **hang** the boy."

He took Oliver away and shut him in a dark room. The next morning a notice appeared on the workhouse **gate**. Five pounds were offered to anybody who would take Oliver Twist.

Oliver was a prisoner in that cold, **dark** room for a whole week. Every morning he was taken outside to wash, and Mr Bumble beat him with a **stick**. Then he was taken into the large hall where the boys had their soup. Mr Bumble beat him in front of everybody. He spent every day crying. When night came he tried to sleep, but he was **cold**, lonely and **frightened**.

One day, outside the high workhouse gate, Mr Bumble met Mr Sowerberry. Mr Sowerberry was a tall, thin man who wore black clothes and made **coffins**. Many of his coffins were for the poor people who died in the workhouse.

"I have prepared the coffins for the two women who died last night," he said to Mr Bumble.

"Good," said Mr Bumble. "You will be rich one day, Mr Sowerberry! Do you know anybody who wants a boy? And five pounds?" He raised his stick and pointed to the notice on the gate.

The arrangements were soon made, and Mr Bumble took Oliver to Mr Sowerberry's shop that evening. Oliver did not want to go.

"I will be good, sir!" he said. "I am a very little boy and it is so – so – lonely! Please don't be angry with me, sir!" To Mr Bumble's surprise, Oliver had **tears** in his eyes. He told the boy not to complain, to dry his eyes and to be good. He took Oliver's hand, and they continued walking in silence.

Mr Sowerberry had closed the shop, and he was writing by the light of a candle when they arrived.

"Here, Mr Sowerberry, I have brought the boy," said Mr Bumble. Oliver **bowed**.

"Oh, that is the boy, is it?" said Mr Sowerberry. "Mrs Sowerberry, come here, my dear." A short thin woman with a narrow face came out from a little room behind the shop. "My dear," said Mr Sowerberry, "this is the boy from the workhouse that I told you about."

Oliver bowed again.

"Oh!" said the woman. "He is very small."

"Yes, he is rather small!" said Mr Bumble. "But he will grow, Mrs Sowerberry, he will grow."

"Yes, I expect he will," said the lady **angrily**, "on our food and our drink. Here, get downstairs, you little bag of **bones**. You can have some of the cold meat that we saved for the dog. The dog hasn't come home since this morning."

Mrs Sowerberry opened a door and pushed Oliver down some stairs into a dark room.

Oliver's eyes shone at the thought of meat. They gave him a plate of the dog's food, and he ate very quickly. Mrs Sowerberry was not pleased that he was so **enthusiastic**.

"Come with me," she said, taking a dirty lamp and leading him upstairs again. "Your bed is in the shop."

Oliver was left alone in the shop. He was alone in a strange place. He climbed quickly into his narrow bed and fell asleep.

From "Oliver Twist" in the Penguin Readers series, retold by Deborah Tempest

---

☐ The boys sat down at the tables in the big hall.
☐ Mr Bumble came into the room.
☐ Oliver went to the master.
☐ The master called out for help.

b. Match the characters with the descriptions. What do you think Mr Bumble looks like? Why do you think so?

Oliver Twist	fat and healthy
The master	tall and thin with black clothes
Mr Sowerberry	short and thin with a narrow face
Mrs Sowerberry	pale, thin and very small

46 a. Make a list of the things that happened in the story, then take turns to retell the story in your own words.

b. Discuss what you would have done in Oliver Twist's place.

Project

Choose one of the scenes from the extract and draw a picture for your class's *Oliver Twist Drawing Competition*.

Writing an assessment report

Tip

An assessment report is usually written for someone in authority such as your employer. It presents and evaluates the positive and negative qualities of a place, person, etc in order to make some kind of judgment or recommendation. Reports always contain factual information.

We always begin a report by saying who the report is for and their position, the writer's name and position and what the report is about.

Introduction
In the **first paragraph** we present the purpose and content of the report.

Main Body
In the **main body**, we present each topic in detail under separate sub-headings.

Conclusion
In the **last paragraph** we summarise the information and state our general assessment or evaluation.

We usually write reports in a formal, impersonal style. We write short sentences containing factual language so that the information can be understood easily. We normally use present tenses in assessment reports as well as the passive voice and full verb forms.

Analysing the Rubric

47 Read the rubric, underline the key words, and answer the questions.

> The editor of the magazine where you work as an assistant editor has asked you to write a report assessing the good and bad points of the Taj Mahal Indian restaurant. Write your report describing the restaurant's food, prices, service, and atmosphere.

1 Who is going to read your report?
 a The restaurant's staff.
 b Your editor.
 c The restaurant's customers.
2 What is your position according to the rubric?
3 What subheadings should the report have?
4 Match the nouns to the adjectives, then say which of these are positive and which are negative.

slow	menu
high	service
helpful	atmosphere
warm	prices
varied	staff

slow service (negative)

5 What should(n't) a good restaurant have? Use your answers to make up sentences, as in the example.

A good restaurant should not have slow service. However, it should have ...

Analysing a Model Text

48 Read the report and fill in the appropriate subheadings from the list.

- Conclusion • Service • Introduction
- Atmosphere • Food and Prices

To: Mr C. James, Editor
From: Al Thompson, Assistant Editor
Subject: Taj Mahal restaurant

1) ....
The purpose of this report is to assess the good and bad points of the Taj Mahal restaurant.

2) ....
The Taj Mahal offers a wide range of Indian cuisine, all of which is beautifully cooked and presented. What is more the meals are good value for money as the prices are quite reasonable.

3) ....
The waiters are very polite and friendly and they are able to make helpful suggestions about the menu. However, the service is a little slow, especially when the restaurant gets busy.

4) ....
The restaurant has a tasteful Eastern-style décor and thick carpets. In addition, the soft ethnic music helps to give the Taj Mahal a very pleasant atmosphere. Nevertheless, the lighting is poor, so it is difficult to read the menu.

5) ....
In conclusion, although the service can be slow and the lighting poor, the Taj Mahal is a pleasant restaurant that offers excellent food at reasonable prices. Therefore, I would certainly recommend it to anyone who enjoys Indian food.

- Which are the positive/negative points that the writer makes? What linking words has he used to link contrasting ideas? similar ideas?

Style

49 Replace the informal phrases with appropriate formal ones.

Informal	Formal
I've written this report to tell you ...	*The aim of this report is to assess ...*
There are lots of Indian dishes.	....
It's a bit pricey.	....
We couldn't see well.	....
If you like Italian food, you should go there.	....

50 Which of the following can you use to start/end a report?

The purpose/aim of this report is to assess …
On the whole …
I would (not) recommend …
The report was carried out to assess
In spite of the (dis)advantages …
As requested, this report is to assess …
To sum up …

Clauses of Concession

51 Join the sentences using words from the list, as in the example.

- furthermore • however • despite the fact
- in addition • although • what's more

1 The staff were courteous and helpful. The service was slow at times.
*The staff were courteous and helpful **although** the service was slow at times.*
***Despite the fact** that the staff were courteous and helpful, the service was slow at times.*
*The staff were courteous and helpful. **However**, the service was slow at times.*

2 The restaurant offers a wide variety of main courses. There was little choice for dessert.
3 The food was very reasonably priced. Drinks were cheap.
4 It is in a poor location. The exterior of the building looks shabby and run down.
5 The lights were too bright. The restaurant has a pleasant atmosphere.
6 It offers a wide variety of Japanese and Thai food. There are some English dishes for the less adventurous.

Discuss & Write

52 a. Which of the following would you expect to find in a *fast food* restaurant?

- fast service ☐
- clean tables ☐
- helpful, friendly staff ☐
- low prices ☐
- silver cutlery ☐
- wide variety of foods ☐
- white tablecloths ☐

b. Listen to the customers talking about Marco's fast food restaurant and tick (✓) the comments that they make.

- The prices are reasonable. ☐
- The staff are friendly and helpful. ☐
- The service is slow when it's busy. ☐
- There are not many dishes to choose from. ☐
- The restaurant opens early. ☐
- There are too many waiters. ☐
- The restaurant is old and not very clean. ☐
- There is nowhere to park your car. ☐
- It has long opening hours. ☐
- It has a friendly relaxed atmosphere. ☐

53 a. Read the rubric, underline the key words and answer the questions in the plan.

You are the assistant manager of Marco's, a fast food restaurant which is part of a large chain. The manager has asked you to write a report assessing the food and prices, service and atmosphere, and suggesting any changes that you think need to be made.

plan

To: *Who are you writing to?*
From: *Who are you?*
Subject: *What are you going to write about?*

Introduction
(Para 1)   *Why are you writing the report?*

Main Body
(Paras 2-4)   *What information about food and prices, service, atmosphere and facilities will you include?*
What are the good and bad points?
Can you make any suggestions?

Conclusion
(Para 5)   *What is your overall impression?*
What are your recommendations?

b. Now write your report (120-180 words). You can use the report in Ex. 48 as a model.

54 Try to explain these quotations in your own words. How do they relate to the theme of the unit?

Famous words

- The proof of the pudding is in the eating.
  Miguel de Cervantes (Spanish writer)
- A balanced diet is a cookie in each hand.
  Barbara Johnson (American cook and author)

129

Self-Assessment Module 4

Vocabulary & Grammar

1 Fill in the missing word.

1 Grilled chicken accompanied .... steamed vegetables is a very healthy meal.
2 He is dedicated .... his family.
3 The restaurant offers a three-.............................. meal for £10 per person.
4 Have we got .... milk left?
5 Would you like still or .... water, sir?
6 She gave her mum a .... of flowers as a birthday present.
7 She has always been prone .... ear infections.
8 Do you prefer wearing formal or .... clothes?
9 That new suit fits you like a ....!
10 The store caters .... people of all ages.
11 Can you buy me a .... of biscuits, please?
12 He is hopeless at .... decisions.
13 Luckily, the headmaster .... him off with a warning.
14 Virgos are creatures of habit, so they like to .... routines.
15 She never buys her perfumes here. She always has them .... from France.
16 That's interesting. The same idea occurred .... me!
17 I'm afraid horror films are not really my cup of ....
18 She was on the .... of playing the video when the electricity was cut off.
19 The test was really easy. It was a .... of cake.
20 Then you .... the eggs with the whisk.

(10 marks)

2 Circle the correct item.

1 Your energy level is at its .... in the early afternoon.
    A top   B high   C peak   D summit
2 We'll have strawberries and .... for dessert.
    A butter   B milk   C yogurt   D cream
3 Tom .... going for a picnic.
    A invited   C suggested
    B offered   D asked
4 Milk products are .... in calcium.
    A rich   B wealthy   C full   D plentiful
5 His fee is just a drop in the .... compared to the cost of the whole project.
    A river   B lake   C ocean   D sea
6 Keep a(n) .... out for a parking space.
    A hand   B eye   C nose   D ear
7 John .... his car serviced last month.
    A has had   C will have
    B had   D had had
8 He can't afford a holiday; he's on a .... budget.
    A wacky   B low   C strong   D tight
9 Your body needs time to .... the vitamins and minerals in your food.
    A absorb   B attract   C stock   D keep
10 Those old photographs have great .... value to me.
    A emotional   C expressive
    B sentimental   D sensitive

(10 marks)

Use of English

3 Complete the second sentence using the word in bold. You must use two to five words including the word given. Don't change the word given.

1 The cupboards are practically empty.
    hardly   There .... in the cupboards.
2 That's the garage where they fixed Ann's car.
    had   Ann .... at that garage.
3 There are only a few strawberries left.
    many   There .... left.
4 "Why don't we go to the park?" Tony said.
    suggested   Tony .... to the park.
5 "Are you interested in Biology?" Laura asked Tim.
    if   Laura .... interested in Biology.

(5 marks)

4 Fill in the correct word derived from the word in bold.

1 Fill your full name in the .... form.   **APPLY**
2 Did you have any .... doing the exercise?   **DIFFICULT**
3 It's .... to cross a street without looking both ways.   **DANGER**
4 He likes .... music.   **TRADITION**
5 Drain the vegetables ....   **THOROUGH**

(5 marks)

Self-Assessment Module 4

5 Read the sentences. If a sentence is correct put a tick (✓). If it has a word which should not be there, write this word on the line.

1. Nowadays the more and more people ....
2. tend to eat junk food. The main reason ....
3. is that people have less of time for eating. ....
4. If we don't improve of our eating habits, ...
5. we are more likely to suffer from diseases in the short term. ....

(5 marks)

Communication

6 Put the dialogue into the correct order.

☐ No problem. I'm happy to help you. Goodbye.
☐ Oh, really. That's great news. Sorry to have troubled you.
☐ Let me see. Here it is. The items you ordered were sent out today.
☐ What seems to be the problem Ms Madoc?
☐ Hello. This is Ruth Madoc, Customer number XJI2459. I'm calling about my order.
☐ I haven't received any goods yet and I placed my order over three weeks ago.
☐ Hello, BMS customer services, Lyn speaking. How may I help you?

(5 marks)

7 Complete the exchanges.

1. A: ....?
   B: Of course. The fitting rooms are over there.
2. A: .... this radio.
   B: Certainly. Would you like an exchange or a refund?
3. A: I'm having a pool party on Saturday. Would you like to come?
   B: ....
      I've got to study for my exams.
4. A: ....?
   B: Yes, I'd like half a kilo of Stilton cheese, please.
5. A: What do you think? ....
      .... these sunglasses?
   B: Yes, but only if you can afford it.

(5 marks)

Listening

8 🎧 You will hear an interview with an owner of an organic food restaurant. For questions (1-10), complete the sentences.

Organic food is produced without the use of
[1]_____.
Diane's first introduction to organic food was as a
[2]_____.
Her grandmother used [3]_____
fertilizers on her fruit and vegetables.
[4]_____ products can also be organic.
A lot of people go to the restaurant [5]_____.
Later in the day, there is a different
[6]_____.
In the summer the café has [7]_____.
People are realising that organic food tastes
[8]_____.
The [9]_____ also benefits from organic food.
The chemicals used in fertilizers and pesticides
[10]_____ the soil.

(10 marks)

Speaking

9 Describe the pictures. Then, in pairs discuss the following:

- Which type of food do you prefer eating? Why?
- Where do you enjoy going out to eat? How often do you go there? Why do you like it?

(10 marks)

131

Reading

10 You are going to read an article about the history of the British monetary system. Choose the most suitable heading from the list (A-I) for each part (1-7) of the article. There is one extra heading which you do not need to use. There is an example at the beginning.

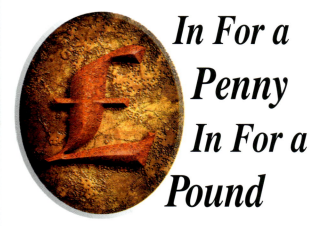

In For a Penny In For a Pound

0 | C

England has enjoyed a relatively stable single national currency with an unbroken history of over 900 years. The origins of the pound sterling date even further back. In fact, the pound as a unit of currency has never had to be replaced by a new currency, in contrast to many European currencies. The pound has also been preferred and widely accepted in international trade for two hundred years. As a result, other countries had to adapt their currency arrangements to fit in with sterling.

1 |

Economic activity in the very earliest civilizations had to do with trading or "bartering". Services were traded to meet individual needs. For example, a master would reward his servant with food and shelter. Goods of equal value were also exchanged. People then began to use items that had the same value to everyone. In the earliest civilizations cattle, grain, salt, leaves, and seeds were traded to buy necessities. England has returned to barter several times over the course of its history.

2 |

The Ancient Britons used sword blades as currency before they started minting coins. The designs of the earliest coins, dating back to 125 BC, were imitations of Macedonia's pure gold coins. As their experience of minting grew the designs became more original. The coins started to reflect their lifestyle and interests. The horse was a common feature as they were a rural people. Their love of hunting and farming can be seen in the designs of boars and ears of wheat.

3 |

Coins continued to be used in Britain while it was part of the Roman Empire. The Romans did, however, impose their own coinage on Britain. Small brass and copper "minissimi" coins were used for low value purchases. When the Roman Empire collapsed in the 5th century and Britain was invaded by the Anglo-Saxons, minting and the use of coins ceased in England for over 200 years. The island went back to bartering and using other, more primitive, standards of value.

4 |

With the Viking invasions of England came an enormous increase in the production of coins. Alfred the Great, who prevented the Vikings from conquering all of England, had eight mints built so that he would have enough coins to pay his soldiers and to build forts and ships. The kings who came after Alfred had to keep increasing the number of mints in order to pay for the defense of the country. It became so complicated, that in 928, King Athelstan passed a law stating that there was to be only one single type of money or currency in England, and there has been just one ever since. This occurred many centuries before other major European countries such as France, Germany and Italy had their own national currency.

5 |

The pound was introduced into England by the Normans even before William I conquered and united England in 1066. It was originally an amount of silver weighing a pound and became the basis of the monetary systems throughout the British colonies. With Britain's head start in the Industrial revolution, developments in banking, her military victories and the spread of the British Empire during the 19th century, the pound sterling became the world's most important currency.

6 |

In 1816 the standard of value for the sterling changed from silver to gold and other countries followed the British example, making the gold standard an international one. During the worldwide economic crisis in 1931, Britain was forced to abandon the gold standard. The US dollar replaced the pound sterling as the key global currency. Other countries then fixed their exchange rates against the dollar, the value of which remained defined in terms of gold.

7 |

After the Norman Conquest, the pound was divided into twenty shillings. The shillings were made of silver and the weight of twenty shillings was exactly that of one pound. The shillings were then divided into twelve pence or pennies. The pennies were made of copper, and the weight of twelve pennies was exactly the weight of one shilling. On 15th February, 1971, Britain introduced the decimal system. This meant that the pound (£) was equal to 100 pence (p) which made it much easier to use.

- **A** The strongest currency worldwide
- **B** Deciding on a single currency
- **C** The long history of the pound
- **D** Using goods to buy and sell
- **E** Coins showed the ancient way of life
- **F** The oldest money in the world
- **G** Making it simpler for all
- **H** From coins to trade again
- **I** Changing the way the pound is measured

(15 marks)

Self-Assessment Module 4

Writing an assessment report

11 You have a part-time job in the cafeteria in your college. The manager wants you to write a report assessing the cafeteria and suggesting any changes that you think need to be made to make it more popular with the students. Use the notes as well as your own ideas to write your report (120-180 words).

To: *The Manager, Hillside Community College Cafeteria*
From: *your name*
Subject: *College Cafeteria*

Introduction
(Para 1)   *purpose of report – assess college cafeteria – suggest changes*

Main Body
(Para 2)   *food is inexpensive – suitable for students on a tight budget – well-cooked – not a very wide range of food – menu is boring*

(Para 3)   *cafeteria is bright and cheerful – long tables no comfortable chairs*

(Para 4)   *during the week – opens from 8am to 6pm – more and more students have lessons at night – study in the library at night and weekends*

Conclusion
(Para 5)   *inexpensive student cafeteria with a pleasant atmosphere – expand menu – buy new furniture – extend opening hours to 8am to 9pm – open on Saturdays and Sundays – attract more students*

(20 marks)
(Total = 100 marks)

12 a. Look at the picture and name the foods. Which are healthy? Which are unhealthy?

b. What do you usually have for: breakfast? lunch? dinner? Are you a healthy eater? Why/Why not?

Sing Along!

🎧 Listen and fill in. Then, listen again and sing.

Eat a **1)** .... breakfast
Before you start your day
2) .... is what you need
To help you work and play

You've got to be
food wise
And watch what's on
your plate
The right food at the
right time
Can keep you feeling
great.

Snacking burns off
3) ...., so
It can be good for you
But choose foods that are healthy
A **4)** .... bar won't do!

You've got to be food wise ...

When it comes to lunchtime
Go for something **5)** ....
A salad or a **6)** ....
Will make you feel just right

You've got to be food wise ...

A good **7)** .... in the evening
Will make your day complete
With vegetables and **8)** ....
A tasty evening treat

You've got to be food wise ...

Progress Update

How do you rate your progress? Tick (✓) the box that applies to you.

	Excellent ****	Good ***	OK **	Could do better *
Vocabulary & Grammar				
Listening				
Speaking				
Reading				
Writing				
Communication				

Sports & Free-time Activities

UNIT 9 Every Man to his Taste

UNIT 10 Spread the News

Module 5

Units 9-10

Before you start ...

Where do you usually do your shopping? Why?
What clothes do you like wearing?
What's your favourite food? How do you cook it?
Do you have a healthy lifestyle?

Listen, read and talk about ...

- sports
- sports qualities
- free-time activities
- entertainment
- the media
- the news
- disasters
- TV Guide
- cinema

Learn how to ...

- make suggestions/agree - disagree
- express likes/dislikes
- prioritise
- ask for permission
- polite requests
- take a phone message
- invite someone to an event
- express regret
- gossip
- make arrangements
- make excuses

Phrasal verbs

- run
- set
- take
- turn
- stand

Write ...

- instructions for a magic trick
- an article about an important sporting event
- a letter to the editor
- an article about a disaster
- a short story
- a formal transactional letter

Practise ...

- conditionals Type 2/3
- wishes
- would rather
- future perfect
- linkers
- quantifiers (both, all, none, neither, either, every, each)

Every Man to his Taste

Lead-in

1 a. Look at the pictures, then listen to the three music extracts. Which best matches how you feel about the pictures?

b. Use the phrases to describe the pictures. Can you name any other extreme sports? Have you ever participated in any of these sports? If so, how did you feel?

- extreme kayaking • snowboarding • goggles
- bungee cord • free-fall parachuting
- slope • solo jump • crane/bridge
- wet suit • bungee jumping

Picture 1 shows a man bungee jumping ...

c. Which of these sentences best describes your feelings about each of the sports above?

I wish I could do it more often.
If I weren't too scared, I would give it a try.
If only I could turn my fear into positive energy.
I'm not sure if I could do it.
I've never wanted to do it.

2 Which of these qualities should people have in order to do high-risk sports? Discuss.

- fear • positive energy • courage • survival instinct
- ability to evaluate risks • sense of adventure
- physical strength • quick reactions • mental energy
- determination

Reading

3 a. The people in the pictures are called 'daredevils'. What does this mean? Do you think what they do is sheer lunacy? How do you think these people feel?

b. Read the article and choose the correct answer, A, B, C or D, then explain the words in bold.

Shaun Baker has two equally crazy ways of **descending** through the **torrents** of a waterfall in a small kayak. He either **paddles** through a series of **boulders** that could smash him and his boat to pieces, or **pushes** his boat out
5 into the air so that he **free-falls** through the air into the water below.
    He calls this extreme kayaking. Others may be tempted to translate this as **sheer** lunacy. However, everyone agrees that it is a **high-risk** sport.
10 When Baker, a 32-year-old professional white water rodeo champion from just outside Maidenhead, explains what he does, it sounds impossible. When he actually shows you, it is truly amazing how, each time, he **emerges** from the waters below, a little bruised, but
15 in one smiling, **triumphant** piece.
    One of his favourite areas to perform these **daredevil feats** is in a valley of waterfalls on the edge of the Black Mountains in central Wales. A breathtakingly beautiful but dangerous spot, it provides
20 Baker with as **nerve-wracking** a challenge as any he has faced in the twenty years he has been in some kind of canoe.
    "It's **in my blood**," he explains, preparing himself both physically and mentally for the challenge ahead.
25 "I don't do this for any **macho** reasons, I do it for myself. If I'm honest, it **scares the life out of me**, especially when I start to **tip** over the edge and I know there's no turning back."
    "The trick is to turn the fear into positive energy.
30 You are frightened at the top of the fall, but this changes into a **survival instinct**. You need every ounce of mental energy and reaction to survive. The real **kick** is when you hit the bottom and reappear from under the water. That's when you know you've made it, and
35 that is the moment when you have **a sense of elation**."

Daredevil Shaun

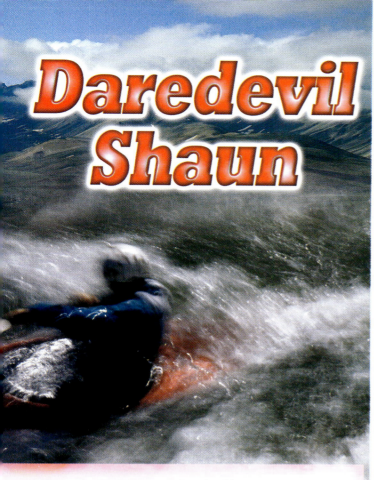

Apart from various national white water rodeo championship wins, Baker also holds the record for the highest free-fall waterfall drop in a kayak, as well as the world speed **altitude** drop of 50 metres. He is just about the only regular extreme kayaker in the world.

"The reason why I still do this," he says, "is that I have the ability to work out whether I can survive or not. If I think something is too risky, I won't do it."

'Too risky' in Baker's language is, of course, totally different to my or your **interpretation**. As he **steadies** himself for his first descent, a slide down a fall of around 60 feet, with dangerous rocks at the bottom, you are left wondering just how he is going to succeed. In his tiny, 2.2-metre-long 'Eskimo' kayak, the smallest in the world, Baker begins.

It is all over in a few seconds. He drops, like a stone, down the fall, and is then forced to his left and onto a totally different route than he had planned.

He then moves **downstream** to his second challenge in order to perform an actual free fall.

"The trick here is to punch the water with the nose of the kayak," Baker explains. "If you have a flat landing, it could kill you."

Baker holds his arm in the air, shoots his thumb up, and then leaps out into the sky before falling down and under the river. There is a second's silence before he emerges again – wet, a little bruised, but safe.

"It's a whole way of life for me," he explains, as we climb our way out of the valley and back to the cars. "It's not that I go out to **impress** anyone, or try to say I'm better. It's just the wonderful experience of testing myself against nature and the **elements**. And each night I look back on a day like today and realise there's nothing I would rather be doing with myself."

1 What does the passage suggest about the two methods Shaun uses to kayak down waterfalls?
   A One is much safer than the other.
   B Both involve free-falling from the top of the waterfall.
   C One is called 'extreme kayaking'.
   D Both are very dangerous.

2 Why does Shaun enjoy kayaking in the waterfalls on the edge of the Black Mountains?
   A It is very beautiful there.
   B It offers him a great challenge.
   C He has lived there for 20 years.
   D Kayaking is very easy there.

3 What does 'it' in line 26 refer to?
   A Shaun's kayak
   B a waterfall
   C extreme kayaking
   D feeling frightened

4 When does Shaun feel best about a descent?
   A before he starts kayaking
   B at the top of the waterfall
   C during the descent
   D when he emerges at the bottom of the fall

5 Shaun still does extreme kayaking because …
   A he doesn't take any risks.
   B he is always able to work out if a descent is too dangerous.
   C he will do anything no matter how dangerous it is.
   D he doesn't care if he survives or not.

6 Shaun enjoys his sport because …
   A he is very good at it.
   B it impresses other people.
   C it doesn't scare him at all.
   D he enjoys testing himself.

c. Match the highlighted words to their synonyms.

• pure • come down • jump • hit • appear
• victorious • thrill

Follow-up

4 Read the article again and list the reasons Shaun does this sport and how this makes him feel. Then, in pairs, talk about whether you would like to try this sport, and explain why/why not.

Vocabulary Practice

Sports

5 Use the adjectives to act out dialogues, as in the example.

- exciting • challenging • thrilling • relaxing
- competitive • dangerous • frightening • risky
- exhausting • nerve-racking • demanding

A: I'd love to try hang-gliding.
B: Really? Why?
A: I'm sure it would be exciting. What about you?
B: No, I wouldn't like to try hang-gliding. I think it would be too frightening.
A: What would you like to try then?
B: Scuba diving ... etc

Qualities

6 a. Fill in the correct word

- competitive • accurate • co-operative • daring
- graceful • careful • determined • courageous

1. A footballer needs to be .... to play as part of a team.
2. A person needs to be .... to try sky surfing because it is quite a dangerous sport.
3. An archer needs to be .... to hit the centre of the target.
4. A long distance runner needs to be .... to finish the race because they get very tired.
5. A racing driver needs to be very .... because he has to drive very fast and take a lot of risks.
6. You need to be .... when you are rock climbing because you could fall and seriously injure yourself.
7. A successful sports person has to be .... and do their best to beat other athletes.
8. An ice-skater needs to be .... so that they can glide across the ice with style and ease.

b. In pairs, discuss what qualities each of the sports below requires.

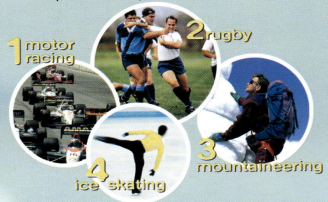

A: In my opinion, you need to be daring to be a racing driver, because it is a dangerous sport.
B: That's true. You also have to be careful or you could get seriously injured.

7 a. Match the columns, then, make up sentences.

Sports	Place	Equipment
football	table	gloves, boots
archery	range	ball
badminton	ring	bow, arrows
snooker	course	racquet, shuttlecock
boxing	court	clubs, ball
golf	pitch	cue, balls

We do archery on a range, using a bow and arrows.

b. What do we call the people who take part in the sports in the table above?

archery – archer   football – footballer

c. Complete the sentences with words from Ex. 7a & b. Which sport does each of these sentences refer to? Which words tell you this?

1. The cheers from the crowd were deafening as the .... ran onto the pitch.
2. I've always loved .... , so my parents gave me a cue for my fifteenth birthday.
3. He got a hole in one on the 17th hole of the ....
4. Janet took aim at the centre of the target, pulled back the string of her .... and fired.
5. At the end of each round, each .... has to return to his corner of the ring.

Game

One student chooses a sport, and says a sentence. In teams, try to guess what the sport is. Each correct guess gets one point. The team with the most points is the winner.

Leader: I'm wearing shorts.
Team A S1: Are you playing tennis?
Leader: No.   etc

Free-Time Activities

8 a. In pairs, think of two more items in each category.

Free-Time Activities	
collecting	stamps, antiques, ...
making	furniture, models, ...
games	cards, chess, backgammon, ...
the Arts	painting, photography, ...
others	watching TV, surfing the net, ...

b. Which of these do you find *interesting*? *challenging*? *boring*? Why?

I find collecting antiques quite interesting, because I can learn about how people lived in the past.

9 In pairs, use the vocabulary from Ex. 8 and the useful language below to act out short dialogues, as in the example.

Making Suggestions	Agreeing/ Disagreeing
Why don't we …?	That's a good/great idea.
How about …?	Yes, let's do that.
What about …?	I don't really feel like it.
Let's …	Oh, it's too boring.
I think we should …	It's a nice idea but …
We could always …	I don't (really) like …

A: How about a game of cards?
B: I don't really feel like it.

A: What about watching TV, then?
B: Yes, let's do that.

Entertainment

10 a. Listen and cross out the phrases you don't hear.

1
- huge tent
- funny clowns
- incredible animals
- excellent show

2
- luxurious theatre
- top class venue
- excellent sound effects
- expansive stage
- unforgettable experience

3
- talented band
- smash-hit tunes
- explosive shows
- nerve-racking experience

b. Use the phrases from Ex. 10a to make up a sentence about each form of entertainment.

I enjoy going to concerts to see talented bands play.

c. Which of these forms of entertainment do you like best? Why? Describe the last time you went.

My favourite form of entertainment is going to …

11 a. Do you like magic tricks? Which is your favourite one?

b. Read the steps involved in the magic trick, and put them in the correct order. Which steps do the pictures show?

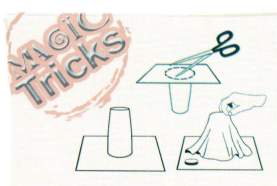

Preparation

..... Cut around the glass, so that its mouth is covered by a paper circle.

1 Take a clear glass and two sheets of white paper.

..... Put some glue on the rim of the glass and stick it down on the paper.

Performance

..... Cover the glass with a cloth and move it over the coin.

..... Put the cloth back over the glass.

..... Move the covered glass away to make the coin 'magically' reappear.

..... Remove the cloth and it will look as if the coin has disappeared.

..... Place a coin on the second sheet of paper and place the glass upside down next to it.

Writing Project

Think of a magic trick and write instructions. Write what you need, the preparation and the procedure you have to follow.

Grammar in use

Conditionals type 2/3
Grammar Reference

12 Match the sentences to the meaning. How do we form type 2/3 conditionals?

- 1 If I **had** £100, I **would** buy tickets for the concert.
- 2 If I **had driven** more carefully, I **wouldn't have** crashed the car.

a imaginary situation in the past
b unreal situation in the present/future

13 Match the parts of the sentences, then say what type of conditional each sentence is.

If we had played better, we	would do the parachute jump with you.
If he had been more careful, he	would join a gym.
If I wasn't so scared, I	wouldn't have lost the game.
If you had said you wanted to come, I	would have got an extra ticket.
If she had more time, she	wouldn't have been injured.

14 Complete the sentences using a type 2 or type 3 conditional.

1 If we had told her about it, ...
2 She would have agreed ...
3 If we had more time, ...
4 We would have arrived in London by now if ...
5 Caroline would tell me ...
6 I would buy it if ...
7 If she had passed her exams, ...
8 If Chris had come, ...
9 We would have won if ...
10 If I knew where it was, ...

Game

In teams, make up as many conditional sentences for each picture as you can. Each correct sentence gets a point. The team with the most points is the winner.

1 I didn't hear the alarm.
2 I didn't study for the exam.

Team A S1: *If he had heard the alarm, he would have woken up on time.*
Team B S1: *If he had woken up on time, he wouldn't have been late for work ... etc*

Wishes
Grammar Reference

15 Study the sentences. Which refer to the present, and which refer to the past? How do we form wishes?

1 I wish I knew more people.
2 If only he were here.
3 I wish I could play the guitar.
4 I wish I hadn't sprained my ankle.

16 Write wishes about these situations, as in the example.

1 You have to work today; you'd rather stay in bed.
   I wish I didn't have to work today.
   If only I could stay in bed.
2 Your team lost the match; you wanted to play in the final.
3 You don't have enough money to go on holiday; you'd like to go to Spain with your friends.
4 You painted your living room green; now you'd rather you had painted it blue instead.

17 a. Use Jane's "wish list" to write full sentences.

- move into new flat / have more space
- find new job / earn more money
- go on diet / fit into my old clothes
- be brave / go scuba diving

Jane wishes she could move into a new flat. If she moved into a new flat, she would have more space.

b. Write down your own wish list and then tell your wishes to the class.

I wish I had lots of money.

18 Look at the pictures and think of relevant wishes, as in the example.

house — money — mobile phone — car

If only/I wish I owned a car.
If I owned a car, I could drive to work/ wouldn't need to take the bus.   etc

138

Would rather

Grammar Reference

19 a. Study the examples. Which refer to the present/future? Which refer to the past?

1. **I'd rather play** squash with Richard, but I promised to have a game with Andy tonight.
2. **I'd rather have spent** longer in bed this morning.
3. **I'd rather Andy played** squash with John tonight.
4. **I'd rather you hadn't done** that.

b. Compare sentences 1 and 3. Who is the subject of *play*? Who is the subject of *played*? What is the difference in the structures?

20 Put the verbs in brackets into the correct tense.

1. We went to the cinema last night, but I'd rather .... **(stay)** at home and watched TV.
2. "Can I borrow your Sociology notes tonight?" "I'd rather you .... **(borrow)** them tomorrow instead. I want to study them tonight."
3. I suggested Ben take up fishing as a hobby, but he said he'd rather .... **(take up)** golf.
4. She'd rather you .... **(not / tell)** Ian about that – it was going to be a surprise.
5. Kate would rather .... **(go)** to the gym after work than go home and relax.
6. I would rather .... **(play)** football last Saturday.
7. Our coach said it didn't matter that we lost the match, but he'd rather we .... **(win)**.

21 Look at the pictures and think of as many sentences as you can using *would rather*.

I'd rather live in a nice cottage than a flat in town.
I'd rather have a big garden with lots of flowers.

Prepositions

Appendix 1

22 a. Underline the correct preposition, then explain the phrases in bold.

1. The burglar was **sentenced** *to/for* a year in prison.
2. I'm **terrible** *at/with* chess. Can't we play another game instead?
3. That's **typical** *to/of* Steve. He's always doing that.
4. The coach wasn't **satisfied** *at/with* his team's performance.
5. Teachers should be **sensitive** *at/to* students' needs.
6. She was **shocked** *at/for* the way Tony spoke to her.
7. Tim can't afford to come with us. He's a bit **short** *with/of* money this month.
8. Will is determined to **succeed** *to/in* the competition this year.
9. The other players **suspected** him *of/to* cheating but they couldn't prove anything.
10. This restaurant **specialises** *in/with* seafood.

b. Fill in the correct preposition, then choose any five phrases and make sentences using them.

1 to emerge .... the water; **2** .... the edge of; **3** to provide sb .... sth; **4** to be .... sb's blood; **5** to change sth .... sth else; **6** to hold the record .... sth; **7** .... a few seconds; **8** to be armed .... sth

Phrasal Verbs

Appendix 2

23 a Fill in the correct particles to form phrasal verbs, then explain their meaning.

1. I hadn't seen Bob for months, but yesterday I **ran** .... him in the street.
2. We went to the airport to **see** Gill ....
3. They want to **run** .... the script one last time before the first performance.
4. He **set** .... his own business when he was 21.
5. Gary's in hospital. He was **run** .... by a car.
6. The bakery had **run** .... brown bread, so we had to get white.
7. I suppose this cold weather means that winter is finally **setting** ....
8. The project took ages – we kept **running** .... **against** unexpected problems.
9. We've **set** .... some money so that we can afford to go on holiday this summer.

b Write a story using as many of the phrasal verbs from Ex. 23a as possible.

As I left home yesterday morning, I ran into Jenny ... etc

139

Grammar in use

Multiple Choice Cloze

24 Read the text and decide which answer, A, B, C or D, best fits each space. There is an example at the beginning.

THE PARALYMPICS

The Paralympics is the largest sporting event **0)** *for* disabled athletes in the world. Athletes from six disability groups take **1)** .... during the eleven days of competition. However, both the **2)** .... and the athletes stress that the sporting performance is what's important, **3)** .... than the participant's disabilities. The Paralympics have **4)** .... a long way since 1948, when a sports competition was first **5)** .... in England for World War II veterans with spinal **6)** .... Competitors from Holland joined a few years **7)** .... , and in Rome in 1960 the **8)** .... official, Olympic-style Paralympics was first organised. The Paralympics include **9)** .... Summer and Winter Games and now take place **10)** .... the Olympics at the same venue in the same year. Events such as wheelchair rugby are very **11)** .... with spectators and require great skill. Another favourite is three-track skiing. Here disabled competitors ski on one leg while **12)** .... themselves on two crutches which also have small skis attached to them. In **13)** .... years the Paralympics have grown dramatically, both in popularity and in the **14)** .... of athletes taking part. This growth will **15)** .... in the future as more and more countries send representatives to the Games.

	A	B	C	D
0	of	with	**for**	about
1	part	place	action	play
2	organisers	presenters	directors	coordinators
3	more	other	rather	instead
4	been	gone	done	come
5	done	fixed	arranged	agreed
6	illnesses	injuries	problems	wounds
7	after	later	then	previously
8	most	many	more	much
9	both	all	either	neither
10	nearby	between	together	alongside
11	precious	popular	worth	famous
12	putting	leaning	holding	supporting
13	last	recent	late	modern
14	addition	group	number	amount
15	keep	continue	stay	expand

Idioms & Fixed phrases

25 a. Match the idioms to the sports in the pictures. What do you think each idiom means?

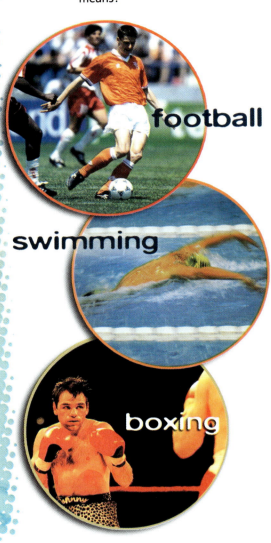

1. to be thrown in at the deep end — *swimming*
2. to be on the ropes — ....
3. to throw in the towel — ....
4. to hit (somebody) below the belt — ....
5. to move the goalposts — ....
6. to box somebody into a corner — ....
7. to be out of one's depth — ....
8. to be on the ball — ....

b. Use the correct idiom from Ex. 25a to complete each of these sentences.

1 We're never going to get this finished on time. We might just as well .... now.
2 Jack always manages to avoid answering any questions. I will have to ....
3 It seems like every time we think we've finished, they .... and we have to make more changes.
4 She was really .... when she said those nasty things about him.
5 The company is .... They will be closing down any day now.
6 We weren't given any training. We were just .... and expected to get on with it.
7 She doesn't like all the extra responsibility that comes with her new job. I think she feels a bit ....
8 The company is really .... They keep up with the latest market changes, so they stay ahead of their competitors.

26 Underline the correct word, then explain the phrases in bold.

1 I've been very busy – in fact, I've **been rushed off my *feet/legs***.
2 It's getting late – perhaps it's time we **hit/kicked the road**.
3 We had a **close *save/shave*** on the way here; a truck nearly crashed into the back of the car.
4 If you can't decide what to do, you should **dream/sleep on it** and see how you feel in the morning.
5 He's the best player in the team. He is **second to *none/nothing***.
6 He is definitely going tomorrow, **come rain or *sun/shine***.

27 Complete the second sentence so that it has a similar meaning to the first. Use between two and five words, including the word in bold.

1 I'm tired of Susan's irresponsible behaviour.
  up I'm .... behaviour.
2 He didn't wake up on time, so he missed the bus.
  have He .... the bus if he had woken up on time.
3 If you want to see the start of the match you haven't got much time left.
  running You .... if you want to see the start of the match.
4 He didn't score from the penalty, so we didn't win the game.
  won If he'd scored from the penalty, ... the game.
5 I'm disappointed that she didn't come to the party.
  wish I .... the party.
6 We'll have a barbecue if it doesn't rain this afternoon.
  unless We'll have a barbecue .... this afternoon.
7 I wish I hadn't gone out last night.
  not I'd .... out last night.
8 I wish our team had won the match.
  only If .... the match.
9 I'd prefer to go to the cinema tomorrow.
  rather I .... to the cinema tomorrow.
10 It's getting cold and the days are shorter. Winter is definitely starting.
  in It's getting cold and the days are shorter. Winter ....

Error Correction

28 Read the text below and look carefully at each line. If the line is correct, put a tick (✓). If it has an extra word, write this word on the line, as in the examples.

Terror on the Terraces

You expect excitement at a football match, so when   0   ✓
I first arrived at the stadium everything seemed to   00   to
normal and under control. The fans beside to me   1   ....
were wearing in their team's colours and chanting   2   ....
football anthems. The atmosphere was a bit tense, but   3   ....
that was because of the two teams playing were   4   ....
being great rivals. As the match went on, though, the   5   ....
crowd became the more and more bad tempered.   6   ....
The trouble really started when the referee made a   7   ....
decision that many of us disagreed with it. Before   8   ....
I knew what was happening, supporters from the   9   ....
opposing teams had been run onto the pitch and were   10   ....
attacking each the other. All around me people started   11   ....
panicking and pushing at frantically to escape. I felt   12   ....
like I was going to get crushed up, and I could hear   13   ....
some of people screaming and crying. It was a   14   ....
such terrifying experience that I will never forget.   15   ....

Listening & Speaking skills

29 a. Listen and fill in the sports event advertisement.

NORTHWOODS TO CAPITOL TOUR

The tour begins on [1] _____ and finishes on [2] _____. Altogether [3] _____ people will take part. Participants will cycle along two-lane [4] _____. The tour will pass through [5] _____ and _____. The tour is for riders of [6] _____ ability. There will be [7] _____ days of cycling altogether. The tour will cost [8] _____ for each person. The participants will sleep in a [9] _____.

b. Look at the pictures. In pairs, discuss what you will/won't need to take with you in order to join the cycling tour.

A: I think we need to take a helmet to protect our heads.
B: I agree. We definitely don't need to take hiking boots, though, because we won't be walking.

30 a. Listen to a radio programme about violent sports and mark the correct box, **Yes** or **No**.

		YES	NO
1	There was a recent sporting injury.	☐	☐
2	Boxing is the most dangerous sport.	☐	☐
3	Boxers are often arrested outside the ring.	☐	☐
4	Violent sports make sports fans behave violently.	☐	☐
5	Competition in sports can be a good thing.	☐	☐
6	Dr Taylor thinks the players themselves should decide whether it is worth the risk.	☐	☐

b. Look at the pictures and describe them.

Picture A shows two boxers in a boxing ring. The boxer in blue is punching the boxer in red. The boxers are wearing ...

In pairs, discuss the following.

- Do you like going to such sporting events?
- Which is your favourite sport? Give reasons.
- Which sporting event would you (not) take young children to? Why (not)?

A: I enjoy going to watch live sporting events. Do you?
B: Yes, I do. I like going to watch football matches, because the atmosphere in the stadium makes it more exciting.
A: I agree – but I wouldn't take young children, because ... etc

31 a. Listen to people talking about their hobbies, and match the statements (A-F) to the speakers. There is one extra letter which you do not need to use.

A They have won a prize for their hobby.
B They collect glass objects.
C They took over a relative's hobby.
D They keep their collection in albums.
E They collect something that makes them laugh.
F They collect things they find in the ground.

Speaker 1 ☐
Speaker 2 ☐
Speaker 3 ☐
Speaker 4 ☐
Speaker 5 ☐

b. Look at the pictures showing various hobbies. Discuss which would be appropriate for the people listed below, and explain why.

A Mr Henderson – 68-year-old retired businessman
B Jimmy Swenson – 13-year-old schoolboy
C Suzy Bellows – 6-year-old schoolgirl
D Hank Goodman – 28-year-old lawyer

A: I think gardening or painting would be good hobbies for Mr Henderson.
B: Yes, I agree.

Now answer the following questions.
- What are your hobbies?
- How did you get started?
- What do you enjoy about them?
- Do you think it's important for people to have hobbies? Why/why not?

Asking for Permission; Polite Requests

32 a. Listen to the dialogues and write *P* (asking for permission) or *R* (polite request).

Dialogue 1 .... Dialogue 3 ....
Dialogue 2 .... Dialogue 4 ....

b. Read the dialogues and fill in the missing words.

1 A: Excuse me – .... you tell me where the tennis club is?
   B: Certainly. Just walk to the end of this road and turn left.

2 A: .... I open the window? It's getting a bit stuffy in these changing rooms.
   B: I'd rather you didn't – I'm feeling a little cold.

3 A: .... I leave the training session early? I've got a dentist's appointment.
   B: Of course.

4 A: .... you give me a lift to football practice, Dad?
   B: All right, but you'll have to take the bus home.

c. In pairs, act out similar dialogues using the following prompts and expressions from the table below.

- Ask a colleague if they can lend you some money.
- Ask the flight attendant if you can change seats.
- Ask the person next to you on the bus if they know where the local gym is.
- Ask your English teacher if you can miss a class in order to take part in an important sports event.

Asking for permission/a favour	Could I/you ... Would it be OK if I ...
Granting permission/a favour	Certainly. (Yes,) of course. OK. All right.
Refusing permission/a favour	Actually, I ... Sorry, but ... I'm afraid that ... I'd rather you didn't.

Taking a phone message

33 a. Listen to the dialogue. Who is calling?

b. Read the dialogue and put Speaker B's replies in the correct order.

A
1 ☐ Good morning. Dixon & Co – how can I help you?
2 ☐ Who is speaking, please?
3 ☐ One moment, please ... I'm afraid Mr Jackson isn't in his office at the moment. Would you like to leave a message?
4 ☐ Right. I'll make sure Mr Jackson gets the message.

B
a Yes, please. Could you tell him that I won't be able to meet him tomorrow, as I'll be in Moscow?
b My name is Helen Baxter.
c Hello – can I speak to Colin Jackson, please?
d Thank you very much.

c. Use the prompts to act out similar dialogues.
- The football match has been cancelled.
- The cricket bat he ordered has arrived.

Inviting a friend to a sporting event

34 a. Listen to the dialogue. What is Duncan going to do?

b. Read the dialogue and fill in the gaps with the words/phrases from the list below.

- Another time, perhaps? • Why do you ask?
- What are you doing this weekend?

A: Hi, Paul – it's Duncan. 1) ....
B: Hi, Duncan. Er, I haven't got any plans. 2) ....
A: I was wondering if you'd like to come and watch a football match. Manchester United are playing on Saturday and I've got an extra ticket.
B: Oh no! I wish I could go to the match with you, but I've just remembered I *do* have plans after all.
A: Never mind. 3) ....
B: I hope so. Thanks for asking me, anyway.

c. Use the prompts to act out similar dialogues.
- basketball game / Sheffield Sharks
- cricket match / Lancashire

Intonation – regrets

35 Listen and repeat.

- I wish I'd won the game.
- If only I'd taken his advice.
- If only I'd made it to the Olympics.
- I wish I had gone to the match.
- If only I hadn't missed the penalty.

143

TROPHY HUNTERS

A Wimbledon

Wimbledon is the most famous tennis **championship** in the world, and over the years it has become a British **institution**. Held every summer at the All-England Lawn Tennis and Croquet Club, the competition lasts for two weeks.

Wimbledon was first held in 1877. In those days, it was an **amateur** event which only men could enter. Today, both men and women, professionals or amateurs can take part in the championship, which is followed in the media by millions of people.

Tennis players come from all over the world to **compete**, hoping to win a **trophy** and a **substantial** amount of money. The prize for winning the Gentlemen's Singles Championship is a large silver **gilt** cup. The winner of the Ladies' Singles gets a silver **salver** called the 'Rosewater Dish'. There are also competitions in both men's and ladies' doubles. The prizes are traditionally presented by the Duchess of Kent.

What makes Wimbledon special is the tradition involved. It is the only international tennis tournament which is still played on **grass**, and the only competition open to both amateurs and **professionals**. The best tradition of all, though, is the **spectators'** custom of eating strawberries and cream while they watch the tennis.

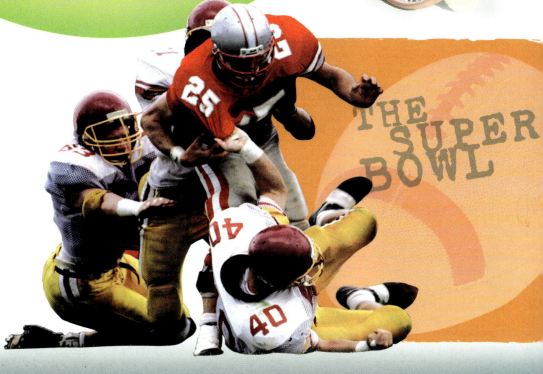

THE SUPER BOWL

Culture Clip 9

36 a. Look at the title and the pictures. What do you think these sportsmen compete for?

b. In which context do you expect to find these words in the articles?

Article A
- tennis championship • held every summer • amateur event
- win a trophy • prizes are presented • played on grass

Article B
- football fans • top teams • play matches
- go through to the playoffs • sing the national anthem
- cheerleaders and marching bands

Wimbledon is a famous tennis championship.

c. Do you know when Wimbledon and the Super Bowl started? In which countries? Which of the two competitions is older? Read the texts to find out.

37 Read the texts and, for each question, choose the sporting event (A-B). Then, explain the words in bold.

Which sports event

• is open to both professionals and non-professionals?	1) ....
• asks a well-known person to perform?	2) ....
• includes appearances by top celebrities?	3) ....
• is an international competition?	4) ....
• is more than 100 years old?	5) ....
• allows participants to play alone or in pairs?	6) ....
• has several other non-sporting activities as part of the event?	7) ....
• gives a reward to both the winners and the losers?	8) ....

38 a. Match the words to their meaning.

amateur	• an important part of sth
honour	• last in a series of stages
feature	• a fixed period when a sport is played
open to	• not professional
final round	• a special privilege
season	• may be entered by

b. What sporting organisations do these initials stand for?

• NFL • NBA • UEFA • FIFA
• PGA • WBC

Speaking

39 Read the texts again and find three differences between each event.

Wimbledon is held in England, whereas the Super Bowl is held in the USA.

Writing

40 Think about your country's most important sporting event. Write an article for a sports magazine. Include:
- when/where it is held
- the event's history
- description of the event
- the prize

B THE SUPER BOWL

The Super Bowl is the **highlight** of the year for American football fans. It is the final round in a competition between the top teams in the National Football League, as well as a national celebration.

The 30 professional teams in the NFL play matches against each other all season to determine who will go through to the **playoffs**. Then, the two winning teams face each other to compete for the Super Bowl Trophy, which is a model of a football in kicking position made of silver. The trophy is presented by the NFL **commissioner**. All players from both teams receive a special commemorative silver ring.

The first Super Bowl was played in 1967. Since then, the event has gradually become more **elaborate** and more popular. These days, the competition is watched by millions of people worldwide, and is more than just a football game. In fact, it is an entertainment **extravaganza**, with a pre-game show and a half-time show which both **feature** famous bands and singers. A big-name star is always asked to sing the national **anthem**, which is considered to be a great honour. The shows also have plenty of cheerleaders and marching bands. Everyone who takes part in the event, from the spectators to the players, has a fantastic time.

Writing a letter to the editor

Tip

We usually write a letter to the editor when we want to express our opinion about a topic that is of interest to the general public, to agree or disagree with something that has been reported, or to discuss a problem and suggest solutions. We usually write a letter to the editor in a formal or semi-formal style.

- We start our letter with *Dear Sir/Madam,*

Introduction
- In the **first paragraph**, we present our reason for writing and our opinion about the topic.

Main Body
- In the **second** and **third paragraphs**, we present our arguments/the problems, together with consequences/suggestions/results, in separate paragraphs.

Conclusion
In the **last paragraph** we summarise our opinion or write it again using different words.

We end with *Yours faithfully,* and **our full name**.

USEFUL EXPRESSIONS

- **To begin the letter:** I am writing to express my support for/(dis)approval of …; I am writing with regard to …; I am writing about …; I have just read …; etc
- **To state an opinion:** In my opinion, …; I (do not) feel/believe/think …; I am (totally) opposed to/in favour of …; I strongly (dis)agree with …; etc
- **To express the consequences/results:** This will/would mean …; Then …; Therefore, …; As a result, …; Consequently, …; If we/they do/did this, …; Obviously, …; Clearly, …; etc
- **To list points:** Firstly, …; First of all, …; Secondly, …; Furthermore, …; What is more, …; Finally, …; etc
- **To end the letter:** I hope my comments/suggestions/points will be taken into consideration; I hope the government/local council/we will …; I hope something will be done about this urgently; etc

Analysing the Rubric

41 Read the rubric, underline the key words and answer the questions.

> The local council has decided to build a new sports centre in your home town where an old factory used to be. Write a letter to the editor of your local newspaper, expressing your support for the plan.

1. Who is going to read your letter?
   a. The local council.
   b. The editor of the local newspaper.
   c. The newspaper's readers.
2. What is your opinion of the plan?
3. How should you begin/end your letter?
4. Should the letter be written in a formal or informal style?
5. Which of the following might you use in the letter? Tick (✓).
   - In my opinion, this is an excellent idea. ☐
   - I am totally opposed to the council's plan. ☐
   - I hope the council won't … ☐
   - I don't think we should … ☐
   - I strongly agree with the council's plan. ☐
6. Which points might you make in your letter? What advantages might a new sports centre have? Tick (✓).
   - More people will be able to play sports. ☐
   - There will be less traffic on the roads. ☐
   - People will have somewhere new to go. ☐
   - It will bring new jobs to the town. ☐
   - It will make the town centre cleaner and tidier. ☐

Analysing a Model Text

42 a. Read the letter and choose sentences to complete it. Why did you decide on them?

A Firstly, it will provide a number of job opportunities.
B To start with, the town has very few sports facilities.
C All in all, I must state that I am in total agreement with the council's decision.
D To sum up, I think it is a very bad idea.
E Furthermore, the new centre will be in an excellent location.
F Also, the location is fantastic.

Dear Sir,

I am writing about the recent article in your newspaper regarding the decision to build a new sports centre in our town. In my opinion, this is an excellent idea which will have many advantages for our town.

1 ☐ Many people do not get the chance to play sports when they want. A new sports centre will give more people the opportunity to play sports. It will also give children and teenagers access to better facilities than they have at school, as well as somewhere to go at weekends. At the moment there is very little for them to do.

2 ☐ It is in the centre of town, near the railway station and several major bus routes. Consequently, it will be very easy to get to. What is more, the fact that it will be built on the site of the old factory means that the town's appearance will be improved.

3 ☐ I hope that the plan is put into effect as soon as possible.

Yours faithfully,
James Marshall
James Marshall

b. How does the writer support his arguments?

c. Underline the linkers the writer uses to: **list points**; **express an opinion**; **express a result**. Replace them with other appropriate ones.

d. Find examples from the letter showing it is written in a formal style.

Style

43 Match the informal phrases/sentences (1-6) to the formal ones (a-f).

1. ☐ I am writing about ...
2. ☐ I think that ...
3. ☐ I hate what they decided to do.
4. ☐ I don't like the idea of ...
5. ☐ So, then ...
6. ☐ I like this idea very much.

a I wish to express my disapproval of ...
b The consequence would be that ...
c I am strongly in favour of ...
d I am writing with regard to ...
e It is my opinion that ...
f I strongly disagree with this decision.

Joining Sentences

44 Match the arguments to the consequences, then write full sentences using the useful expressions from the table on p. 146.

Arguments
1. ☐ If the park is sold there will be no open spaces left.
2. ☐ There will be very few green areas in town.
3. ☐ The town will be crowded and built up.

Consequences
a There will be more traffic and pollution, and the town will no longer be a nice place to live.
b Children will not be able to play freely, and people will have nowhere to walk their dogs, ride their bicycles and so forth.
c This is very unhealthy, as people need fresh air and natural surroundings for good health.

Discuss & Write

45 a. Read the rubric, then use information from Ex. 44 to answer the questions in the plan.

> You read the article below in Tuesday's edition of the *Westvale Herald*. You have decided to write a letter to the editor to express your opposition to the plan and to urge the council to reconsider its decision.

At yesterday's meeting, after a long discussion, Westvale Council finally made a decision on what to do with Longheath Park. The park has been neglected for many years and it would require a large sum of money to improve facilities and to carry out other restoration work. Despite the popularity of the park with local residents, the council decided that they could not afford to do this. Instead, in a controversial move, they have chosen to sell the land to a property developer. It is thought that the developer plans to build an estate of 50 houses on the land.

Dear Sir,

Introduction
(Para 1)   Why are you writing?
           What is your opinion?

Main Body
(Paras 2-3) What are your arguments/the problems?
             What are the consequences or suggestions and results?

Conclusion
(Para 4)   What is your opinion again?
           What do you think should happen next?

Yours faithfully,
Your full name

b. Use your answers to Ex. 45a to write your letter (120-180 words). You can use the letter in Ex. 42 as a model.

46 Explain the quotations below in your own words.

- A man sits as many risks as he runs.
  Henry David Thoreau (US poet)
- Always do what you are afraid to do.
  Ralph Waldo Emerson (US philosopher)
- Everything is sweetened by risk.
  Alexander Smith (Scottish poet)
- Sports do not build character. They reveal it.
  Heywood Hale Broun (US broadcast journalist)

Spread the News

Lead-in

1 Read the title. What do you expect the unit is about?

2 a. How do you keep yourself informed?
• newspapers • magazines • Internet • TV
• radio • other

b. Are you a bookworm? What do you like reading? What form of books do you prefer: *hardcover*? *paperback*? *e-book*? Give reasons. Think about:

• cost   • convenience   • binding

I prefer reading paperbacks because they are cheap and easy to carry.

c. Look at the survey results in the table. What do the percentages tell you? Is the printed word dying?

	No. of people who use	
	printed word	electronic media
newspapers	36%	64%
magazines	54%	46%
encyclopaedias	74%	26%
dictionaries	78%	22%

The percentages tell us that more people use electronic media to read newspapers than the printed word.

3 a. In pairs, tick (✓) the arguments in favour of electronic media.

access information without leaving your desk	....
carry it around with you	....
take longer to read	....
good graphics and layout	....
it is cheaper	....
can fit in your pocket	....
get up-to-date information instantly	....
read sth over and over	....
lasts a long time, doesn't need replacing	....

b. Use arguments from above to express your opinion.

Thanks to electronic media, I can access any information I want to without even leaving my desk. Sadly, I can't carry it around with me in the same way I can with traditional books.

Reading

4 a. Read the title. Is this possible? Why/Why not? Read and find out.

b. Read the article again and choose the most suitable sentence from the list (A-I) for each gap. There is one extra sentence which you do not need to use. There is an example at the beginning.

E-books the books of the future?

A few years ago, nobody could have imagined buying a whole dictionary or encyclopaedia on CD-Rom – but we do now, and it's a **booming** business. Are e-books set to take over from the printed word? Well, some multimedia companies are **predicting** that, in a few years' time, production of newspapers and magazines will have been **halved**, as we will be turning to our computers to get the latest news. But how do people feel about reading their daily newspaper, or even their favourite novels, on their computer screens? **0 E**

It is certainly a question that we are going to have to think about soon. Technology produces new products every day and the **publishing industry** is already showing great interest in the future of the e-book. **1** ☐

As for e-books, despite the fact that the technology has not been fully developed yet, and an e-book that you can carry about with you is still much more expensive than an ordinary book, researchers claim that soon e-books will become much cheaper than paper versions, and will be much more popular.

2 ☐ Stephen King, the best-selling writer of horror books, **posted** his newest short story on the Internet and it sold more copies in its first days than many of his printed novels had. **3** ☐

Well, is this really the end of the book and the newspaper? I **doubt** it, and it seems that even Stephen King agrees. Despite his success on the Internet, he does not seem to think anything can replace the book! This is partly because, although we like to think that technology is capable of anything, it isn't. At least, not yet! **4** ☐ It took 25 hours for Associated Press to **download** Stephen King's story. This is because lack of **band width** makes it very slow to send material, **especially** pictures, over the Internet. Even though work is constantly being carried out to solve this problem, demand for the Internet is increasing too fast for scientists to keep up. What is more, it takes much longer for us to read on the net. **5** ☐

There is another problem, too, which has nothing to do with technology. People simply prefer paper. It doesn't matter how many books, magazines or newspapers are

148

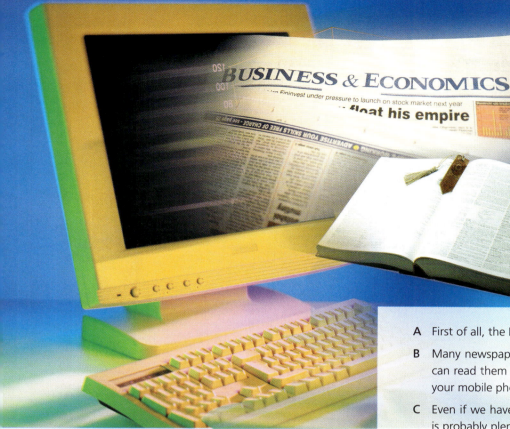

A First of all, the Internet is slow.

B Many newspapers are already online; and you can read them on screen at home, or even on your mobile phone.

C Even if we haven't, it doesn't matter, as there is probably plenty of room for both books and screens.

D To publishers, this meant the arrival of the e-book!

E Would you be happy to get your newspaper on the screen, or do you still prefer turning those pages?

F Did you know that we can read 50% more quickly on paper than we can on a computer screen?

G It looks as if people are already interested in the general idea.

H We like to decorate our rooms with them, too.

I More than half of today's newspapers now have websites.

produced – we never stop buying them. It seems that we like the feel of books and magazines – we like to put them in our bags or pockets and take them out on the bus or the train on the way to work. We like to sit and read in the park or on the beach.

6   How many of us would **exchange** what we have now – a **row** of books in a bookcase, or a pile of magazines on the coffee table – for a row of little screens? For many of us, the idea of Sunday morning without a cup of coffee and a pile of newspapers is impossible.

Nevertheless, by the time e-books have become as widely available as printed ones, it is likely that at least some of us will have changed our minds.

7   Publishers will be delighted to **cater** for those who prefer to use a screen, but paper lovers shouldn't worry, as the printed page will **undoubtedly** keep its place in our lives. There is even news that MIT will have come up with a **compromise** soon – a **system** where we can tell our computers what we want to read, and then they will print our own personal newspaper for us. The difference will be that we will only have to read about things which interest us. Just think – if you hate the **business section**, you don't have to order it. If you dislike tennis, you can request only the football results. It sounds like this could be good news for everyone!

c. Find the phrasal verbs in the text, which mean: *think of, place inside, remove, do, move at the same speed, replace*. Then, explain the words in bold and suggest synonyms for the highlighted words.

Follow-up

5 Which of the following best describes the author's main point? Give reasons.

a Books are old fashioned.
b The printed word will never die.
c E-books will replace paper books.

How far do you agree with the author?

Vocabulary Practice

The News

6 a. Match the newspaper headlines to the sections. Can you think of any other sections? Which is your favourite section of the newspaper? Why? Which do you never read?

Poland hit by more bad weather	UK news
Mobile phone company makes bid for rival	world news
Russian satellites launched	politics
Poor results force England's cricket captain to quit	business
Cancer screening benefits praised	education
A MAGICAL PERFORMANCE	sports
TV standards falling	science/technology
UK backs peace plan	entertainment
SOUTH-EAST ASIAN LEADERS MEET FOR NEW TALKS	health
Education spending key to next election	reviews

I like reading the sports section the most.
I never read the politics section. I'm not interested in it.

b. How often do you buy a newspaper? Is it a *daily* or a *weekly* paper? Is it a *tabloid* (popular press) or a *broadsheet* (quality press)? What is its circulation?

7 Listen to each of the people and match them to the newspaper sections they are talking about.

Lyn	horoscopes
Stacey	letters to the editor
Bob	classifieds
Tony	crossword

8 a. The following words often appear in newspaper headlines. Match them to their meanings.

quit	the important factor
bid	to try to buy/take over sth
cut	support
back	reduce
hit	affect sb/sth badly
talks	resign
key	formal discussions

b. Find the above words in the headlines in Ex. 6a then re-write each headline without using them.

*Poland **hit** by more bad weather.*
*Poland **has been badly affected** by more bad weather.*

Disasters

9 a. Look at the headlines. Which disasters are mentioned here? Which are natural and which are man-made? Can you think of any other disasters?

1. MASSIVE EARTHQUAKE LEAVES THOUSANDS HOMELESS IN INDIA
2. Village flooded as river breaks banks
3. Malawi declares famine emergency
4. Arsonists blamed for forest fires
5. Evacuation underway as Mount Etna erupts again
6. Gas explosion kills family of four

b. Listen to the radio report and fill in the table. Which of the headlines from Ex. 9a does it match?

Where?	• small village of .... in Warwickshire
When?	• last ....
What happened?	• river broke its .... village ....
Results:	• Thousands of pounds worth of damage; up to .... people evacuated their homes.
Action taken:	• The .... was called in. They used .... to build up river banks.
	• Council look at ways of making .... it never happens again.

c. Imagine you are the newsreader at your local TV station. Report the flood in Ex. 9b.

The small village of Upton in Warwickshire was flooded yet again last Tuesday when ...

Writing Project

Use the plan in Ex. 9b to write a news report about a recent disaster in your country for the school magazine. Start by giving the *summary of the event* (where, when, what, etc.), and then *describe the event* in detail. Finish your news report by writing the *action that will be taken*.

10 Match the columns to form compound nouns, then use them to complete sentences 1-6.

magazine	films
radio	effects
black and white	broadcast
special	station
current	covers
live	affairs

1 Photographs of her have appeared on *magazine covers* all over the world.
2 I always listen to that .... in the morning because I really like the DJ.
3 We'll go over now to a .... from the Houses of Parliament where the Prime Minister is about to give his speech.
4 I love watching old .... Some of them are classics.
5 We should watch that new .... programme on TV tonight; it looks like it will be really interesting.
6 The plot was a bit silly but the .... were amazing.

TV Guide

11 a. Look at the extract from the TV guide section of a magazine and in pairs make up dialogues.

5.35	**Neighbours:** Danny confronts Steve. Australian soap.	**BBC1**
6.00	**BBC News:** Presented by David Hawkins.	
6.30	**Regional News: Weather**	
7.00	**Animal Hospital:** Real life stories of animals in crisis presented by Rolf Harris.	
7.30	**EastEnders:** A case of mistaken identity for Kat and Ian goes too far. Soap.	
8.00	**Weird Nature:** New series which looks at strange behaviour in the animal kingdom.	
8.30	**This is your life:** Michael Aspel presents an unsuspecting celebrity with their life story.	
9.00	**Manhunt:** Police drama. Borne and his team manage to arrest most of the smugglers. Starring David Suchet.	

A: Is there anything good on TV tonight?
B: I quite fancy watching Manhunt.
A: What's that?
B: You know, the police series. It's normally really good.
A: What time does it start? / I don't think so, it's not my style. etc

b. How often do you watch TV? What do you enjoy watching on TV? Which of the series on BBC 1 can you watch in your country?

Cinema

12 a. In pairs, think of as many words as possible related to the cinema.

b. Look at the pictures. Which is *an animated film, an action film, a romance, a science-fiction film*? In pairs, use the prompts to make up dialogues, as in the example.

A: Would you like to go and see a film tonight?
B: Yes sure. Any suggestions?
A: How about that action film?
B: Which one?
A: Lethal Weapon 3.
B: What is it like?
A: The newspaper says it's exciting … etc

Lion King ★★★★
Incredible animation and full of lovable characters, this is one of Disney's best-ever films. For children and adults alike.

Lethal Weapon 3 ★★★★
Exciting action sequences and a funny, well-written script make this film well worth watching.

Star Wars Episode 1: The Phantom Menace ★★★★
Spectacular special effects, a star studded cast along with fast paced action make this the greatest space adventure of all time.

You've Got Mail ★★
Despite its predictable plot, this is an enjoyable romantic comedy with a happy ending.

Project

13 Think of a film which you have recently seen and talk about it, then write a short review. Write about: *type of film, cast, plot, directing, photography and special effects*. Finally make your *recommendation*.

Game: Charades

Think of a film/TV programme. Indicate the number of words in the title, then mime each word. Students try to guess what the title is. The student who guesses correctly becomes the leader and you continue the game.

Grammar in use

Future Perfect
Grammar Reference

14 Study the sentences. Which is used to describe an action that will be finished before a stated future time? Which is used to emphasise the duration of an action up to a certain point in the future?

*He **will have been working** there for more than forty years by the time he retires.*
*He **will have had** his novel published by the end of the month.*

15 a. Rachel is thinking about her future. What does she hope she will have done by the time she is thirty years old?

- graduate from music college
- play in big orchestras
- play with other great musicians
- become a famous cellist
- give concerts around the world

Rachel hopes she will have graduated from the music college by the time she is thirty years old.

b. What do you think you will have done by the time you are thirty years old?

I hope I will have set up my own business by the time I am thirty years old.

16 Use the prompts to make up sentences, as in the example.

1. Helen/play the flute/4 years
2. Luke/drive a taxi/6 years
3. Sam/study Computer Science/18 months
4. Stella/work as a florist/2 years

By the end of the year, Helen will have been playing the flute for four years.

17 Look at the newspaper headlines. Which do you think will have happened in twenty years' time?

1 Another huge leap as first man walks on Mars.
2 GMX announces the invention of the world's first hover car.
3 First woman president of the USA celebrates victory.
4 Scientists claim they can now cure all major diseases.
5 New global currency to be adopted by more than 100 countries.

I don't think man will have walked on Mars in twenty years' time.

18 Put the verbs in brackets into the future perfect simple or continuous.

1 A: Why don't we meet at the restaurant at 7 o'clock?
   B: That's a bit early. I'm not sure if I 1) .... (finish) by then.

2 A: Do you think we should call John and tell him that we're going to be late.
   B: No, there's no point. He 2) .... (leave) by now.

3 A: Did you hear that Lucy is moving at the end of the month?
   B: Really? But by the end of the year she 3) .... (live) in that flat for ten years!

4 A: I think Dave's really looking forward to retiring.
   B: I'm not surprised. By the summer he 4) .... (teach) for more than thirty years.

Linkers

19 Study the sentences. Which of the words in bold show: *contrast*? *positive addition*? *negative addition*? Can you think of other synonymous words?

Neither of the two girls like/likes horror films.
Although he's rich, he isn't happy.
Besides being beautiful she is **also** talented.

20 Join the sentences using the words in bold.

1 John has lived here for six months. Sue has lived here all her life. **whereas**
   John has lived here for six months, whereas Sue has lived here all her life.

2 The play opens next week. Nick isn't at rehearsals. **despite**

3 The film is excellent. The special effects are stunning. **furthermore**

4 Stuart doesn't play the guitar. Mary doesn't play the guitar either. **neither**

5   He is a very talented actor. He is a good singer. **besides**
6   The article was very interesting. The writer was a little biased. **however**

21 Circle the correct word A, B, or C.

1   .... I normally enjoy detective stories, I found that one a bit predictable.
    A   However   B   Although   C   But
2   Fiona speaks neither Spanish .... French.
    A   not   B   no   C   nor
3   Dad always reads .... the international news and the sports section.
    A   neither   B   both   C   either
4   Dan doesn't want to move, ... his house was damaged by the earthquake.
    A   however   B   but   C   although
5   He's a very talented actor .... I don't think he's good enough to win the Oscar.
    A   but   B   and   C   or
6   Andrea loves romantic films, ... Joe prefers thrillers.
    A   besides   B   moreover   C   while
7   In .... to being an excellent journalist, he is also a newsreader.
    A   addition   B   spite   C   order
8   Which programme do you want to watch? There is .... the news or a documentary.
    A   either   B   also   C   both
9   .... the play's excellent reviews, we didn't enjoy it very much.
    A   Despite   B   Apart   C   Whereas
10 Although she is best known for her role in the soap opera, she has .... appeared in some serious dramas.
    A   more   B   neither   C   also

Quantifiers

22 a. Underline the correct word.

1   The film has **both/all** a star-studded cast and a very well-written script.
2   Claire, Zoe and Carol all tried to get tickets for the concert but **none/neither** of them had any luck.
3   **Every/Either** footballer dreams of winning the world cup.
4   **Both/Each** Adam and Joe work at the radio station as sound technicians.
5   **Neither/Either** of the boys has seen that film yet.
6   Paul buys a newspaper **all/every** day.
7   We could watch TV or we could rent a video, **every/either** is fine with me.

8   **All/Either** of the people in the audience were clapping and cheering.
9   **Each/Every** of his books has been a bestseller.
10 I was surprised that **every/none** of the major newspapers reported the story.

b. Look at the pictures. Then make up sentences using appropriate quantifiers and the prompts, as in the examples.

• comedy   • science-fiction   • exciting   • thriller
• special effects   • characters   • romantic
• animated

*Both D and E are science-fiction films.
Neither B nor C are comedies/is a comedy.*

Prepositions

Appendix 1

23 a. Fill in the correct preposition.

1   The ticket can be used on all buses and trains in the city centre and is **valid** .... one week.
2   Paula **wastes money** .... clothes and CDs.
3   I didn't **vote** .... him in the last election but I actually think he's done a good job.
4   The film was definitely **worthy** .... all the awards that it won.
5   You shouldn't **worry** .... things so much. Everything's going to be OK.
6   He couldn't **get used** .... working at the station.

b. Fill in the missing preposition, then choose any five phrases and make up sentences using them.

1) .... CD-ROM; 2) the feel .... sth; 3) to read .... a computer screen; 4) to think .... sth; 5) to show interest .... sth; 6) capable .... sth; 7) .... least; 8) lack .... sth; 9) to exchange sth .... sth else; 10) to cater .... sth/sb

153

Grammar in use

Open Cloze

24 Read the text below and think of the word which best fits each space. Use only one word in each space. There is an example (0) at the beginning.

HOT OFF THE PRESS

Millions of people **0)** *from* all around the world buy a newspaper every day. Some people read a broadsheet **1)** .... its analysis of world events. Others just flick **2)** .... a tabloid for the latest celebrity gossip or to glance **3)** .... the horoscopes or TV listings. Whatever the reason, your paper can provide you **4)** .... all sorts of useful and entertaining information. In the past, newspapers played an even **5)** .... important role, as they helped to improve literacy and encouraged people to fight **6)** .... freedom and human rights.

The concept of newspapers can be traced as **7)** .... back as ancient Rome, where each day handwritten notices would **8)** .... put up around the city and its provinces. They would give news about government decisions, important marriages, births and deaths, and even the results **9)** .... gladiatorial contests. Printed reports of news events started **10)** .... appear in the 16th century, and **11)** .... the late 18th century newspapers were common in Europe and the USA. In fact, many newspapers which are still going strong today, **12)** .... *The Observer* and *The Times* in London, date back to this period. As printing technology has improved, newspapers have **13)** .... able to increase circulation, and now individual newspapers can sell millions of copies. Even **14)** .... the introduction and development of other media, such as TV and radio, newspapers still **15)** .... an important part in our lives.

Phrasal Verbs
Appendix 2

25 Fill in the correct form of **take**, **turn** or **stand** and then explain each of the phrasal verbs.

1. I disagree with everything he .... **for**. He represents everything I hate.
2. It's amazing how much Jack .... **after** his father.
3. The radio's a bit loud, could you .... it **down**?
4. Rick will be earning a lot more although he'll have to .... **on** more responsibility as well.
5. She .... **up** skiing while she was living in France.
6. I'm really proud that he .... **up for** what he believes in.
7. Emma .... **over** control of the company when her father retired.
8. Do you think Rebecca will .... **up** at the party tonight?
9. The company is committed to .... **out** high quality goods at the lowest possible price.
10. They had already given him the money before they realised they had been .... **in** by a conman.

26 Try to explain the abbreviations. You can use your dictionary.

1. Fan mail should be sent **c/o** the TV studios. *care of*
2. I didn't have any money so I had to give Tom an **IOU**.
3. Helen works as a **PA** for a famous film producer.
4. Julia works in the **PR** department.
5. Please send an **SAE** with your application form.
6. He bought his new TV on **HP**.
7. What's the **ETA** of that flight?
8. We need to finish this report **ASAP**.
9. Simon really enjoys watching **DIY** programmes but he never does anything around the house.
10. The new cinema will be opened by a **VIP**.

Word Formation

27 Use the words in capitals to form words that fit in the text below. There is an example (0) at the beginning.

CAN'T GET enough TV

Is TV 0) *addiction* becoming Britain's new problem? New figures from the 1) .... Office of Statistics 2) .... suggest that this might be the case. Their 3) .... have found that watching TV is the nation's 4) .... pastime. Britons on average, watch an 5) .... amount of TV each week. The 6) .... couch potatoes 7) .... watch more than six hours of TV every day. The 8) .... of these people enjoy soap operas, 9) .... series and game shows and can't wait for 10) .... TV with all the new channels it will offer.

ADDICT
NATION
CERTAIN
RESEARCH
FAVOUR
BELIEVE
BAD
REGULAR
MAJOR
ENTERTAIN
DIGIT

Key-word Transformations

28 Complete the second sentence using the word in bold. You must use between two and five words including the word given. Don't change the word given.

1 Do you think Frank is going to come tonight?
   up   Do you think Frank ....
   .... tonight?

2 Disney Studios produce a fantastic animated film every couple of years.
   out   Every couple of years ....
   .... a fantastic animated film.

3 Chloe was completely fooled by the practical joke they played on her.
   taken   Chloe ....
   .... the practical joke they played on her.

4 We enjoyed the film even though it got poor reviews.
   spite   We enjoyed the film ....
   .... reviews.

5 Jim has known how to drive since last August.
   driving   By next August, Jim ....
   .... one year.

6 Sally was the only one who didn't enjoy the film.
   apart   Everyone ....
   .... Sally.

7 The article she is writing will be finished by three o'clock.
   have   She ....
   ....
   the article by three o'clock.

8 I don't think John is still at work.
   will   I think John ....
   ....
   .... now.

Idioms & Fixed phrases

29 Fill in *eye(s)*, *ear(s)* or *nose* and then explain what each of the phrases in bold means.

1 We haven't planned what we're going to do, we'll just **play it by** ....

2 Shall we get the bill? I'll try and **catch the waiter's** ....

3 Apparently Mark offered to lend her his old car but she **turned her** .... **up** at the idea.

4 Kate's house is beautifully decorated; she **has a** really **good** .... **for** colour.

5 It felt like Pete **was looking down his** .... **at** us because he thinks he's more intelligent.

6 When I told her how I might be able to get her a ticket to the concert, she **was all** ....

7 I don't know exactly what happened but I think **there's more to it than meets the** ....

8 It's Neil's first real job and he's still a bit **wet behind the** ....

9 He's thinking about moving, he has a great flat but he's **paying through the** .... **for it**.

10 I looked everywhere for my glasses only to find they were **under my** .... all the time.

Listening & Speaking skills

30 Listen and match the days to the events. There is one event which you do not need to use.

- A On this day you can watch old films.
- B On this day you can visit an art exhibition.
- C On this day you can see a musical.
- D On this day you can hear a concert on the radio.
- E On this day you can buy handmade products.
- F On this day you can meet a famous writer.

1	Tuesday	4	Friday
2	Wednesday	5	Saturday
3	Thursday		

31 a. Look at the pictures and in pairs discuss the following.

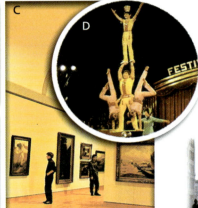

1. What do you think the pictures show? How do you know?
2. What do you normally do in these places?
3. When was the last time you went to one of these places? Talk about your experience.
4. Which of these places would you take a visitor from another country? Why?

1 A: I think picture A shows inside a theatre.
   B: That's right. There are actors on stage.

b. Describe the pictures.

Picture A shows a theatre. There are actors in costume. They are on the stage. It looks like the play is set in an office.

c. Think of questions that match the answers.

 1 I'd love to. / Not really.

(musical) 2 No, not at all. / Yes, I love them.

(art exhibitions) 3 It depends. / I do, actually.

 4 Yes, I have. / No, but I'd love to.

1 *Would you like to go to the cinema?*

d. You and your friend want to go out somewhere. Use the prompts in part c and the useful language to act out dialogues.

Useful Language	
How about …?	What do you think of …?
Would you prefer …?	Why don't we …?
Shall we …?	Do you fancy … -ing?

A: How about going to the cinema?
B: Why not? Is there anything good on?
A: Well, not really.
B: In that case, why don't we go to … etc

32 Listen and mark the sentences *Yes* or *No*.

		YES	NO
1	Angela thinks that the news should be censored.	☐	☐
2	Bernand disagrees that violent scenes should be shown later at night.	☐	☐
3	Angela thinks children copy what they see on TV.	☐	☐
4	The rating system only tells people how violent a programme is.	☐	☐

33 a. Describe the pictures. How do they make you feel?

The first picture shows a car exploding. …

b. In pairs, discuss the following:

- Should the news show violent scenes?
- Does violence in the media have an effect on children? What effect could it have on them?

34 Listen and fill in the instructions leaflet.

Safety Instructions for Natural Disasters

EARTHQUAKE
- Protect yourself under a [1] _____ or _____ .
- Be sure to cover [2] _____ .
- Carry a [3] _____ with you.

HURRICANE
- Board up all the [4] _____ .
- Take shelter in the [5] _____ .
- Keep supplies such as [6] _____ bottled water and tinned food.

FLOOD
- Wear clothing that is [7] _____ .
- Climb onto your [8] _____ and wait to be rescued.

35 Look at the pictures and, in pairs, decide which of the following are needed in case of an earthquake giving reasons.

A: I think the most important thing to have is a torch.
B: You're right. This will help us … . We would also need … .

Gossip

36 a. Listen to the dialogues. Which is about: someone the speakers know? a famous person?

b. Read the dialogues. Which of the phrases in bold: passes on gossip? responds to gossip? In pairs, act out the dialogues.

- A: **Did you hear that** Katie won a new car?
  B: **Are you sure?**
- A: **Guess what!** The lead singer of Soundbytes is buying a house near here.
  B: **No, really?** That's fantastic!
- A: **I've got the most amazing news. You'll never believe it** when I tell you! But you didn't hear it from me.
  B: **Tell me. I won't tell a soul.**
  A: Peter and Janet are finally getting married!

c. In pairs, use the phrases in bold to gossip about:
- a friend of yours who is going to have a baby.
- a neighbour who is going to appear on a TV quiz show.

Intonation (Word Stress)

37 Listen and underline the stressed word. Listen again and repeat.

- A: You'll never believe what happened. Stacey just got fired!
  B: No, really?
- A: Don't tell anyone I told you, but I saw Jim cheat on the test.
  B: I won't say a word.
- A: Did you hear about Al? He's moving away.
  B: Are you sure?

Making arrangements

38 a. Listen to the dialogue. What time are the speakers going to meet?

b. Match the exchanges to form a dialogue.

1	Hi Joanne, it's Rachel here. Listen, do you still want to go to an Internet café this afternoon?	a	Well, there's one in Church Street.
2	Great! Where shall we go?	b	What time shall we meet?
3	Alright. We'll go there, then.	c	Hi Rachel. Erm yes, if you do.
4	How about six o'clock?	d	Okay. See you there.
5	We could meet at the bus station.	e	That's fine. Where?

c. Use the prompts to act out similar dialogues.
- library/in the town centre/3pm/outside
- cinema this evening/the Odeon on Shelley Road/8 o'clock/in the café over the road

Making excuses

39 a. Listen to the dialogue. Where had Danny planned to go?

b. Read the dialogue and fill in the missing phrases.

A: Hi, Danny. I'm calling about going to the cinema tomorrow night. **1)** ……………………………… I can't make it.
B: Oh no. What's **2)** ………………………………?
A: Well, to be honest I'd forgotten that I promised I would babysit for my sister.
B: I see. Well, **3)** ……………………………… time, then.
A: Yeah. **4)** ……………………………… Friday?
B: No problem.

c. Take roles and act out a similar dialogue.

A	B
greeting/cancel plans	ask for a reason
give excuse	offer to reschedule
accept and suggest when	agree

Robinson Crusoe

Daniel Defoe (1660-1731) was an important English author, who many consider to be one of the founders of the English novel. During his lifetime, he published some 200 works of **non-fiction** and 2000 short essays as well as his novels and other **works of fiction**. His many works reflect his own varied interests and experiences. After he left university, he became involved in **trade and politics**, and travelled widely in Europe, publishing his first poem in 1701. His most famous novel, *Robinson Crusoe*, was published in 1719, when he was 60 years old, and was partly based on the **memoirs** of travellers and **castaways**. *Robinson Crusoe* is about a young Englishman who dreams of going to sea. When his father refuses to let him make even one journey, he runs away to sea. A terrible shipwreck occurs and Crusoe ends up on a **desert** island. With a few supplies from the shipwreck, he builds a house, a boat and a new life. Crusoe has many adventures, and even rescues a native who eventually becomes his servant, Man Friday. Twenty-seven years after the shipwreck, Crusoe is finally rescued.

The Earthquake

I had found a cave to live in and had spent three or four months building a wall around its entrance. It meant that I had to enter my home by using a ladder, but at least I would be safe from the wild animals and any other creatures which may live on the island.

When I had finally finished building, I **pitched my tent** in the space between the cave mouth and the wall and felt very comfortable and content. However, this feeling did not last long. The very next day, when I was busy in my new home, just inside the entrance to the cave, I saw some earth falling from the roof of my cave, and I heard two of the supporting posts, which I had put up, make a frightening, cracking noise. I was afraid that the roof of the cave was about to fall in and **bury me alive**, so I ran to my ladder and climbed over the wall to get clear of any falling rocks which might roll down the hill.

The moment I stepped down onto the ground, I realised that a terrible earthquake was taking place. The ground I was standing on **shook** three times, with a pause of about eight minutes between each **tremor**. The shaking was so strong that it would have brought down the strongest building in the world. Huge waves were crashing on the **shore** and making a terrible noise as the earthquake shook the water. I think that the shocks must have been stronger under the water than they were on land.

The experience frightened me so much that I was stunned, and could do nothing but stare around me. I felt sick from the shaking of the earth, as if I was in a boat on a rough sea. Then, suddenly, I heard a crash as rocks fell from the hill, and I was filled with fear. I was worried that my months of work would have been destroyed in a few minutes and that my few **belongings** would be destroyed. This thought made me so sad that I felt **my heart sink in my chest**.

I sat on the ground until I was sure that the earthquake had stopped. When there was no shaking for some time, and it seemed that my wall had not been damaged by the earthquake, I began to feel my courage returning. However, I was still afraid to go back into my cave in case the roof **collapsed** on top of me. I did not know what to do.

As I sat there, the sky became grey and rain clouds **gathered** overhead. The wind began to blow, and grew stronger and stronger, until, in no more than half an hour, a dreadful **hurricane** was blowing. The sea was rough, and trees were being pulled up by their roots. It was a terrible **storm**. After three hours, the wind dropped and the rain started. Through all this, I stayed sitting on the ground, afraid to move.

Suddenly, I realised that this strange weather must be a result of the earthquake and therefore, it must mean that the earthquake was over. If I was right, then it was safe to return to my cave. I felt happier at this thought, and went and sat in my tent, where I could **shelter** from the rain. However, my tent was being beaten so hard by the storm that I was forced to go into my cave, although I was still nervous and unsure about the safety of the roof.

After some time, I began to feel calmer. There had been no more shaking, but I had made a new plan. If earthquakes happened often on this island, then I would have to build a new home. A cave was not a safe place to live. This time, I would make a hut, **surrounded by** a wall, and I would live there without fear.

Literature Corner 10

40 a. Read the author's biography and answer the questions.

- Where did Robinson Crusoe come from?
- Why did he run away?
- What happened?
- Where did he end up?
- How long was he there?

b. What problems do you think he experienced on the island?

41 a. Listen and number the sounds in the order you hear them. Which of these would you expect to find in the extract? Why?

...... supporting posts making a cracking noise
...... huge waves crashing
...... thunder
...... rocks rolling down the hill
...... leaves rustling
...... wind blowing
...... raining
...... lions roaring

b. Read the story and find out if your guesses were correct.

42 Read the extract again and mark the sentences **C** (correct) or **I** (incorrect). Then, explain the words in bold.

1. Crusoe built a cave to live in. ....
2. The tremor made the cave crash down. ....
3. Crusoe's belongings were destroyed. ....
4. Crusoe stood near the wall during the earthquake. ....
5. There was a terrible storm. ....
6. Crusoe started to repair the cave. ....

43 a. Find the words which mean:

- doorway (l. 2) • put up (l. 6) • satisfied (l. 8)
- dirt (l. 11) • astonished (l. 27) • drop (l. 33)
- nerve (l. 37) • fell down (l. 39) • pounded (l. 54)

b. Underline the paragraph which best matches the picture.

44 Make a list of the things that happened during and after the earthquake. Then, describe the event. Do you agree with Robinson Crusoe's plan? What would you do in his place?

Writing

45 Your local literature club has announced a short story competition. To enter the competition, you have to describe a typical day in the life of somebody who has been shipwrecked on a desert island. Write your story.

159

Writing a formal transactional letter

> **Tip**
>
> We usually write a formal transactional letter to respond to written information in the form of advertisements, letters, invitations, notes etc.
>
> **Introduction**
> In the **first paragraph**, we write our opening remarks and explain the reason for writing the letter.
>
> **Main Body**
> In the **second** and **third paragraphs** we ask questions or give the information required. We always ask our questions in a formal indirect way.
>
> **Conclusion**
> In the **last paragraph** we write our closing remarks.
> It is important to include all the facts provided in the rubric and the notes. However, we need to rewrite the information in our own words as much as possible. We do not use abbreviations, contracted types or colloquialisms for this type of transactional letter.

Analysing the Rubric

46 Read the rubric and underline the key words. Then, answer the questions.

> You are an author and you have received the following invitation. Write a letter accepting the invitation and ask for details regarding the location, time and whether you can bring any guests with you.

> Dear Mrs Stephens,
> We would be delighted if you would accept our invitation to present the awards at the Book Society's 5th annual awards dinner.
> ....
> ....
> Yours sincerely,
> Peter Van De Vere

1. What is the written information given?
   a a note
   b an invitation
   c an advertisement
2. What will the letter be about?
   a asking for more information
   b refusing invitation
   c accepting an invitation and asking for more information
3. Who are you writing to?
   a someone you know well
   b someone you've never met
   c a friend
4. Will your letter be formal/informal? Why?
5. What questions do you need to ask?

Analysing a Model Text

47 a. Read the letter and underline the questions Mrs Stephens asks. Has she included all the points?

> Dear Mr Van De Vere,
>
> Thank you for your kind invitation. I would be honoured to present the awards at the Book Society's 5th annual awards dinner. Unfortunately, you failed to mention a few important details.
>
> Firstly, I would be grateful if you could let me know the exact date of the event, so that I can rearrange my schedule. I assume that you are holding the event at the Regency Hotel in London, as you did last year. However, I would be grateful if you could let me know if the location has changed. I also need to know what time the event starts.
>
> In addition, I was wondering if it would be possible to bring my daughter as my guest. Finally, I would like to mention that I am a strict vegetarian, therefore I would be grateful if you could let me know whether there will be any vegetarian dishes on the menu.
>
> Thank you again for choosing me to host such a worthwhile event. I am looking forward to it immensely.
>
> Yours sincerely,
> *Jane Stephens*
> Jane Stephens

b. Answer the questions.

1. What is each paragraph about?
2. Find examples to suggest that the letter is formal.
3. Have any extra questions been asked?

Indirect Questions

48 a. Use the phrases to form indirect questions.

> - I would be grateful/appreciate it if ...
> - I was wondering if it would be possible (to/for) ...
> - Could you please let me know/tell me (if/whether) ...
> - I would like to know (if/whether) ...

1. Where is the awards ceremony?
   Could you please let me know where the awards ceremony will be held?
2. Where is my seat?
3. What time is the last train?
4. Should I bring my own supplies?
5. Can I park my car nearby?

b. Rewrite the formal indirect questions in other words, as in the example.

1. *Could you please let me know the location of the awards ceremony?*

Content analysis

49 a. Match the formal indirect questions with the type of letter, then change them to direct questions, as in the example.

1. ☐ Could you please let me know the whereabouts of the statue I ordered and paid for over a month ago?
2. ☐ I would like to know the price of front row seats.
3. ☐ We were wondering if you would be our guests at the concert next Saturday night.
4. ☐ We would be grateful if you would accept these backstage passes and signed CDs as compensation for any inconvenience you might have suffered.

A letter of apology
B letter of complaint
C letter requesting information
D letter of invitation

Where is the statue I ordered and paid for a month ago?

b. Which of the following closing remarks are appropriate for each type of letter? Which are formal?

Please write back soon with your answers.
I would like this matter to be resolved as soon as possible.
Hope you can come.
Please accept our sincere apologies once more.

Error Correction

50 Read the paragraph and correct the mistakes. (There are four mistakes.) What type of letter is it taken from?

> I was wondering if it can be possible for you to send me a copy of your calendar of events. Also, could you please let me to know whether you accept children under the age of 10? In addition, I would be appreciating it if you could say me if you offer any courses during the winter.

Discuss & Write

51 a. Read the rubric and extract below, then listen to the dialogue and complete the notes you have made.

> You have just received a letter informing you that you have won a competition. Write a letter to the competition organisers asking for the information you require.

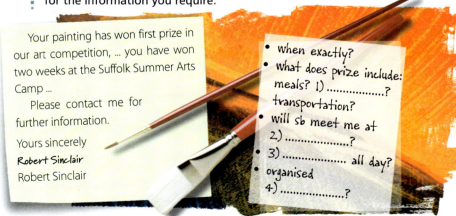

b. Change your notes into formal indirect questions.

Could you please let me know the exact dates of the camp?

c. Read the rubric again, then answer the questions in the plan.

Introduction
(Para 1) What are your opening remarks?
What is your reason for writing?

Main Body
(Paras 2-3) What questions do you have to ask?
Do you have any other questions to ask?

Conclusion
(Para 4) What are your closing remarks?

d. Which of the following are appropriate to begin/end your letter?

1 Dear + Sir/Madam,
   Yours faithfully,
2 Dear first name,
   Lots of love,
3 Dear Mr/Miss/Ms + last name,
   Yours sincerely,

52 Write your letter to the competition organisers using your answers from Ex. 51. You can use the letter in Ex. 47a as a model.

53 Try to explain these quotations in your own words.

- A room without books is like a body without a soul.
  Marcus Tullius Cicero (Roman statesman)
- A community needs news for the same reason that a man needs eyes. It has to see where it is going.
  Dame Rebecca West, (British author)
- TV is chewing gum for the eyes.
  Frank Lloyd Wright, (US architect)
- The public is like a piano. You just have to know what keys to poke.
  Al Capp (US cartoonist)

161

Self-Assessment Module 5

Vocabulary & Grammar

1 Fill in the missing word.

1. Earthquakes are .... disasters.
2. The arsonist was .... to twelve years in prison.
3. We play football on a football ....
4. I don't know if I will .... finished the report by noon.
5. He has been .... stamps since he was six years old.
6. If I had a computer, I .... play computer games in my free time.
7. .... the bad weather, they decided to go out.
8. There is a lot of demand .... the new computer game.
9. Bungee jumping is a ....-risk sport.
10. He is suspected .... stealing the car.
11. He isn't a professional tennis player. He's an ....
12. He couldn't get .... to living in such a cold country.
13. Bill isn't afraid to .... up for what he believes in.
14. The castle was surrounded .... a dense forest.
15. The competition is .... twice a year.
16. Players from all over the world .... in the Championship events, hoping to win a prize.
17. Tony and Jim both entered the competition, but .... of them were successful.
18. Daniel Defoe wrote many .... of fiction.
19. Who did you vote .... in the last election?
20. I think we should .... the road before it gets dark.

(10 marks)

2 Circle the correct item.

1. Huge waves were .... on the shore.
   A cracking B crashing C jumping D dropping
2. A basketball player must be .... so he can work with the other members of his team.
   A graceful   C courageous
   B competitive   D co-operative
3. The competitors all sing the .... anthem before the game starts.
   A state   C national
   B country   D countryside
4. I'll read about the economy in the .... section.
   A business B politics C health D education
5. If he .... the report on time, he wouldn't have to do overtime.
   A finished   C had been finished
   B had finished   D would have finished
6. The wind was .... hard.
   A rolling B blowing C rustling D roaring
7. Let's try and catch the waiter's .... so we can pay the bill.
   A ear B nose C hand D eye
8. That new game is really second to ....
   A nothing B no C zero D none
9. Sports Day is the .... of the school year.
   A focus B highlight C peak D feature
10. We .... some money to buy a new car.
    A set up   C set in
    B set to   D set aside

(10 marks)

Use of English

3 Complete the second sentence using the word in bold. You must use two to five words including the word given. Don't change the word given.

1. She didn't study enough so she failed the test.
   have She .... if she had studied enough.
2. I wish he hadn't misbehaved in class.
   rather I .... misbehaved in class.
3. He's tired of Ann's lies.
   fed He .... lies.
4. He was the only one who didn't call.
   apart Everyone.................................. him.
5. The book he is working on will be finished by the end of next month.
   have He .... book by the end of next month.

(5 marks)

4 Fill in the correct word derived from the word in bold.

1. Her house is .... decorated. **BEAUTIFUL**
2. "Friends" is my .... TV series. **FAVOUR**
3. He bought a .... camera last week. **DIGIT**
4. The .... of people enjoy watching soap operas. **MAJOR**
5. What's your .... of the story? **INTERPRET**

(5 marks)

Self-Assessment Module 5

5 Read the sentences. If a sentence is correct put a tick (✓). If it has a word which should not be there, write this word on the line.

1 "Three Men" is a great film. The ....
2 cast they are excellent and the ....
3 script is much clever. The plot has an ....
4 unexpected twist and the end is ....
5 rather surprising. Don't be miss it. ....

(5 marks)

Communication

6 Ask as many questions as possible to match the answers.

1 (cinema)? — Sorry, I can't make it. / Yeah, why not.
2 (new bike)? — No, really? / Are you sure?
3 (newspaper)? — Sure, go ahead. / Well, no.
4 (tennis)? — Thanks but no. / Why not?
5 (kayaking)? — Me too. / I don't.

(5 marks)

7 Write questions to complete the exchanges.

1 A: .... the window?
　 B: No, not at all.
2 A: .... a football match?
　 B: I'd love to.
3 A: .... Ms Johnson, please?
　 B: I'm afraid Ms Johnson isn't in her office at the moment.
4 A: .... Jenny won a trip to Italy!
　 B: Really! That's fantastic!
5 A: .... meet?
　 B: We could meet in front of the restaurant.

(5 marks)

Listening

8 🎧 You will hear a radio interview with an agent who represents musicians. For questions (1-5), choose the best answer A, B or C.

1 Peter has come on the show to talk about
　A the group U4.
　B the problems famous people have.
　C how to become famous.

2 Peter says that famous people
　A are always perfect.
　B can't have any privacy.
　C enjoy meeting people.

3 Overenthusiastic fans sometimes
　A ask for autographs.
　B break into the stars' houses.
　C put things into the stars' rubbish bins.

4 Famous people's children often
　A pretend to have friends.
　B want to get close to their teachers.
　C meet people who pretend to be their friends.

5 A famous person
　A can have financial problems.
　B has no privacy.
　C can suffer from a nervous breakdown.

(10 marks)

Speaking

9 In pairs, talk about how the people are feeling in each situation. Which photograph is the best image of success? Why?

(10 marks)

Self-Assessment Module 5

Reading

10 You are going to read an article about lightning. Choose the most suitable sentence from the list (A-H) to complete each gap (1-6) in the article. There is one extra sentence which you do not need to use. There is an example at the beginning.

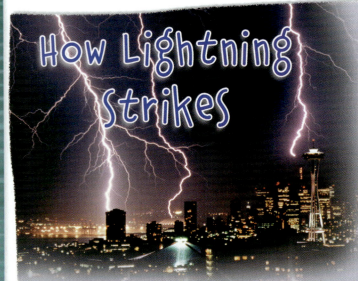

How Lightning Strikes

A thunderstorm is one of the most impressive sights in nature with huge menacing black clouds producing hot bright flashes of lightning and booming thunder as well as torrential rain or hail. But what causes these dramatic storms and what exactly are thunder and lightning?

Clouds are formed when a mass of cold air meets a mass of warm air. **0 F** Water vapour in the warm air condenses to form clouds. Thunder clouds are typically very tall, dark and deep. Thunder and lightning are both caused when electrical charges build up in these clouds. **1** However they believe that it has something to do with charged water droplets and tiny pieces of ice colliding inside the cloud. Normally a positively charged area forms in the upper region of the cloud and a negatively charged region forms in the lower region of the cloud.

These charges are incredibly large and so thunderstorms contain an enormous amount of energy. A voltage of more than 100 million volts can be generated between the cloud and the ground. **2** Air will not normally conduct electricity but when such huge voltages are generated, the resistance of the air breaks down. We get a sudden spark, called an electrical discharge, which can occur inside the cloud, between the cloud and the ground, or between two different clouds. **3** Because it is so powerful, lightning generates a lot of heat. A lightning strike can heat the air around it to more than 30,000 °C. That's five times hotter than the surface of the sun! The heat causes the air to expand incredibly quickly and we get the loud explosive sonic boom known as thunder.

So lightning and thunder are created at more or less the same time. If you have been caught in a thunder storm, though, you will know that we normally see the lightning first and then hear the thunder a few seconds later. **4** The light travels so quickly that it gets to us almost instantaneously but, in air, sound takes around three seconds to travel one kilometre. This means that if we count the number of seconds between seeing the lightning and hearing the thunder and divide by three we can find out how many kilometres away the storm is from us.

It can be very dangerous to be caught outside in a thunder storm. More than 100 people are killed by lightning strikes each year in the USA alone, and many more are seriously injured. If you do find yourself in this situation the safest thing to do is to crouch down close to the ground. **5** Lightning tends to strike at the highest point in an area so you are much more at risk near a tree, pole, or any other tall structure. You will be safer inside a metal-bodied car, or even better inside a building. If you are inside though, it is best not to take a shower or use the phone since lightning can strike phone lines or water pipes. Whatever you do, you shouldn't believe the saying that lightning never strikes the same place twice. **6** Scientists observing thunder storms have noticed that certain tall buildings or trees can be struck a number of times, even during a single storm.

A Whatever you do, don't take shelter under a tree.
B This flash of electricity is a lightning strike.
C In fact lightning can be attracted to the same spot over and over again.
D Compare that to the voltage of the electricity supply in your home which is only about 200 volts.
E This is why lightning has its distinctive forked shape.
F The warmer air is forced to rise quickly above the colder air.
G Scientists don't understand exactly how the charges are generated.
H This is because light travels faster than sound and so the light from the lightning reaches us before the sound from the thunder.

(15 marks)

Self-Assessment Module 5

Writing a letter to the editor

11 You read an article about a proposal to build a new cinema complex in your town. Write a letter to the editor expressing your support. (120-180 words)

Dear Sir,

Introduction
(Para 1)   *I am writing – recent article – proposed cinema complex – in my opinion – excellent idea – many advantages*

Main Body
(Para 2)   *many people – have the chance – watch new films when they are released – provide children and teenagers – somewhere to go at weekends*

(Para 3)   *provide many jobs – building, maintaining and running the complex – be of great benefit to the whole town*

Conclusion
(Para 4)   *wonderful idea – I hope – start building the complex – as soon as possible*

Yours faithfully,
(your full name)

(20 marks)
(Total = 100 marks)

Sing Along!

12 a. In pairs, talk about what is taking place in each of these pictures and decide whether these situations would make a good news story and why. Think about:

- where the event took place
- what kind of event each one was
- what happened next

b. What happened today? In pairs, talk about today's news headlines and how the events will affect your country.

c. Listen and fill in. Then, listen again and sing.

I've got the **1)** .... so bad
That I want the world to see
I'm going to tell you all about it
Are you **2)** .... to me?

I'm spreading the news
That I've got the blues
There's so many ways to tell you all
That I can pick and choose
Which method to use
When I'm spreading the news

You can read it in the **3)** ....
Or in a **4)** ....
You can see it in a **5)** ....
On your TV screen

I'm spreading the news ...

I'm going to send the **6)** .... an e-mail
To let everybody know
Then I'm going to give an **7)** ....
On the **8)** ....

I'm spreading the news ...

I've got to find a way
To make the world sit up and look
I'm going to **9)** .... my troubles
In an electronic **10)** ....

I'm spreading the news ...

Progress Update

How do you rate your progress? Tick (✓) the box that applies to you.

	Excellent ****	Good ***	OK **	Could do better *
Vocabulary & Grammar				
Listening				
Speaking				
Reading				
Writing				
Communication				

Grammar Reference

Unit 1

Present Simple and Present Continuous

We use the present simple for:
- facts and permanent states. *Frank **works** for an insurance company.*
- general truths and laws of nature. *Oil floats on water.*
- habits and routines (with **always**, **usually** etc). *She usually **goes** to the supermarket on Thursdays.*
- timetables and programmes (in the future). *His flight **arrives** at six o'clock tomorrow morning.*
- sporting commentaries, reviews and narrations. *Beckham **wins** the ball, **crosses** and Owen **scores**.*
- feelings and emotions. *I **love** Venice, it's a beautiful city.*

The time expressions we use with the present simple are: *Usually, often, always, every day/week/month/year etc, in the morning/afternoon/evening, at night/the weekend, on Fridays, etc*

We use the present continuous (to be + verb -ing):
- for actions taking place at or around the moment of speaking. *The kids **are watching** a video in the living room.*
- for temporary situations. *We **are decorating** the kitchen this week.*
- for fixed arrangements in the near future. *I**'m going** to a party at Jack's house tonight.*
- for currently changing and developing situations. *The sea **is becoming** more and more polluted.*
- with adverbs such as always to express anger or irritation at a repeated action. *She **is** always **talking** on the phone when I want to use it.*

The time expressions we use with the present continuous are: *Now, at the moment, at present, these days, nowadays, still, today, tonight, etc*

State Verbs

Stative verbs are verbs which describe a state rather than an action, and so do not usually have a continuous tense. These verbs are:
- verbs of the senses (**see, hear, smell, taste, feel, look, sound, seem, appear** etc) *The material **feels** really soft.*
- verbs of perception (**know, believe, understand, realise, remember, forget** etc) *I **know** exactly what she means.*
- verbs which express feelings and emotions (**like, love, hate, enjoy, prefer, detest, desire, want** etc) *Helen **enjoys** going to the theatre.*
- and some other verbs (**be, contain, include, belong, fit, need, matter, cost, own, want, owe, weigh, wish, have, keep** etc) *That jumper she bought me **doesn't fit** very well.*

Some of these verbs can be used in continuous tenses but with a difference in meaning.

Present Simple	Present Continuous
THINK *I **think** she's a very good teacher.* (= believe)	*We **are thinking** about going on holiday.* (= are considering)
HAVE *He **has** hundreds of CDs.* (= own, possess)	*I **am having** a great time.* (= experiencing) *She **is having** a shower.* (= taking) *We **are having** dinner.* (= eating)
SEE *I can **see** our house from up here.* (= it is visible) *I **see** what you mean.* (= understand)	*I'm **seeing** the optician at ten o'clock.* (= am meeting)
TASTE *The dessert **tastes** delicious.* (= it is, has the flavour of)	*Bill **is tasting** the curry to see if it is spicy enough.* (= is testing)
SMELL *The food **smells** very good.* (= has the aroma)	*She **is smelling** the flowers.* (= is sniffing)
APPEAR *He **appears** to know what he's doing.* (= seems to be)	*She **is appearing** in a play at the Grand.* (= is performing)
FIT *The dress **fits** her perfectly.* (= it's the right size)	*Mike **is fitting** a new lock on the door.* (= is attaching)

Note:
- The verb enjoy can be used in continuous tenses to express a specific preference.
  *Doug really **enjoys** going to the theatre.* (general preference)
  BUT: *She's **enjoying** the party very much.* (specific preference)
- The verbs **look** (when we refer to somebody's appearance), **feel** (experience a particular emotion), **hurt** and **ache** can be used in simple or continuous tenses with no difference in meaning.
  I feel very happy. = *I am feeling very happy.*

Adverbs of Frequency

These include **always, frequently, often, once, twice, sometimes, never, usually, ever, hardly ever, rarely, occasionally** etc.
- Adverbs of frequency are normally placed before the main verb. *I rarely drive to work. I hardly ever go to the theatre.*

Grammar Reference

- However, adverbs of frequency are placed after the verb to be and after auxiliary verbs. *Janet is often late for meetings. I have always wanted to go to Cuba.*

Present Perfect

We use the present perfect (have + past participle) for:
- an action that happened at an unstated time in the past. The emphasis is on the action, the time that it occurred is unimportant or unknown. *I **have washed** the car. Mary **has been** to Italy twice.*
- an action which started in the past and continues up to the present, especially with stative verbs (see above) such as **be, have, like, know**, etc. *I **have known** her for six years.*
- a recently completed action. *I **have finished** my geography essay.*
- personal experiences or changes. *She **has dyed** her hair.*

> The time expressions we use with the present perfect are: *for, since, already, always, just, ever, never, so far, today, this week/month etc, how long, lately, recently, still (in negations), etc*

Present Perfect Continuous

We use the present perfect continuous (have + been + verb -ing):
- to put emphasis on the duration of an action which started in the past and continues up to the present. *We **have been cleaning** the house all morning.*
- for an action which started in the past and lasted for some time. It may still be continuing or has finished already with the result visible in the present. *He's tired because he **has been working** really hard recently.*
- to express anger, irritation, or annoyance. *She **has been using** my computer without asking me.*
- for repeated actions in the past continuing to the present. *She has lost weight because she **has been going** to the gym every night after work.*

> The time expressions we use with the present perfect continuous are: *for, since, how long ...?, all day/morning/month etc, lately, recently*

Note: with the verbs **live, work, teach** and **feel** we can use the present perfect or the present perfect continuous with no difference in meaning. *He **has lived/has been living** in Liverpool for the last five years.*

Prepositions of Place

Prepositions of place are prepositions which describe where someone or something is. These prepositions include:

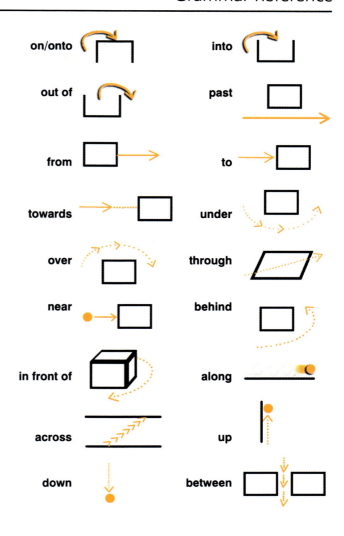

Unit 2

Past Simple

We use the past simple:
- for an action that occurred at a definite time (stated or implied) in the past. *The postman **delivered** the parcel at 8 o'clock this morning.*
- for actions that happened immediately after one another in the past. *She **opened** the curtains and **looked** out of the window.*
- for habits or states which are now finished. *Mr Jones **worked** in a factory when he was younger.*
  Note that **used to** can also be used instead of the past simple for habits/repeated actions in the past (see p. 168).

> The time expressions we use with the past simple are: *yesterday, then, when, How long ago ...?, last night/week/month/year/Friday/October etc, three days/weeks etc ago, in 1999 etc*

167

Grammar Reference

Past Continuous

We use the past continuous:

- for an action which was in progress when another action interrupted it. We use the past continuous for the action in progress (the longer action) and the past simple for the action which interrupted it (shorter action). *We **were playing** football in the garden when it started to rain.*
- for two or more simultaneous actions in the past. *I **was cooking** dinner in the kitchen while Mary **was watching** TV in the living room.*
- for an action which was in progress at a stated time in the past. We don't mention when the action started or finished. *At 11 o'clock last night I **was driving** home from the party.*
- to describe the atmosphere, setting etc and to give background information to a story. *The birds **were singing** and the sun **was shining**, I **was sitting** outside in the garden when something strange happened ...*

Note: When there are two past continuous forms in a sentence with the same subject we can avoid repetition by just using the present participle (-ing form) and leave out the verb to be. *He was walking along, he was whistling a tune. = He was walking along, whistling a tune.*

The time expressions we use with the past continuous are: *while, when, as, all morning/evening/day/week etc*

Past Perfect

We use the past perfect (had + past participle):

- for an action which happened before another past action or before a stated time in the past. *Lucy **had finished** her homework by six o'clock.*
- for an action which finished in the past and whose result was visible at a later point in the past. *He **had sprained** his ankle a few days earlier and he was still limping slightly.*
- for a general situation in the past. *Everything **had seemed** normal at first.*

The time expressions we use with the past perfect are: *before, after, already, just, for, since, till/until, when, by the time, never etc*

Past Perfect Continuous

We use the past perfect continuous:

- to put emphasis on the duration of an action which started and finished in the past, before another action or stated time in the past, usually with for or since. *I **had been walking** for about half an hour when I realised I was completely lost.*
- for an action which lasted for some time in the past and whose result was visible in the past. *She **had been swimming** and her hair was still wet.*

The time expressions we use with the past perfect continuous are: *for, since, how long, before, until etc*

Used to

We use **used to** + infinitive to refer to past habits or states. In such cases **used to** can be replaced by the past simple with no change in meaning. *When the children were younger they **walked/used to walk** to school every day.*

But for an action that happened at a definite time in the past we use the **past simple** not **used to**. *I walked to work yesterday.* (NOT: ~~I used to walk to work yesterday.~~)

Time expressions to talk about the past:

ago	(= back in time from now) is used with the past simple *I finished work about an hour ago.*
since	(= from a starting point in the past) is used with the present perfect (simple and continuous) *I haven't seen Rick since he got married.*
for	(=over a period of time) is used with the present perfect (simple and continuous) *They've been playing that computer game for hours.*
already	is used in statements and questions (to show surprise) *I have already spoken to Nick. Have you finished your essay already?*
yet	is used with the present perfect in questions and negations. *Have you paid the rent yet? I haven't finished eating yet.*

Unit 3

Future Simple

We use the future simple (will + bare infinitive) for:

- decisions made at the moment of speaking. *It's hot in here, I**'ll open** a window.*
- predictions about the future, based on what we think, believe or imagine, using the verbs **think, believe, expect** etc, the expressions **be sure, be afraid** etc, and the adverbs **probably, certainly, perhaps** etc. *He **will probably** call you later.*
- promises, threats, warnings, requests, hopes, and offers. ***Will** you **help** me clean up this mess?*
- actions, events, situations which will definitely happen in the future and which we can't control. *Sue **will be** three years old in June.*

Grammar Reference

Be going to

We use **be going to**:
- for plans, intentions or ambitions for the future. *I'm going to be a doctor when I finish university.*
- actions we have already decided to do in the near future. *Steve is going to work with his dad during the summer holidays.*
- predictions based on what we can see or what we know, especially when there is evidence that something will happen. *The sky is very clear, it's going to be cold tonight.*

The time expressions we use with the future simple and **be going to** are: *tomorrow, the day after tomorrow, tonight, soon, next week/month/year/summer etc, in a week/month etc*

Future Continuous

We use the future continuous (will be + present participle of the verb):
- for actions which will be in progress at a stated future time. *I've got a new job, this time next month I'll be working in the bank.*
- for actions which will definitely happen in the future as the result of a routine or arrangement. *I will be visiting my grandparents at the weekend.*
- when we ask politely about someone's plans for the near future. *Will you be finishing with that book soon?*

For future perfect and future perfect continuous see unit 10.

Time clauses when talking about the future:

When we are using the **present simple** or **present perfect**, but NOT future forms, we use words and expressions such as *while, before, after, until/till, as, when, whenever, once, as soon as, as long as, by the time*, etc to introduce time clauses. *By the time we get there the film will have started.* (NOT: *By the time we will get there ...*)

We also use the **present simple** and **present perfect** but NOT future forms after words and expressions such as *unless, if, suppose/supposing, in case* etc. *Take an umbrella in case it rains later.* (NOT: *... in case it will rain later.*)

We use **future forms** with:
- **when** - when it is used as a question word. *When will you be going shopping next?*
- **if/whether** – after expressions which show uncertainty/ignorance etc, such as *I don't know, I doubt, I wonder, I'm not sure*, etc. *I don't know whether he will get the job.*

Type 0/1 Conditionals

Type 0 conditionals are used to express a general truth or a scientific fact. In this type of conditional we can use **when** instead of **if**.

If-clause	Main Clause
If/when + present simple →	present simple
If/When you mix red and yellow paint, you get orange.	

Type 1 conditionals are used to express a real or very probable situation in the present or future.

If-clause	Main Clause
If + present simple →	future simple, imperative, can/must/may etc + bare infinitive
If I finish this essay tonight, I will/might/etc go to the cinema with Julie.	

When the hypothesis comes before the main clause, we separate them with a comma. When the main clause comes before the if-clause, then we do not use a comma to separate them.

Note: With type 1 conditionals we can use **unless + affirmative verb** (= if + negative verb). *I will not be able to come unless Jack gives me a lift.* (= if Jack does not give me a lift, ...)

Clauses of purpose

Clauses of purpose are used to explain why somebody does something. They are introduced with the following words/expressions.

- **to - infinitive** – *Colin went to the library to borrow a book.*
- **in order to/so as to + infinitive** (formal) – *The boss requested that everyone work overtime in order to finish the project on time.*
- **so that + can/will** (present/future reference) – *I will give you my number so that you can call me if there are any problems.*
- **so that + could/would** (past reference) – *He left at 5 o'clock, so that he would be at the airport in plenty of time.*
- **in case + present tense** (present or future reference) – *Leave the answer machine on in case anyone calls when we are out.*
- **in case + past tense** (past reference) – *She had made some sandwiches in case we got hungry.*
  Note: **In case** is never used with **will** or **would**.
- **for + noun** (expresses the purpose of an action) – *We went to Marco's for a pizza.*
- **for + -ing form** (expresses the purpose of something or its function) – *Microwaves are used for heating up food.*
- **with a view to + -ing form** – *The Wilson's bought the old farmhouse with a view to renovating it.*

We can express **negative purpose** by:
- **in order not to/so as not to + infinitive** – *I wrote a list of the things I had to do so as not to forget anything.*
- **prevent + noun/pronoun + (from) + -ing form** – *The teacher covered up what was written on the board to prevent the students from reading it.*

169

Grammar Reference

The definite article *the*

We use **the**:

- with nouns when talking about something specific. *Jo owns a car and a motorbike.* **The** *car is blue and* **the** *motorbike is red.*
- with nouns that are unique. (**the** *sun,* **the** *Earth etc*)
- with names of newspapers (**the** *Times*), cinemas (**the** *Odeon*), theatres (**the** *Empire*), museums/art galleries (**the** *Louvre*), ships (**the** *Titanic*), organisations (**the** *United Nations*).
- with the names of rivers (**the** *Thames*), groups of islands (**the** *Seychelles*), mountain ranges (**the** *Pyrenees*), deserts (**the** *Kalahari*), oceans (**the** *Pacific*) canals (**the** *Panama canal*), countries when they include words such as States, Kingdom, Republic (**the** *USA*), and names or nouns with of (**the** *Houses of Parliament*), in geographical terms such as **the** *Antarctic/Arctic/equator,* **the** *North of Spain,* **the** *North/East/South/West.*
- with the names of musical instruments and dances (**the** *piano,* **the** *tango*).
- with the names of families (**the** *Smiths*) and nationalities ending in **-sh**, **-ch**, or **-ese** (**the** *Chinese*). Other nationalities can be used with or without the (**the** *Egyptians/Egyptians*).
- with titles (**the** *ambassador,* **the** *President*) but not with titles including a proper name (*Prince Charles*).
- with adjectives/adverbs in the superlative form (**the** *best book I have ever read*) but when most is followed by a noun it doesn't take the (*most people enjoy going to the cinema*).
- with the words **day, morning, afternoon** and **evening**. *It was late in* **the** *afternoon and the sun was starting to set.* BUT: **at night, at noon, at midnight, by day/night**
- with historical periods/events (*the last Ice Age, the Vietnam war*) BUT: **World War I**
- with the words **only, last** and **first** (used as adjectives). *She was* **the** *only one who understood me.*
- with the words **station, cinema, theatre, library, shop, coast, sea(side), beach, country(side), city, jungle, world, ground, weather.** *We went for a drive along* **the** *coast.*

We do not use **the**:

- with uncountable and plural nouns when talking about something in general. **Cars** *release harmful gases into the atmosphere.* **Coffee** *is a very popular drink.*
- with proper nouns. **Harry** *works in a bookshop.*
- with the names of sports, games, activities, days, months, celebrations, colours, drinks and meals. *We are going to have* **dinner** *on* **Monday**.
- with languages unless they are followed by the word **language**. *Veronica speaks* **Spanish, Italian** *and* **English** *fluently.* BUT: **The French language** *is spoken in parts of Canada.*
- with the names of countries which don't include the word **State, Kingdom** or **Republic**. *Germany, India, Australia.* BUT there are some exceptions: **the Netherlands, the Gambia, the Vatican.**
- with the names of streets (*Oxford Street, Penny Lane* BUT: **the M6, the A42**), squares (*Trafalgar Square*), bridges (*London Bridge* BUT: **the Golden Gate Bridge**), parks (*Central Park*), railway stations (*Euston, King's Cross*), mountains (*Mount Everest*), individual islands (*Sardinia*), lakes (*Lake Windermere*) and continents (*Africa*).
- with possessive adjectives or the possessive case. *That is* **my car**.
- with the names of restaurants, shops, banks, hotels etc which are named after the people who started them (**Harrods, Luigi's Restaurant**).
- with the words **bed, hospital, college, court, prison, school, university** when we refer to the purpose for which they exist. *The injured girl had to be taken to* **hospital**. BUT: *We went to* **the hospital** *to visit Tina.*
- with the word **work** (= place of work). *I need to be at* **work** *by 10 o'clock.*
- with the words **home, mother, father** etc when we talk about our own home/parents.
- with **by** + means of transport (*by bus/ferry/train/car etc*) *They travelled to Glasgow* **by train**.
- with the names of illnesses. *He's got* **pneumonia**. BUT: flu/**the flu**, measles/**the measles**, mumps/**the mumps**.

Unit 4

Infinitive

The **to-infinitive** is used:

- to express purpose. *Carl called* **to talk** *about our plans for tomorrow.*
- after certain verbs (agree, appear, decide, expect, hope, plan, promise, refuse, etc). *They expect* **to finish** *the building work this afternoon.*
- after **would like, would prefer, would love** etc to express a specific preference. *I would prefer* **to go** *out for dinner tonight.*
- after adjectives which describe feelings/emotions (happy, sad, glad, etc); express willingness/unwillingness (willing, eager, reluctant etc); refer to a person's character (clever, kind etc) and the adjectives lucky and fortunate. *I was very sad* **to hear** *that Carol had lost her job.* Note: With adjectives that refer to character we can also use an impersonal construction. *It was kind of you* **to help** *Andrea with her essay.*
- after **too/enough**. *It isn't warm* **enough to go** *out without a coat.*
- to talk about an unexpected event usually with **only**. *I finally arrived at the airport* **only to find** *that my flight had been cancelled.*
- with **it + be + adjective/noun**. **It was easy to find** *the house after all.*
- after **be + first/second/next/last** etc. *She* **was the first person to congratulate** *me after the game was over.*
- after verbs and expressions such as **ask, learn, explain, decide, find out, want, want to know** etc when they are followed by a question word. *The maths teacher* **explained how to solve** *the problem.*

Grammar Reference

Note: **why** is followed by **subject + verb**, NOT an infinitive. *I wonder **why she didn't tell** us.*
- in the expressions **to tell you the truth, to be honest, to sum up, to begin with** etc. ***To tell you the truth** I didn't expect that you would come.*

Note: If two **to-infinitives** are linked by **and** or **or** the **to** of the second infinitive can be omitted. *I would like **to go and see** what is happening for myself.*

The **infinitive without to** is used:
- after modal verbs. *Beth **can speak** German and Italian.*
- after the verbs **let, make, see, hear,** and **feel**. *They made him fill out a lot of forms.* BUT: we use the **to-infinitive** after **be made, be heard, be seen** etc (passive form). *He **was made to fill** out a lot of forms.*
Note: When **see, hear** and **watch** are followed by an **-ing form** there is no change in the passive. *He **saw me talking** to Anna. I **was seen talking** to Anna.*
- after **had better** and **would rather**. *We **had better take** the train because the traffic is very bad at the moment.*
- **help** can be followed by either the **to-infinitive** or the **infinitive without to**. *She **helped** me **(to) choose** the carpet for the living room.*

-ing form

The **-ing form** is used:
- as a noun. ***Smoking** is very bad for your health.*
- after certain verbs: **admit, appreciate, avoid, continue, deny, fancy, go** (for activities), **imagine, mind, miss, quit, save, suggest, practise, consider, prevent**. *Can you **imagine winning** the lottery?*
- after **love, like, enjoy, prefer, dislike, hate** to express general preference. *Jamie **enjoys talking** to his friends on the phone.* BUT: for a specific preference (would like/ would prefer/would love) we use a **to-infinitive**.
- after expressions such as **be busy, it's no use, it's (no) good, it's (not) worth, what's the use of, can't help, there's no point in, can't stand, have difficulty (in), have trouble** etc. ***There is no point in talking** to the boss about it, he never listens to us.*
- after **spend, waste,** or **lose** (time, money, etc). *He **spent** a lot of time and money **repairing** his car.*
- after the preposition **to** with verbs and expressions such as **look forward to, be used to, in addition to, object to, prefer** (*doing sth to sth else*). *He **prefers swimming to playing** football.*
- after other prepositions. *He was thinking **of quitting** his job.*
- after the verbs **hear, listen to, notice, see, watch,** and **feel** to describe an incomplete action. *I **heard** Nicky **talking** to Chris. (I only heard part of the conversation.)* BUT: we use the **infinitive without to** with **hear, listen to, notice, see, watch,** and **feel** to describe the complete action. *I **heard** Nicky **tell** the story. (I heard the whole story.)*

Difference in meaning between the **to-infinitive** and **-ing form**

Some verbs can take either the **to-infinitive** or the **-ing form** with a change in meaning.

- **forget + to-infinitive** = not remember – *He **forgot to lock** the door.*
  forget + -ing form = not recall – *I'll never **forget travelling** around India.*
- **remember + to infinitive** = not forget – *Did you **remember to turn** off all the lights?*
  remember + -ing form = recall – *I **remember talking** to Jane at the party.*
- **mean + to-infinitive** = intend to – *I'm sorry I never **meant to upset** you.*
  mean + -ing form = involve – *If I get this job I'm afraid it will **mean moving** nearer to the city centre.*
- **regret + to-infinitive** = be sorry to (normally used in the present simple with verbs such as **say, tell, inform**) – *We **regret to inform** passengers that the British Airways flight to Heathrow has been cancelled.*
  regret + -ing form = feel sorry about – *I **regret losing** touch with my old friend Stuart.*
- **try + to-infinitive** = do one's best, attempt – *She **tried to call** you but she couldn't get through.*
  try + -ing form = do something as an experiment – *Why don't you **try changing** the batteries?*
- **stop + to-infinitive** = stop temporarily in order to do something else – *After a couple of hours we **stopped to have** a rest.*
  stop + -ing form = finish doing something – *At five o'clock everyone **stopped working** and went home.*

Comparisons

As / Like

We use **like**:
- with nouns/pronouns/-ing form to express similarity. *She treats him **like a servant**. (He isn't a servant.)*
- with **feel, look, smell, taste**. *He **looks like** his brother.*

We use **as**:
- to say what somebody or something really is. *He works **as a personnel manager** for that accounting firm.*

Comparatives and Superlatives

We use the **comparative** to compare one person or thing with another. We use the **superlative** to compare one person or thing with more than one person or thing of the same group. We often use **than** after a comparative and **the** before a superlative. *He is **older than** me. He's **the oldest** person in the room.*

Formation of comparatives and superlatives from adjectives and adverbs:
- with one-syllable adjectives, add **-(e)r** to form the comparative and **-(e)st** to form the superlative.
  *close – clos**er** – clos**est***
  Note: for one syllable adjectives ending in **a vowel + a consonant**, we double the consonant.
  *big – big**ger** – big**gest***

171

Grammar Reference

- with two-syllable adjectives ending in **-ly, -y, -w**, also add **-er / -est**. *narrow – narrower – narrowest*
  Note: for adjectives ending in **a consonant + y** we replace the **-y** with an **-i**. *tiny – tinier – tiniest*
- with other two-syllable adjectives or adjectives with more than two syllables, comparatives and superlatives are formed with **more/most**.
  *intelligent – **more** intelligent – **most** intelligent*
- with adverbs that have the same form as their adjectives we add **-er/-est**. *hard – harder – hardest*
- two-syllable or compound adverbs take **more/most**.
  *slowly – **more** slowly – **most** slowly*
  Note: **clever, common, cruel, friendly, gentle, pleasant, polite, shallow, simple, stupid, quiet** can form their comparatives and superlatives either with **-er/-est** or with **more/most**
- Irregular forms:
  good – better – best / bad – worse – worst / much – more – most / little – less – least / far – farther/further – farthest/furthest / many/lots – more – most

Types of comparisons:

- **as + adjective + as** (to show that two people or things are similar in some way) In negative sentences we use **not as/so ... as**. *The blue skirt is **as expensive as** the red one.*
- **less + adjective + than** (expresses the difference between two people or things) The opposite is **more ... than**. *Paul is **less successful than** his brother.*
- **the least + adjective + of/in** (compares one person or thing to two or more people or things in the same group. The opposite is **most ... of/in**. *She is **the least ambitious** person in the company.*
- **much/a lot/far/a little/a bit/slightly + comparative** (expresses the degree of difference between two people or things) *Brian is **slightly older than** Claire.*
- **comparative** and **comparative** to show that something is increasing or decreasing *The traffic gets **worse and worse** every day.*
- **the + comparative ..., the + comparative** (shows that two things change together or that one thing depends on another thing) ***The longer** the day went on, **the more** tired she became.*
- **by far + the + superlative** (emphasises the difference between one person or thing and two or more people or things in the same group) *Last year was **by far the best** the company has ever had.*

Unit 5

Present/Past Participles

We use **present participles** to describe something. *It was a **boring** lecture.* (How was the lecture? Boring.)

We use **past participles** to say how someone felt. *We were **bored**.* (How did we feel? Bored.)

Logical Assumptions/Deductions

Must: Sure/Certain that sth is true.
Must is used in affirmative sentences and expresses positive logical beliefs. *You've been travelling all day, you **must** be exhausted!*

Can't/couldn't: Certain that sth is not true/real.
Can't and **couldn't** are used in negations and express negative logical assumptions. *That **can't** be Jason, he's on holiday in Spain at the moment.*

Possibility

Can + present infinitive: General possibility, sth theoretically possible. Not used for a specific situation. *For the main course you **can have** pasta or pizza.*

Could/May/Might + present infinitive: It is possible/likely, perhaps. Used to show sth is possible in a specific situation. *You should keep that picture, it **may be** valuable one day.*
Note: we can use **can/could/might** in questions BUT NOT **may**. *Do you think that you **can/could/might** fix it?*

Could/Might/Would + perfect infinitive: Refers to the past, sth that was possible but didn't happen. *She **might have** passed the exam if she had studied harder.*

Obligation/Duty/Necessity

Must: Expresses duty, strong obligation to do sth. Sth is essential. We generally use **must** when the speaker has decided that sth is necessary. *I **must** pay the electricity bill today.*

Have to: Expresses strong necessity/obligation. We usually use **have to** when somebody other than the speaker has decided that sth is necessary. *The teacher said we **have to** hand our homework in tomorrow.*
Note: **Must** and **have to** have different meanings in questions. *Do I **have to** wash the car now? (Is it necessary for me ...?) **Must** I wash the car now? (Do you insist that I ... ?)*

Should/Ought to: Express duty, weak obligation. These are less emphatic than **must/ have to**. *We **should** redecorate the living room soon.*

Need: It is necessary to. ***Need** I apply for the job in writing?*
Note: **Need** can be used as a modal verb or as a main verb with no change in meaning. ***Need** I finish the report today? (Do I need to finish the report today?)*

Absence of necessity

Needn't/Don't have to/Don't need to + present infinitive: It isn't necessary to do sth (in the present/future). *You **don't need to** take the dog for a walk, I will do it.*

Didn't need to/Didn't have to: It wasn't necessary to do sth. We don't know if it was done or not. *She **didn't need to/have to** pay the whole amount today. (We don't know if she paid it or not.)*

Grammar Reference

Needn't + bare perfect infinitive: It was not necessary to do sth but it was done. *You **needn't have typed** the whole thing again it was saved on the computer. (You did type it all.)*

Prohibition

Mustn't/Can't: It is forbidden to do sth; it is against the rules/law; you are not allowed to do sth. *You **mustn't/can't** drive if you haven't got a licence.*

Criticism

Could/Should/Might/Ought to/ + perfect infinitive: Used to criticise someone's actions or lack of action (in the past). It would have been better if you had ... (past). *They **could have thanked** me for everything I've done for them.*

Question Tags

- **Question tags** are formed with an auxiliary verb and the appropriate personal pronoun. They take the same auxiliary as in the statement or, if there isn't an auxiliary in the statement they take **do/does** (present simple) or **did** (past simple).
- After affirmative statements we use a negative interrogative tag and after negative statements we use an ordinary interrogative tag.
  He works in the bank, doesn't he?
  She couldn't remember his phone number, could she?
  Note:
  Let's has the tag **shall we?** – ***Let's** put some music on, **shall we**?*
  Let me/him has the tag **will you/won't you?** – *You'll **let me** borrow this shirt, **won't you**?*
  I have (possess) has the tag **haven't I?** BUT **I have** (used idiomatically) has the tag **don't I?** – ***He has** a blue car, **hasn't he**? Last week **he had** a cold, **didn't he**?*
  This/That is has the tag **isn't it?** – ***This** restaurant is very cheap, **isn't it**?*
  I am has the tag **aren't I?** – ***I am** late **aren't I**?*
  A negative imperative has the question tag **will you?** – ***Don't** tell anyone, **will you**?*

Unit 6

The Passive

We form the passive with the verb **to be** in the appropriate tense and the **past participle** of the main verb. Only transitive verbs (verbs which take an object) can be used in the passive. (*live* does not have a passive form).

We use the passive:

- when the person or people who do the action are unknown, unimportant or obvious from the context. *Jim's bike was stolen. (We don't know who stole it.) The house is being redecorated. (It's unimportant who is doing it.) The thief has been arrested. (It's obvious that the police arrested him.)*
- when the action itself is more important than the person/people who do it, as in news headlines, newspaper articles, formal notices, advertisements, instructions, processes etc. *The annual general meeting will be held on June 25th.*
- when we want to avoid taking responsibility for an action or when we refer to an unpleasant event and we do not want to say who or what is to blame. *Three people were seriously injured in the accident.*

Changing from the active to the passive:

- the **object** of the active sentence becomes the **subject** in the passive sentence
- the active verb remains in the same tense but changes into a passive form
- the **subject** of the active sentence becomes the **agent**, and is either introduced with the preposition **by** or is omitted.

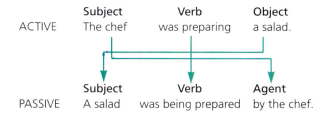

- Only transitive verbs (verbs that take an object) can be changed into the passive. **Active:** *Jackie lives on the third floor (intransitive verb)* **no passive form:** ~~*The third floor is lived on by Jackie.*~~
  Note: Some transitive verbs (*have, exist, seem, fit, suit, resemble, lack* etc) cannot be changed into the passive. *Rick has a red jumper.* **NOT:** ~~*A red jumper is had by Rick.*~~
- we can use the verb to get instead of the verb to be in everyday speech when we talk about things that happen by accident or unexpectedly. *He got injured when he was playing rugby. (Instead of he was injured…)*
- **By + the agent** is used to say who or what carries out an action. **with + instrument/material/ingredient** is used to say what the agent used. *The pasta sauce was made **by** Tony. It was made **with** fresh tomatoes from the garden.*
- The agent can be omitted when the subject is they, he, someone/somebody, people, one, etc. *Somebody has cleaned the car. = The car has been cleaned.*
- The agent is not omitted when it is a specific or important person, or when it is essential to the meaning of the sentence. *The film was directed by David Lynch.*
- With verbs which can take two objects such as *bring, tell, send, show, teach, promise, buy, sell, read, offer, give, lend,* etc, we can form two different passive sentences.
  Lucy gave the letter to me. (active)
  I was given the letter by Lucy. (passive, more usual)
  The letter was given to me by Lucy. (passive, less usual)
- If in an active sentence a preposition follows a verb, then in the passive it is placed immediately after the verb. *The ball **hit** Charlie **on** the head. Charlie was **hit on** the head by the ball.*

Grammar Reference

- The verbs **hear, help, see,** and **make** are followed by the bare infinitive in the active but by the to-infinitive in the passive. *Tina's mum **made** her clean her room. Tina **was made to** clean her room by her mum.*
- **Let** becomes be allowed to in the passive. *The teacher let the children leave early. The children **were allowed** to leave early.*
- To ask questions in the passive we follow the same rules as for statements, keeping in mind that the verb is in the interrogative form. *Have they opened the new shopping centre yet? Has the new shopping centre been opened (by them) yet?*
- When we want to find out who or what performed an action, the passive question form is **Who/What … by?** *Who was the book written by?*

Relative Clauses

Relative clauses are introduced with either a **relative pronoun** or a **relative adverb**.

Relative Pronouns

We use:
i. **who(m)/that** to refer to people.
ii. **which/that** to refer to things.
iii. **whose** with people, animals and objects to show possession (instead of a possessive adjective).

- **Who, which,** and **that** can be omitted when they are the object of the relative clause. *He's the person (who) I am going to be working for.*
- **Whom** can be used instead of **who** when it is the object of the relative clause. **Whom** is always used instead of **who** or that after a preposition. *That's the girl to whom Rob was speaking at the party last night.*
- **Who, which,** or **that** is not omitted when it is the subject of a relative clause. *The woman who owns that restaurant is French.*
- **Whose** is never omitted. *That's the man whose son had the accident.*

Relative adverbs

We use:
i. **when/that** to refer to a time (and can be omitted) *That was the year **(when/that)** we finished school.*
ii. **where** to refer to a place. *The hospital **where** I was born is closing down.*
iii. **why** to give a reason, usually after the word reason (why can be omitted). *The reason **(why)** he did this is still not clear.*

Identifying and Non-Identifying Relative Clauses

An identifying relative clause gives necessary information essential to the meaning of the main sentence. It is not put in commas and is introduced with **who, which, that, whose, where, when,** or the **reason (why)**. *The man **who** sold me the car said it had never broken down.*

A non-identifying relative clause gives extra information and is not essential to the meaning of the main sentence. It is put in commas and is introduced with **who, whom, which, whose, where,** or **when**. *The man, who was very persuasive, sold me the car for £1000.*

Unit 7

Causative form

- we use **have + object + past participle** to say that we have arranged for someone to do something for us. The past participle has a passive meaning. *Jackie **had her jacket cleaned** at the dry cleaner's.* (She didn't clean it herself.)
- Questions and negations of the verb **have** are formed with **do/does** (present simple) or **did** (past simple). *Did you **have** the photographs developed yesterday?*
- We also use **have something done** to talk about an unpleasant experience that somebody had. *Last night Neil **had** his mobile phone **stolen**.* (= his phone was stolen)
- We can use the verb **get** instead of **have** in informal conversation. *I'm going to **get** a new lock fitted on the front door.*

Note: The word order is very important. **Tony had his car repaired** and **Tony had repaired his car** have very different meanings. In the first case Tony arranged for someone else to do the repairs whereas in the second case he carried out the repairs himself.

	Regular active form	Causative form
Present Simple	She **washes** the windows.	She **has** the windows **washed**.
Present Continuous	She **is washing** the windows.	She **is having** the windows **washed**.
Past Simple	She **washed** the windows.	She **had** the windows **washed**.
Past Continuous	She **was washing** the windows.	She **was having** the windows **washed**.
Future Simple	She **will wash** the windows.	She **will have** the windows **washed**.
Future Continuous	She **will be washing** the windows.	She **will be having** the windows **washed**.
Present Perfect	She **has washed** the windows.	She **has had** the windows **washed**.
Present Perfect Continuous	She **has been washing** the windows.	She **has been having** the windows **washed**.
Past Perfect	She **had washed** the windows.	She **had had** the windows **washed**.
Past Perfect Continuous	She **had been washing** the windows.	She **had been having** the windows **washed**.
Infinitive	She should **wash** the windows.	She should **have** the windows **washed**.
-ing form	It's worth **washing** the windows.	It's worth **having** the windows **washed**.

Grammar Reference

Reported Speech - Statements

Reported speech is the exact meaning of what someone said, but not the exact words. We do not use quotation marks. The word **that** can either be used or omitted after the introductory verb *(say, tell, suggest, etc)*.
She said **(that)** she wouldn't be back until 10 o'clock.

Say - Tell

- say + no personal object – He **said** he was very tired.
- say + to + personal object – He **said to us** he was very tired.
- tell + personal object – He **told us** he was very tired.

Expressions used with **say**, **tell** and **ask**.

Say	hello, good morning/afternoon etc, something/nothing, so, a prayer, a few words, no more, for certain/sure etc
Tell	the truth, a lie, a story, a secret, a joke, the time, the difference, one from another, somebody one's name, somebody the way, somebody so, someone's fortune, etc
Ask	a question, a favour, the price, after somebody, the time, around, for something/somebody, etc

Reported Statements

- In reported speech, personal/possessive pronouns and possessive adjectives change according to the meaning of the sentence.
  John said, "I'm having my bike repaired."
  John said (that) **he** was having **his** bike repaired.
- We can report someone's words either a long time after they were said (out-of-date reporting) or a short time after they were said (up-to-date reporting).

Up-to-date reporting

The tenses can either change or remain the same in reported speech.
Direct speech: Tim said, "I still **haven't done** my homework."
Reported speech: Tim said (that) he still **hasn't/hadn't done** his homework.

Out-of-date reporting

The introductory verb is in the past simple and the tenses change as follows:

Direct speech	Reported speech
Present Simple → Past Simple	
"My train arrives at 3 o'clock."	He said (that) his train arrived at 3 o'clock.
Present Continuous → Past Continuous	
"I am playing chess this afternoon."	He said (that) he was playing chess that afternoon.
Present Perfect → Past Perfect	
"I have made lasagne."	He said (that) he had made lasagne.
Past Simple → Past Simple or Past Perfect	
"I paid five pounds for the book."	He said (that) he paid/had paid five pounds for the book.
Past Continuous → Past Continuous or Past Perfect Continuous	
"I was walking to the bus stop."	He said that he was walking/had been walking to the bus stop.
Future (will) → Conditional (would)	
"I will return the videos tomorrow."	He said that he would return the videos the next day.

- Certain words and time expressions change according to the meaning as follows:
  now → then, immediately
  today → that day
  yesterday → the day before, the previous day
  tomorrow → the next/following day
  this week → that week
  last week → the week before, the previous week
  next week → the week after, the following week
  ago → before
  here → there
  come → go
  bring → take
- The verb tenses remain the same in reported speech when the introductory verb is in the present, future or present perfect.
  Ann **has said**, "Breakfast **is** ready."
  Ann **has said** (that) breakfast **is** ready.
- The verb tenses can either change or remain the same in reported speech when reporting a general truth or law of nature.
  The teacher said "Malta **is** an island."
  The teacher said (that) Malta **is/was** an island.

Reported Questions

- Reported questions are usually introduced with the verbs **ask**, **inquire**, **wonder** or the expression **want to know**.

175

Grammar Reference

- When the direct question begins with a question word (**who**, **where**, **how**, **when**, **what**, etc), the reported question is introduced with the same question word.
  What time is it, please? (direct question)
  *She asked me **what** the time was.* (reported question)
- When the direct question begins with an auxiliary (**be**, **do**, **have**), or a modal verb (**can**, **may**, etc), then the reported question is introduced with **if** or **whether**.
  Are there any oranges left? (direct question)
  *He asked me **if/whether** there were any oranges left.* (reported question)
- In reported questions, the verb is in the affirmative. The question mark and words/expressions such as **please**, **well**, **oh**, etc are omitted. The verb tenses, pronouns and time expressions change as in statements.
  Can you tell me when the next bus to Leeds is, please? (direct question)
  She asked me when the next bus to Leeds was. (reported question)

Reported Orders

To report orders we use the introductory verbs **order** or **tell + sb + (not) to - infinitive**.
Cease fire! (direct order)
*He **ordered** them **to cease** fire.* (reported order)
Stop talking! (direct order)
*She **told** me **to stop** talking.* (reported order)

Unit 8

Reported Commands, Requests, Suggestions, etc

To report commands, requests, suggestions, instructions etc. we use a special introductory verb followed by a **to-infinitive**, **-ing form**, or **that-clause**, depending on the introductory verb.

Introductory verb	Direct speech	Reported speech
+ to infinitive		
agree	"Yes, I'll lend you the CD."	He agreed to lend me the CD.
*claim	"I'm working on a top secret project."	He claimed to be working on a top secret project.
*demand	"I want to be served immediately."	He demanded to be served immediately.
offer	"Would you like me to buy tickets for the concert?"	He offered to buy tickets for the concert.
*promise	"I promise I'll call you as soon as I get home."	He promised to call me as soon as he got home.
refuse	"No, I won't do what she wants."	He refused to do what she wanted.
*threaten	"Be quiet or I'll give you extra homework."	He threatened to give us extra homework if we weren't quiet.

Introductory verb	Direct speech	Reported speech
+ sb + to-infinitive		
advise	"You should try to get more exercise."	He advised me to try to get more exercise.
allow	"You can watch the film on TV."	He allowed me to watch the film on TV.
ask	"Where do you live?"	He asked me where I live.
beg	"Please, please, you have to do something."	He begged me to do something.
command	"Put the gun down."	He commanded her to put the gun down.
encourage	"You should come to the party."	He encouraged me to go to the party.
forbid	"You cannot listen to your music at this time of night."	He forbade me to listen to my music at that time of night.
invite	"Will you come to my wedding reception?"	He invited me to go to his wedding reception.
order	"Do twenty press ups at once!"	He ordered me to do twenty press ups immediately.
*remind	"Don't forget to lock the door when you leave."	He reminded me to lock the door when I left.
*warn	"Be careful, don't believe everything she says."	He warned me not to believe everything she says.
+ -ing form		
accuse sb of	"She told Mary my secret."	He accused her of telling his secret to Mary.
*admit (to)	"Yes, I dropped the glass."	He admitted to dropping/ having dropped the glass.
apologise for	"I'm sorry I am late."	He apologised for being late.
*boast about/of	"I'm an excellent singer."	He boasted of being an excellent singer.
*complain (to sb) of/about	"I feel very hungry."	He complained (to me) of feeling very hungry.
*deny	"I didn't steal the money!"	He denied stealing/having stolen the money.
*insist on	"I am going to give you a lift home."	He insisted on giving me a lift home.
*suggest	"Why don't we play badminton tomorrow?"	He suggested playing badminton the next day.
+ that clause		
explain	"It is quicker to take the train because the traffic is bad."	He explained that it was quicker to take the train because the traffic was bad.
inform sb	"The flight has been cancelled due to bad weather."	He informed us that the flight had been cancelled due to bad weather.

Grammar Reference

* The verbs marked with an asterisk can also be followed by a that-clause in reported speech. *He claimed that he knew nothing about it. etc*

Note: To report negative commands and requests we usually use **not + to-infinitive**.
Direct: *Mum said, "**Don't touch** the iron, it's hot!"*
Reported: *Mum told us **not to touch** the iron because it was hot.*

- In conversation we use a mixture of statements, commands and questions. When we turn them into reported speech, we use **and, as, adding that** and **he/she added that, because, but, since** etc. Words such as **oh!, oh dear, well** etc are omitted in reported speech.
Direct: *"Oh! That's a nice dress," Cathy said to me, "It suits you perfectly."*
Reported: *Cathy said that it was a nice dress and added that it suited me perfectly.*

Countable – Uncountable Nouns

- **Countable** nouns are those that can be counted (*one apple, two apples* etc). **Uncountable** nouns are those that cannot be counted (*water, bread* etc). **Uncountable** nouns take a singular verb and are not used with a/an.

Groups of uncountable nouns include:
- mass nouns (*orange juice, butter, sugar* etc)
- subjects of study (*chemistry, history, maths* etc)
- sports (*football, rugby, cricket*)
- languages (*Italian, Japanese, Arabic*)
- diseases (*chickenpox, malaria, asthma*)
- natural phenomena (*rain, snow, mist*)
- collective nouns (*baggage, money, furniture*)
- certain other nouns (*accommodation, anger, luck*)

Some/Any/No

Some, any and **no** are used with uncountable nouns and plural countable nouns. *some water, some potatoes.*
- **Some** and its compounds (somebody, someone, something, somewhere etc) are normally used in affirmative sentences. *There is some water left in the bottle.*
- **Some** and its compounds are also used in interrogative sentences when we expect a positive answer, for example when we make an offer or request. *Would you like something to eat?*
- **Any** and its compounds (anyone, anything etc) are usually used in interrogative sentences. *Has anyone seen Pat today?* **Not any** is used in negative sentences. *There isn't any petrol in the tank.* **Any** and its compounds can also be used with negative words such as **without, never, rarely**. *I have never met anyone like her before.*
- When **any** and its compounds are used in affirmative sentences there is a difference in meaning. *We can go anywhere you like.* (it doesn't matter where)
Anyone could have told you that. (it doesn't matter who)

- **No** and its compounds are used instead of **not any** in negative sentences. *Dora didn't do anything.* (= She did nothing) *There wasn't anybody there.* (= There was nobody there)
Note: We use a singular verb with compounds of **some, any** and **no**. *There **is** nothing we can do.*

Every/Each

Each and **every** are used with singular countable nouns. We normally use **each** when we refer to two people or things and **every** when we refer to three or more people or things. *She was carrying a suitcase in each hand. Every house in the street has a blue front door.*
- The pronouns **everyone, everybody, everything** and the adverb **everywhere** are used in affirmative, interrogative and negative sentences, and are followed by a singular verb. We normally use every when we are thinking of people or things together, in a group to mean all, everyone etc. *Every person in the room was listening to the speech.* (all together). Whereas we normally use **each** when we are thinking of people or things separately, one at a time. *He spoke to each person in turn.* (one at a time)
- We use **every** to show how often something happens. *The train leaves every hour.*
- We use **every** but **not** each with words and expressions such as **almost, nearly, practically**, and **without exception**. *In winter it rains almost every day.*

A few/Few – A little/Little

A few and **few** are used with plural countable nouns. **A little** and **little** are used with uncountable nouns.
- **A few** means not many but enough. *We have a few hours before we need to be at the station, shall we go and get something to eat.* **Few** means hardly any, almost none and can be used with very for emphasis. *There were (very) few people left in the office after 5 o'clock.*
- **A little** means not much, but enough. *There is a little coffee left, would you like another cup?*
- **Little** means hardly any, almost none and can be used with very for emphasis. *There is (very) little milk left. I'll go and buy some.*

A lot of/lots of – much – many

- **A lot of/lots of** are used with both plural countable and uncountable nouns. They are normally used in affirmative sentences. The **of** is omitted when **a lot/lots** are not followed by a noun. *Were there a lot/lots of apples on the tree? Yes there were lots.*
- **Much** and **many** are usually used in negative or interrogative sentences. **Much** is used with uncountable nouns and **many** is used with plural countable nouns. *There aren't **many parks** in the centre of the city. Did you spend **much money** at the market?*

177

Grammar Reference

- **How much** and **how many** are used in questions and negations.
  How much + uncountable noun → amount
  How many + countable noun → number
  How much salt shall I put in the sauce?
  How many children does she have?
- **Too much** is used with uncountable nouns. It has a negative meaning and shows that there is more of something than is wanted or needed. *I couldn't sleep, the workmen were making too much noise.*
- **Too many** is used with plural countable nouns. It has the same negative meaning as too much. *It was very crowded. There were too many people there.*
- We **use many/much/some/any/most/(a) few/(a) little/ several/one/two** etc. **+ of** followed by **the/that/this/ these/those** and then a noun when talking about a specific group. *Some of the houses in that street are very expensive.* (houses in that street) **but:** *Some houses are very expensive.* (houses in general)

Unit 9

Type 2 and 3 Conditionals

- **Conditionals Type 2 (unreal present)** are used to express imaginary situations, which are contrary to facts in the present, and, therefore, are unlikely to happen in the present or the future. We can use either were or was for all persons in the if-clause. We can also use the structure If I were you ... to give advice.

If-clause	Main Clause
If + past simple/past continuous	would/could/might + present bare infinitive

If I watched that serial, I would know what they were talking about.
If Jack was playing today, we would have a much better chance of winning.
If I were you, I would tell her the truth.

- **Conditionals Type 3 (unreal past)** are used to express imaginary situations which are contrary to facts in the past. They are also used to express regrets or criticism.

If-clause	Main Clause
If + past perfect/past perfect continuous	would/could/might + perfect bare infinitive

If they had invited me, I would have gone to the party.
If it hadn't been raining today, we would have gone to the beach.

Wishes

- We can use **wish /if only** to express a wish.

Verb Tense		Use
+ past simple/ past continuous	*I wish I was on holiday now. (but I'm not) If only I were going to the party. (but I'm not)*	To say that we would like something to be different about a present situation.
+ past perfect	*I wish I had started my essay earlier. (but I didn't) If only she hadn't given away my secret. (but she did)*	To express regret about something which happened or didn't happen in the past.
+ subject + would + bare inf.	*I wish you would behave better in class. If only it would stop raining.*	to express: • a polite imperative. • a desire for a situation or person's behaviour to change.

Note:
- **If only** is used in exactly the same way as **wish** but it is more emphatic or more dramatic.
- We can use **were** instead of **was** after **wish** and **if only**. *I wish I were/was on holiday now.*

Had Better/ Would Rather

Had better (= it would be good to) is used to give strong or urgent advice. Had better cannot be used in the past or the comparative.
- had better + a bare infinitive → immediate future
  You had better apologise to Sonya.

Would rather (= would prefer to) expresses preference. When the subject of would rather is also the subject of the following verb, we use the following constructions:
- would rather + present bare infinitive → present/future.
  I'd rather help you with that later.
- would rather + present perfect bare infinitive → past
  I went to the club last night but I'd rather have stayed at home.
- would rather + bare infinitive + than (+ bare infinitive)
  Since it's such a beautiful day, I'd rather play football than (play) squash today.

When the subject of **would rather** is different from the subject of the following verb, we use the following constructions;
- would rather + past tense → present/future
  I'd rather John told you about the plan because it was his idea.
- Would rather + past perfect → past
  I'd rather we had left home a bit earlier, then we wouldn't have been caught in the rush hour traffic.

Grammar Reference

Unit 10

Future Perfect → will have + past participle

- We use the **future perfect** for actions that will have finished before a stated time in the future. *We **will have finished** our course by the end of June.*

> The time expressions we use with the future perfect are: *Before, by, by then, by the time, until/till (only in negative sentences).*

Future Perfect Continuous → will have been + verb + -ing

- We use the **future perfect continuous** to emphasise the duration of an action up to a certain time in the future. The future perfect continuous is used with: by…for. *By the end of the May Luke **will have been living** in Manchester **for** five years.*

Linking Words

Linking words show the logical relationship between sentences or parts of sentences.

Positive addition:
and, both … and, too, besides (this/that), moreover, what is more, in addition (to), also, as well as (this/that), furthermore etc. *The assistant was **both** friendly **and** helpful.*

Negative addition:
neither (… nor), nor, neither, either etc. ***Neither** Sam **nor** I went to the meeting.*

Contrast:
but, although, in spite of, despite, while, whereas, however, even though, on the other hand, yet, still etc. ***Even though** we played very well we still lost the match.*

Giving examples:
such as, like, for example, for instance, especially, in particular etc. *The weather has been excellent this week. Saturday **in particular** was very hot and sunny.*

Cause/Reason:
as, because, because of, since, for this reason, due to, so, as a result (of) etc. *He had to take the bus **because** his car had broken down.*

Condition:
if, whether, only if, in case of, in case, provided (that), providing (that), unless, as/so long as, otherwise, or (else), on condition (that) etc. *Amy's dad said she could go to the party **as long as** she was home by 11 o'clock.*

Purpose:
to, so that, so as (not) to, in order (not) to, in order that, in case etc. *Dan went to the bank **to** get some money.*

Effect/Result:
such/so … that, so, consequently, as a result, therefore, for this reason, etc. *She doesn't really like her flat **so** she is looking for somewhere else to live.*

Time:
when, whenever, as, as soon as, while, before, until/till, after, since etc. *We'll go out **as soon as** you get here.*

Exception:
except (for), apart from etc. *I've paid all of the bills **except for** the electricity one.*

Relatives:
who, whom, whose, which, what, that. *That's the girl **who** works in the bookshop.*

Listing points/events

To begin:	initially, first, at first, firstly, to start/begin with, first of all etc. ***First** he packed his suitcase.*
To continue:	secondly, after this/that, second, afterwards, then, next etc. ***Next** he called for a taxi.*
To conclude:	finally, lastly, in the end, at last, eventually, etc. ***Eventually** we left for the station.*
Summarising:	in conclusion, in summary, to sum up, on the whole, all in all, altogether, in short etc. ***All in all** it was one of the best holidays of my life.*

Both/Neither – All/None – Either

- **Both** refers to two people, things or groups. It has a positive meaning and is followed by a plural verb. ***Both** men used to live in Brighton.*
- **Neither** refers to two people, things or groups and has a negative meaning. It is followed by a singular countable noun. However the **Neither of + plural noun phrase** structure can be followed by either a singular or plural verb in the affirmative. ***Neither** shop had the CD I was looking for. **Neither of them** has been to Paris before.*
- **All** refers to more than two people, things or groups. It has a positive meaning and is followed by a plural verb. ***All** of the rooms have en-suite bathrooms and air conditioning.*
- **Both/All** can go (a) after the verb to be or (b) after an auxiliary verb but before the main verb. *They **are both/all** very tired. They have all/both been working very hard.*
- **Whole** is used with singular countable nouns. We use a/the/this/my etc + whole + noun. Whole is not used with uncountable nouns. *She ate **the whole pizza**. She ate **all of the pizza**. She spent **all of her money**.* NOT: *She spent the whole of her money.*
  All + day/morning/week/year etc = the whole + day/morning/week/year etc. *She's been working in the restaurant all morning/the whole morning.*
- **None of** refers to two or more people, groups or things and has a negative meaning. It is used with nouns or object pronouns and is followed by either a singular or a plural verb. ***None of** the islands is inhabited.*

179

Grammar Reference

- **Either** refers to two people, things or groups and is followed by a singular countable noun. However the **Either of + plural noun phrase** structure can be followed by either a singular or plural verb. *Either dress is fine. Either of the dresses is/are fine.*
  We can use **not ... either (of)** instead of **neither (of)**. **Either** can also be used at the end of a negative sentence. *"I have never seen Andy's flat." "I have never seen it either."*
- **Both ... and** is followed by a plural verb. *Both Rob and John go to the café every day.*
  Neither ... nor/Either ... or are followed by either a singular or plural verb. ***Neither** Italy **nor** Spain is/are going to sign the treaty.*

Rules for Punctuation

Capital Letters

A capital letter is used:
- to begin a sentence. *This is a pen.*
- for days of the week, months and public holidays. *Monday, January, New Year*
- for names of people and places. *My friend's name is Mary and she's from Leeds, England.*
- for people's titles. *Mr and Mrs Smith; Dr Parker; Professor Jones etc*
- for nationalities and languages. *They are Portuguese. He's fluent in Spanish and Russian.*

Note: The personal pronoun I is always a capital letter. *Tony and I are going out tonight.*

Full Stop (.)

A full stop is used:
- to end a sentence that is not a question or an exclamation. *We're having a wonderful time. We wish you were here.*

Comma (,)

A comma is used:
- to separate words in a list. *We need butter, milk, flour and eggs.*
- to separate a non-identifying relative clause (i.e. a clause giving extra information which is not essential to the meaning of the main clause) from the main clause. *Steve, who is a teacher, lives in Australia.*
- after certain linking words/phrases (e.g. in addition to this, moreover, for example, however, in conclusion, etc). *Moreover, Sue is very kind to children.*
- when if-clauses begin sentences. *If you have any queries, don't hesitate to ask.*

Note: No comma is used, however, when the if-clause follows the main clause.
- to separate question tags from the rest of the sentence. *Mr Jones is your physics teacher, isn't he?*

Question Mark (?)

A question mark is used:
- to end a direct question. *Where is Tanya?*

Exclamation Mark (!)

An exclamation mark is used:
- to end an exclamatory sentence, i.e. a sentence showing admiration, surprise, joy, anger, etc. *That's not true! What horrible news!*

Quotation Marks (' ' " ")

Quotation marks are used:
- in direct speech to report the exact words someone said. *'The bus arrives at 11:45am,' said Tony. "What's your address?" he asked her.*

Colon (:)

A colon is used:
- to introduce a list. *There were three of us on the train: my sister, my friend Peter and me.*

Brackets ( )

Brackets are used:
- to separate extra information from the rest of the sentence. *The most popular magazines (i.e. National Geographic, Focus, Fair Lady, etc) can be found almost anywhere in the world.*

Apostrophe (')

An apostrophe is used:
- in short forms to show that one or more letters or numbers have been left out. *I'm (= I am) sending you ... He left for Russia in the spring of '99. (=1999)*
- before or after the possessive -s to show ownership or the relationship between people.
  Tom's cat, my sister's husband (singular noun + 's)
  my grandparents' friends (plural noun + ')
  men's hats (Irregular plural + 's)

Irregular Verbs

Infinitive	Past	Past Participle	Infinitive	Past	Past Participle
be	was	been	lie	lay	lain
bear	bore	born(e)	light	lit	lit
beat	beat	beaten	lose	lost	lost
become	became	become	make	made	made
begin	began	begun	mean	meant	meant
bite	bit	bitten	meet	met	met
blow	blew	blown	pay	paid	paid
break	broke	broken	put	put	put
bring	brought	brought	read	read	read
build	built	built	ride	rode	ridden
burn	burnt (burned)	burnt (burned)	ring	rang	rung
burst	burst	burst	rise	rose	risen
buy	bought	bought	run	ran	run
can	could	(been able to)	say	said	said
catch	caught	caught	see	saw	seen
choose	chose	chosen	seek	sought	sought
come	came	come	sell	sold	sold
cost	cost	cost	send	sent	sent
cut	cut	cut	set	set	set
deal	dealt	dealt	sew	sewed	sewn
dig	dug	dug	shake	shook	shaken
do	did	done	shine	shone	shone
dream	dreamt (dreamed)	dreamt (dreamed)	shoot	shot	shot
drink	drank	drunk	show	showed	shown
drive	drove	driven	shut	shut	shut
eat	ate	eaten	sing	sang	sung
fall	fell	fallen	sit	sat	sat
feed	fed	fed	sleep	slept	slept
feel	felt	felt	smell	smelt (smelled)	smelt (smelled)
fight	fought	fought	speak	spoke	spoken
find	found	found	spell	spelt (spelled)	spelt (spelled)
flee	fled	fled	spend	spent	spent
fly	flew	flown	split	split	split
forbid	forbade	forbidden	spread	spread	spread
forget	forgot	forgotten	spring	sprang	sprung
forgive	forgave	forgiven	stand	stood	stood
freeze	froze	frozen	steal	stole	stolen
get	got	got	stick	stuck	stuck
give	gave	given	sting	stung	stung
go	went	gone	stink	stank	stunk
grow	grew	grown	strike	struck	struck
hang	hung (hanged)	hung (hanged)	swear	swore	sworn
have	had	had	sweep	swept	swept
hear	heard	heard	swim	swam	swum
hide	hid	hidden	take	took	taken
hit	hit	hit	teach	taught	taught
hold	held	held	tear	tore	torn
hurt	hurt	hurt	tell	told	told
keep	kept	kept	think	thought	thought
know	knew	known	throw	threw	thrown
lay	laid	laid	understand	understood	understood
lead	led	led	wake	woke	woken
learn	learnt (learned)	learnt (learned)	wear	wore	worn
leave	left	left	win	won	won
lend	lent	lent	write	wrote	written
let	let	let			

Verbs, Adjectives, Nouns with Prepositions

Appendix

A

absent from (adj)	allergic to (adj)	apply (to sb) for sth (v)
abstain from (v)	amazed at/by (adj)	approve of (v)
according to (prep)	amount to (v)	argue with sb about sth (v)
account for (v)	amused at/with/by (adj)	arrest sb for sth (v)
accuse sb of (v)	angry at what sb does (adj)	arrive at (a small place) (v)
accustomed to (adj)	angry with sb about sth (adj)	arrive in (a town) (v)
acquainted with (adj)	angry with sb for doing sth (adj)	ashamed of (adj)
advantage of (n)	annoyed with sb about sth (adj)	ask for (v) (but: **ask sb a question**)
advice on (n)	(in) answer to (n)	astonished at/by (adj)
afraid of (adj)	anxious about sth (adj)	attend to (v)
agree with sb on sth (v)	apologise to sb for sth (v)	(un)aware of (adj)
aim at (v)	appeal to/against (v)	

B

bad at (adj) (but: He was very **bad to** me.)	belong to (v)	blame sth on sb (v)
base on (v)	benefit from (v)	boast about/of (v)
beg for (v)	bet on (v)	bored with/of (adj)
begin with (v)	beware of (v)	borrow sth from sb (v)
believe in (v)	(put the) blame on sb (n)	brilliant at (adj)
	blame sb for sth (v)	busy with (adj)

C

capable of (adj)	comment on (v)	connect to/with (v)
care about (v)	communicate with (v)	conscious of (adj)
care for sb (v) (= like)	compare with (v) (how people and things are alike and how they are different)	consist of (v)
(take) care of (n)		contact between (n) (but: **in contact with**)
care for sth (v) (= like to do sth)	compare to (v) (show the likeness between sb/sth and sb/sth else)	content with (adj)
careful of (adj)		contrary to (prep)
careless about/with (adj)	comparison between (n)	contribute to (v)
cause of (n)	complain of (v) (= suffer from)	convert to/into (v)
certain of (adj)	complain to sb about sth (v) (= be annoyed at)	cope with (v)
charge for (v)		correspond to/with (v)
charge sb with (a crime) (v)	compliment sb on (v)	crash into (v)
cheque for (n)	comply with (v)	crazy about (adj)
choice between/of (n)	concentrate on (v)	crowded with (adj)
clever at (adj) (but: It was very **clever of** you to buy it.)	(have) confidence in sb (n)	cruel to (adj)
	congratulate sb on sth (v)	cure for (n)
	connection between (n) (but: **in connection with**)	curious about (adj)
close to (adj)		

D

date back to (v)	depart from (v)	disagree with (v)
date from (v)	departure from (n)	disappointed with/about (adj)
deal with (v)	depend on/upon (v)	disapprove of (v)
dear to (adj)	describe sb/sth to sb else (v)	discourage from (v)
decide on/against (v)	description of (n)	discussion about/on (n)
decrease in (n)	die of/from (v)	dismiss from (v)
dedicate to (v)	die in an accident (v)	dissatisfied with (adj)
deficient in (adj)	differ from (v)	distinguish between (v)
delay in (n)	(have) difference between/of (n)	dream about (v)
delight in (v)	different from (adj)	dream of (v) (= imagine)
delighted with (adj)	difficulty in/with (n)	dressed in (adj)
demand for (n)	disadvantage of (n) (but: **there's a disadvantage in doing sth**)	
demand from (v)		

Verbs, Adjectives, Nouns with Prepositions

Appendix 1

E	eager for (adj) (put) effort into sth (n) emphasis on (n) engaged in sth (adj) engaged to sb (adj) enthusiastic about (adj) equal to (adj) escape from (v) example of (n) excellent at (adj) exception to (n)	(make an exception of sth/sb = treat sb/sth as a special case take exception to sth = object to sth) exchange sth for sth else (v) excited about (adj) exclaim at (v) excuse for (n) excuse sb for (v) expel from (v) experienced in (adj)	experiment on/with (v) expert at/in (sth/doing sth) (n) (= person skilled at) expert at/in/on (sth/doing sth) (adj) (= done with skill or involving great knowledge) expert with sth (n) (= good at using sth) expert on (n) (= person knowledgeable about a subject)
F	failure in (an exam) (n) faithful to (adj) familiar to sb (adj) (= known to sb) familiar with (adj) (= have knowledge of)	famous for (adj) fed up with (adj) fill sth with sth else (v) fond of (adj) forget about sth (v) forgive sb for (v)	friendly with/to (adj) frightened of (adj) full of (adj) furious with sb about/at sth (adj)
G	genius at (n) glance at (v) glare at (v)	good at (adj) (but: He was very **good to** me.) grateful to sb for sth (adj)	guilty of (adj) (but: He felt **guilty about** his crime.)
H	happen to (v) happy about/with (adj) hear about (v) (= be told) hear from (v) (= receive a letter/phone call)	hear of (v) (= know that sth or sb exists) hope for sth (v)	(no) hope of (n) hopeless at (adj)
I	idea of (n) identical to (adj) ill with (adj) impressed by/with (adj) (make an) impression on sb (n) include in (v)	increase in (n) indifferent to (adj) information about/on (n) insist on (v) (have no) intention of (n) interest in (n) interested in (adj)	interfere with/in (v) invest in (v) invitation to (n) invite sb to (v) involve in (v)
J	jealous of (adj)		
K	knock at/on (v) know about/of (v) keen on sth (adj)	keen to do sth (adj) kind to (adj)	key to (n) knowledge of (n)
L	lack in (v) lack of (n) laugh at (v)	lean on/against (v) lend sth to sb (v) listen to (v)	look at (v)
M	married to (adj) mean to (adj)	mention to (v) mistake sb for (v)	mix with (v)
N	name after (v) necessary for (adj) need for (n)	nervous about (adj) new to (adj) nice to (adj)	(take) (no) notice of (n)
O	obedient to (adj) object to (v) objection to (n)	obliged to sb for sth (adj) obvious to (adj) occur to (v)	operate on (v) opinion of/on (n)

Appendix

Verbs, Adjectives, Nouns with Prepositions

P	part with (v) patient with (adj) persist in (v) (take a) photograph of (n) picture of (n) pity for (n) take pity on sb (phr) pleasant to (adj) pleased with (adj) (take) pleasure in (n)	(have the) pleasure of (n) point at/to (v) (im)polite to (adj) popular with (adj) praise sb for (v) prefer sth to sth else (v) prepare for (v) present sb with (v) prevent sb from (v) (take) pride in (n)	pride oneself on sth/on doing (v) prohibit sb from doing sth (v) prone to (adj) protect against/from (v) protection from (n) proud of (adj) provide sb with (v) punish sb for (v)
Q	quarrel about sth/with sb (v/n)	qualified for (adj) quick at (adj)	quotation from (n)
R	ready for (adj) reason for (n) reason with (v) receive from (v) (keep) a record of (n) recover from (v) reduction in (n) refer to (v) (in/with) reference to (n) refrain from (v) regardless of (prep)	related to (adj) relationship between (n) (but: a **relationship with** sb) relevant to (adj) rely on (v) remind sb of/about (v) remove from (v) replace sth with sth else (v) reply to (n/v) report on (n/v) reputation for/of (n)	respect for (n) respond to (v) responsiblity for (n) responsible for (adj) result from (v) (= be the consequence of) result in (v) (= cause) result of (n) rich in (adj) rise in (n) rude to (adj)
S	safe from (adj) same as (adj) satisfied with/by (adj) save sb from (v) scared of (adj) search for (v/n) (be) in search of (n) sensitive to (adj) sentence sb to (v) separate from (v) serious about (adj) shocked at/by (adj) short of (adj)	shout at (v) shy of (adj) sick of (adj) similar to (adj) smell of (n/v) smile at (v) solution to (n) sorry about (adj) (= feel sorry for sb) (but: I'm **sorry for** doing sth) specialise in (v) spend money on sth (v) spend time in/doing sth (v) stare at (v)	subject to (adj/v) submit to (v) (but: **submit sth for** publication) subscribe to (v) succeed in (v) suffer from (v) superior to (adj) sure of/about (adj) surprised at/by (adj) suspect sb of (v) suspicious of (adj) sympathise with (v)
T	(have) taste in (n) taste of (v) terrible at (adj) terrified of (adj) thank sb for (v)	thankful for (adj) think about/of (v) threaten sb with sth (v) throw at (v) (in order to hit) throw to (v) (in order to catch)	tire of (v) tired of (adj) (= fed up with) translate from ... into (v) typical of (adj)
W	wait for (v) warn sb against/about/of (v) waste (time/money) on (v)	weak in/at (adj) wonder about (v) worry about (v)	worthy of (adj) write to sb (v)

Phrasal Verbs

Break

break down = 1) (int) (of machinery) stop working; 2) (int) (of a person) lose control of feelings; 3) (int) (of talks/negotiations etc) fail; 4) (tr) separate under headings
break in = (int) enter by force or illegally
break into = 1) (tr) enter by force; 2) (tr) interrupt
break off = (tr) end a relationship/agreement
break out = (int) (of war, etc) begin suddenly
break through = (int) advance (in spite of opposition)
break to = (tr) tell (usu bad news) to sb in a kind way
break up = 1) (int) (of schools, etc); stop for holidays 2) (int) end a relationship

Bring

bring about = (tr) cause to happen
bring back = (tr) cause to recall
bring down = (tr) cause to fall
bring forward = (tr) move sth to an earlier date or time
bring in = (tr) create profit/money
bring on = (tr) cause, usu sth unpleasant
bring out = (tr) put on the market
bring round = 1) (tr) cause to regain consciousness; 2) (tr) persuade; **bring over (to)**
bring up = 1) (tr) raise a child; 2) (tr) mention/introduce a subject

Carry

be carried away = be very excited
carry off = (tr) handle a difficult situation successfully
carry on (with) = (tr) continue with
carry out = (tr) conduct an experiment
carry through = (tr) complete successfully in spite of difficulty

Come

come across = (tr) find/meet by chance
come by = (tr) obtain
come down to = (tr) be passed on to sb by inheritance
come down with = (tr) become ill; **go down with**
come into = (tr) inherit
come off = (int) succeed
come out = 1) (int) (of flowers) begin to blossom; 2) (int) be published; 3) (int) (of stains) be able to be removed
come round = 1) (int) visit casually; 2) (int) recover consciousness
come to = (tr) amount to a total
come up = 1) (int) be mentioned; 2) (int) arise; occur
come up to = 1) (tr) approach; 2) (tr) equal; (of expectations) be up to
come up with = (tr) find (an answer, solution, etc)

Cut

cut across = (tr) take a shorter way
cut back (on) = (tr) reduce (expenses, production); **cut down on**
cut in = 1) (int) move suddenly in front of another car; 2) (int) interrupt
cut into = (tr) interrupt
cut off = 1) (tr) disconnect; 2) (tr) isolate (usu places)
cut out = (tr) omit
be cut out for/to be = be suited for (a profession)
cut up = (tr) cut into small pieces

Do

do away with = (tr) abolish
do down = (tr) speak badly of sb
do in = (tr) kill
do up = (tr) fasten; tie
do with = (tr) want
do without = (tr) live or continue without having sth/sb

Fall

fall apart = (int) come to pieces
fall back on = (tr) turn to sb/sth for help when other plans have failed
fall behind with = (tr) fail to keep up with
fall for = 1) (tr) fall in love with sb; 2) (tr) be deceived
fall in = (int) collapse
fall in with = (tr) agree with
fall into = 1) (tr) be divided into (categories); 2) (tr) begin; enter a state
fall on = 1) (tr) attack; 2) (tr) eat hungrily
fall out with = (tr) quarrel
fall through = (int) fail to be completed

Appendix

Get

get across = (tr) successfully communicate ideas
get along = (int) continue despite difficulties
get along with = (tr) be on friendly terms; **get on with**
get at = (int) mean
get away with = (tr) escape punishment for a wrongful, illegal act
get back = (tr) recover possession of
get down = 1) (tr) swallow with difficulty; 2) (tr) depress
get down to = (tr) start doing sth seriously
get on = 1) (tr) enter (bus, train, etc); 2) (int) make progress
get on with = (tr) be on good terms with
get out = (int) (of news) become known
get over = (tr) recover from
get round = (tr) persuade; **bring round**
get round to (tr) = find time to do sth
get through = 1) (tr) finish (a piece of work); 2) (tr) go on living through difficult times
get through to = (tr) reach by phone
get up = (int) rise from bed

Give

give away = 1) (tr) reveal; 2) (tr) give sth free of charge
give back = (tr) return
give in = (int) surrender; yield
give off = (tr) emit (smells, heat, fumes, etc)
give out = 1) (int) come to an end; 2) (tr) distribute
give up = 1) (tr) abandon an attempt/habit; 2) (tr) surrender

Go

go after = (tr) pursue
go ahead = (int) be allowed to happen
go away = (int) stop; cease
go back on = (tr) break a promise/agreement
go by = (tr) base one's ideas on
go down with = (tr) become ill
go for = 1) (tr) attack; 2) (tr) apply for (a job)
go in for = (tr) take part in (a competition)
go off = 1) (int) (of a bomb) explode; 2) (of an alarm) ring; 3) (int) (of food) spoil
go on = 1) (int) continue; **carry on**; 2) (int) happen
go out = (int) stop burning
go over = 1) (tr) examine details; **go through**; 2) (tr) repeat
go round = 1) (int) be enough for everyone to have a share; 2) (int) (news/disease) spread; circulate; **get round**
go through = 1) (tr) experience; 2) (int) (of a deal/arrangement) be completed with success; 3) (tr) discuss in detail
go up = (int) (of prices) rise
go with = (tr) match
go without = (tr) endure the lack of sth; **do without**

Hold

hold back = 1) (tr) control (tears, laughter); 2) (int) hesitate
hold in = (tr) restrain
hold off = (tr) keep at a distance
hold on = (int) wait (esp on the phone)
hold out = 1) (int) last; 2) (int) persist
hold to = (tr) follow exactly; keep to (a promise, etc)
hold up = 1) (tr) delay; 2) (tr) use violence in order to rob

Keep

keep after = (tr) continue to pursue
keep away (from) = (tr) stay away
keep back = (tr) conceal
keep down = (tr) cause to remain at a lower level
keep in = (tr) make sb stay indoors (as punishment)
keep off = (tr) stay away from; avoid
keep on = (int) continue despite difficulties
keep out = (tr) exclude sb/sth
keep up (with) = (tr) stay at the same level as sb/sth
keep up with = (tr) continue to be informed

Let

let down = 1) (tr) (of clothes) lengthen (≠ **take up**); 2) (tr) disappoint
let in(to) = allow sb to enter a place
let off = (tr) not punish
let on = (int) reveal a secret
let out = 1) (tr) release; 2) (tr) (of clothes) make larger (≠ **take in**)
let up = (int) become less strong

Look

look after = (tr) take care of
look back (on) = (tr) consider the past
look down on = (tr) despise (≠ **look up to**)

Phrasal Verbs

look forward to = (tr) anticipate with pleasure
look in on sb = (tr) pay a short visit to
look into = (tr) investigate
look on = (int) observe
look out = (int) be careful
look out for = (tr) be alert in order to see/find sb/ sth
look over = (tr) examine carefully; **go through**
look round = (tr) inspect a place
look through = (tr) look at quickly
look up = (tr) look for sth in an appropriate book/list

Make

be made for = suit exactly
make for = (tr) go towards
make out = 1) (tr) distinguish; 2) (tr) write out; fill in
make over = (tr) give possession of sth to sb else
make up = 1) (tr) invent; 2) (tr) put cosmetics on; 3) (int) reconcile
make up for = (tr) compensate
make up one's mind = decide

Pass

pass away = (int) die
pass off as = (tr) pretend to be sth/sb else successfully
pass out = (int) lose consciousness

Pay

pay back = 1) (tr) return money owed; 2) (tr) take revenge on sb
pay down = (tr) pay part of the price for sth and the rest over a period of time
pay for = (tr) receive punishment
pay off = (tr) pay sb to leave employment
pay up = (tr) pay (a debt) in full

Pull

pull down = (tr) demolish
pull in = (int) (of trains) arrive (≠ **pull out**)
pull oneself together = bring one's feelings under control
pull through = (int) succeed despite difficulties
pull up = (int) stop

Put

put aside/by = (tr) save
put across = (tr) communicate successfully; **get across/over**
put away = 1) (tr) store; 2) (tr) put sb into prison/ mental hospital
put down = 1) (tr) write down; **take down**; 2) (tr) suppress forcibly
put down to = (tr) attribute to
put forward = (tr) propose
put off = (tr) postpone
put on = 1) (tr) dress oneself in; 2) (tr) increase (in weight); 3) (tr) cause to take place (show/performance)
put out = (tr) extinguish (fire etc); 2) cause trouble
be put out = be annoyed
put through = (tr) connect by phone
put up = 1) (tr) erect; build; 2) (tr) offer hospitality; 3) (tr) show in a public place
put up with = (tr) tolerate

Run

run across/into = (tr) meet/find by chance
run after = (tr) chase
run away with = (tr) steal
run down = 1) (tr) knock down (with a vehicle); **run over**; 2) (tr) speak badly of sb
run in = (tr) bring a new car engine into full use (by driving it slowly for a set period)
run off = (tr) make prints/copies
run out of = (tr) no longer have a supply
run through = 1) (tr) use up; 2) (tr) rehearse, check or revise quickly
run up = (tr) accumulate
run up against = (tr) encounter (difficulties/opposition)

See

see about = (tr) deal with; **see to**
see off = (tr) accompany a traveller to his/her plane, train, etc
see out = (tr) accompany sb to the door/exit of a house/building
see over = (tr) inspect a place; **look round**
see through = (tr) not be deceived

Set

set aside = (tr) save for a special purpose
set in = (int) (of weather) start and seem likely to continue
set off = (int) start a journey
set out = 1) (int) begin a journey; 2) intend to do sth
set up = (tr) start a business

Appendix

Stand

stand by = 1) (tr) support sb, esp in difficulties; 2) (int) be ready for action
stand for = 1) (tr) represent; 2) (tr) tolerate; **put up with**
stand in for = (tr) replace sb temporarily
stand out = (int) be noticeable
stand up = 1) (int) rise to one's feet; 2) (tr) fail to meet
stand up for = (tr) support
stand up to = (tr) resist

Take

take after = (tr) resemble
take away = (tr) remove
take back = (tr) apologise
take for = (tr) identify wrongly
take in = 1) (tr) give accommodation; 2) (tr) make clothes narrower (≠ **let out**); 3) (tr) fully understand
take off = 1) (tr) remove clothes (≠ **put on**); 2) (int) (of planes) leave the ground (≠ **come down**); 3) (tr) imitate 4) (tr) (of time) take time as a holiday
take on = 1) (tr) undertake work/responsibility; 2) (tr) employ
take out = 1) (tr) remove; 2) (tr) clean (mark, dirt)
take over = (tr) gain control of sth
take to = 1) (tr) begin a habit; 2) (tr) like
take up = 1) (tr) begin a hobby, sport, job; 2) (tr) fill (time, space)
be taken aback = be strongly surprised
be taken in = be deceived

Turn

turn away = (tr) refuse admittance
turn down = 1) (tr) refuse an offer; 2) (tr) reduce loudness (≠ **turn up**)
turn in = 1) (int) go to bed; 2) (tr) give to the police
turn off = (tr) switch off (≠ **turn on**)
turn out = 1) (tr) produce; 2) (int) prove to be
turn over = (int) turn to a new page; change the TV channel
turn to = 1) (tr) go to sb for help/advice; 2) (tr) begin (a way of life or doing sth)
turn up = 1) (int) arrive or appear (unexpectedly); 2) (int) (of an opportunity) arise

Tapescripts

UNIT 1

Tapescript for Exercise 2c (p. 6)

A: There was a really interesting programme on TV last night about strange houses.
B: Oh yeah? I saw a really unusual house once in Suffolk in England. It was five storeys high and it looked like a house on top of a block of flats.
A: I know which one you mean. It's called 'The House in the Clouds' and it was on that programme. It's a clapboard building with a pitched roof and big chimney.
B: Yes, that's the one. And there's another weird house in Britain with a shark in the roof, isn't there?
A: Yeah. It looks just like a normal terraced house – you know – a brick wall around the front garden, a porch and panelled windows and all that and then there's this great big shark in the roof!
B: Well, there's no accounting for some people's taste. So, what other houses were featured on that programme, then?
A: Well, there was this funny-looking hut on stilts in Zimbabwe that had a thatched roof and was on stilts with steps up to the front door, but my favourite was this really tiny little rock house in Portugal.
B: What was so unusual about it?
A: It had a low roof which was a big rock, stone walls, one small window and a small door. I can't imagine anyone living there.
B: Like I said, there's no accounting for some people's taste.

Tapescript for Exercise 5b (p. 8)

John: How are you settling in to your new home, Ann?
Ann: Fine, thanks John. Now I've got the home I've always wanted, a traditional cottage in the country.
John: Sounds lovely. How big is it?
Ann: Oh, it's only small, but it's really cheap.
John: It sounds great.
Ann: It is. And it's very comfortable, too.
John: Does it need a lot of fixing up?
Ann: No, actually it is quite well maintained. The only problem I have is that it's rather cold. Anyway, how's your house hunting going? Have you found anywhere yet?
John: I have actually, thanks for asking. I'm moving into my nice new modern flat next month.
Ann: That's great news! Tell me all about it.
John: Well, it's part of a 3 storey building in the suburbs.
Ann: Is it far from the city?
John: No, not at all. It's really spacious, too. There's a huge living room.
Ann: It sounds expensive.
John: Well, it is a bit expensive, but it's worth it because it's very luxurious.
Ann: Oooh it sounds very nice. I suppose it comes fully furnished?
John: It certainly does. You'll have to come round and see it when I've moved in.
Ann: I'd love to.

Tapescript for Exercise 11a (p. 9)

What colours are the rooms in your house painted? Would it surprise you to learn that the colours around you can affect how you feel? Well, it's true, colour can drastically affect your mood. So it makes sense to surround yourself with colours that you like and ones that will put you into a positive frame of mind.

Red, for example, is a strong colour, so too much of it in a room can be overwhelming. But, in small amounts red is energising and can make us feel active and excited. Red is best used outside or in a room where we spend a short amount of time each day.

Orange can make us feel enthusiastic and talkative. Extroverts usually prefer this colour because it makes them feel adventurous. Orange stimulates our appetites too, so it would be perfect for the kitchen or dining room.

Yellow is an uplifting colour and can make us feel cheerful and happy. However, it is a colour that should be used sparingly because too much can make us feel impatient.

Blue is the colour that is the most universally preferred, and blue rooms instil peacefulness so it is a good choice for studies or doctors' waiting rooms. Blue can also help us feel calm and confident, but it suppressess our appetites so it's only a good choice for the kitchen if you are on a diet.

Green is often used in hospitals because of its soothing properties. It has the power to make us feel relaxed and refreshed. Therefore, don't paint a work area green because you won't get much work done. Green is a good choice for bedrooms.

White is often used in doctors' offices because it gives us an impression of cleanliness. However, it does nothing to relax us – we just feel cautious and nervous. It can also make us feel isolated and withdrawn.

Therefore, we should think carefully about our colour schemes when the time comes to redecorate because different colours can affect how we feel in a number of ways. That said, though, we should rely on our own taste and surround ourselves with the colours we like and feel comfortable with. Use your favourite colours to create a colour scheme you know you can live with.

Tapescripts

 Tapescript for Exercise 32 (p. 14)

Speaker 1

Hello ... is that Murray and Sons? Right ... Well ... I'm phoning to ask if you can help me. The problem? Oh, yes ... Well, I had some new tiles put on last month – not everywhere, only on one part where the wind had blown off some of the old ones. Anyway, the men who did the work can't have done a very good job because now every time it rains we have to put buckets in the room below to catch the water. Do you think you could come and sort it out, please?

Speaker 2

It needs complete resurfacing. There are big holes all over and when it rains they fill with water and I get soaked just walking to the front door. I park the car on the street now because I don't want to damage it any more. So the sooner you come and do it the better.

Speaker 3

Well, I only had the double glazing put in six months ago and I didn't notice it in summer, but now it's cold outside and I can really feel the draught. It's the one in the lounge. It looks like it's closed but it's not and there's a gap and that's where the cold air comes in.

Speaker 4

Yes, it's a very nice flat, two big rooms and a big balcony. It's got a good view, too – over the park towards the river, so you don't feel closed in at all, the feeling of space is wonderful. So it was fine for just the two of us, but now that we're going to have a family – twins, too – we really have to move. It's a pity, but there you are!

Speaker 5

We've had someone in to check it – he says there's nothing wrong, but it's still not working properly. I mean, it's really hot outside, and I think to myself, well, at least it's going to be cool at home. But when I switch it on, it just sends out warm air. We'll have to take it back to the shop. In this heat I need something to keep me cool.

 Tapescript for Exercise 34a (p. 14)

Host: Today on "Family Life" we will be talking about child safety in the home. Here with us to answer your questions and to talk about the dangers children can face in the home is Marsha Ward, mother of two and author of "Secure your home; Save your child." Welcome, Marsha.
Marsha: Thank you. It's great to be here.
Host: Well, we all know to keep children away from hot stoves, irons and sharp objects, but I think there is a lot more to child safety in the home than that, isn't there?
Marsha: Definitely. Did you know that more than a million children in Britain every year require hospital treatment for accidents that happen in the home?
Host: Really? No, I had no idea that the number was that high.
Marsha: Yes – and almost all of those accidents could have been prevented.
Host: So, what are the most common causes of injuries and how can we prevent them from happening?
Marsha: Falling, burns, drowning, choking and poisoning are the main causes of injuries in the home and small children are the most at risk. Parents can prevent children from falling down the stairs by fitting safety gates at the top and bottom. They can use rubber mats to prevent children slipping on floors, especially in the bathroom. However, children should never be left alone in the bath. A child can drown in only two inches of water.
Host: Would you say that the bathroom is the most dangerous room in the house?
Marsha: It's true that a lot of accidents happen in the bathroom, but the most dangerous room by far is the kitchen. This is where there are the most hidden dangers. Parents should never allow children to play alone in the kitchen. Also, they should keep all appliance cords, knife blocks and hot foods out of reach and put safety catches on all the cupboards and drawers, especially where cleaning items and medicines are kept.
Host: This is great advice, and I think now is a good time to go to the phones and answer some of our listeners' questions. Hello, line 1 ... [fade]

 Tapescript for Exercise 36 (p. 14)

Estate Agent: Good morning. Rutland Homefinders. Can I help you?
Client: Yes, hello, my name is Markham, Celeste Markham. I spoke to you last Monday about buying a house and you asked me to phone back this morning to see if anything suitable had come up.
Estate Agent: Ah yes ... Just a moment. Yes, we have got something which might be suitable. You especially wanted a big garden, didn't you?
Client: Yes, that's right. My husband and I are both keen gardeners.
Estate Agent: Well, that's usually difficult here, but I think we're in luck. There is a detached house near the river – quite a prestigious area, really, with large front and back gardens.
Client: Hmm ... that sounds interesting. How much is it?
Estate Agent: They are asking for £400,000. Quite a good price for the area.
Client: I see. What sort of age is the house?
Estate Agent: Well, it was built in the 1930s so it's fairly typical of the time – very well built.
Client: What about parking? Those old houses often don't have a garage and we don't want to leave the car on the street.
Estate Agent: No problem. There's a large double garage.
Client: Good! Now, how about the inside?
Estate Agent: Well, there are four bedrooms ...
Client: That would be fine, but what about bathrooms? There are five of us and the children definitely need their own.

Tapescripts

Estate Agent: Yes, the main bedroom has an en-suite bathroom and there is also another one upstairs.
Client: What about downstairs? Does it have a TV room?
Estate Agent: Well, it's the usual arrangement: sitting room, separate dining room, large kitchen which could also be used as a family room – I suppose you could put the TV there. Oh, and the present owners have recently put in a pool, which is an extra feature that I'm sure your family will appreciate.
Client: Well, it does sound just what we're looking for. When can I see it?
Estate Agent: Let's say … [fade]

Tapescript for Exercise 49b (p. 19)

A: Morris and Green. Can I help you?
B: Good morning, yes. I saw an advert in the paper for a house you have to rent on Beech Lane. I was wondering if you could give me some more details about it.
A: Oh yes, of course. I'll just find the file…..
   Ah OK, its number 32 Beech Lane. Do you know where that is?
B: I think so. It's a couple of miles out of town, towards Deighton, isn't it?
A: That's right. A very nice location, it's out in the countryside but it's only about 15 minutes' drive into the centre of town. There's a regular bus service as well, which will be handy if you don't drive.
B: Does the house have a garden then?
A: Yes, the house backs on to a small wood but there's a large garden at the front of the property.
B: Now the ad said that there are two bedrooms and that the whole house is fully furnished. Is that right?
A: Yes that's correct. Let's see, there are two very spacious bedrooms and a bathroom upstairs. Then downstairs there is another bathroom, and the living room, which has a beautiful old fireplace. Then there's the dining room, and a large modern kitchen. Ah and there's a door from the kitchen directly into the garage.
B: That sounds perfect. Can I ask you about the rent?
A: Of course, if you decide to take the property you would be asked to sign a six month contract and the rent would be £800 a month. A very good price for this property I think.
B: Yes, that sounds excellent. Could I make an appointment to come and see the house?
A: Of course madam, if I can just take some of your details …

UNIT 2

Tapescript for Exercise 2a (p. 20)

Marta

We moved house a week ago and now I'm miles away from all my friends. Mum says I'll make new ones when I start my new school, but that won't be for ages because it's still the summer holidays. I don't like not having anyone to play with. I've got my computer and all my toys in my new room, but I've had enough of being all by myself all the time.

Steve

Oh, it's no use. I've been buying all the newspapers every day and going through the job sections, but I still haven't had any luck. I've sent off dozens of application letters, but I just get rejected every time. I did get one interview, but they didn't call me back afterwards. I'm starting to lose my self-confidence as well. What with being made redundant when the factory closed and having to claim unemployment benefit, I'm afraid I'm feeling a bit sorry for myself.

Laura

I couldn't wait until I finished my exams. I thought it would be the best feeling ever. You know, having plenty of time to relax, getting a job and earning some money for the first time. It sounds brilliant, doesn't it? The thing is though, now that I've actually left school I've got no idea what I want to do. I've been reading about different careers, but none of them really appeal to me. I'm getting tired of doing nothing because my friends are either at university or working, so I'll have to think of something soon.

Tony

Most people think that old people have an easy life. They don't have to work, they get a pension from the state, and they have time to take up all kinds of hobbies. Well, let me tell you that the truth is rather different. I've worked all my life, since I was sixteen years old and I really enjoyed it. Now that I've retired, I don't know what to do with myself. I miss all my old work mates. I miss the daily routine. Now that I'm not working I feel that there's a big hole in my life. The pension isn't that great either, so I've had to change my lifestyle and get by on much less money than before. Don't be in such a hurry to retire, that's what I say!

Bill and Terry

Nothing prepares you for being a new parent. It doesn't matter how many books you read, or how many experienced mums and dads you might talk to, you will never be ready. Having a baby in our lives has made a huge difference. We rarely go out now, we never get a good night's sleep anymore, and we certainly never have a lie-in on Sunday mornings anymore, but we just don't care! The joy that our tiny baby has brought us is greater than we could ever have

Tapescripts

imagined.

Tapescript for Exercise 7b (p. 22)

Speaker A

Sting is one of the most popular solo artists in the world and has had huge success with his latest world tour. Sting, or, to use his real name, Gordon Sumner, has always loved guitar music, although he was trained as a pianist from a young age. He did not become a professional musician straight away, though. He had jobs as a ditch digger and as an English teacher before he left his hometown of Newcastle and moved to London to pursue his dream.

Speaker B

Many of Hollywood's greatest stars seem to have come from poor backgrounds only to make it big on the silver screen. Harrison Ford's life story is just one of these rags to riches tales. In his early career, Harrison had very little money and even had to teach himself carpentry in order to find work. These days, however, he is one of Hollywood's biggest names with millions of dollars in the bank and a never-ending supply of leading roles.

Speaker C

I just love Michelle Pfeiffer. I think she's a fantastic actress and I've seen all her films. In my opinion, she just gets better and better. It must be really hard to become a successful film star. You have to be very ambitious. Michelle Pfeiffer was a checkout clerk in her local supermarket before she went to Hollywood to seek her fortune, so she can't have had much acting experience. Some people are just naturally talented, though, aren't they?

Speaker D

There aren't many rock stars who could manage to stay in the charts for four decades, but Rod Stewart is not just any rock star. He began his musical career in the early sixties and has been a member of several different bands, including *The Faces* and *Shotgun Express*. Rod says that music is his first love, but football is his second. In fact, he once played as an apprentice professional for Brentford Football Club.

Speaker E

Who's my favourite actor? Well, I'd have to say John Malkovich. He's been working in the film industry for almost twenty years and he has still got that special quality that makes a brilliant actor. He can take on any role and really make it work, if you know what I mean. He's had a very interesting life, as well. Did you know that he used to work as a forest fire fighter in a national park in Canada? It's true. He also had jobs as a dishwasher and bus driver before he became famous.

Tapescript for Exercise 8a (p. 22)

A: So, what do you think of life in England, Amy?
B: Oh, I don't think it's all that different from life in America, really.
A: Oh? How's that?
B: Well, people tend to do the same things at the same stages in their lives. We have the same milestones, if you know what I mean.
A: Hmm, I'm not sure I do. Give me an example.
B: OK. Well, children here in Britain start elementary school at the age of five, don't they?
A: Yes, that's right.
B: Well, it's the same in the US.
A: Oh, I see. But then things are a little different after that, aren't they?
B: Yes, I suppose so. In America, children go to junior high school between the ages of 12 and 14, and you don't have junior high schools here, do you?
A: Not usually, no. Children here go straight from primary, or elementary school to secondary school.
B: Yes, but they leave school at the same age as children in the US.
A: Really?
B: Yes. In America, you can leave school when you are 16, or you can wait until you graduate at 18. If you leave school at 16, you can get a job right away, but if you leave at 18, you can either get a job, or you can go to college. It's the same here, isn't it?
A: Yes, you're right. So, for how long do people go to college in the US?
B: Well, they usually stay in college for four years, which means that they leave when they are twenty-two, but they can also go to junior college, which means that they can leave when they are twenty.
A: I see. So the education systems are similar in both countries.
B: Yes, but it's not only that. People in the US and in Britain tend to leave home, get married and have children at around the same ages, too.
A: Do they?
B: Yes. People usually leave home at 18 in both countries, because that's when they move away to go to college.
A: That makes sense. So, how old are people in the States when they get married, then?
B: The average age for men is about 27, but women are usually a little bit younger than that - around 25 so that's an average age of about 26. Women tend to have their first child at about 27 on average.
A: Hmm, that's interesting. I think things are pretty similar here.
B: They are. I've studied this a lot, you know!
A: I didn't realise you were so interested in social issues. What other things have you found out?

B: Well, I can tell you that people in America usually buy their first house when they are in their mid thirties at about 35.
A: Really? I would have thought they would be in their twenties.
B: No, most people want to wait before buying property these days, so they rent houses or apartments for a few years first.
A: And what about retirement? How old are people when they stop working?
B: Well, you can stop working when you are 55, but most people don't retire until they are 65 or older. You can get social security benefits from the age of 62, though.
A: I can't believe you know so much about all this.
B: Well, it's just something I find interesting. I like to find out about how people live around the world and compare life in different countries.
A: And which country would you most like to live in?
B: Oh, I would have to visit them all before I could decide on something like that!

◆ Tapescript for Exercise 10 (p. 23)

Speaker 1

I don't know how it happened. I was at the bank and had been waiting for ages. Noboby seemed to be doing any work, let alone serving the customers. Suddenly, something just snapped. I totally lost control of myself and started shouting at the top of my voice. I shouted at the teller and banged on the counter with my fist demanding service. I didn't calm down until they had dealt with me and I left the building!

Speaker 2

It was the last thing I expected. I'd arrived home late from work and I was tired and hungry. The house was unusually dark and quiet. I let myself in and walked into the lounge. Suddenly, the lights went on and everyone jumped up and shouted "Surprise!" We had a fantastic time. It was the best birthday I've ever had.

Speaker 3

Today's lecture was really the worst. Every time Professor Brown opened his mouth, this guy put up his hand and asked a question. It wouldn't have been so bad if every question hadn't taken the professor off the topic, but it was just one irrelevant question after another. By the end of the lecture, I was so irritated that I just had to say something to this guy. Then, when I did, I found out he wasn't even a student, just a visitor!

Speaker 4

It was fantastic. It's the biggest roller coaster in the country, you know! Anyway, when we went down the first big dip, my stomach felt like it was in my mouth. I just couldn't stop screaming. I thought we were going to fly off the tracks. It was really scary.

Speaker 5

It's such a waste of time! I just sit there all day in front of a computer screen. It's always the same, day in, day out. I have a pile of cards and I punch the keys and enter the data and when I've finished I go home. The next day there's another pile of cards. I really must find a more interesting job.

◆ Tapescript for Exercise 18b (p. 25)

Sam: You know Sarah, things are really different today.
Sarah: Oh that's so true. Kids today seem to spend all their time alone. You know, playing with computers and watching TV. We never did any of that in our day. We were always doing something with our friends.
Sam: Yes, that's true. And have you noticed that they're always on the phone as well? Some kids even have their own private line. Can you imagine that?
Sarah: We'd never have been able to do that! We didn't even have a phone when I was young. We used to use the phone at old Mrs Mantry's house. Do you remember how she used to listen in on us?
Sam: I sure do. I also remember we'd spend a lot of time running around and playing out in the fresh air. Do you remember the games we used to play with our friends in the street? And during summer Dad would take us fishing in the river.
Sarah: That's right, but he would never let us swim there. He said the current was too dangerous.
Sam: Yes, I remember. Those were the good old days. We didn't have to worry about safety either. We would always leave our doors unlocked.
Sarah: It was certainly much safer then.
Sam: But it wasn't a bed of roses either. We had to do everything by hand, even the washing. Mum and Dad were pretty strict with us, too. We had to do all our chores every day.
Sarah: Mmm. I used to feed the chickens and collect the eggs.
Sam: And I had to chop the wood every day for the stove.
Sarah: Yes. We all had to pull our weight around the house.
Sam: And Mum and Dad made us go to bed early every night.
Sarah: Yes, especially on school nights. The teachers at school were rather strict too, weren't they?
Sam: Yes, we couldn't talk or do anything.
Sarah: Do you remember the school uniforms we used to wear? They were awful, weren't they?
Sam: Yes, I had to wear a tie all year round! It was terrible!
Sarah: But we were always free on Saturdays and Sundays, though. And school holidays were always a lot of fun, too. We used to visit Grandma and Grandpa on the farm and spend the whole summer with the animals.

Tapescripts

Tapescript for Exercise 27a (p. 28)

Speaker 1

I work to live. I don't live to work. I'm lucky because in my job I can work from home so I get to spend more time with my kids than most people. We eat together, we play together and I get to see all the things that many working parents miss out on. We are very close, we love each other very much and we would do anything for each other and that's the way it should be. After all, your family will still be there for you long after all your friends have come and gone. Besides, I think a person who has a strong family behind them is more secure and confident and can deal with life better.

Speaker 2

Most people spend a third of their lives at work so obviously it helps if you enjoy what you do. I'm lucky because I love my work and there's nothing else I would rather be doing. I've worked very hard to get where I am, but it was worth it. I get a lot from my job. I enjoy the responsibility of my position, the respect from my colleagues and I get paid a lot of money. The main reason why it's so important to me though is that feeling of great satisfaction I get when I have achieved my goals after a difficult day or week. It's a fantastic feeling.

Speaker 3

There's a saying that talks about how you can't choose your family but you can choose your friends. I think that's totally true and my friends certainly mean a lot to me. I spend most of my time with them, but if I don't see them for a while, when we meet again it's like we were never apart. I care what they think and I can talk to them about anything. I have a small circle of good friends and we are always there for each other if any one of us needs anything. It's a good feeling.

Speaker 4

The most important person in my life at the moment is my fianceé. We met at university and got engaged three months ago. We just clicked, you know, right from the start. We have so much in common. Sometimes we talk for hours on end. We share everything and we tell each other everything. I think it is important to have a partner that you can rely on and who will support you. Someone who you can share all your experiences with.

Speaker 5

You can be as rich as Bill Gates but if you only spend your money on doctors and medical bills, then what's the point? Being healthy means you can enjoy living. You can do anything you want and live life to the fullest. Without good health you have nothing – that's my opinion.

Tapescript for Exercise 29a (p. 28)

Rachel

I don't really mind being an only child. At least it means that my parents give me lots of attention. They only have me to look after, so they have plenty of time to spend with me. I think some children are spoilt because their parents give them whatever they want, but mine aren't like that. They are quite strict. I wouldn't mind if my parents had another child, though, because I do spend more time than I would like by myself. Sometimes, when my parents are at work, or when I want to play with someone and all my friends are busy I think about it. I wouldn't want a brother, but a sister might be nice. Sometimes I think it would be nice to have someone nearer my own age at home to talk to and share clothes and stuff with. Of course, if I had a sister we would have to move to a bigger house because the house we live in now only has two bedrooms. I wouldn't want to have anyone else sleeping in my room. I've got lots of good friends, so all in all I'm happy being the only child in my family. I think that if you really have a good friend then it's not so bad being an only child.

Tapescript for Exercise 31 (p. 28)

Speaker 1

I'll never forget that day. I was terrified as I walked through those huge gates and joined the crowd of screaming five-year-olds. I was very shy at that age, so I didn't want to talk to anyone. I stood on my own in a corner of the playground and felt as though I was going to burst into tears at any minute. Luckily, I was soon rescued and taken to my desk, where I could sit and read a book quietly so that no one would bother me! Of course, it got much better after that first experience and I made lots of friends. Now, I honestly believe that those were the best days of my life, but I didn't know that at the time!

Speaker 2

My strongest childhood memory is from when I was six or seven years old. I'd got a brand new bike for my birthday, and I couldn't wait to ride it. It was red and shiny and I was really proud of it. It had been raining outside and my parents wanted me to wait before I tried it out, but of course, I wouldn't take no for an answer. I set off along the path, wobbling bravely on my new bike. Then, the front wheel skidded on a wet patch and I went flying. I had cuts and bruises all over my legs. Look, you can still see one of the scars!

Speaker 3

I thought it was the end of the world when my parents told me that we were going to live in Scotland. My dad had got a job there and it meant that he would earn much more money, but I didn't care. All I thought about was the fact that

I would be leaving all my friends behind. I hated the idea of changing schools, too, as I didn't want to have to get used to a whole new set of teachers and children. In the end, though, it wasn't that bad. I was a bit sad for a few weeks, but I soon made new friends and everything was fine.

Speaker 4

I remember, when I was four years old, my father woke me up in the middle of the night. He told me that we were taking Mum to hospital and that I should come too. He dressed me and then helped Mum to go downstairs. We got in the car and Dad drove to the hospital - speeding, if I remember correctly. As soon as we arrived, my mother was taken away and my father and I waited nervously. I don't know how long we waited. It must have been ages, because I know I fell asleep at one stage. Finally my father was called in. Then we went in and I saw my mum holding a tiny bundle wrapped in a blanket. I looked and saw a little person with a wrinkled face. I couldn't believe it! I had a new brother!

Speaker 5

There are certain things which you never forget. For me, the one occasion which stands out in my memory is the time my parents took me to Italy. I was only about eight years old, but I remember seeing the Colosseum and listening to my big brother telling me about the fights that had taken place there. I was very impressed, I can tell you. I've been there since, but that first visit will always be the most memorable to me.

◆ Tapescript for Exercise 39b (p. 30)

Jack and Jill decided to try again. They walked up to the top of the slope and quickly jumped on their sled. They were still talking excitedly, so Jill forgot to hold tight and Jack forgot to steer carefully. They kept going faster and faster. They crashed through the fence, went over the steep bank and flew into the air. With two loud cries, they landed in the middle of the road.

"We knew this would happen," the other children cried out as they ran over to help. They found Jack sitting up. He had a dazed look on his face and a deep cut on his forehead. "Where's Jill?" he asked in a worried voice. They all looked for Jill. Finally, they found her lying quietly in the snow. Her face was white and very shocked.

When Jack tried to stand up, he cried out loudly. He couldn't move. "I think I've broken my leg!" Ed Devlin tied his handkerchief around Jack's head while the other children ran over to help Jill.

Jill was lying in the snow. She was in a lot of pain, but she tried very hard not to cry. Just then, a sled arrived driven by Mr Grant, a farmer. He gently lifted Jack and Jill onto his sled and covered them with a coat. Then, the sad group set off home.

Module Self Assessment 1

◆ Tapescript for Exercise 8b (p. 35)

Speaker 1

Even though our house was small, it was very cosy. Mum was good at sewing so there were lovely colourful curtains and matching cushions everywhere. She also had a pet dog, Chester, who was always lying about and that added to the warm homely feeling of the house that I grew up in.

Speaker 2

Our house was big and very neat. There was always a lot of space in the rooms, and the whole place had a light and airy feel. There was little furniture and what we had was all white. Our house was never cluttered and there was never any mess. I must admit it did feel a bit bare at times, though. I used to wish my house was a bit more like other people's – you know, more lived in.

Speaker 3

Well, we had two houses. In the city, we lived in a flat. Nothing fancy really, just a typical two-bedroomed place. But our country house was fantastic. It was a cosy little cottage made of old red bricks and had an enormous garden. There was a fireplace in it and lots of comfortable, old furniture. We couldn't wait for the weekend to arrive so that we could head down there to our country retreat.

Speaker 4

I can't really say that I remember one particular home as standing out. You see, Dad was in the army, so we travelled quite a bit. We moved every year or so. Oh, there were some interesting houses, like the one with a frog pond in the front yard. There was also a strange, three-storey, tall, narrow house, that was painted bright pink. I couldn't wait to get out of there. I was too embarrassed to invite my friends over!

Speaker 5

My parents were artists and our house was an old, renovated warehouse. The ceiling was high and there were wooden beams holding up the roof. There was really only one huge room with beaded curtains and plants separating the various sections of the house like the kitchen. It wasn't a traditional house, compared to the ones other children live in. But we had lots of space to run and play in so we were never bored!

Tapescripts

 **UNIT 3**

◆ Tapescript for Exercise 2a (p. 38)

Carl

I've been dreaming about going to Russia for ages. When I was young, I read a book about St Petersburg, the Venice of the north, and since then I've had a yearning to actually see it for myself. At last, I'm off – the day after tomorrow. It's a cultural tour so we'll spend lots of time at the Hermitage Museum, the largest art gallery in Russia. We'll also visit the fabulous Grand Palace which dates from the 18th century and take a tour of the gardens and pavillions that are scattered through the park. St Petersburg is the home of the Kirov Ballet, too, so I'm definitely going to try to get tickets. I can't wait. It's going to be a fantastic trip.

Sonya

I've always wanted to visit Australia and finally this year I've managed to save up enough money to do it. It's going to be brilliant! I'm flying in to Cairns and then I'm going to visit Dunk, Lizard and Bedarria Islands. I can't wait to walk along the white sandy beaches and go surfing off the beach. I'm going to go snorkelling and scuba diving around the Great Barrier Reef. There's a glass bottom boat tour that I'm going to take too, I'll see lots of exotic tropical fish and the spectacular coral gardens in the reef. The highlight of my holiday though, is definitely going to be swimming with the giant potato cod on Lizard Island. I may even get the chance to touch it!

Rick

I'm going to the Czech Republic this year. It's somewhere that I've never been but I've heard good things about it and my travel agent set me up with a really good package deal. I'm going to stay in Prague for two days and visit the historic Prague Castle with its magnificent gallery and treasury. I'm going to sit in the Old Town square and admire the interesting mix of different styles of architecture that Prague is famous for and visit some of the museums. Then I'm going to visit one or two of the many medieval chateaux and ancient castles in Bohemia and some picturesque traditional villages where people still wear traditional folk costumes. I'll be eating lots of traditional food while I'm away too, like goulash, dumplings and sauerkraut. I can't wait!

Moira

I'm a very active person and not the sort who can sit still for very long, so that's why I'm going to Canada. I'm going hiking through the forests and mountains near Lake Superior where I expect to see lots of animals like moose, deer, beavers and maybe even a bear! It'll be great to enjoy the beautiful unspoilt countryside. I'll be camping out every night, which I think adds to the adventure. I'm going to visit Algonquin Park and spend a few days crisscrossing the park's many trails. Then, I'm going kayaking and white-water rafting and after that I am going to see the spectacular Niagara Falls. I am really looking forward to it. It's going to be the trip of a lifetime!

◆ Tapescript for Exercise 5a (p. 40)

Weather forecaster:

Good afternoon. I'm Gail Winters with the weekly worldwide weather forecast. Let's start off in Latin America. Here, you can see Havana, Cuba, where the weather is beautiful at the moment. Anyone heading off to Cuba for their holidays this summer will be pleased to hear that this is the perfect time to go. There are no signs of the tropical storms which sometimes hit the island at this time of year. It's hot, dry and sunny, with temperatures expected to be in the high thirties all week. Taking a look at the rest of the continent, now, you can see that ... (fade) ...

... we're going to head right across the Pacific Ocean now and take a look at Hong Kong where it's the beginning of the rainy season and the rains are expected at any time, although they haven't arrived yet. At the moment, it's very hot and humid there with temperatures reaching 35°C. The weather is also fairly hot and sticky in the rest of Asia ... [fade] ...

... let's move down into the southern hemisphere again and see what the weather is like in South Africa. Now, as you can probably tell from the chart, the rain has certainly arrived here. On the west coast the weather is very wintry indeed. In Cape Town it has been raining and windy all week. They're having very wet, cool weather there and last night the temperature fell to below freezing for the first time this year. The temperatures are much the same throughout the rest of South Africa ... [fade] ...

... so we'll head back up to Europe for a look at the weather there. As you can see, the weather in the Swiss Alps here is very mild at the moment. I know many people hear the words "Swiss Alps" and conjure up images of snow on the mountains and all the great skiing that goes with it, but at this time of the year the climate is much more pleasant, although it can be quite changeable. In Geneva today it is warm and dry, if a little bit breezy. A high temperature of 18°C is expected. So to take a quick look at the rest of Europe, then, ... [fade] ...

◆ Tapescript for Exercise 9a (p. 41)

Speaker 1

This year I will be staying at the Regent again. All the staff are friendly and co-operative, from the manager to the chambermaid. The facilities are excellent, too. There's a heated swimming pool, and a fully equipped gym, so I can keep fit during my stay. The restaurant is fantastic and there's a very cosy lounge where I like to relax in the evenings. I think I'll just book myself into my usual suite, order room service and completely relax for my entire stay. Well, I deserve a bit of luxury!

Speaker 2

In two weeks we are going on an all expenses paid trip to the Bahamas. We've booked a first class cabin and I can't wait to set sail. Brian is a bit nervous, though. I've told him that there's nothing to worry about. After all, there will be a fully-trained and very experienced crew on board. He says that we will probably get bored, but there's going to be plenty of entertainment. I'm especially looking forward to dining at the captain's table, which is a special privilege for first class passengers. I just can't wait till we are sitting by the pool soaking up the sun.

Speaker 3

We are the kind of people who like our home comforts. So, whenever we go on holiday, we take them all with us! We just pack up our belongings, hook up to the car and get out on the open road. We have everything we need with us. We've even got a fully equipped kitchen. Everything is very compact. The furniture either converts into something else, or folds away to make extra space. It's really liberating, too. If we don't like a certain area, we can simply move on. The beauty of being mobile is that we can tour a whole area and choose the best places to stop.

Speaker 4

Well, my friends and I are all at university, and we don't have a lot of money to spend on holidays. We have a budget to stick to every day, so we try to find the cheapest places to stay. Of course, the accommodation is very basic. We usually have to share rooms and sleep in narrow bunks and we use our own sleeping bags, as sheets and blankets are not provided. The good thing about them is that they have cooking facilities and communal dining halls, where you can meet travellers from all over the world. That's great, because you can sometimes pick up tips on other places to stay, as well as on places to avoid!

◆ Tapescript for Exercise 10a (p. 41)

Claire

I was very worried about travelling on my own because that's usually when things go wrong. I had tried to prepare for every eventuality. I thought I might get airsick so I took a travel sickness pill, which didn't work. I considered the possibility that my luggage might get lost so I had a spare change of clothes in my hand luggage. I even worried that the flight might be delayed so I had a book to read to pass the time. Nevertheless, I had no idea that my worst fears would come true and the plane would have to set down in the middle of nowhere due to engine trouble.

Tim

I can assure you I won't be staying there again. It started off quite well. I checked in all right and I was pleased to find the room was quite spacious and clean. I can't stand staying in tiny rooms. The other guests kept to themselves and didn't make too much noise. I only ordered room service once because the food was so terrible, but when I got the bill I nearly had a heart attack. I couldn't believe how much I had to pay. It was disgraceful!

Pam

I never thought something like that would happen to me. I am a very organised person and I always carry a spare tyre in case I get a flat. I also have an extra gas bottle for the cooker in case I run out. Little did I know, though, that the main battery would go flat and I would be unable to recharge it on site because there was a general power cut in the area. I had to use candles for the rest of my stay and wait for the power to come back on so I could recharge the battery and go home.

◆ Tapescript for Exercise 31 (p. 46)

Why not treat your family to a great winter weekend in Wales this month? Breakaway is offering special family weekend breaks with luxury accommodation in the Snowdonia region, for just £200.

With its relaxing log fires, stunning lakeside view, extensive gardens and woodland walks, the beautiful 18th century Bron-y-Byth Hotel is the ideal base for visiting Snowdonia's many attractions. Take a ride on the Welsh Highland Railway or visit one of Snowdonia's many castles – some as much as 800 years old. Snowdonia is also renowned for walking and rock climbing, offering some of the most spectacular routes in the world.

The hotel's suberb facilities include a heated indoor swimming pool, and a fully equipped gym. There is also a supervised games room to keep the children happy. All en-suite rooms are attractively decorated and provide air-conditioning, a colour television, telephone and even a hairdryer. Other facilities include 24-hour room service as well as a laundry service. Guests are particularly recommended to take advantage of the Bron-y-Byths' excellent restaurant which boasts delicious traditional Welsh dishes. Be sure not to miss a taste of roast Welsh lamb with mint sauce or a fine selection of tasty Welsh cakes and cheeses.

Breakaway's unbeatable offer is available from now until January 4th. It is all inclusive and suitable for 2 adults and 2 children. To book, call Breakaway on 0180 2278954.

Tapescripts

Tapescript for Exercise 33 (p. 46)

Janet: Dave, I thought you were still in Brazil!
Dave: No. I got back last week.
Janet: What was the trip for; business or pleasure?
Dave: I went for Carnival, and it was fantastic. Definitely the trip of a lifetime.
Janet: Ooh! Tell me all about it.
Dave: Well, the flight was a bit tiring. It took 10 hours, but when I arrived I was whisked straight to a luxury hotel in Rio de Janeiro near the Copacabana Beach where I had a swim after my nap.
Janet: That sounds lovely. Tell me about the carnival. Was it as good as everyone says?
Dave: It's fantastic. The parades were really spectacular. The dancers were brilliant – I don't know where they got their energy from. They danced the samba all night long. The costumes were incredible, too. I went to the *Sambodromo*, a street which is specially designed for samba parades, and danced the night away, too.
Janet: Wow, I'm really jealous. How long were you there for?
Dave: I went for 10 days. Carnival only lasts for 5 days, though, so after the festival was over I tried to spend the rest of my holiday relaxing on the beach.
Janet: What do you mean you tried?
Dave: Well, the nightlife is so good it's difficult not to go out all the time. There are some great restaurants and really fantastic nightclubs, too. It's a really exciting city with such a mix of nationalities. I met lots of interesting people.
Janet: Don't tell me you need a holiday to recover from your holiday!
Dave: Yes, something like that! I've got my photos developed, though if you'd like to pop round one evening and have a look at them.
Janet: I'd love to, thanks.

Tapescript for Exercise 35 (p. 46)

News Item 1

LOST LUGGAGE FOUND 3 YEARS LATER

Bob Williams, 43, from Birmingham, England, got a surprise this week when his lost luggage finally turned up 3 years after he went on holiday. Bob went to Mexico in August, 1998, with his wife, Sheila, on Air America flight 257. They had no idea at the time that one of their suitcases would go on a magical mystery tour around the world for the next three years.

Apparently, the suitcase was mislabelled at Birmingham airport and went to Malaga, in Spain. From there it was redirected to LA International, where the Williams had changed planes, and someone in the lost property office there forwarded it to Melbourne, Australia, on the basis of an old label, where it sat unclaimed for the next 18 months. Finally, the case was opened and it was forwarded to Mr Williams at his home address.

"It took me totally by surprise," said Mr Williams. "I thought it was lost forever. I'm just a bit worried now about what to tell the insurance company."

News Item 2

DESERT ISLAND DREAMERS

Two British tourists stranded for 3 days on a deserted Thai island, were rescued yesterday by a local fisherman. Brothers Paul and Darren Asquith from Merseyside say they will not be taking legal action against boatman, Mr Nok Sor, who waited 1 1/2 hours for the boys to show up on the beach of Ko Phan before he left them there last Friday. Six other tourists who made the trip back to the mainland with Mr Sor claim he was extremely anxious to sail home before dangerous weather conditions made their return journey impossible. When asked why they had missed the boat, Darren explained that he and Paul had fallen asleep while sunbathing on a beach on the other side of the island.

Tapescript for Exercise 50b (p. 51)

Kate: Okay. I think we're ready to write a reply to this fax, now. Do you have the details in front of you?
Sarah: Yes, I'm ready.
Kate: Right now, can I just double-check those dates, then?
Sarah: The um, the 6th to the 16th September, that's 10 days and eleven nights.
Kate: Right, I'll just make a note of that. Oh and have you booked the bus?
Sarah: Yes, I called them yesterday, so that's all organised. They'll pick us up at the school at 9 so we should arrive at Hawthorn Park at around 12:45. Just in time for lunch.
Kate: Great. Now, lets look at the rooms. There'll be the two of us, and 15, no 16 girls altogether. So we'll need one twin room for the teachers and I think we should put the girls in four, four-bed rooms. According to the brochure that Joe sent us, that will work out the cheapest; especially with their school discount. Oh, do we need another room for the driver?
Sarah: No, he's going to stay with someone locally, so we don't have to worry about him. Just the five rooms.
Kate: That's something to be grateful for. Now I just have to remember to ask them what sports facilities they have.
Sarah: Yes, and do we have to book these facilities before we use them?
Kate: Good idea.
Sarah: Don't forget to ask for information about the local area. Joe said that they could organise some things for us. Can he arrange a visit from a local historian?
Kate: Right. I've written that down, too. I think I've got everything I need now to write to Joe with the final details.

198

Tapescripts

UNIT 4

 Tapescript for Exercise 2b (p. 52)

Speaker 1

Solar power is safe and clean. It does not pollute the environment and it is a very powerful, cheap renewable resource. Solar power has always given us light and heat but now thanks, to solar technology, we are finding ways to store this power and use it as an alternative source of energy. Solar energy can be turned into electricity and used to run small gadgets like calculators. It is also used to heat water and to heat and cool factories, warehouses and other large buildings. Solar power batteries are also available. They capture and store the sun's energy so that it can be used when needed.

Speaker 2

We have been using windmills for hundreds of years to pump water so this form of energy is nothing new. However, today we are using wind turbines to turn this energy into electricity. The wind turbines have large blades which catch the wind. These blades are connected to a generator which produces electricity. Wind factories or farms are used to create enough electricity to run homes and communities. Unfortunately, areas which don't get enough wind have to use other sources of power as well.

Speaker 3

Hydropower is another natural source of energy. Fast moving streams or rivers have been used for hundreds of years to power grain and saw mills. Now they are used to create electricity. They can even create electricity for whole cities. By building dams across bodies of water we can redirect the flow through hydroelectric plants. Some hydroelectric power plants can even store the power to be used later. Hydropower is a safe and natural way to produce electricity as long as care is taken not to flood the surrounding areas or interfere too much with the natural flow of the water.

 Tapescript for Exercise 5 (p. 54)

Children's TV presenter:

Now it's time for 'Did you know'. Today all our interesting facts are about our own planet - the Earth. Okay, here we go. Did you know that the Earth is the fifth biggest planet in our solar system? It has a circumference of 40,000 km and a diameter of about 12,760 km although this changes depending on where you are because the Earth isn't perfectly round.

Did you know that from outer space the Earth looks blue because of all its water? 70% of our planet's surface area is covered by seas and oceans, 97% of the world's water is salt water and only 1% is good enough for us to drink.

Okay, now let's read some viewers' letters and see how much you know about the Earth. Here's one from Sarah Brown in Bolton who says: "Did you know that the highest point on Earth is the top of Mount Everest at 8848 m above sea level?" Well done Sarah. That's very interesting. "Do you know what the lowest point is, though?" Well, Ryan Jones from Leeds does. He tells us that it's the Dead Sea which is 400m below sea level. Thank you Ryan. Sarah and Ryan will both recieve a 'Did you know' pen.

Now it's time for this week's competition ...

◆ Tapescript for Exercise 31 (p. 60)

Janet: Sandra, did you hear the smog alert on the news this morning?
Sandra: No, what did it say?
Janet: That people with breathing difficulties should stay indoors all day today.
Sandra: Oh dear. You know the air used to be so clean here on the island. That's why I moved here.
Bill: Yes, me too. Ever since they built that factory over on the east coast, the air we breathe has been getting dirtier and dirtier. Yesterday it was pumping out enormous clouds of thick grey smoke, so I'm not surprised there's a smog warning today.
Janet: It's more than just the factories, though. I think we're all partly to blame. We all drive when we could walk or even catch the bus. And the tourists coming to the island don't help either.
Bill: What do you mean, Janet?
Janet: Well, you know, they all bring their cars across or hire them here, and that doesn't help the situation at all.
Sandra: It's not just the air pollution, though. It seems that the whole island is becoming one big environmental disaster.
Bill: You're right, there, Sandra. Whenever I go to the beach or take a walk in the countryside, I see rubbish wherever I go. I really don't know why people have to dump their rubbish in such beautiful areas. It makes me really mad!
Janet: I know what you mean, Bill. I saw someone throwing some litter out of the window of their car as they were driving past. I shouted after them, but they didn't take any notice of me.
Bill: I pick up rubbish when I see it and I try to recycle when I can, but it's just not enough to make a difference.
Sandra: And on top of everything, there are more trees being cut down every day. Do you know that they're clearing the land over near the lake to build another tourist resort?
Janet: It won't be long before we don't have any forests left on the island at all. And that means all the birds and animals that live in the forest will disappear as well. Everything that's beautiful will disappear and then no-one will want to come here anymore.
Bill: Come on, you lot. Moaning isn't going to change anything. We have to do something to get our beautiful island back.

Tapescripts

◆ **Tapescript for Exercise 33 (p. 60)**

Fran: Our guest speaker this morning is the famous animal rights activist John McKenzie. He is here today to discuss the growing problem of our endangered animals. Welcome to the show John, and thanks for joining us today.

John: Hello, Fran. Thanks for inviting me onto the programme.

Fran: I understand, John, that you are working with several different environmental agencies to try to increase people's awareness of how serious the problem of our endangered species really is.

John: You're absolutely right Fran. Most people are aware that certain animals are in danger of becoming extinct but, unfortunately, the media tends to focus only on the exotic animals like elephants, pandas and tigers. There are countless other animals, birds and fish that are also becoming extinct. In fact, there are very few animals on our planet which are not in danger!

Fran: Really? Are things that bad?

John: Oh yes. We can see the signs everywhere. For example, we all know how polluted our planet has become. Well, if pollution is affecting our air and water, then naturally all the creatures who breathe the air and live in the water are also suffering. Cutting down trees to grow crops or build houses is another major factor. We are destroying the animals' natural habitats so there is nowhere for them to live or find food.

Fran: OK John. So what the listeners and I need to know, is what we can do about it.

John: One important thing we can all do, is to be more careful about the souvenirs we buy when we are abroad. Many countries are still selling leopard skin coats and crocodile bags, belts and shoes. They are also using animal shells, such as the sea turtle's, to make sunglasses and jewellery. Although most of these products are officially banned, they are still being made and sold. But, if we stop buying these products, they will have to stop killing animals to produce them.

Fran: What about at home, is there anything we can do in our own neighbourhoods?

John: There most definitely is Fran. First of all, we can try to clean up our environment. The less pollution we produce, the more chance animals have of surviving. We can also keep an eye on what is happening around us. It is illegal to hunt or kill many animals in the UK, so if you notice anyone breaking these laws you must report them to the authorities. Also, if there is a zoo in your area, you can make sure that the animals are being well looked after. If you notice that the animals are not healthy and happy or are being mistreated, make sure you tell someone in charge. And don't forget, if you notice a problem has not been fixed, you can always go to your local newspaper, radio or TV station. There is nothing like negative publicity to get something done quickly.

Fran: Well John, I think we have all learned a lot today. Good luck in your continuing struggle to save our endangered species. Thank you for coming in and I hope you will come back.

◆ **Tapescript for Exercise 35 (p. 60)**

Speaker 1

One of the most successful recycling programmes around today is that of the aluminum can. This programme, which began in 1968, has shown us the value and importance of recycling. Recycling aluminum helps the environment in two ways. Firstly, 95% less energy is used to recycle a can than to make a new one. Secondly, by recycling them, we are keeping cans out of our overflowing rubbish dumps and landfill sites.

Speaker 2

Last weekend thousands of people showed up at Centre City zoo. The unusually large turnout was due to 'plastic recycling day'. In an effort to help the environment, the zoo offered 50% off the cost of admission to anyone who brought in a clean, empty plastic bottle for recycling. Visitors to the zoo watched plastic recycling demonstrations and learnt about all the recycled products available. It was such a successful event that similar events are planned for the near future.

Speaker 3

Summer is nearly over and, this September, as the children get ready to head back to school, here are some environmentally friendly tips to keep in mind. Firstly, try to reuse whatever your can from last year. You may be able to buy second hand books as well. Then, make sure you buy only recycled paper and notebooks. If you really must buy something new, make sure it's something that can be used again next year – and the next.

Speaker 4

A UK based charity has found a way to use cardboard recycling to help adults with learning disabilities. The scheme involves a shop called 'Scrap for Play' where shredded cardboard is made into bedding for horses and farm animals. The trainees are sent to pick up the used cardboard from local businesses and taught how to use the shredding machine. The shredded cardboard is then sold to local farmers, who use it to make warm bedding for their animals. This scheme is providing job training and employment for people in need, while at the same time helping the environment.

Speaker 5

The next time you use your phone card to call a friend or make dinner reservations, you could be helping to feed a starving child in India. A new scheme means that each card can be traded in by a child at a soup kitchen for a meal of bread, lentils, vegetables and dessert. So, save your old phone cards and recycle them. You could be saving a child's life.

Tapescripts

Module Self-Assessment 2

◆ Tapescript for Exercise 8 (p. 67)

Interviewer: Welcome to today's programme. Today, we have as our guest Mr Dan Singer, who began the 'Act Now' group. Hello Dan. You have often been called an 'eco-warrior'. What do you think of that?
Guest: Well I don't mind being called an eco-warrior, but some people might think that the warrior bit means being aggressive or even violent, and I'm not at all like that at all. Nor is any member of the 'Act Now' group.
Interviewer: Some people think that the time you ripped up pavements was quite aggressive, though. What was that all about?
Guest: What we did was, dig up a street and plant flowers there. We did it to prove a point – that we're not going to put up with living in a concrete jungle with no trees or flowers. Humans are only part of the greater system of things. It's about time people stopped being selfish and realised that it's not just about now, I mean, the present. It's also about the future. What will our children have left to enjoy if we take away nature's beauty?
Interviewer: So, the term 'eco-warrior' comes from these views and actions.
Guest: I suppose people give it different meanings, but from my point of view, you can call me an 'eco-warrior' if it means someone who loves and respects nature and the environment. The 'warrior' bit is about fighting to protect it.
Interviewer: One of your main concerns is obviously the environment, but what exactly does 'Act Now" do?
Guest: OK. Let's take it from the start. We want to balance the relationship between people and their natural environment. At 'Act Now" we believe in working together as a community. We provide people with information and try to educate them about environmental issues like endangered species and the use of toxic fertilizers and pesticides. As our name suggests, we then show people that they can join us and *act now* to prevent the destruction of our planet.
Interviewer: So, how do you protect the environment? I mean, what are some of your projects?
Guest: We organise protests against whatever we consider to be harmful to the environment. For example, Newton Council has decided to begin work on a new highway in the area. So, we're making protest signs and we're holding a march outside the Town Hall tomorrow.
Interviewer: Do you have much public support during your protests?
Guest: Oh yes. We make brochures and flyers that we give out, and we find that most people are curious and friendly. Many also attend the protests.
Interviewer: Yes, last week I watched you being interviewed on the news, when you were protesting against killing animals for their fur.

Guest: That was a very successful event. In fact, we even got support from the mayor as well as a famous rock group and a film star! We have also given clothing designers and manufacturers information on fur substitutes.
Interviewer: So it's not all about marches and demonstrations. It sounds like you do quite a bit of research too.
Guest: Indeed we do. Through the Internet, books, that sort of thing.
Interviewer: Thank you for taking the time to speak with us today Dan, and good luck with 'Act Now'.
Guest: Thank you.

UNIT 5

◆ Tapescript for Exercise 10b (p. 73)

A Oh no! I've got a letter from the company I applied for a job with. It says they've found someone else! Oh, what a shame! I was sure I'd get that job!

B Wait a minute. I don't understand this. The manual says put plug A in socket B, but I can't find a socket B. It doesn't make any sense.

C Ah! I could really get used to this! There's nothing like lying by the pool on a sunny day with a waiter bringing you cool refreshing drinks! This is the life!

◆ Tapescript for Exercise 31 (p. 78)

Speaker 1

I used to be the most stressed man on earth. I was working for a large company in the city and I used to spend up to twelve hours a day in my office, struggling with mountains of paperwork. I got up at six every morning and didn't usually get home until late in the evening. My family never saw me. I never had time to meet up with my friends. It was no kind of life, really. Then one day, I suddenly realised that I was letting life pass me by. I decided that there are more important things in this world than a fat pay packet. That was it. I gave up my job and found work in a much smaller firm, where there was much less pressure. I took quite a big drop in salary, but it was worth it. Having a well-paid job is not the only measure of success, is it? I believe that if you are happy with your life, then you are truly successful.

Speaker 2

When you become a parent, you have all kinds of plans. Everybody does. We all think we will be the best parent ever; that we will be there for our children as they grow up and that we will give them all the attention they need. In reality, though, it is not as simple as that. Most of us have to work, so we are away from our homes for most of the day. When I

Tapescripts

had my eldest daughter, I knew that my life would have to change if I was going to be the parent I wanted to be. I gave up my job with a large fashion company and began to work from home, designing and making clothes. It meant that I could still work, and I also had the opportunity to be at home with my children. I think we're all much happier as a result.

Speaker 3

Life in the city was so hectic that I was always stressed out. It took me over an hour to get to work on the train and the bus, and by the time I got to the office I felt worn out. Then there were all the traffic fumes and the noise. It really wasn't very healthy. Then last year, I went to visit some friends who live in a tiny village, miles away from anywhere. Their lifestyle was so much more relaxed and peaceful that I decided there and then to move out to the country. Now I live in a little cottage, surrounded by fields and trees. I work from home, so there are no more tiring journeys on public transport and I am a far more positive person.

Speaker 4

My view is that, if you really want to improve your life, you should try to improve the lives of others. I started doing charity work about five years ago and, since then, I have raised thousands of pounds and made life better for hundreds of people around the world. It is a truly wonderful feeling to know that you are using your life, your time and your energy for those in need. It also makes you realise how lucky you are to have a roof over your head, food and clean water to drink. There are so many people in the world who are less fortunate than I am, so I think it is only right to try and give something back.

◆ Tapescript for Exercise 33 (p. 78)

1 **A:** How are you feeling?
   B: Oh, not too bad. A little bit shaken.
   A: I'm not surprised! It must have been terrifying.
   B: Well, yes. My whole life flashed before me. I've never been so scared in all my life as when I saw that bicycle in front of me.
   A: Well, you'd better get used to being scared.
   B: What do you mean?
   A: You've still got to tell Mum what you did to her car, remember!

2 **A:** Are you alright?
   B: No. I feel awful. It must have been the seafood. I don't think it was 100% fresh.
   A: Well, I had the prawns and lots of them, and I'm OK. Are you sure you're not allergic?
   B: No way. I'm sure you just have a stronger stomach than me. Oh, my stomach! That's it! I'm never eating at that seafood restaurant again.

3 **A:** Hi! I'm back!
   B: Oh, it's so early. I don't know how you can do that every morning.
   A: Well, it's a great start to the day. I feel fighting fit and ready to face anything!
   B: Good. You can get the kids ready for school, then.
   A: No problem. You know, you'd have much more energy if you took regular exercise. I dare you to join me tomorrow. A good run will really set you up for the day.
   B: Hmm…we'll see.

4 **A:** Well, it looks as though someone has been overdoing it.
   B: Oh dear. Is it bad news?
   A: Not really. Just a pulled muscle. Have you been doing any strenuous exercise?
   B: Well, I do quite a bit of weightlifting.
   A: Ah, well. There's your answer. I would try to ease up a bit if I were you.

5 **A:** Ow! Be careful! That's my bad hand!
   B: What do you mean, your bad hand? What's wrong with it?
   A: I've got a blister on it and it really hurts. Look.
   B: Ooh, that is nasty. How did you do that?
   A: I caught it on the oven door when I was making dinner.
   B: Well, that was silly. Why didn't you use the oven gloves?

◆ Tapescript for Exercise 35a & b (p. 78)

A: Do sit down. Now, what seems to be the trouble?
B: Well, I'm just feeling very stressed. It's becoming a bit of a problem really.
A: How do you mean?
B: Well, it's affecting my whole life, and I don't seem to have a social life anymore. I just worry all the time and I can't seem to relax.
A: I see. What do you think is causing this stress?
B: Well, I suppose it's my job, mainly. I've had to do a lot of overtime recently. My boss keeps giving me impossible deadlines to meet and I'm scared that he'll give me the sack if I don't get everything done on time.
A: Hmm. That's not good. Have you considered changing your job?
B: Oh, yes! I think about it all the time! The trouble is, there's just nothing available right now, and I really do need the job.
A: Well, in that case, perhaps you should talk to your boss and ask to cut down on the hours you work.
B: Oh, I don't think he would like that at all. Isn't there anything else you can suggest?
A: Well. If you really want to beat stress, the best thing you can do is make more time for yourself. You need to make

sure you use that time to do something just for you, to help you relax, and put your problems aside.

B: I see. Well, it's true I don't have much free time at the moment. When I'm not at work I have to take care of my two children.

A: Why don't you consider child minding or day care for your children. That might be the answer to your problem.

B: I suppose I could do something like that. But the thing is, I really need a cure now. Aren't there any pills you can give me?

A: Of course, there are pills to help people deal with stress, but taking medicine is not the best solution. My advice to you would be to try to take things easier for a while. Cut down on the overtime, put your children in day care. Oh, and try to find time to relax.

B: I'll try that and see how I go. Well, thank you for your advice.

A: No problem. I hope things start to get easier for you.

UNIT 6

◆ Tapescript for Exercise 12a (p. 87)

A: Can I help you, sir?
B: Yes. I'd like to report a missing bag. I'm sure it's been stolen. I turned my back on it just for a moment to buy some magazines for the flight... and it was gone.
A: I see, sir. First, I'll need your name and address so we can contact you if it's found.
B: Yes, of course. It's Henry Benson, and my address is 13 Court Road, Muchly.
A: Right, sir. Can you describe the bag for me?
B: Well, it's a blue trolley bag with a retractable handle. About medium sized.
A: And when and where did you lose it?
B: It was just minutes ago, at the magazine stand in the departure lounge.
A: And the contents of the bag? Can you remember what was inside?
B: Well, let me think. Mostly clothes for the trip, but... yes, there's a brown leather wallet with some credit cards and some extra ID in case my passport got lost.
A: ... leather wallet, credit cards, ID. Anything else? Money, travellers cheques, camera or other luxury items?
B: Oh yes. An old black instamatic, you know, one of those easy to use things. But I wouldn't say it was valuable.
A: OK.
B: And a pocket calculator. White, with a digital display window and grey push buttons. I find it comes in useful when I travel abroad, to work out how much I'm spending and if I'm getting a fair rate when I change money. Well ... that's about it, I think. Except, of course for the clothes. There's a rather expensive new suit that I... [fade]

◆ Tapescript for Exercise 31 (p. 92)

Martha: Sorry I'm late. There was a problem with one of the computers at work and I had to stay and sort it out.
Sally: Oh, don't talk to me about computers, Martha. Those machines are more trouble than they're worth!
Bob: What makes you say that, Sally?
Sally: Well, we've just got a new computer at the doctor's surgery where I work. It's supposed to make my job as a receptionist much easier, because all the patient's files will be stored on computer and I won't have to deal with piles of paper anymore.
Bob: So, what's the problem?
Sally: Well, guess who has to type in all the information. Me, of course. I've been working late every night for a week trying to get through it all.
Martha: Yes, but when you're done everything will be organised and you'll be able to find everything very easily.
Sally: Hmm. I suppose you're right.
Martha: It's like our computers in the office. I mean, they do go wrong every now and then, and I suppose we do spend a lot of time fixing problems, but most of the time they make life a lot easier. On top of that we don't have to have so many filing cabinets taking up all the space because all our files are on disc.
Bob: Exactly. I admit, when I first got the computer I use at the garage, it did take me a long time to learn how to use it properly, but now I don't have half the trouble I used to have with jobs like doing my accounts, or billing customers. And I get everything done so much faster. I think they're wonderful machines, really. Working with cars, as I do, you see just how useful they can be.
Martha: What do you mean?
Bob: Well, they have computers in cars these days, don't they? It means that people can use them while they are driving to keep up with all the travel news or to find maps of whatever area they want.
Sally: Really? I didn't know that. Computers are everywhere, aren't they? Perhaps I shouldn't get angry with my kids for spending so much time in Internet cafés.
Martha: Oh, no. They should use computers as much as possible. They will need their computer skills if they want to get jobs when they leave school.
Sally: I know that. I just wish they would spend more time reading and less time surfing the net. They need reading skills, too. Anyway, they have computer lessons at school, so they are learning all the useful stuff there.
Bob: I'm afraid I'll have to disagree with you there, Sally. Most schools don't have enough computers for all the kids to get enough practice. Things are getting better, but I think that the more practice children can get in their free time, the better. If they aren't familiar with computers, they won't have a future. It's as simple as that.
Martha: Bob's right. Using computers may not be very good for their eyesight, but it is good for their marks!

Tapescripts

Sally: Oh well. Perhaps I should get a computer at home and get connected to the Internet, then!
Bob: Definitely you won't regret it and you can check they're not shopping online with your credit cards!
Sally: Oh, don't! I won't sleep tonight now you've said that!
All: Hahaha!

◆ Tapescript for Exercise 33 (p. 92)

A: With me in the studio this afternoon is Police Inspector Neal Mitchell, who will be telling us about certain things we can do to protect our homes while we are away on holiday, or just out for the evening. Inspector Mitchell, thank you for joining us.

B: Oh, you can call me Neal. I'm not on duty at the moment!

A: Haha. Alright, Neal. So, what is the main thing we should remember when we leave our homes for any period of time?

B: Well, the first thing I'd like to suggest is fairly obvious, but you'd be surprised how many people forget to do it. You should always make sure that your doors and windows are locked securely when you are getting ready to go out. An open window is an invitation to a burglar.

A: Of course.

B: You should also check that all valuables are locked up safely. If you have valuable jewellery, for example, it is a good idea to invest in a safe. Burglars will help themselves to anything they can get their hands on, so never leave anything precious just lying around.

A: That's good advice, Neal. A lot of people think that their belongings are safe just because their doors are locked, but it doesn't hurt to be extra careful, does it?

B: It certainly doesn't. Another good idea is to leave a light on in the house when you go out for the evening, but it's important to remember that burglars are not stupid. I know a lot of people who leave their hall light on, but how many people do you know who spend the evening sitting in the hall?

A: Not many!

B: Exactly! Leave a light on where you would normally be, let's say, in the living room, or in the bedroom. That way it looks as though you are actually in the house. As an extra safety measure, you could leave the radio on, or the television, so that there is some noise to scare off the burglars. Don't leave it on too loud, though, or your neighbours won't be too happy - especially if you are late home!

A: Good point!

B: Now, obviously, the best thing you can do to prevent your house from being burgled is to install a burglar alarm. These are fairly expensive, but they are by far the best way to secure your home. It's best to do this through a reputable security firm in your area.

A: Right. And then of course you need to remember to set it every time you leave the house!

B: Haha! Yes. Another thing you can do, which I strongly recommend, is to let your neighbours know when you are going to be away and ask them to keep an eye on your house. You can offer to do the same for them, too.

A: Like a neighbourhood watch scheme, you mean?

B: Exactly. Neighbourhood watch schemes are extremely successful in preventing crime. It's important that we all work together for the good of the community.

A: Yes. Now, Neal, it's not only burglars who put our homes at risk while we are away, is it?

B: No, you're absolutely right. We also have to protect our homes from fire. Now, I know this is really the fire department's job, but I would like to advise all your listeners to fit a smoke alarm in their homes. These are essential gadgets and have saved thousands of homes from fire damage.

A: Neal, I'm afraid we're running out of time, but I'd like to thank you very much for joining us today. If you need any more information about protecting your home, ... [fade]

◆ Tapescript for Exercise 35 (p. 92)

Speaker 1

I've never really enjoyed passive forms of entertainment. I find that the best way to unwind at the end of a long day is to do something active. The minute I get home from work, I put on my trainers and go for a run in the park. It really gets rid of all the tension that builds up in me through the day. I go to the gym four times a week, too. My friends don't understand why I don't just lounge in front of the TV like they do, but the truth is that I just don't feel relaxed when I'm sitting around doing nothing.

Speaker 2

This machine has got to be the best thing I've ever bought. It was expensive, of course, but it was worth every penny. Now I spend almost all my free time watching films. I had a video before, of course, but this is the next step up and much better. The quality is fantastic, for a start, and you also get interviews with the actors, and information about the making of the film, which you never get on videos. The digital quality is just so much better than videos, and of course the discs don't take up nearly as much room. My favourite way to relax in the evenings these days is to curl up on the sofa with the remote in my hand.

Speaker 3

I was never a big fan of modern technology until I bought my computer and got online. Now I spend most of my evenings checking out different websites - just surfing, you know. There's so much information out there - it's amazing. I've learnt so many new things and I've even made some new friends in the chatrooms I've visited. Some people say that it's an antisocial way of passing the time, but I don't agree. My social life has improved, actually. I've found lots of brilliant sites and I've learnt all sorts of things that I never knew before.

Speaker 4

It might seem a bit old-fashioned in this world of computers and high-tech gadgets, but I have to say that I prefer to make my own entertainment. My family agree with me. We hardly ever watch television and we don't even own a computer. In the evenings, when the kids have finished their homework and we've all had dinner, we usually get together and play something fun. I think it's better for the kids. They can practise their spelling with Scrabble, and they learn all kinds of useful facts when we play Trivial Pursuit. It's a great way to improve your general knowledge. It's relaxing, but it exercises our brains at the same time.

Speaker 5

My mum bought me this for my birthday and now I hardly ever put it down. I think it's much better than a computer because you can take it everywhere with you. I've got loads of games for it, and I swop them with my friends at school, so I get to play lots of different things and I never get bored. I find it very relaxing. I just sit and play with it in my room after school and at the weekends. I'm always trying to beat my last score for each game and to get a higher score than all of my friends.

◆ Tapescript for Exercise 39 (p. 93)

Student A

Int: (indistinct, because of background noise throughout - eg phone/voices outside/etc) What changes do you think we'll see in computers of the future?
A: I'm sorry – I didn't catch what you said.
Int: I wondered in what way you expect computers of the future to be different.
A: Oh, I really haven't got a clue, I'm afraid. They'll be faster, probably, and much smaller ... other than that, I can't say.
Int: Do you use the Internet much?
A: Yes, quite a lot.
Int: So would you say it's very important in your life?
A: It's not – oh, what's the word? – it's not *essential*. Is that right? In other words, I think it's useful, but I can live without it.
Int: Do you use it for recreation more than information?
A: I'm afraid I'm not sure what you mean.
Int: Sorry – what I was trying to say was, *(fade)* do you use it for ...

Student B

Int: (indistinct, because of background noise throughout - eg phone/voices outside/etc) What changes do you think we'll see in computers of the future?
B: What?
Int: I wondered in what way you expect computers of the future to be different.
B: (pause) I don't know. (pause) Faster, maybe ... much smaller ...

Int: Do you use the Internet much?
B: Yes, quite a lot.
Int: So would you say it's very important in your life?
B: (pause) It's ... er ... er ... (pause) I think it's useful, but I can live without it.
Int: Do you use it for recreation more than information?
B: (long pause) What?
Int: Sorry – what I was trying to say was, *(fade)* do you use it for ...

◆ Tapescript for Exercise 52 (p. 97)

Jill: Hi, Frank.
Frank: Oh hi, Jill.
Jill: How are you? Are the kids OK?
Frank: Yes, we're fine. The kids are really excited at the moment.
Jill: Oh why's that?
Frank: Their school has just bought a lot of new computers for the kids to use in their lessons.
Jill: That's a great idea. It's so useful for the kids to be learning computer skills. They'll really need them when they start looking for a job.
Frank: That's true. They love using computers as well. The teachers can use films, cartoons and sound effects to teach things.
Jill: It sounds more like a game than a lesson. It must be more interesting than those boring old classes we used to sit through.
Frank: I wonder where the school found the money, though. It must have cost a fortune for all those computers, not to mention the new software as well.
Jill: And they'll need to hire some technical support staff. You know how often things can go wrong.
Frank: It's strange, I heard that the school was going to hire a new Music teacher or Art teacher last year but they decided they couldn't afford it.
Jill: It would be a shame if the more creative subjects get ignored because of this new technology.
Frank: I suppose they think the kids can be creative with the computer. Artists in the future will be using special effects and computer graphics instead of paint and canvasses... but I think you're right – they need to find a balance ...

Module Self-Assessment 3

◆ Tapescript for Exercise 6 (p. 99)

1   *Man:* I don't think we'll have to wait very long today. I've never seen the acupuncturist's waiting room so empty.
    Woman: Oh, I don't mind waiting. I've never tried this therapy before, and I can't imagine what it feels like.
    Man: (laugh) Don't worry. Mr Lim is very experienced and besides, acupuncture really works. The needles are very fine so you hardly feel them.

Tapescripts

Woman: You know what. Maybe this wasn't such a good idea. Um, I think I might leave it for today. Apologise to Mr Lim for me please. Er, well, uh, goodbye.

2   **Man**

Thanks for taking my call. I realise that you're busy. Er, I was just wondering if you could tell me the name of that sweet-smelling oil which you used during my last treatment. It made my migraine disappear immediately and I'm sure it was because of its smell. It would be great to have some to use at home. I hope it's not hard to find, as I wouldn't mind getting some.

3   *Man:* Er, yes, hello. I just wanted to say that I think this alternative medicine business is all a load of rubbish.
Presenter: Well, this show is all about expressing your opinion. (laugh) But do tell us, what makes you say that?
Man: Well, for starters I spent a fortune on bottles of vitamin pills from the health food shop, as the assistant advised, and well, they didn't work.
Presenter: You mean the vitamins didn't help with your health problem?
Man: That's right. I still suffer from arthritis, but now I also have to put up with indigestion thanks to those vitamin pills!

4   **Girl**

Hello, I'm a student from the College of Alternative Therapies and I'm doing a research project on the influence of colour on people's psychology. This will only take a few moments. Are you ready? OK. Now, I'm going to show you some cards, each with a different colour and I'd like you to tell me in one word, how the particular colour makes you feel.

5   **Man**

... and by practicing yoga every day, you will find it easier to relax and unwind. Your level of fitness doesn't really matter at first, nor does your age. The exercises are all gentle and mainly involve stretching, to help your body gradually become more flexible. Yoga also focuses on breathing techniques. This can help to free your body and mind from everyday pressures.

6   *Receptionist:* No, it's not too late, we are still accepting applications.
Man: That's great. I've always been interested in plants and their ability to heal. I hope I'll be accepted.
Receptionist: I'm sure you'll have no trouble sir. There are a few requirements, but the very fact that you're so interested in what we teach is very important.
Man: Well, I want to start my own business one day, and then perhaps teach others about the advantages of natural therapies.

UNIT 7

◆ **Tapescript for Exercise 3a (p. 102)**

Tony

The best present ever given to me? Oh that's easy. It was from my parents on my 20th birthday. I had just passed my driving test but I was really short of money so I was still taking the bus to and from work each day. Mum and Dad had dropped a few hints before my birthday and when the big day arrived I was really excited. It was really hard to hide my disappointment when all mum gave me was a small box but when I opened it and found the keys inside, I was so happy. It was the perfect present, so useful and exactly what I wanted.

Linda

It's so difficult to think of just one present. My best friend Amy always gets perfect gifts for me. We're so similar that she knows that if she likes something, then I'm bound to like it too. Maybe it's because we're both Librans. You can see what she got for me last year. It's hanging on the wall over there. Isn't it beautiful? I look at myself in it all the time.

Helen

A couple of Christmases ago some of my friends were going on a skiing holiday. I was so jealous you wouldn't believe it. I had just moved house though so I couldn't afford to go with them. Imagine my surprise when the day before they were supposed to go, they all came round to see me. They said they had clubbed together to get a special present for me and gave me the ticket. It was a major panic to get everything organised in time but it was definitely the best present I have ever had.

◆ **Tapescript for Exercise 8a (p. 105)**

Hello shoppers! Welcome to Lewston Shopping Centre! On the ground floor, you will find W H Smith, the newsagent's, Boots, the chemist's and Tesco supermarket. Why not stop for a coffee at Starbucks or grab a bite to eat at McDonald's – which are also on the ground floor? Next is having its end of season sale so why not pop in and check out the clothing bargains before you head upstairs?

On the first floor, Debenhams department store also has up to 40% off selected items. Habitat furniture shop has lots of great deals, too, as does Dixons where this month's special deal is a DVD player for only £199! Fancy a spot of DIY this weekend? Then, Homebase has everything you need. Or, if you would rather relax and listen to some music, HMV can satisfy every taste from Mozart to Marilyn Manson. And if you're looking for something special for the lady in your life, Payne & Son has an extensive range of gold and silver jewellery for you to choose from. Whatever you want to buy – you're sure to find it here at Lewston Shopping Centre. Happy shopping!

Tapescripts

Tapescript for Exercise 10a (p. 105)

Salesperson: Good morning Sir. Can I help you?
Customer: I hope so. My wife bought me this jacket for my birthday but there are quite a few problems with it.
Salesperson: What kind of problems, Sir?
Customer: Well, first of all there are two missing buttons. Secondly the lining is torn and there is a stain on the sleeve, right there, look!
Salesperson: Yes Sir, I can see the problem. We can repair the damage and have it cleaned for you if you would like to keep it.
Customer: Unfortunately, there is another, more serious, problem. When I tried it on, I noticed that one sleeve is longer than the other. I'll try it on and show you!
Salesperson: No Sir, that won't be necessary. I can see for myself that the sleeves are uneven. I am terribly sorry the jacket is obviously defective. Would you like to exchange it for something else or would you prefer a refund?
Customer: A refund, please.

Tapescript for Exercise 10b (p. 105)

Mgr: Good afternoon Madam, can I help you?
Woman: I certainly hope so. Your salesgirl wasn't very helpful at all. In fact, I found her to be rather rude!
Mgr: Yes Madam, I do apologise. Now, what seems to be the problem.
Woman: Well, last week I came in here and bought a few things for the house. We've just had it redecorated you know and I wanted to splash out a bit ... Anyway, the delivery van came yesterday and after I had unpacked everything, I noticed that several pieces were damaged. First of all, the table was badly scratched. In fact, there were quite a few scratches on it.
Mgr: May I ask if it was scratched when you bought it?
Woman: Of course it wasn't. And there's more! There was a large crack running down the left side of the mirror.
Mgr: I see. Well obviously we ...
Woman: Wait a minute I haven't finished yet. Where was I? Let me see.. scratched table, cracked mirror, what else? Oh yes, the carpet. There was a nasty stain on the carpet, it looks like someone has spilt tea or coffee on it. It looks awful! Oh yes and the cushions! Well, the brown ones are okay but the cream coloured ones are both badly torn... And as for the TV, it just doesn't work! We plugged it in, switched it on and…nothing. No sound, no picture nothing! I really don't know how you can sell merchandise in such awful condition. You should be ashamed! What am I supposed to do with torn cushions, a stained carpet and a broken TV?
Mgr: I really am most dreadfully sorry Madam. Naturally we will replace all the damaged items and please accept my sincere apologies ...
Woman: Well, to be honest, I was going to demand a full refund but ...

Tapescript for Exercise 28 (p. 110)

At Gibson's Mall we treat our customers as welcome guests. With over 100 free parking spaces, a roof garden coffee shop, a gas station and an indoor play area for children, Gibson's has a great deal to offer.

On the right of the main entrance is Kay's Supermarket. You can count on Kay's for value and freshness. They have the largest organically grown produce section in the area and their baked goods are baked fresh daily in their in-store bakery. Opposite Kay's you will find Baxter's Hardware Store. Baxter's is your one-stop shop for all your household needs. As well as power tools you will find a large selection of house wares and hardware. Next to Baxter's is Carter's Chemist's where you can get help and advice as well as a huge range of medicines.

These are just a few of the many stores and businesses that you will find at Gibson's Mall. You will also find dress stores, toy stores, shoe stores, boutiques, bookstores, a deli, a photo shop, a hair salon and much much more.

To help you enjoy your shopping experience at Gibson's our friendly staff are happy and willing to assist you in any way they can.

We are open from Monday to Saturday 9am - 9pm and Sunday 10am - 6pm. So come on down to Gibson's Mall where you will find whatever you want!

Tapescript for Exercise 30 (p. 110)

Radio Host: Welcome back. My next guest on today's show is writer and documentary filmmaker, Donna Farnham, who has just published a new book all about the harmful effects of advertising. Now, in your book you say that, in general, advertising harms us all. Can you tell us what you mean by this?
Donna: Certainly. I mean that advertising makes us dissatisfied with our lives, our relationships, our houses, our jobs, and especially our own appearance. Advertisers show us images of perfection and make us feel inadequate. Then, they tell us if we buy a certain product we can be perfect, too, and the problem is we believe them even though it is obviously a lie.
Radio Host: I see. But aren't there laws against dishonest advertising?
Donna: Yes. Advertisers can't say a mouthwash will give you fresh breath if it doesn't. But the real lies in advertising are in the images that promise that buying the mouthwash will transform your life and make you popular and attractive.
Radio Host: And when it doesn't, this is when we get dissatisfied?
Donna: Precisely. We are encouraged to buy things that will never really do what we want them to do, such as, solve our problems, make us beautiful, rich, intelligent and so forth and so we are constantly disappointed and dissatisfied.

Tapescripts

Radio Host: I see. But do you really think that people actually pay that much attention to ads?

Donna: If you ask people if they pay attention to ads and if they think they are affected by them, they will instantly say 'No'. But the truth is that we are all influenced by ads without even realising it. For instance, did you know that the top selling brand of washing powder is also the one that is the most heavily advertised?

Radio Host: So, is all advertising bad?

Donna: No. There is nothing wrong with adverts that give us honest information about products we need – it's just difficult to name one that does that.

Radio Host: Ha ha. Well, that's all we have time for ... [fade]

◆ Tapescript for Exercise 32 (p. 110)

1 You are in a shop and you hear a conversation between a customer and a sales assistant. How does the customer pay for the jumper?

Customer: I'll take this jumper, please.
Shop assistant: Will that be cash or credit?
Customer: Umm cash, I think. No, wait, I don't have enough on me. You don't take cheques, do you?
Shop assistant: No, I'm sorry we don't.
Customer: Then I suppose it'll have to be credit. Here you are.
Shop assistant: Thank you. Sign here, please. Thank you.

2 You hear someone talking about his shopping habits. Why does he shop in his own neighbourhood rather than in a superstore?

You know I much prefer to go shopping at my neighbourhood stores rather than those enormous new superstores. They might charge a little more, but they know me there and the people are so much friendlier. They always have time for a neighbourly chat and they even carry my groceries out to my car.

3 You hear a conversation between two girls in a clothing shop. One of them is trying on a pair of jeans. Why does she decide to buy them?

Girl 1: So, what do you think of this pair of jeans then? I think they might be a bit tight.
Girl 2: No, they're fantastic. You look great!
Girl 1: Really? How much are they? £45! That's far too much.
Girl 2: But they really do look great. I think you should go for it.
Girl 1: You think so? Mmm, maybe you're right. They do look good. I'll get them!

4 You hear an advertisement on the radio for a new mobile phone. What features does it have?

It's finally here the new Talk Back mobile phone just in time for the holidays. It's small, light and comes with six brightly coloured mix and match covers. You can download ring tones, send text and picture messages to your friends and it has five built-in computer games to choose from. Voice activated dialling lets you phone someone by just saying their name and with caller ID you can see who's calling you before you answer. It's fun and affordable so what are you waiting for?

◆ Tapescript for Exercise 38a (p. 112)

Speaker 1

Hot and tasty like Mum's. Apple and cherry just out of the oven.

Speaker 2

Lovely to look at, lovely to hold. But, if you break it consider it sold!

Speaker 3

Step up, step up! So fresh they're still swimming!

Speaker 4

Lovely posies, sweet-smelling posies! Only 50p a bunch!

◆ Tapescript for Exercise 46b (p. 114)

Cynthia: Hi Sharon, have you been to that new supermarket yet?

Sharon: Oh yes, I went last week. It's wonderful, isn't it? I particularly like the 'Foods of the World' section, it looks so colourful with all those flags and posters from around the world and it has so many interesting and exotic products.

Cynthia: I like the deli counter, I've never seen so many different kinds of cheeses and all those patés and salamis look very appetising. They even let you sample some of them if you don't know what they taste like.

Sharon: Did you visit the bakery section? They bake all their own bread, biscuits and cakes, so the smell is irresistible!

Cynthia: I know, and those pies look delicious, too. How about the tea and coffee section? You can even ask them to grind the beans for you, and there is nothing like the marvellous aroma of freshly-ground coffee.

Sharon: I can't get over how clean and bright the place is, and the scent of the freshly cut flowers from the stall at the front entrance is heavenly. It's much more pleasant than our old supermarket in town, isn't it.

Cynthia: Definitely, and the staff are so polite and helpful. The young man in the cafeteria even carried my tray for me because my hands were full!

Sharon: What's the cafeteria like? I didn't have time to go in there but it looked very nice. It's on the second floor, isn't it?
Cynthia: Yes, that's right, it's just behind the toy department. The food is fresh and tasty and the coffee is wonderful. It's very reasonably priced too. Look, I've got to go again tomorrow and pick up some groceries for the weekend, why don't we go together?
Sharon: That's a great idea. I'll call you in the morning and we can meet at the bus stop.
Cynthia: OK, see you tomorrow.

UNIT 8

◆ Tapescript for Exercise 9b (p. 119)

1. A: How would you like your steak?
   B: Oh, well done please, I can't eat it if it's rare.

2. A: Could I have a bottle of mineral water?
   B: Would you like still or sparkling sir?

3. A: Can I have a loaf of bread?
   B: There's no white left I'm afraid, you'll have to have brown.

4. A: Can you get breakfast at the hotel?
   B: Yes they do either a continental or a full English.

5. A: Is there any tea left?
   B: Yes, there's still some in the pot. Would you like milk and sugar?

◆ Tapescript for Exercise 12a (p. 119)

1. A: Little Italy. Can I help you?
   B: Hello, this is Jane Hoskins from 12, Station Road. I phoned for a delivery about 45 minutes ago and it still hasn't arrived.
   A: Let me check on that for you. ... Yes I'm sorry Mrs Hoskins, we've been very busy tonight. The driver has just left with your order, he should be with you any minute.
   B: OK, great. Thank you.

2. A: Are you ready to order?
   B: Yes, but I was wondering if it would be possible for you to move us to another table. It's very dark in this corner.
   A: Of course Madam, right away. How about that table next to the window?
   B: Yes, that would be fine.

3. A: Good morning sir. How can I help you?
   B: Hello, I came in yesterday and bought some of these frozen dinners because I thought they were on sale.
   A: Yes, that's right they're half price at the moment.

   B: Well, when I got home and looked at the receipt I noticed that I'd been charged full price for them.
   A: Can I see the receipt sir ... oh I'm terribly sorry. I don't know how that could have happened. I'll get you a refund straight away.

4. A: Is something wrong sir?
   B: Yes, I'm afraid this isn't what I ordered. I asked for a cheese burger but you've given me a chicken burger instead.
   A: Oh I'm sorry. I must have misheard you ... there you are sir.
   B: Thank you.

◆ Tapescript for Exercise 31 (p. 124)

Gary: Do you want to go out for dinner tonight?
Sarah: Again! That's the third time this week. Don't you ever eat at home Gary?
Gary: Yes, sometimes I get take out or order pizza.
Sarah: Don't you ever cook anything?
Gary: Not often, I don't really know how to and I'm usually too busy.
Frank: Do you have any idea how unhealthy it is to eat out so often?
Gary: Why do you say that Frank?
Frank: Well, first of all you can never be sure how fresh the ingredients are and it's a well known fact that most restaurants don't buy the best quality produce because it costs too much.
Gary: So how come the food is always so tasty?
Frank: That's because they use a lot of fat and seasonings like salt, pepper and spices to improve the flavour.
Sarah: Besides, eating out all the time can get expensive, think of all the money you could save, Gary, if you ate at home.
Gary: I suppose so, but the menu would be rather boring, I can only make easy things like spaghetti and omelettes.
Sarah: So, get a cook book! There are lots of easy recipes that you could follow.
Gary: But then I'd have to go to the supermarket, buy the ingredients, come home, cook and then do all that washing-up afterwards. I certainly don't have the time to do that every day.
Frank: Stop making excuses Gary. If you plan your meals in advance you only have to shop once or twice a week and washing-up doesn't take that long to do!
Sarah: I think you are just being lazy, Gary.
Frank: I know, let's start a dinner club. We each cook twice a week, that way we can have home cooked food 6 times a week and go out for dinner once a week. What do you say?
Sarah: I think that's a great idea Frank, don't you Gary?
Gary: I suppose so, but you'd better bring your indigestion tablets when it's my turn to cook!

Tapescripts

◆ Tapescript for Exercise 33 (p. 124)

Interviewer: Now, Welcome to 'You and Your Health'. Today on our show we have the famous cardiologist Dr Shaw. He is here to give us some advice about how to keep our hearts in good condition. Thanks for taking the time to come on our show Dr Shaw. A lot of our listeners have written in with questions and concerns regarding their health and the health of their loved ones. First of all maybe you could explain to us why the numbers of people suffering from heart attacks seem to be on the increase these days?

Dr Shaw: Well, I think the answer to that is, unfortunately, our modern lifestyle.

Interviewer: Could you be a little more specific please doctor?

Dr Shaw: Yes, of course. What I mean is that we live in a fast paced, demanding world today. We all seem to be in a terrible hurry, under a lot of stress with less and less time to relax and take care of our health. For example, how many times have you been too busy to eat a proper meal and so end up eating some unhealthy take out food full of salt, fat, preservatives and colourings? Most people underestimate the importance of a healthy diet. We all know that we should eat more fresh fruit, and vegetables, but when we are busy we tend to forget and go for something quick, convenient and filling which is often quite unhealthy.

Interviewer: So, what you're telling us is that if we all make an effort to eat healthier food we are less likely to suffer from heart problems.

Dr Shaw: Of course a healthier diet is going to help, however, diet alone is not enough to guarantee a healthy heart. Exercise is also important. We should all make sure we get a regular moderate amount of daily exercise.

Interviewer: You mean we should all join a gym or buy exercise machines?

Dr Shaw: Only if you have the time and the money. If not just spend thirty minutes a day doing a physical activity such as walking, cycling, gardening or even dancing, you will be helping your heart as well as strengthening your muscles and increasing your lung capacity. Which brings me to another important lifestyle change that is quite hard for a lot of people to make and that of course is to try and cut down on caffeine and nicotine. In fact, if I had to describe a potential heart attack victim it would be a man in his 50's with a stressful job and a family to support, who drinks a lot of coffee, smokes cigarettes doesn't eat proper balanced meals and gets very little physical exercise.

Interviewer: Well, thanks Dr Shaw, you have certainly given us a lot to think about. We are now going to open up the phone lines and allow our listeners the chance to ask their questions ...

◆ Tapescript for Exercise 35 (p. 124)

Young People's eating habits

Most young people today, unfortunately, have very unhealthy eating habits. Studies have shown that teenagers today eat more processed foods than ever before. When eating out they choose fast food restaurants for the obvious reasons. They are cheap, noisy and usually filled with people their own age. However, fast food restaurants are not their only source of unhealthy food. The modern day family usually has both parents working outside the home and this means parents don't often have the time to prepare healthy nutritious meals for their family. Supermarkets today are filled with prepackaged, instant foods. For example you can get mashed potatoes in a packet (just add water), tinned or packaged soups as well as a large variety of frozen ready made dishes such as lasagna, meat pies, and many others. Therefore even home cooked meals might not be that nutritious.

Another contributing factor to young people's unhealthy eating habits is the fact that there seem to be no regular meal times these days. Most people skip breakfast because they don't have time or, if they do have something, it is usually of little nutritious value such as toast and jam or a doughnut or croissant. Lunch is also a problem, if you have a lunch break a lot of people use their lunch hour to socialise or run errands and they don't want to spend a lot of time eating. As a result the most popular foods at lunchtime are snacks. These come in the form of burgers, fries, hotdogs or sandwiches which are usually on white bread with plenty of mayonnaise or butter and processed foods, such as cheese or luncheon meats. After school, most young people are hungry so they fill up on biscuits, crisps or other unhealthy snacks. If they end their day with a meal of pizza or some other ready made food they have not had anything fresh or nutritious to eat all day. Combined with sugary soft drinks the average young person's diet is unhealthier now than it has ever been!

◆ Tapescript for Exercise 37a (p. 125)

1 **A:** We're all going out to that new Chinese restaurant tonight, would you like to join us?
  B: Sure, why not? I don't have anything else to do tonight.

2 **A:** I'm having a party on Saturday night, I hope you can make it.
  B: Thanks, I'd love to come.

3 **A:** I'm having a dinner party on Tuesday, everyone has to bring a dish. Would you like to come?
  B: Um, I guess so.

4 **A:** It's my 6 year old daughter's birthday party on Sunday and all the children from her class will be there, you are coming aren't you?
  B: Yes, I suppose so.

Tapescripts

5 A: Do you want to come to my parent's house for dinner on Sunday?
B: Ok, I might as well. I don't want to stay here all by myself.

◆ Tapescript for Exercise 39a (p. 125)

A: Have you been served?
B: No, I haven't.
A: What can I get you?
B: Erm, 2 cheeseburgers and 2 large Cokes, please.
A: Would you like any fries with that?
B: Yes, 2 medium fries and a child's portion of chicken nuggets.
A: OK. Anything else?
B: No, that's it, thanks.
A: That's £6.20, then, please.
B: Here you are.
A: Thank you. It'll just be a couple of minutes.

◆ Tapescript for Exercise 52b (p. 129)

Ben

I go to Marco's a couple of time a week because it's so close to the office. There's not a wide variety of food, but it's good and really cheap as well. Sometimes at lunchtime, though, it gets a bit crowded. When that happens, the service is really slow. They definitely need extra staff for the busy periods. But apart from that, its OK. Fine for a quick lunch.

Joey

No, I've never been in here before but today I was just looking for somewhere I could grab a quick bite to eat. The food's good, though, and the man behind the counter was friendly and helpful. Mind you the place looks like it could do with being decorated, doesn't it? It's a bit dirty and dingy. What's more, it's so dark that you can hardly see the menu.

Rachel

What I like the most about Marco's is that it's always here when I need it. I finish work at 2 o'clock in the morning and I like to go for something to eat before I go home. Everywhere else in town is closing at that time but not this place. There's a really friendly and relaxed atmosphere in here as well. I can sit, chatting with my friends, for hours and you never feel any pressure to finish up and leave. I wish they had a car park, though. It's a little scary going back to my car so late when everything is dark and deserted.

Module Self-Assessment 4

◆ Tapescript for Exercise 8 (p. 131)

Interviewer: Let's welcome Diane Hall, owner of the organic food restaurant, *Nature's Way*. So, Diane, what exactly is organic food?
Diane: Organic food is food that is natural. It hasn't been grown using chemicals. Only natural fertilizers and no pesticides.
Interviewer: And how did you first become interested in organic food?
Diane: Well, as a teenager I remember going to my grandmother's house. She had a wonderful garden where she grew fruit and vegetables. I remember picking an apple from her tree, and thinking it was delicious. When she had us over for dinner, her salads were also very tasty. She used no chemical fertilizers you see. So I suppose it was from there that I became fascinated with organic food.
Interviewer: So, are fruit and vegetables the only types of organic food?
Diane: Oh, no. And I'm glad you've bought up that point Stuart, because organic food includes meat, as well as fruit, vegetables, grains, pulses and even dairy products.
Interviewer: That's interesting. I didn't know that meat and dairy products could be organic.
Diane: Well, organic beef comes from cattle that are fed grass grown in soil that hasn't been treated with chemicals.
Interviewer: I see. Do you use only organic products in your café?
Diane: Yes, and we serve a wide variety of foods, for different people. During the week, a lot of business people come in for lunch or a snack. In the evenings, we have a different menu for people who want a 3-course meal.
Interviewer: And are you open at weekends?
Diane: We are and we offer late breakfasts or brunch, as well as dinner. In summer we open the patio and have barbecues.
Interviewer: So, do you find that organic food is becoming more popular?
Diane: Yes, it is. Most people prefer food that has been grown without using chemicals. They're also noticing that organic food tastes better.
Interviewer: I've heard that organic food is also better for the environment. Is this true?
Diane: Well, think of the chemical fertilizers and pesticides poison the soil and end up in our water. Our wildlife becomes affected and so do we. Organic means natural which is better for us and our planet!

Tapescripts

UNIT 9

◆ Tapescript for Exercise 10a (p. 137)

A The fun, the colour, the entertainment. Come and see the greatest show on earth with the Ringling Brothers, coming to you all the way from the USA on August 2nd, 3rd and 4th. This amazing show will be held in a huge circus tent, on the grounds of Sheffield Football Stadium. There will be funny clowns, daring acrobats, incredible animals and extraordinary performers ... Gates open at 7 pm, and the show goes on for three exciting hours. Buy tickets at the door, for £5 per adult and £2 for children under 12. But tickets are limited, so get there early ...

B Come and experience a night of mystery and passion, as the luxurious La Roix, at Queen's Hill, brings you the classic romance *In The Dawn*. This top-class venue, with comfortable seating and first-rate views of the expansive stage, provides an unforgettable theatrical experience. *In The Dawn* stars Katherine Ross, along with an impressive cast of brilliant actors, all of whom have recently returned from a popular run of the play on Broadway. The play opens on December 15th for two weeks. For enquiries and ticket reservations, call Style Bookings on 3247621.

C Let *The Storm* begin. Yes, they're here. This talented rock band, will soon be on stage near you. *The Storm* have had a number of smash-hit tunes lately but haven't toured for over 5 years. So all you screaming fans, get ready – because at last they're coming to the Entertainment Hall, for 2 explosive shows, on Saturday, March 10th & Sunday, March 11th. Tickets go on sale on Monday 3rd February at the Ticket Box – £3 for students and £5 for others. Get ready for a wild party!

◆ Tapescript for Exercise 29a (p. 142)

Come on out and join us for the Northwoods to Capitol cycling tour. From June 22-June 30, travel with us on our cycling adventure through the spectacular scenery of Central and Eastern Wisconsin.

300 participants will pedal along quiet two-lane roads from Middleton to the beautiful shores of Green Bay and Lake Michigan, in Door County. Along the way cyclists will pass through some of the most beautiful hills and forests in Wisconsin.

You don't have to be a professional cyclist to participate in this tour. It has been designed for cyclists of average ability, with terrain ranging from flat roads to rolling hills. This seven-day tour includes six days of cycling plus one day to explore the scenic Door County area.

At only $205 per person, this tour is a bargain! The cost covers everything you need, including maps, a tent and the use of showers at the rest stops. Meals are extra, but there are cooking facilities available. So, don't miss out on the fun – bring the family and have a blast!

◆ Tapescript for Exercise 30a (p. 142)

Phil: Today on Lookabout we are looking at the problem of violent sports. Our guest is sports psychologist Dr Moira Taylor. Thank you for coming today, Doctor.
Dr Taylor: Good morning, Phil. Great to be here.
Phil: As another professional boxer was seriously injured at the weekend, is it time to stop violent sports?
Dr Taylor: Well, violence in sports does cause problems, but there are a number of things we need to think about. For example, which sports should we ban?
Phil: Sports like boxing, which are the most dangerous, I suppose.
Dr Taylor: Well, that's only partly true. In boxing there are strict rules which protect the participants. When these safety rules and regulations are followed, boxing isn't as dangerous as it looks. Far more people hurt themselves playing football. In fact, you are more likely to suffer a serious injury while horse riding than while boxing.
Phil: Maybe the reason so many people pick out sports like boxing and wrestling as being particularly violent is that the athletes are deliberately trying to injure their opponents. Apart from anything else, do boxers make good role models for young sports fans?
Dr Taylor: That's certainly a good argument, and we should remember that if boxers behaved like that outside the ring they would be arrested. However, even in ice hockey and rugby, players are encouraged to be as physical as possible. We have to decide whether violent sports encourage fans to behave more violently. Personally I don't think that violence in society can be explained so easily.
Phil: So you wouldn't be in favour of banning violent sports?
Dr Taylor: No, I think that competitive sports can be a positive influence on young people as long as they are encouraged to behave in an acceptable sporting way. Of course we shouldn't encourage violence, and we need to make sure that all sports are as safe as possible. This is especially important with the increase in popularity of extreme sports in recent years. However, whatever sport we're talking about, as long as the competitors understand the risks involved then it should be their decision.
Phil: And so you would take your children to watch, say a boxing match?
Dr Taylor: Yes, of course.

◆ Tapescript for Exercise 31a (p. 142)

Speaker 1

Ever since I was a young child I can remember being fascinated by my Aunt Edies' teaspoon collection. Each one was different; some were brass, some were silver and she even had one beautiful tiny gold one. What made them so interesting was the fact that they all had different designs on them. When Aunt Edie passed away she left me her collection. She had fifty spoons from all around the world and I now have over a hundred. Personally, I find it a fascinating hobby, as most spoons were made to commemorate a particular historical event. I find it a very rewarding as well as educating pastime.

Speaker 2

People sometimes laugh when I tell them I collect unusual paper napkins, but I'm quite serious about it. I have an amazing collection of different ones from all over the world. I even keep them in photo albums so they don't get damaged. I have travelled to many different countries and I always manage to find unique and interesting napkins to bring back with me. My favourites are the ones I picked up in Taiwan; they are brightly coloured and they have beautiful elaborate designs on them. I've also got some interesting ones from some expensive restaurants, but quite often they use cloth napkins and they won't let me keep those!

Speaker 3

Most of the pieces in my rock collection are ones you can find in any backyard. I clean them with a special solution and this brings out their unusual colours and shapes. I found two very unusual rocks at a relatives' property in the country and when I cleaned them I realised that they were actually quartz crystals. I must admit I wouldn't mind adding a gold nugget to my collection, but, unfortunately, those are very rare and hard to find.

Speaker 4

I've always enjoyed watching comedy films, so it was only natural that I should start a comedy video collection. My favourite has to be the one called "The Road to Italy" starring Mel Winters, it's one of the funniest films I have ever seen. I hope one day to have at least one film starring a famous comedian from each decade. For example, I have a silent Charlie Chaplin film as well as Laurel and Hardy, Abbot and Costello all the way to the present with Eddie Murphy and even Billy Connolly. To date, I have over 110 videos and I keep them in alphabetical order on bookshelves in my living room. My wife complains that our front room looks like a video library, but it's a hobby that the whole family can enjoy!

Speaker 5

I never used to enjoy dancing much, probably because I'm not too keen on the music that is popular in the clubs these days, but ballroom dancing is something different. You get to dress up in fancy clothes and meet interesting people who share your hobby. It also keeps you fit and improves your coordination. The hardest part is finding someone to dance with. Luckily I have a really good dance partner called Ted. We even won a trophy in last year's competition. I began ballroom dancing five years ago and it looks as though I'll be doing it for a long time.

UNIT 10

Tapescript for Exercise 7 (p. 150)

Lyn

Ah, this could be what you're looking for. A fully-furnished two-bedroomed flat, in the city centre. Five minutes walk from the railway station. Just £400 a month. Shall we ring up and arrange to go and see it?

Stacey

Do you want to hear yours? You're Capricorn aren't you? It says it's a good week for you to meet new people and that on the 12th you're going to have some unexpected good news.

Bob

I'm totally stuck. I can normally finish it in about 20 minutes but today it's really difficult. Have you got any idea what 17 across could be?

Tony

I see someone's written in complaining about the council's plan to build that new supermarket. He says it's going to mean much more traffic in the city centre and that all our small local shops are going to suffer. I certainly agree with him about that.

Tapescript for Exercise 9b (p. 150)

Radio news reporter

The bad weather that has been sweeping the country for the last two months has taken its toll again on the unlucky inhabitants of the small village of Upton, in Warwickshire. They woke up on Tuesday to find that most of the village had been flooded for the second time in less than three weeks. The village lies on the River Severn, which has been at a dangerously high level all month. The flood defences had been reinforced after the first floods but they didn't prove to be strong enough. Early on Tuesday morning the river broke its banks again. Within hours, low lying parts of the village were submerged in more than a metre of water. Local councillor, Bill Jameson said that it was a total disaster for the town, as things were just getting back to normal after the first floods. The flood has caused thousands of pounds worth of damage, and up to a hundred people have had to be evacuated from their homes. The army has been called in, and has been working all day using sandbags to try to build up the banks of the river again. However, Jameson says that in the long term, more serious action will have to be taken. He said that the local council will be looking at ways of making sure that this never happens again. Even if it means such drastic action as diverting the course of the river away from the village …

213

Tapescripts

◆ Tapescript for Exercise 30 (p. 156)

Tuesday

As part of a special programme of events, Millford Art Centre brings you an exhibition of some of the finest local artwork produced in the last century. This week, you can view work by a different artist every day, including a display of original paintings and sculptures by Millford's own David Thornby, on Tuesday. For a full programme, visit the Art Centre in Sanding Road, or call us on 01432 678439.

Wednesday

The Millford Annual Arts and Crafts Fair will be held in the Town Hall on Wednesday from 10 am until 5pm. There will be a variety of stalls selling quality handmade goods to suit all tastes, including clothing, ornaments, jewellery and toys. Homemade refreshments will also be available throughout the day. The entrance fee is £1 for adults, and 50 pence for children, senior citizens and students.

Thursday

Come along to Milestones Bookshop in Millford Shopping Centre this Thursday and you will have the chance to meet the author of this year's best-selling novel: *Summer Skies*. For one day only, Helen Blake will be in the store, reading extracts from her book and signing copies for every customer as part of a three-month promotional tour. She will also be taking part in a question and answer session, so you can find out all you need to know about the author and her work. Milestones will be open from 9 am until 6 pm.

Friday

Movie lovers won't want to miss Friday's unique programme at the Odeon Cinema. Three Alfred Hitchcock favourites will be playing in an afternoon of classic thrillers. *The Birds* will be shown at 2 pm, followed by *Psycho* at 4 pm and *Vertigo* at 6 pm. View the movie of your choice for the special price of £2.50, or, if you dare, see all three for just £5!

Saturday

If you didn't manage to get tickets to see Soundbytes live at Millford Stadium, then you'll be pleased to know that you don't have to miss out on the biggest musical event of the year! We'll be bringing the concert live to your living room on Saturday night. Tune in to Millford FM at eight o'clock, and turn up the volume for an evening of live entertainment and incredible music. 96 – 98FM.

◆ Tapescript for Exercise 32 (p. 156)

Angela: Turn that off Bernard! That's not suitable for the children to see.
Bernard: But I'm only watching the news.
Angela: I don't care what it is. It's too violent.
Bernard: Yes, you're right, but I suppose it's a sign of the times we're living in. We live in a violent world and so it's only logical that there will be scenes showing violent events on the news.
Angela: Yes, but I don't want to see it. They should cut those bits out.
Bernard: Now you're talking about censoring the news. We don't want to do that, Angela. Journalists have a moral responsibility to report the truth. If we allow them to distort the truth or change the facts just because it may offend or upset some people then we will be asking for trouble.
Angela: That may be so but they shouldn't show such violence early in the evening when there is the possibility that young children may be exposed to it. They could simply report the news and then show the pictures on a later edition.
Bernard: That's a good idea. You know some people say that if children are exposed to violence in the media they develop aggressive behaviour. They say this is why there is so much violence in our society. The violence in society is reflected by the media and shown on TV. Children see it and copy it, and so we have a vicious circle.
Angela: I think they're right. Parents have to be responsible and make sure their children don't watch violent programmes.
Bernard: That's why we have a rating system so people know before a film or TV programme starts what age group it is suitable for and whether it contains violence or sex or bad language.
Angela: Yes, but I don't expect the news to be X-rated!

◆ Tapescript for Exercise 34 (p. 156)

A: Guess what, Dad! I got an A on my Geography project.
B: Well done! What did you end up doing your project on?
A: You remember, it was all about what we should do in case of a natural disaster.
B: Oh yes, that's right. It was all about floods and earthquakes, wasn't it?
A: … and hurricanes.
B: Ok, so tell me, what should I do in an earthquake?
A: Well, the best thing to do is to get under a table or a bed and cover your head, in case there is any falling glass. Oh yes, and if you live in an area where there are a lot of earthquakes you should make sure you carry a whistle with you so that you can whistle for help if you get stuck.
B: That makes sense, but what about a hurricane?
A: There is usually some warning when a hurricane is coming so you must board up all your windows and go to the basement. You should also make sure that you have a supply of candles, bottled water and tinned food, just in case you have to stay down there for a while.
B: Ah ha, I see. And what should I do if there is a flood? Keep a boat in the garage, just in case?
A: Come on Dad, this is serious. You should make sure you wear waterproof clothing so that you won't get too wet while you are waiting to be rescued. Then, you must get as high up as you can, like on the roof of your house or the top of a hill.

B: Well, I am impressed, you obviously did a lot of work for this project. You deserve a good grade. You know, I'm really glad there's *someone* in the family who knows what to do in case of an emergency!

◆ Tapescript for Exercise 51 (p. 161)

Julie: Mum, look at this! I won that painting competition! I got first prize.
Mum: That's wonderful. Well done! What did you win?
Julie: Two weeks at the Suffolk Summer Arts Camp.
Mum: What's that?
Julie: It's a place where you go to learn new techniques and take part in workshops so you can improve your painting skills and learn new things. They teach you all about oils, acrylics and watercolours and other things like how to make jewellery and pottery.
Mum: Wow. That sounds perfect for you. So, when do you go?
Julie: I don't know when it is exactly, it doesn't say. I hope I get all my meals, accommodation and transportation paid for, too.
Mum: I expect you will, but you'd better ask and make sure.
Julie: Yes, I will and I don't know how to get there exactly, so I will ask if somebody is going to pick me up from the airport.
Mum: That's a good idea. It will save you a lot of trouble.
Julie: Yes, and I wonder if we will have lessons all day or if we will have time to do some sightseeing. Perhaps there will be some organised trips, too. I have a lot of questions to ask.
Mum: Yes, you'd better make some notes so you can write a letter and ask them everything you need to know.
Julie: Yes, I'll do that now. Oh, this is really exciting. I've never won anything before.

Module Self-Assessment 5

Tapescript for Exercise 8 (p. 163)

Interviewer: Welcome to the second part of our show. Before the break we were talking to the group "U4", the winner of our local talent competition. They are very talented and we hope that one day we will see them at the top of the charts. However, I have with me now an agent who has worked with many famous musicians and has come to give us some information regarding the problems of being famous. Welcome to the show, Peter.
Peter: Thanks for inviting me.
Interviewer: Now, Peter, perhaps you could explain to us exactly what you mean when you say that famous people have problems. It is certainly hard for us ordinary people to imagine that famous people have any serious problems when most of them have enough money to live a very comfortable life. They also have lots of people taking care of them, like their agents, record companies and so on.
Peter: Well, it might seem like that to the rest of us but when you consider the pressure there is on a famous person to always look good and be polite and friendly you can begin to get an idea of how being famous can sometimes cause a celebrity serious problems.
Interviewer: Ummm... well... I mean, it must be great to be able to walk into a shop or restaurant, be instantly recognized and get the best service. I don't think I would have a problem with people stopping me on the street and asking for my autograph!
Peter: Yes, but unfortunately it doesn't stop there! Imagine you want to go jogging in the park, meet some friends at a café, or even just go shopping with your family on a Saturday afternoon. Your hair, make up and clothes must always look perfect, because you never know when you will be photographed. Not to mention the fact that people constantly come up to you, ask for your autograph and want to tell you how they feel about you and your work!
Interviewer: Well, that still doesn't sound so terrible to me!
Peter: Ok, how would you like to have to have a security system installed to prevent over-enthusiastic fans from breaking into your house, stealing your laundry off the washing line or taking souvenirs from your rubbish bin!
Interviewer: You've got a point. I don't think I'd like that very much!
Peter: Then, of course, there's the paparazzi, the photographers who secretly follow you around, hoping to get a picture of you doing something embarrassing like taking out the rubbish with curlers in your hair. Your family and friends will also find they have very little privacy. The children of famous people have a particularly hard time because their classmates and even teachers will sometimes pretend to be their friend just to get closer to their parents.
Interviewer: That's awful! But there must be some advantages to being famous. For example, having all that money would be nice!
Peter: Even the money can sometimes cause problems. You can certainly afford to live a comfortable lifestyle but the press will always criticize you. Let me give you an example. If you buy an expensive car, they will say you are showing off. If you buy an inexpensive car, they will say you are cheap or having financial problems. You also have to make sure that you have a trustworthy accountant because the tax department will be keeping a strict eye on you!
Interviewer: That's a point, I hadn't thought of that!
Peter: And don't forget, your personal life will become everybody's business. For instance, if you take time off to relax there will be rumours that you are having a nervous breakdown, and if you ever have to go into hospital everyone will know your personal health details.
Interviewer: As you see, being famous can be quite complicated. You see, most people think celebrities are rich, successful people enjoying the attention of the public. Only a few realise that they are people too, who deserve some privacy. Thanks a lot, Peter, for helping us understand a little better what celebrities go through. I suppose you really do have to pay a price for fame.

Word List

UNIT 1

abandon (v) /əbændən/
absent (adj) /æbsənt/
accuse of (v) /əkjuːz əv/
accustomed (adj) /əkʌstəmd/
active (adj) /æktɪv/
adventurous (adj) /ədventʃərəs/
airy (adj) /eəri/
apologise (v) /əpɒlədʒaɪz/
appeal to (v) /əpiːl tu/
appliance (n) /əplaɪəns/
apply (v) /əplaɪ/
approve (v) /əpruːv/
attic (n) /ætɪk/
badly fitting (phr) /bædli fɪtɪŋ/
barrack (n) /bærək/
basement (n) /beɪsmənt/
battlements (n) /bætəlmənts/
become short of (phr)
beg (v) /beg/
bird-watcher (n) /bɜːrd wɒtʃər/
brand-new (adj) /brænd njuː/
built-in (adj) /bɪlt ɪn/
caterer (n) /keɪtərər/
cellar (n) /selər/
centrally located (phr) /sentrəli loʊkeɪtɪd/
chimney (n) /tʃɪmni/
choke (v) /tʃoʊk/
confident (adj) /kɒnfɪdənt/
conservative (adj) /kənsɜːrvətɪv/
convert (v) /kənvɜːrt/
convince (v) /kənvɪns/
cramped (adj) /kræmpt/
creative (adj) /krieɪtɪv/
decay (v) /dɪkeɪ/
depressed (adj) /dɪprest/
detached (adj) /dɪtætʃt/
draughts (n) /drɑːfts/
drawbridge (n) /drɔːbrɪdʒ/
driveway (n) /draɪvweɪ/
druid (n) /druːɪd/
dwelling (n) /dwelɪŋ/
electrocution (n) /ɪlektrəkjuːʃən/
eloquent (adj) /eləkwənt/
evict (v) /ɪvɪkt/
experience (v) /ɪkspɪəriəns/
extension (n) /ɪkstenʃən/
feature (n) /fiːtʃər/
fence (n) /fents/
fibreglass (n) /faɪbərglɑːs/
fitted (adj) /fɪtɪd/
fortress (n) /fɔːrtrɪs/
from scratch (idm) /frəm skrætʃ/
fuel bill (phr) /fjuːəl bɪl/
fully furnished (phr) /fʊli fɜːrnɪʃt/

guard rail (phr) /gɑːrd reɪl/
harsh (adj) /hɑːrʃ/
hay fever (phr) /heɪ fiːvər/
humidifier (n) /hjuːmɪdɪfaɪər/
hut (n) /hʌt/
impractical (adj) /ɪmpræktɪkəl/
in authority (phr) /ɪn ɔːθɒrɪti/
indigestion (n) /ɪndɪdʒestʃən/
intact (adj) /ɪntækt/
isolated (adj) /aɪsəleɪtɪd/
keep (n) /kiːp/
landmark (n) /lændmɑːrk/
leaking (adj) /liːkɪŋ/
lodging (n) /lɒdʒɪŋ/
lounge (n) /laʊndʒ/
memorable (adj) /memərəbəl/
moat (n) /moʊt/
mop (v) /mɒp/
move out (phr v) /muːv aʊt/
mow (v) /moʊ/
occupy (v) /ɒkjupaɪ/
outcrop (n) /aʊtkrɒp/
outskirts (n) /aʊtskɜːrts/
peaceful (adj) /piːsfʊl/
pitched (adj) /pɪtʃt/
prevent (v) /prɪvent/
rear patio (phr) /rɪər pætioʊ/
rename (v) /riːneɪm/
rental details (phr) /rentəl diːteɪlz/
residential area (phr) /rezɪdentʃəl eəriə/
resist (v) /rɪzɪst/
rubber mat (phr) /rʌbər mæt/
safety catches (phr) /seɪfti kætsɪz/
safety cover (phr) /seɪfti kʌvər/
safety gate (phr) /seɪfti geɪt/
scalding (adj) /skɔːldɪŋ/
sculpture (n) /skʌlptʃər/
set up (phr v) /set ʌp/
setting (n) /setɪŋ/
shadow (n) /ʃædoʊ/
sheer cliff (phr) /ʃɪər klɪf/
sliding (adj) /slaɪdɪŋ/
spacious (adj) /speɪʃəs/
spare room (phr) /speər ruːm/
spiral (adj) /spaɪərəl/
spruce (n) /spruːs/
stable (n) /steɪbəl/
stand out (phr v) /stænd aʊt/
stilt (n) /stɪlt/
storehouse (n) /stɔːrhaʊs/
storey (n) /stɔːri/
suburb (n) /sʌbɜːb/
suitable for (phr) /suːtəbəl fər/
terraced (adj) /terəst/
thatched (adj) /θætʃt/

tiled (adj) /taɪəld/
tiny (adj) /taɪni/
watch group (phr) /wɒtʃ gruːp/
well-maintained (adj) /wel meɪnteɪnd/
winding (adj) /waɪndɪŋ/
withdrawn (adj) /wɪðdrɔːn/

UNIT 2

abruptly (adv) /əbrʌptli/
absorbed in (phr) /əbzɔːrbd ɪn/
achieve (v) /ətʃiːv/
allow (v) /əlaʊ/
anatomy (n) /ənætəmi/
announce (v) /ənaʊns/
announcement (n) /ənaʊnsmənt/
arched (adj) /ɑːrtʃt/
avid (adj) /ævɪd/
balance (v) /bæləns/
banner (n) /bænər/
bark (v) /bɑːrk/
barrel (n) /bærəl/
basement (n) /beɪsmənt/
best seller (phr) /best selər/
Board of Education (phr) /bɔːrd əv edʒukeɪʃən/
brace (v) /breɪs/
break in (phr v) /breɪk ɪn/
bring up (phr v) /brɪŋ ʌp/
broad (adj) /brɔːd/
broad-shouldered (adj) /brɔːd ʃoʊldərd/
build (n) /bɪld/
bump (v) /bʌmp/
bushy (adj) /bʊʃi/
bustling (adj) /bʌslɪŋ/
candy-scrape (n) /kændi skreɪp/
capable of (phr) /keɪpəbəl/
centre parting (phr) /sentər pɑːrtɪŋ/
chap (n) /tʃæp/
charge with (phr v) /tʃɑːrdʒ wɪð/
chat room (phr) /tʃæt ruːm/
cheek (n) /tʃiːk/
cheer (v) /tʃɪər/
cheerful (adj) /tʃɪərfəl/
chilly (adj) /tʃɪli/
cling (v) /klɪŋ/
comment on (phr) /kɒmənt ɒn/
concentrate on (phr) /kɒnsəntreɪt ɒn/
congregate (v) /kɒŋgrɪgeɪt/
cope with (phr) /koʊp wɪð/
crash (v) /kræʃ/
criticise (v) /krɪtɪsaɪz/

crooked (adj) /krʊkɪd/
crowd (n) /kraʊd/
curl (n) /kɜːrl/
damsel (n) /dæmzəl/
deaf (adj) /def/
deafening (adj) /defənɪŋ/
declare (v) /dɪkleər/
dedicate to (phr) /dedɪkeɪt tu/
depend on (phr) /dɪpend ɒn/
determined (adj) /dɪtɜːrmɪnd/
devoted (adj) /dɪvoʊtɪd/
diary (n) /daɪəri/
dimple (n) /dɪmpəl/
disappointed (adj) /dɪsəpɔɪntɪd/
dismiss from (phr) /dɪsmɪs frəm/
divorce (n) /dɪvɔːrs/
do-or-die expression (phr)
doubtful (adj) /daʊtfʊl/
driving licence (phr) /draɪvɪŋ laɪsəns/
eagerness (n) /iːgərnəs/
ecstatic (adj) /ekstætɪk/
electrical wire (phr) /ɪlektrɪkəl waɪər/
emoticon (n) /ɪmoʊtɪkɒn/
encourage (v) /ɪnkʌrɪdʒ/
engagement (n) /ɪngeɪdʒmənt/
excited (adj) /ɪksaɪtɪd/
executive (adj) /ɪgzekjʊtɪv/
experience (n) /ɪkspɪəriəns/
experiment (n) /ɪksperɪmənt/
expressive (adj) /ɪkspresɪv/
feast (n) /fiːst/
field (n) /fiːld/
finances (n) /faɪnænsəz/
financial security (phr) /faɪnænʃəl sɪkjʊərɪti/
financially (adv) /faɪnænʃəli/
finishing line (phr) /fɪnɪʃɪŋ laɪn/
fire brigade (phr) /faɪər brɪgeɪd/
first-rate (adj) /fɜːrst reɪt/
folk (n) /foʊk/
forehead (n) /fɒrɪd/
forgive (v) /fərgɪv/
freckle (n) /frekəl/
frizzy (adj) /frɪzi/
frustrated (adj) /frʌstreɪtɪd/
furious (adj) /fjʊəriəs/
generation (n) /dʒenəreɪʃən/
give up (phr v) /gɪv ʌp/
gloomy (adj) /gluːmi/
goal (n) /goʊl/
good-natured (adj) /gʊd neɪtʃərd/
graduate (v) /grædʒueɪt/
graduation (n) /grædʒueɪʃən/
grin (n) /grɪn/

216

Word List

Guess what! (phr)
handsomely (adv) /hænsəmli/
have an early night (phr)
highly-paid (adj) /haɪli peɪd/
hug (v) /hʌg/
in store (phr) /ɪn stɔːʳ/
inaudible (adj) /ɪnɔːdɪbəl/
increase (n) /ɪnkriːs/
influence (v) /ɪnfluəns/
injury (n) /ɪndʒəri/
iron rod (phr) /aɪəʳn rɒd/
irritated (adj) /ɪrɪteɪtɪd/
join the army (phr)
lad (n) /læd/
lick (v) /lɪk/
living conditions (phr) /lɪvɪŋ kəndɪʃənz/
lose hearing (phr) /luːz hɪərɪŋ/
majority (n) /mədʒɒrɪti/
marriage (n) /mærɪdʒ/
message notification (phr) /mesɪdʒ noʊtɪfɪkeɪʃən/
mischievous (adj) /mɪstʃɪvəs/
molasses (n) /məlæsɪz/
motivated (adj) /moʊtɪveɪtɪd/
moving house (phr) /muːvɪŋ haʊs/
mute (adj) /mjuːt/
nickname (n) /nɪkneɪm/
overjoyed (adj) /oʊvəʳdʒɔɪd/
patent office (phr) /peɪtənt ɒfɪs/
path (n) /pɑːθ/
pinnacle (n) /pɪnɪkəl/
pleased (adj) /pliːzd/
pointed chin (phr) /pɔɪntɪd tʃɪn/
qualify for (v) /kwɒlɪfaɪ fəʳ/
reflect (v) /rɪflekt/
register (v) /redʒɪstəʳ/
repose (v) /rɪpoʊz/
responsibility (n) /rɪspɒnsɪbɪlɪti/
resume (v) /rɪzjuːm/
retirement (n) /rɪtaɪəʳmənt/
run out of (phr v) /rʌn aʊt əv/
scared (adj) /skeəʳd/
scornful (adj) /skɔːʳnfəl/
seem (v) /siːm/
senior citizen (phr) /siːnjəʳ sɪtɪzən/
set off (phr v) /set ɒf/
shake (v) /ʃeɪk/
shield (n) /ʃiːld/
sideburn (n) /saɪdbɜːʳn/
siren wailing (phr) /saɪərən weɪlɪŋ/
slyly (adv) /slaɪli/
snub (adj) /snʌb/
solemn (adj) /sɒləm/

sound transmitter (phr) /saʊnd trænzmɪtəʳ/
sparkle (v) /spɑːʳkəl/
spectator (n) /spekteɪtəʳ/
speech problem (phr) /spiːtʃ prɒbləm/
spiky (adj) /spaɪki/
splash (v) /splæʃ/
spoil (v) /spɔɪl/
sports field (phr) /spɔːʳts fiːld/
spread (v) /spred/
sprint (v) /sprɪnt/
spin (v) /spɪn/
state (v) /steɪt/
stick out (phr v) /stɪk aʊt/
subscription (n) /səbskrɪpʃən/
subside (v) /səbsaɪd/
survey (n) /sɜːʳveɪ/
survive (v) /səʳvaɪv/
tearful (adj) /tɪəʳfʊl/
telegraphy (n) /telɪɡrɑːfi/
That's a pity. (phr)
thrilled (adj) /θrɪld/
thunder (n) /θʌndəʳ/
timid (adj) /tɪmɪd/
tippet (n) /tɪpət/
tiptop (n) /tɪptɒp/
toddler (n) /tɒdləʳ/
transmit (v) /trænzmɪt/
trembler (n) /trembləʳ/
tribe (n) /traɪb/
turn of the century (phr)
unanimity (n) /juːnənɪmɪti/
unbearable (adj) /ʌnbeərəbəl/
vibration (n) /vaɪbreɪʃən/
voice transmitter (phr) /vɔɪs trænzmɪtəʳ/
wage (n) /weɪdʒ/
waste of time (phr)
wave (v) /weɪv/
white plague (phr) /ʰwaɪt pleɪɡ/
whiz (v) /ʰwɪz/
winner's certificate (phr) /wɪnəz səʳtɪfɪkət/
wire (n) /waɪəʳ/
workshop (n) /wɜːʳkʃɒp/
worldwide (adv) /wɜːʳldwaɪd/
worried (adj) /wʌrid/
wrinkle (n) /rɪŋkəl/

UNIT 3

acre (n) /eɪkəʳ/
adventure (n) /ædventʃəʳ/
alike (adv) /əlaɪk/
appreciate (v) /əpriːʃieɪt/

archery (n) /ɑːʳtʃəri/
aspect (n) /æspekt/
aspiring (adj) /əspaɪərɪŋ/
assign (v) /əsaɪn/
award-winning (adj) /əwɔːʳd wɪnɪŋ/
bargain (n) /bɑːʳɡɪn/
boiling hot (phr) /bɔɪlɪŋ hɒt/
bothered (adj) /bɒðəʳd/
break (n) /breɪk/
broaden (v) /brɔːdən/
brochure (n) /broʊʃəʳ/
cable (n) /keɪbəl/
cancel (v) /kænsəl/
chalk (n) /tʃɔːk/
changeable (adj) /tʃeɪndʒəbəl/
chief (n) /tʃiːf/
claim (v) /kleɪm/
clue (n) /kluː/
coastline (n) /koʊstlaɪn/
cobbled (adj) /kɒbəld/
colony (n) /kɒləni/
compact (adj) /kəmpækt/
conference (n) /kɒnfrəns/
confirm (v) /kənfɜːʳm/
consulate (n) /kɒnsjʊlət/
continent (n) /kɒntɪnənt/
continental (adj) /kɒntɪnentəl/
convenience (n) /kənviːniəns/
court (n) /kɔːʳt/
craft (n) /krɑːft/
credit card (phr) /kredɪt kɑːʳd/
cruise (n) /kruːz/
cuisine (n) /kwɪziːn/
date back (phr v) /deɪt bæk/
decade (n) /dekeɪd/
deer (n) /dɪəʳ/
defend (v) /dɪfend/
deposit (n) /dɪpɒzɪt/
destination (n) /destɪneɪʃən/
dine (v) /daɪn/
discount (n) /dɪskaʊnt/
drop sb a line (phr)
due to (prep) /djuː tu/
dye-filled (adj) /daɪ fɪld/
eager (adj) /iːɡəʳ/
elegant (adj) /elɪɡənt/
elk (n) /elk/
embassy (n) /embəsi/
emergency (n) /ɪmɜːʳdʒənsi/
enthusiastic (adj) /ɪnθjuːziæstɪk/
establish (v) /ɪstæblɪʃ/
exceptional (adj) /ɪksepʃənəl/
facility (n) /fəsɪlɪti/
fair (adj) /feəʳ/
fall (n) /fɔːl/
familiar (adj) /fəmɪliəʳ/

fans (n) /fænz/
feel a bit under the weather (idm)
feel up to sth (phr v) /fiːl ʌp tu/
fiesta (n) /fiestə/
fir (n) /fɜːʳ/
first aid kit (phr) /fɜːʳst eɪd kɪt/
flat (adj) /flæt/
float (v) /floʊt/
fortune (n) /fɔːʳtʃuːn/
fossil (n) /fɒsəl/
four-poster (adj) /fɔːʳ poʊstəʳ/
freeze (v) /friːz/
freight (n) /freɪt/
fully equipped (phr) /fʊli ɪkwɪpt/
gather (v) /gæðəʳ/
get a move on (phr)
glamorous (adj) /glæmərəs/
glimpse (n) /ɡlɪmps/
goat (n) /goʊt/
goggle (n) /gɒgəl/
gourmet (adj) /ɡʊəʳmeɪ/
guard (n) /gɑːʳd/
guidebook (n) /gaɪdbʊk/
hamper (v) /hæmpəʳ/
handmade (adj) /hændmeɪd/
hatchback (n) /hætʃbæk/
health spa (phr) /helθ spɑː/
heated (adj) /hiːtɪd/
hot spot (phr) /hɒt spɒt/
in advance (phr) /ɪn ædvɑːns/
in the nick of time (phr)
insect repellent (phr) /ɪnsekt rɪpelənt/
insurance (n) /ɪnʃʊərəns/
interior (n) /ɪntɪəriəʳ/
invasion (n) /ɪnveɪʒən/
journey (n) /dʒɜːʳni/
lantern (n) /læntəʳn/
legendary (adj) /ledʒəndri/
leisurely (adj) /leʒəʳli/
lifetime (n) /laɪftaɪm/
live out of a suitcase (idm)
log fire (phr) /lɒg faɪəʳ/
loom (v) /luːm/
make ends meet (idm)
medieval (adj) /mediːvəl/
mild (adj) /maɪld/
mislabel (v) /mɪsleɪbəl/
mist (n) /mɪst/
money belt (phr) /mʌni belt/
moor (n) /mʊəʳ/
moss (n) /mɒs/
mugger (n) /mʌgəʳ/
non-refundable (adj) /nɒn rɪfʌndəbəl/
orbit (n) /ɔːbɪt/

217

Word List

outer (adj) /ˈaʊtər/
outline (n) /ˈaʊtlaɪn/
overcharge (v) /ˌoʊvərˈtʃɑːrdʒ/
package holiday (phr) /ˈpækɪdʒ ˈhɒlɪdeɪ/
palm-fringed (adj) /pɑːm frɪndʒd/
pastime (n) /ˈpɑːstaɪm/
peak (n) /piːk/
pickpocket (n) /ˈpɪkpɒkɪt/
piñon pine (phr) /ˈpɪnɒn paɪn/
power cut (phr) /ˈpaʊər kʌt/
preliminary (adj) /prɪˈlɪmɪnri/
proposed (adj) /prəˈpoʊzd/
public (adj) /ˈpʌblɪk/
put my feet up (idm)
race (n) /reɪs/
railroad route (phr) /ˈreɪlroʊd ruːt/
range (n) /reɪndʒ/
restore (v) /rɪˈstɔːr/
reusable (adj) /riːˈjuːzəbəl/
ridge (n) /rɪdʒ/
roam (v) /roʊm/
roar (v) /rɔːr/
rucksack (n) /ˈrʌksæk/
rugged (adj) /ˈrʌgɪd/
ruins (n) /ˈruːɪnz/
sample (v) /ˈsɑːmpəl/
sandy (adj) /ˈsændi/
scenery (n) /ˈsiːnəri/
scenic (adj) /ˈsiːnɪk/
seafood (n) /ˈsiːfuːd/
secluded (adj) /sɪˈkluːdɪd/
self-contained (adj) /self kənˈteɪnd/
settler (n) /ˈsetlər/
shipping lane (phr) /ˈʃɪpɪŋ leɪn/
shipwreck (n) /ˈʃɪprek/
short of (phr) /ʃɔːrt əv/
site (n) /saɪt/
ski lift pass (phr) /skiː lɪft pɑːs/
slope (n) /sloʊp/
snorkel (v) /ˈsnɔːrkəl/
soaked (adj) /soʊkt/
spectacular (adj) /spekˈtækjʊlər/
squirrel (n) /ˈskwɪrəl/
stained glass (phr) /steɪnd glɑːs/
stone's throw (phr) /stoʊnz θroʊ/
stopover (n) /ˈstɒpoʊvər/
strategic (adj) /strəˈtiːdʒɪk/
stretch (v) /stretʃ/
stroll (n) /stroʊl/
stun (v) /stʌn/
stylish (adj) /ˈstaɪlɪʃ/
sunscreen (n) /ˈsʌnskriːn/
touch (n) /tʌtʃ/

tour (n) /tʊər/
tower (v) /ˈtaʊər/
track (n) /træk/
travel (n) /ˈtrævəl/
trendy (adj) /ˈtrendi/
trip (n) /trɪp/
tyre (n) /ˈtaɪər/
ultimate (adj) /ˈʌltɪmət/
unspoiled (adj) /ʌnˈspɔɪld/
upscale (v) /ʌpˈskeɪl/
vacancy (n) /ˈveɪkənsi/
volunteer (n) /ˌvɒlənˈtɪər/
wander (v) /ˈwɒndər/
waterfront (n) /ˈwɔːtərfrʌnt/
weather forecast (phr) /ˈweðər fɔːrkɑːst/
white-water rafting (phr) /ˈhwaɪt wɔːtər ˈrɑːftɪŋ/
wild game (phr) /waɪld geɪm/
wildlife (n) /ˈwaɪldlaɪf/
wind (n) /wɪnd/
wintry (adj) /ˈwɪntri/
with regard to (phr)
woodland (n) /ˈwʊdlənd/

UNIT 4

acid rain (phr) /ˈæsɪd reɪn/
address (n) /əˈdres/
afar (adv) /əˈfɑːr/
alternative (adj) /ɔːlˈtɜːrnətɪv/
ant (n) /ænt/
armour (n) /ˈɑːrmər/
array (n) /əˈreɪ/
ballad (n) /ˈbæləd/
ban (v) /bæn/
budget (n) /ˈbʌdʒɪt/
can't help (phr) /kɑːnt help/
can't stand (phr) /kɑːnt stænd/
car pool (phr) /kɑːr puːl/
centipede (n) /ˈsentɪpiːd/
circumference (n) /sərˈkʌmfrəns/
clad (adj) /klæd/
clover (n) /ˈkloʊvər/
coal (n) /koʊl/
community (n) /kəˈmjuːnɪti/
consequence (n) /ˈkɒnsɪkwens/
conservation (n) /ˌkɒnsərˈveɪʃən/
crimson (adj) /ˈkrɪmzən/
daisy tree (phr) /ˈdeɪzi triː/
deceive (v) /dɪˈsiːv/
deforestation (n) /diːˌfɒrɪˈsteɪʃən/
demand (v) /dɪˈmɑːnd/
diameter (n) /daɪˈæmɪtər/
drawback (n) /ˈdrɔːbæk/
drift (v) /drɪft/
emit (v) /ɪˈmɪt/

endangered species (phr) /ɪnˈdeɪndʒərd ˈspiːʃiːz/
energy use (phr) /ˈenərdʒi juːs/
epic (adj) /ˈepɪk/
face (v) /feɪs/
fairy land (phr) /ˈfeəri lænd/
filter (n) /ˈfɪltər/
fluorescent (adj) /flʊəˈresənt/
fossil fuel (phr) /ˈfɒsəl fjuːəl/
fragile (adj) /ˈfrædʒaɪl/
frozen (adj) /ˈfroʊzən/
gadget (n) /ˈgædʒɪt/
gas mask (n) /gæs mɑːsk/
generate (v) /ˈdʒenəreɪt/
global warming (phr) /ˈgloʊbəl ˈwɔːrmɪŋ/
grainmill (n) /ˈgreɪnmɪl/
grateful (adj) /ˈgreɪtfʊl/
greenhouse gases (phr) /ˈgriːnhaʊs ˈgæsɪz/
hold still (phr) /hoʊld stɪl/
hue (n) /hjuː/
hum (v) /hʌm/
humming fly (phr) /ˈhʌmɪŋ flaɪ/
hydropower (n) /ˈhaɪdroʊpaʊər/
imagery (n) /ˈɪmɪdʒri/
industrial (adj) /ɪnˈdʌstriəl/
inspire (v) /ɪnˈspaɪər/
insulate (v) /ˈɪnsjʊleɪt/
Inuit (n) /ˈɪnjuɪt/
knob (n) /nɒb/
lack (n) /læk/
layer (n) /ˈleɪər/
lizard (n) /ˈlɪzərd/
logger (n) /ˈlɒgər/
lose heart (phr) /luːz hɑːrt/
lyric (n) /ˈlɪrɪk/
mahogany (n) /məˈhɒgəni/
mammal (n) /ˈmæməl/
mend (v) /mend/
nuclear (adj) /ˈnjuːklɪər/
objection (n) /əbˈdʒekʃən/
off limits (phr) /ɒf ˈlɪmɪts/
offshore (adv) /ˈɒfʃɔːr/
ozone layer (phr) /ˈoʊzoʊn leɪər/
pedestrian (n) /pɪˈdestriən/
percentage (n) /pərˈsentɪdʒ/
perch (v) /pɜːrtʃ/
permafrost (n) /ˈpɜːrməfrɒst/
pied (adj) /piːd/
poisonous (adj) /ˈpɔɪzənəs/
pole (n) /poʊl/
power (v) /ˈpaʊər/
pump (v) /pʌmp/
push (n) /pʊʃ/
quotation (n) /kwoʊˈteɪʃən/
radiation (n) /ˌreɪdiˈeɪʃən/
rare (adj) /reər/

recycle (v) /riːˈsaɪkəl/
reindeer (n) /ˈreɪndɪər/
rely on (v) /rɪˈlaɪ ɒn/
renewable (adj) /rɪˈnjuːəbəl/
reserve (v) /rɪˈzɜːrv/
resource (n) /rɪˈsɔːrs/
rhetorical (adj) /rɪˈtɒrɪkəl/
rhyme (n) /raɪm/
rhythm (n) /ˈrɪðəm/
rotor blade (phr) /ˈroʊtər bleɪd/
rubbish dump (phr) /ˈrʌbɪʃ dʌmp/
run (v) /rʌn/
safeguard (v) /ˈseɪfgɑːrd/
sanctuary (n) /ˈsæŋktʃuəri/
sawmill (n) /ˈsɔːmɪl/
seed (n) /siːd/
set up (phr v) /set ʌp/
share (v) /ʃeər/
shortage (n) /ˈʃɔːrtɪdʒ/
shower (n) /ˈʃaʊər/
significant (adj) /sɪgˈnɪfɪkənt/
sleepy-head (n) /ˈsliːpi hed/
solar (adj) /ˈsoʊlər/
sorrel (n) /ˈsɒrəl/
sow (v) /soʊ/
stitch (n) /stɪtʃ/
storm (n) /stɔːrm/
swallow (n) /ˈswɒloʊ/
swift (adj) /swɪft/
take advantage of (phr)
take for granted (phr)
tear (n) /tɪər/
timber (n) /ˈtɪmbər/
treasure (n) /ˈtreʒər/
treeless (adj) /ˈtriːləs/
tuck (v) /tʌk/
tundra (n) /ˈtʌndrə/
turbine (n) /ˈtɜːrbaɪn/
ultraviolet (adj) /ˌʌltrəˈvaɪələt/
unoccupied (adj) /ʌnˈɒkjʊpaɪd/
urban sprawl (phr) /ˈɜːrbən sprɔːl/
verse (n) /vɜːrs/
vote (v) /voʊt/
waste (n) /weɪst/
wing (n) /wɪŋ/
wipe out (phr v) /waɪp aʊt/

UNIT 5

accident prone (phr) /ˈæksɪdənt proʊn/
ache (v) /eɪk/
acidic (adj) /əˈsɪdɪk/
acne (n) /ˈækni/
alert (adj) /əˈlɜːrt/

Word List

alkaline (adj) /ˈælkəlaɪn/
allergic (adj) /əˈlɜːrdʒɪk/
annual (adj) /ˈænjuəl/
antacid (adj) /æntˈæsɪd/
arrogant (adj) /ˈærəgənt/
arthritis (n) /ɑːrˈθraɪtɪs/
asthma (n) /ˈæsmə/
average (n) /ˈævərɪdʒ/
awaken (v) /əˈweɪkən/
aware (adj) /əˈweəʳ/
bacteria (n) /bækˈtɪəriə/
blemish (n) /ˈblemɪʃ/
bloated (adj) /ˈbloʊtɪd/
bloodstream (n) /ˈblʌdstriːm/
brain (n) /breɪn/
break the ice (phr)
bubble (n) /ˈbʌbəl/
carbohydrate (n) /ˌkɑːrboʊˈhaɪdreɪt/
cast (n) /kɑːst/
cave (n) /keɪv/
cereal (n) /ˈsɪəriəl/
check-up (n) /ˈtʃek ʌp/
circulate (v) /ˈsɜːrkjʊleɪt/
clumsy (adj) /ˈklʌmzi/
conductor (n) /kənˈdʌktəʳ/
construct (v) /kənˈstrʌkt/
crack of dawn (phr)
cramp (n) /kræmp/
crater (n) /ˈkreɪtəʳ/
cure (n) /kjʊəʳ/
decline (v) /dɪˈklaɪn/
depressed (adj) /dɪˈprest/
deprive of (v) /dɪˈpraɪv əv/
determine (v) /dɪˈtɜːrmɪn/
diarrhoea (n) /ˌdaɪəˈriːə/
digestive system (phr) /daɪˈdʒestɪv sɪstəm/
dizziness (n) /ˈdɪzinəs/
dose (n) /doʊz/
early bird (phr) /ˈɜːrli bɜːrd/
endorphin (n) /ɪnˈdɔːrfɪn/
enquiry (n) /ɪnˈkwaɪəri/
erect (v) /ɪˈrekt/
evolution (n) /ˌiːvəˈluːʃən/
existence (n) /ɪgˈzɪstəns/
fatigue (n) /fəˈtiːg/
feathered (adj) /ˈfeðəʳd/
feel it in my bones (phr)
fever (n) /ˈfiːvəʳ/
flu (n) /fluː/
fluid (n) /ˈfluːɪd/
food poisoning (n) /ˈfuːd pɔɪzənɪŋ/
found (v) /faʊnd/
gene (n) /dʒiːn/
get that off my chest (phr)
geyser (n) /ˈgiːzəʳ/

glucose (n) /ˈgluːkoʊz/
harmony (n) /ˈhɑːrməni/
have itchy feet (phr)
heart attack (phr) /hɑːrt əˈtæk/
heart disease (phr) /hɑːrt dɪˈziːz/
heat stroke (phr) /ˈhiːt stroʊk/
hit the jackpot (idm)
hormone (n) /ˈhɔːrmoʊn/
hot spring (phr) /hɒt sprɪŋ/
humid (adj) /ˈhjuːmɪd/
hypothalamus (n) /ˌhaɪpoʊˈθæləməs/
identical (adj) /aɪˈdentɪkəl/
immune (adj) /ɪˈmjuːn/
in tune with (phr)
indicate (v) /ˈɪndɪkeɪt/
insomnia (n) /ɪnˈsɒmniə/
limestone (n) /ˈlaɪmstoʊn/
lump (n) /lʌmp/
mechanism (n) /ˈmekənɪzəm/
miner (n) /ˈmaɪnəʳ/
mineral (adj) /ˈmɪnərəl/
moody (adj) /ˈmuːdi/
motivate (v) /ˈmoʊtɪveɪt/
mud (n) /mʌd/
muscle contraction (phr) /ˈmʌsəl kənˈtrækʃən/
muscular (adj) /ˈmʌskjʊləʳ/
native (adj) /ˈneɪtɪv/
nausea (n) /ˈnɔːziə/
neuralgia (n) /njʊəˈrældʒə/
night owl (phr) /naɪt aʊl/
nine-to-fiver (phr) /naɪn tə faɪvəʳ/
nocturnal (adj) /nɒkˈtɜːrnəl/
nose bleed (phr) /noʊz bliːd/
outsmart (v) /aʊtˈsmɑːrt/
owl (n) /aʊl/
patient (adj) /ˈpeɪʃənt/
perfectionist (n) /pəˈfekʃənɪst/
physical (adj) /ˈfɪzɪkəl/
pill (n) /pɪl/
pneumonia (n) /njuːˈmoʊniə/
pollen (n) /ˈpɒlən/
practical (adj) /ˈpræktɪkəl/
predictable (adj) /prɪˈdɪktəbəl/
prescribe (v) /prɪˈskraɪb/
priest (n) /priːst/
prospector (n) /prəˈspektəʳ/
psychological (adj) /ˌsaɪkəˈlɒdʒɪkəl/
put my finger on (idm)
put words into my mouth (idm)
queue (n) /kjuː/
random (adj) /ˈrændəm/
rat race (idm) /ræt reɪs/
regulate (v) /ˈregjʊleɪt/

reliable (adj) /rɪˈlaɪəbəl/
relieving (adj) /rɪˈliːvɪŋ/
revolution (n) /ˌrevəˈluːʃən/
rheumatism (n) /ˈruːmətɪzəm/
runny nose (phr) /ˈrʌni noʊz/
scar (n) /skɑːr/
sentimental (adj) /ˌsentɪˈmentəl/
serotonin (n) /ˌserəˈtoʊnɪn/
shift work (phr) /ʃɪft wɜːrk/
side effect (phr) /saɪd ɪˈfekt/
sleep pattern (phr) /sliːp pætərn/
sling (v) /slɪŋ/
slow-paced (adj) /sloʊ peɪst/
sneeze (v) /sniːz/
sociable (adj) /ˈsoʊʃəbəl/
sore eyes (phr) /sɔːr aɪz/
spa (n) /spɑː/
splitting (adj) /ˈsplɪtɪŋ/
spot (n) /spɒt/
sprain (v) /spreɪn/
steam (n) /stiːm/
stethoscope (n) /ˈsteθəskoʊp/
streaming (adj) /ˈstriːmɪŋ/
strict (adj) /strɪkt/
stroke (n) /stroʊk/
stomach (n) /ˈstʌmək/
surface (n) /ˈsɜːrfɪs/
sweet tooth (idm) /swiːt tuːθ/
synchronise (v) /ˈsɪŋkrənaɪz/
tablet (n) /ˈtæblət/
tempo (n) /ˈtempoʊ/
tick (v) /tɪk/
traffic jam (phr) /ˈtræfɪk dʒæm/
travel sickness (phr) /ˈtrævəl sɪknəs/
treatment (n) /ˈtriːtmənt/
ulcer (n) /ˈʌlsəʳ/
viral infection (phr) /ˈvaɪərəl ɪnˈfekʃən/
virus (n) /ˈvaɪərəs/
volcano (n) /vɒlˈkeɪnoʊ/
wakeful (adj) /ˈweɪkfʊl/
weightlifting (n) /ˈweɪtlɪftɪŋ/
wellbeing (n) /ˈwelbiːɪŋ/
wheeze (v) /ʰwiːz/
wildlife reserve (phr) /ˈwaɪldlaɪf rɪzɜːrv/
yawn (v) /jɔːn/

UNIT 6

access (n) /ˈækses/
affair (n) /əˈfeəʳ/
answering machine (phr) /ˈɑːnsərɪŋ məʃiːn/
apparatus (n) /ˌæpəˈreɪtəs/

approve (v) /əˈpruːv/
arsonist (n) /ˈɑːrsənɪst/
ATM (n)
automatically (adv) /ˌɔːtəˈmætɪkli/
aware of (adj) /əˈweəʳ əv/
bare (adj) /beəʳ/
be in the mood (phr)
birth certificate (phr) /bɜːrθ səˈtɪfɪkət/
call direct (phr) /kɔːl daɪrekt/
capture (v) /ˈkæptʃəʳ/
carjack (n) /ˈkɑːrdʒæk/
cheat (v) /tʃiːt/
clay (n) /kleɪ/
closed circuit (phr) /kloʊzd sɜːrkɪt/
commit crimes (phr) /kəˈmɪt kraɪmz/
company (n) /ˈkʌmpəni/
computer graphics (phr) /kəmˈpjuːtəʳ ˈgræfɪks/
contact (n) /ˈkɒntækt/
contain (v) /kənˈteɪn/
couch potato (idm) /kaʊtʃ pəˈteɪtoʊ/
courtroom (n) /ˈkɔːrtrʊm/
courtyard (n) /ˈkɔːrtjɑːrd/
data (n) /ˈdeɪtə/
defence (n) /dɪˈfens/
devote (v) /dɪˈvoʊt/
diary entry (phr) /ˈdaɪəri entri/
discourage (v) /dɪsˈkʌrɪdʒ/
disruptive (adj) /dɪsˈrʌptɪv/
dozen (n) /ˈdʌzən/
drop off (v) /drɒp ɒf/
DVD (n)
elaborate (adj) /ɪˈlæbərət/
enamel (adj) /ɪˈnæməl/
enforce (v) /ɪnˈfɔːrs/
estimate (v) /ˈestɪmeɪt/
face charge (phr) /feɪs tʃɑːrdʒ/
face recognition (n) /feɪs ˌrekəgˈnɪʃən/
fine (n) /faɪn/
finger scanning (phr) /ˈfɪŋgəʳ skænɪŋ/
fingerprinting (n) /ˈfɪŋgəʳprɪntɪŋ/
flame (n) /fleɪm/
floppy disk (phr) /ˈflɒpi dɪsk/
footstep identification (phr) /ˈfʊtstep aɪˌdentɪfɪˈkeɪʃən/
force (v) /fɔːrs/
forefinger (n) /ˈfɔːrfɪŋgəʳ/
forger (n) /ˈfɔːrdʒəʳ/
forth (adv) /fɔːrθ/
framework (n) /ˈfreɪmwɜːrk/
fraud (n) /frɔːd/
hacker (n) /ˈhækəʳ/

219

Word List

hard drive (phr) /hɑːrd draɪv/
hijacker (n) /haɪdʒækər/
ID card (phr) /aɪdiː kɑːrd/
identification (n) /aɪdentɪfɪkeɪʃən/
identify (v) /aɪdentɪfaɪ/
illuminate (v) /ɪluːmɪneɪt/
imitate (v) /ɪmɪteɪt/
in profile (phr) /ɪn proʊfaɪl/
incredible (adj) /ɪnkredɪbəl/
indistinct (adj) /ɪndɪstɪŋkt/
install (v) /ɪnstɔːl/
judge (n) /dʒʌdʒ/
keep in touch (with) (phr)
keep track of (phr)
keyboard (n) /kiːbɔːrd/
keypad (n) /kiːpæd/
kidnapper (n) /kɪdnæpər/
laptop (n) /læptɒp/
lean (v) /liːn/
lever (n) /liːvər/
line up (v) /laɪn ʌp/
liquidise (v) /lɪkwɪdaɪz/
locate (v) /loʊkeɪt/
log off (phr v) /lɒg ɒf/
log on (phr v) /lɒg ɒn/
mailbox (n) /meɪlbɒks/
maintain (v) /meɪnteɪn/
mankind (n) /mænkaɪnd/
mantel (n) /mæntəl/
microwave oven (phr)
  /maɪkroʊweɪv ʌvən/
miniature (n) /mɪnɪtʃər/
mishap (n) /mɪshæp/
mistake sb for (v) /mɪsteɪk fər/
monitor (v) /mɒnɪtər/
mouse (n) /maʊs/
MP3 (n)
mugging (n) /mʌgɪŋ/
name after (v) /neɪm ɑːftər/
network (n) /netwɜːrk/
notorious (adj) /noʊtɔːriəs/
occur (v) /əkɜːr/
odd (adj) /ɒd/
on the alert (phr)
operate (v) /ɒpəreɪt/
opposed to (adj) /əpoʊzd tə/
password (n) /pɑːswɜːrd/
pause (n) /pɔːz/
PIN (n)
plead not guilty (phr)
plug in (v) /plʌg ɪn/
preserve (v) /prɪzɜːrv/
printer (n) /prɪntər/
privacy (n) /prɪvəsi/
proof (n) /pruːf/
property (n) /prɒpərti/
quack (n) /kwæk/
radar (n) /reɪdɑːr/

rag (n) /ræg/
ransom (n) /rænsəm/
recapture (v) /riːkæptʃər/
record (n) /rekɔːrd/
refrain from (v) /rɪfreɪn frəm/
release (v) /rɪliːs/
remote control (phr) /rɪmoʊt
  kəntroʊl/
rental (n) /rentəl/
request (n) /rɪkwest/
restate (v) /riːsteɪt/
reverse (v) /rɪvɜːrs/
robot-pet (n) /roʊbɒt pet/
run one's life (phr)
satellite (n) /sætəlaɪt/
scatter (v) /skætər/
scheme (n) /skiːm/
security (n) /sɪkjʊərɪti/
security guard (phr) /sɪkjʊərɪti
  gɑːrd/
sentence to (v) /sentəns tu/
set fire (phr) /set faɪər/
shoplift (n) /ʃɒplɪft/
skid (v) /skɪd/
smash (v) /smæʃ/
smoke detector (phr) /smoʊk
  dɪtektər/
smuggle (v) /smʌgəl/
soak (v) /soʊk/
sociologist (n) /soʊsiɒlədʒɪst/
software (n) /sɒftweər/
sparkling (adj) /spɑːrklɪŋ/
speed (n) /spiːd/
statement (n) /steɪtmənt/
store (v) /stɔːr/
surveillance (n) /sərveɪləns/
suspect (v) /səspekt/
swing (v) /swɪŋ/
technophile (n) /teknoʊfaɪl/
technophobe (n) /teknoʊfoʊb/
tone (n) /toʊn/
trial (n) /traɪəl/
trickery (n) /trɪkəri/
try sb (v) /traɪ/
twinkling (adj) /twɪŋklɪŋ/
up to date (phr)
vacant (adj) /veɪkənt/
vanish (v) /vænɪʃ/
via (prep) /vaɪə/
viewpoint (n) /vjuːpɔɪnt/
website (n) /websaɪt/
willing (adj) /wɪlɪŋ/
withdraw (v) /wɪðdrɔː/
witness (n) /wɪtnəs/

UNIT 7

ambient advertising (phr)
  /æmbiənt ædvərtaɪzɪŋ/
award (n) /əwɔːrd/
baggy (adj) /bægi/
balance (n) /bæləns/
bank (n) /bæŋk/
bar (n) /bɑːr/
barber (n) /bɑːrbər/
bear in mind (phr)
bleach (n) /bliːtʃ/
boss (n) /bɒs/
brand (n) /brænd/
bunch (n) /bʌntʃ/
button (n) /bʌtən/
canal (n) /kənæl/
cater for (v) /keɪtər fər/
chatter (v) /tʃætər/
checked (adj) /tʃekt/
cheque (n) /tʃek/
clue (n) /kluː/
collectibles (n) /kəlektɪbəlz/
commonplace (adj)
  /kɒmənpleɪs/
counter (n) /kaʊntər/
dedicated (adj) /dedɪkeɪtɪd/
deli (n) /deli/
delicacy (n) /delɪkəsi/
delicatessen (n) /delɪkətesən/
denim (n) /denɪm/
deodorant (n) /dioʊdərənt/
diverse (adj) /daɪvɜːrs/
empty-handed (adj) /empti
  hændəd/
enhance (v) /ɪnhɑːns/
envelope (n) /envəloʊp/
expose (v) /ɪkspoʊz/
fabric (n) /fæbrɪk/
faithful (adj) /feɪθful/
floating (adj) /floʊtɪŋ/
flowery (adj) /flaʊəri/
food court (phr) /fuːd kɔːrt/
fragrance (n) /freɪgrəns/
frame (n) /freɪm/
freshly ground (phr) /freʃli
  graʊnd/
furnishing (n) /fɜːrnɪʃɪŋ/
genuinely (adv) /dʒeniuɪnli/
glassware (n) /glɑːsweər/
guarantee (v) /gærəntiː/
hammer (n) /hæmər/
hand in (phr v) /hænd ɪn/
handicrafts (n) /hændɪkrɑːfts/
hardware (n) /hɑːrdweər/
hawk (v) /hɔːk/
house (v) /haʊz/
hustle and bustle (phr)
hype (n) /haɪp/

import (v) /ɪmpɔːrt/
interest (n) /ɪntrəst/
job-oriented (adj) /dʒɒb ɔːrientɪd/
lamb chop (phr) /læm tʃɒp/
laundrette (n) /lɔːndret/
leggings (n) /legɪŋz/
line (v) /laɪn/
liquid (n) /lɪkwɪd/
loose (adj) /luːs/
loose stitching (phr) /luːs stɪtʃɪŋ/
mango (n) /mæŋgoʊ/
memento (n) /mɪmentoʊ/
merchant (n) /mɜːrtʃənt/
nail (n) /neɪl/
nylon (adj) /naɪlɒn/
object (v) /əbdʒekt/
obsessed (adj) /əbsest/
obsession (n) /əbseʃən/
open-minded (adj) /oʊpən
  maɪndɪd/
optimistic (adj) /ɒptɪmɪstɪk/
ornament (n) /ɔːrnəmənt/
outing (n) /aʊtɪŋ/
pamper (v) /pæmpər/
passion (n) /pæʃən/
pasta (n) /pæstə/
pave (v) /peɪv/
pinstriped (adj) /pɪnstraɪpt/
polish (n) /pɒlɪʃ/
polka-dot (adj) /pɒlkə dɒt/
project (v) /prɒdʒekt/
prone (adj) /proʊn/
rash (n) /ræʃ/
refund (n) /riːfʌnd/
roll (v) /roʊl/
rule (v) /ruːl/
scratched (adj) /skrætʃt/
screwdriver (n) /skruːdraɪvər/
shopping spree (phr) /ʃɒpɪŋ
  spriː/
sleeve (n) /sliːv/
speciality (n) /speʃiælɪti/
spice (n) /spaɪs/
stained (adj) /steɪnd/
stall (n) /stɔːl/
stationery (n) /steɪʃənri/
striped (adj) /straɪpt/
suede (adj) /sweɪd/
superstore (n) /suːpərstɔːr/
tableware (n) /teɪbəlweər/
taste (n) /teɪst/
temptation (n) /empteɪʃən/
thermometer (n) /θərmɒmɪtər/
tight (adj) /taɪt/
tight budget (phr) /taɪt bʌdʒɪt/
tights (n) /taɪts/
tin (n) /tɪn/
toiletries (n) /tɔɪlətriːz/

220

Word List

torn lining (phr) /tɔːrn laɪnɪŋ/
trader (n) /treɪdər/
trend (n) /trend/
unwrap (v) /ʌnræp/
utensil (n) /juːtensəl/
wacky (adj) /wæki/
washing powder (phr) /wɒʃɪŋ paʊdər/
water (v) /wɔːtər/
well mannered (phr) /wel mænərd/
zip (n) /zɪp/

UNIT 8

absorb (v) /əbzɔːrb/
accompany (v) /əkʌmpəni/
appetite (n) /æpɪtaɪt/
aubergine (n) /oʊbərʒiːn/
avocado (n) /ævəkɑːdoʊ/
baked (pp) /beɪkt/
beat (v) /biːt/
beef (n) /biːf/
bitter (adj) /bɪtər/
boast (v) /boʊst/
boiled (pp) /bɔɪld/
bolognaise (n) /bɒləneɪz/
bubbling (adj) /bʌblɪŋ/
cauliflower (n) /kɒliflaʊər/
chillies (n) /tʃɪliz/
chipped (pp) /tʃɪpt/
chop (v) /tʃɒp/
clove (n) /kloʊv/
cod (n) /kɒd/
coffin (n) /kɒfɪn/
coleslaw (n) /koʊlslɔː/
compensate (v) /kɒmpənseɪt/
courteous (adj) /kɜːrtiəs/
cracker (n) /krækər/
croissant (n) /krwæsɒn/
cutlery (n) /kʌtləri/
décor (n) /ceɪkɔːr/
dip (n) /dɪp/
donate (v) /doʊneɪt/
doughnut (n) /doʊnʌt/
drain (v) /dreɪn/
dried fruit (phr) /draɪd fruːt/
eggplant (n) /egplɑːnt/
elevate (v) /elɪveɪt/
energy boost (n) /enərdʒi buːst/
equivalent (adj) /ɪkwɪvələnt/
evaluate (v) /ɪvæljueɪt/
extinguish (v) /ɪkstɪŋgwɪʃ/
factual (adj) /fæktʃuəl/
fat free (phr) /fæt friː/
fibre (n) /faɪbər/
flakes (n) /fleɪks/

flexible (adj) /fleksɪbəl/
forbid (v) /fərbɪd/
fried (pp) /fraɪd/
gang (n) /gæŋ/
gate (n) /geɪt/
ginger (n) /dʒɪndʒər/
gradually (adv) /grædʒuəli/
grain (n) /greɪn/
grapes (n) /greɪps/
grate (v) /greɪt/
grater (n) /greɪtər/
gravy (n) /greɪvi/
grilled (pp) /grɪld/
ground meat (phr) /graʊnd miːt/
hang (v) /hæŋ/
hectic (adj) /hektɪk/
immense (adj) /ɪmens/
ingredient (n) /ɪŋgriːdiənt/
interval (n) /ɪntərvəl/
jelly (n) /dʒeli/
judgment (n) /dʒʌdʒmənt/
junk food (phr) /dʒʌnk fuːd/
kiwi (n) /kiːwiː/
lamb (n) /læm/
lean (adj) /liːn/
leek (n) /liːk/
lentil (n) /lentɪl/
lobster (n) /lɒbstər/
master (n) /mɑːstər/
meat grinder (phr) /miːt graɪndər/
melon (n) /melən/
melt (v) /melt/
metabolism (n) /mɪtæbəlɪzəm/
mixture (n) /mɪkstʃər/
mushroom (n) /mʌʃruːm/
mussel (n) /mʌsəl/
nap (n) /næp/
napkin (n) /næpkɪn/
nod off (phr v) /nɒd ɒf/
notice (v) /noʊtɪs/
nugget (n) /nʌgɪt/
octopus (n) /ɒktəpəs/
olives (n) /ɒlɪvz/
on the rise (phr)
overcooked (pp) /oʊvəkʊkt/
oysters (n) /ɔɪstərz/
packaging (n) /pækɪdʒɪŋ/
pale (adj) /peɪl/
pan (n) /pæn/
parsley (n) /pɑːrsli/
paste (n) /peɪst/
peach (n) /piːtʃ/
pear (n) /peər/
pea (n) /piː/
peel (v) /piːl/
peeler (n) /piːlər/

pickled (pp) /pɪkəld/
pinch (n) /pɪntʃ/
pineapple (n) /paɪnæpəl/
pint (n) /paɪnt/
pity (n) /pɪti/
plain (adj) /pleɪn/
poach (v) /poʊtʃ/
portion (n) /pɔːrʃən/
postpone (v) /poʊspoʊn/
pot (n) /pɒt/
poultry (n) /poʊltri/
poverty (n) /pɒvərti/
pricey (adj) /praɪsi/
protein (n) /proʊtiːn/
pudding (n) /pʊdɪŋ/
quiche (n) /kiːʃ/
raw (adj) /rɔː/
reflex (n) /riːfleks/
refrain (v) /rɪfreɪn/
remind (v) /rɪmaɪnd/
reunite (v) /riːjuːnaɪt/
roasted (pp) /roʊstɪd/
rolling pin (phr) /roʊlɪŋ pɪn/
rye bread (phr) /raɪ bred/
salmon (n) /sæmən/
sauce (n) /sɔːs/
schedule (n) /ʃedjuːl/
shabby (adj) /ʃæbi/
shrimps (n) /ʃrɪmps/
sieve (n) /sɪv/
skimmed (adj) /skɪmd/
skip (v) /skɪp/
smoked (adj) /smoʊkt/
snail (n) /sneɪl/
soft drink (phr) /sɒft drɪŋk/
sour (adj) /saʊər/
spirit (n) /spɪrɪt/
squid (n) /skwɪd/
starve (v) /stɑːrv/
steamed (pp) /stiːmd/
stick (n) /stɪk/
still (adj) /stɪl/
stir (v) /stɜːr/
stock up (phr v) /stɒk ʌp/
stuffed (pp) /stʌft/
tablecloth (n) /teɪbəlklɒθ/
takeaway (n) /teɪkəweɪ/
taskmaster (n) /tɑːskmɑːstər/
tender (adj) /tendər/
threaten (v) /θretən/
tough (adj) /tʌf/
tray (n) /treɪ/
trout (n) /traʊt/
tuna (n) /tjuːnə/
underworld (n) /ʌndərwɜːrd/
unprocessed (adj) /ʌnproʊsest/
upbeat (adj) /ʌpbiːt/
veal (n) /viːl/

vital (adj) /vaɪtəl/
warn (v) /wɔːrn/
whisk (n) /ʰwɪsk/
yogurt (n) /jɒgərt/
zucchini (n) /zuːkiːni/

UNIT 9

altitude (n) /æltɪtjuːd/
amateur (adj) /æmətər/
and so forth (phr)
anthem (n) /ænθəm/
archer (n) /ɑːrtʃər/
arrows (n) /æroʊz/
attach (v) /ətætʃ/
backgammon (n) /bækgæmən/
band (n) /bænd/
boulder (n) /boʊldər/
bow (v) /boʊ/
bungee cord (phr) /bʌndʒi kɔːrd/
carry out (phr v) /kæri aʊt/
challenge (n) /tʃælɪndʒ/
championship (n) /tʃæmpiənʃɪp/
chant (v) /tʃɑːnt/
cheerleader (n) /tʃɪərliːdər/
chess (n) /tʃes/
club (n) /klʌb/
commemorative (adj) /kəmemərətɪv/
commissioner (n) /kəmɪʃənər/
controversial (adj) /kɒntrəvɜːrʃəl/
co-ordinator (n) /koʊɔːrdɪneɪtor/
council (n) /kaʊnsəl/
course (n) /kɔːrs/
crane (n) /kreɪn/
crush up (v) /krʌʃ ʌp/
crutch (n) /krʌtʃ/
cue (n) /kjuː/
custom (n) /kʌstəm/
daredevil (adj) /deərdevəl/
daring (adj) /deərɪŋ/
descend (v) /dɪsend/
disabled (adj) /dɪseɪbəld/
downstream (adv) /daʊnstriːm/
elaborate (adj) /ɪlæbərət/
elation (n) /ɪleɪʃən/
element (n) /elɪmənt/
emerge (v) /ɪmɜːrdʒ/
estate (n) /ɪsteɪt/
expand (v) /ɪkspænd/
explosive (n) /ɪksploʊsɪv/
extravaganza (n) /ɪkstævəgænzə/
fan (n) /fæn/
feature (v) /fiːtʃər/
free fall (phr) /friː fɔːl/

221

Word List

gilt (n) /gɪlt/
glide (v) /glaɪd/
graceful (adj) /greɪsfʊl/
handkerchief (n) /hæŋkəʳtʃɪf/
highlight (v) /haɪlaɪt/
instinct (adj) /ɪnstɪŋkt/
institution (n) /ɪnstɪtjuːʃən/
interpretation (n) /ɪntɜːʳprɪteɪʃ°n/
kick (v) /kɪk/
lean (v) /liːn/
leap (v) /liːp/
lunacy (n) /luːnəsi/
macho (adj) /mætʃoʊ/
media (n) /miːdiə/
mental (adj) /mentəl/
neglect (v) /nɪglekt/
nerve-wracking (adj) /nɜːʳv rækɪŋ/
opposition (n) /ɒpəzɪʃ°n/
paddle (v) /pædəl/
Paralympics (n) /pærəlɪmpɪks/
participate (v) /pɑːʳtɪsɪpeɪt/
pitch (n) /pɪtʃ/
positive (adj) /pɒzɪtɪv/
present (v) /prɪzent/
property developer (phr) /prɒpəʳti dɪveləpəʳ/
punch (v) /pʌntʃ/
range (n) /reɪndʒ/
reconsider (v) /riːkənsɪdəʳ/
representative (n) /reprɪzentətɪv/
require (v) /rɪkwaɪəʳ/
restoration (n) /restəreɪʃ°n/
rewarding (adj) /rɪwɔːʳdɪŋ/
ring (n) /rɪŋ/
rival (n) /raɪvəl/
salver (n) /sælvəʳ/
sheer (adj) /ʃɪəʳ/
sheet (n) /ʃiːt/
shuttlecock (n) /ʃʌtəlkɒk/
sky surfing (phr) /skaɪ sɜːʳfɪŋ/
slope (n) /sloʊp/
smash-hit (adj) /smæʃ hɪt/
solo jump (phr) /soʊloʊ dʒʌmp/
space (n) /speɪs/
specialise (v) /speʃəlaɪz/
steady (adj) /stedi/
substantial (adj) /səbstænʃəl/
support (v) /səpɔːʳt/
surroundings (n) /səraʊndɪŋz/
terrace (n) /terɪs/
three-track (adj) /θriː træk/
thumb (n) /θʌm/
tip (n) /tɪp/
top class (phr) /tɒp klɑːs/
torrent (n) /tɒrent/

tournament (n) /tʊəʳnəmənt/
triumphant (adj) /traɪʌmfənt/
trophy (n) /troʊfi/
tune (n) /tjuːn/
typical (n) /tɪpɪkəl/
urge (v) /ɜːʳdʒ/
valley (n) /væli/
venue (n) /venjuː/
waterfall (n) /wɔːtəʳfɔːl/
wound (n) /wuːnd/

UNIT 10

access (v) /ækses/
adopt (v) /ədɒpt/
animation (n) /ænɪmeɪʃ°n/
back (v) /bæk/
backstage (n) /bæksteɪdʒ/
band width (phr) /bænd wɪdθ/
bid (n) /bɪd/
binding (n) /baɪndɪŋ/
booming (adj) /buːmɪŋ/
broadsheet (n) /brɔːdʃiːt/
bury (v) /beri/
calendar (n) /kælɪndəʳ/
castaway (n) /kɑːstəweɪ/
cater (v) /keɪtəʳ/
chest (n) /tʃest/
circulation (n) /sɜːʳkjʊleɪʃ°n/
clap (v) /klæp/
collapse (v) /kəlæps/
compensation (n) /kɒmpənseɪʃ°n/
compromise (v) /kɒmprəmaɪz/
confront (v) /kənfrʌnt/
contest (n) /kɒntest/
currency (n) /kʌrənsi/
desert (adj) /dezəʳt/
download (v) /daʊnloʊd/
evacuation (n) /ɪvækjueɪʃ°n/
famine (n) /fæmɪn/
fast paced (phr) /fɑːst peɪst/
fiction (n) /fɪkʃ°n/
founder (n) /faʊndəʳ/
gladiatorial (adj) /glædiətɔːriəl/
global (adj) /gloʊbəl/
halved (adj) /hɑːvd/
hardcover (n) /hɑːʳdkʌvəʳ/
honour (v) /ɒnəʳ/
hurricane (n) /hʌrɪkən/
immensely (adv) /ɪmensli/
instantly (adv) /ɪnstəntli/
launch (v) /lɔːntʃ/
layout (n) /leɪaʊt/
leap (n) /liːp/
literacy (n) /lɪtərəsi/
massive (adj) /mæsɪv/

memoir (n) /memwɑːʳ/
overhead (adv) /oʊvəʳhed/
paperback (n) /peɪpəʳbæk/
pile (n) /paɪl/
pitch (v) /pɪtʃ/
post (n) /poʊst/
reschedule (v) /riːʃedjuːl/
resolve (v) /rɪzɒlv/
row (n) /roʊ/
screening (n) /skriːnɪŋ/
script (n) /skrɪpt/
servant (n) /sɜːʳvənt/
shelter (n) /ʃeltəʳ/
sink (v) /sɪŋk/
star studded (phr) /stɑːʳ stʌdɪd/
supporting (adj) /səpɔːʳtɪŋ/
tabloid (n) /tæblɔɪd/
trade (n) /treɪd/
tremor (n) /tremər/
valid (adj) /vælɪd/
whereabouts (n) /ʰweərəbaʊts/